Theories of School Counseling for the 21st Century

Theories of School Counseling for the 21st Century

EDITED BY COLETTE T. DOLLARHIDE

AND

MATTHEW E. LEMBERGER-TRUELOVE

OXFORD
UNIVERSITY PRESS

Oxford University Press is a department of the University of Oxford. It furthers
the University's objective of excellence in research, scholarship, and education
by publishing worldwide. Oxford is a registered trade mark of Oxford University
Press in the UK and certain other countries.

Published in the United States of America by Oxford University Press
198 Madison Avenue, New York, NY 10016, United States of America.

Library of Congress Cataloging-in-Publication
Data Names: Dollarhide, Colette T., author. |
Lemberger-Truelove, Matthew E., 1976– author.
Title: Theories of school counseling for the 21st century /
Colette T. Dollarhide, Matthew E. Lemberger-Truelove.
Description: New York, NY : Oxford University Press, [2019] |
Includes bibliographical references and index.
Identifiers: LCCN 2018018639 (print) | LCCN 2018040292 (ebook) |
ISBN 9780190840259 (updf) | ISBN 9780190840266 (epub) |
ISBN 9780190840242 (pbk.; alk. paper)
Subjects: LCSH: Educational counseling—United States.
Classification: LCC LB1027.5 (ebook) | LCC LB1027.5 .D56 2019 (print) |
DDC 371.4—dc23 LC record available at https://lccn.loc.gov/2018018639

Artwork used for the front cover was contributed by Matthew Lemberger-Truelove.

First, this work is dedicated to the hard-working professional school counselors who answer the call to action every day. It takes courage, faith, and dedication to be a professional school counselor; rather than rescue every "starfish stranded on the beach," a professional school counselor works to "make the entire ocean" a more habitable place. It is only when we can make the school a community, where safety, learning, belonging, and inclusion are constant conditions, that we can say that a school is healthy. Professional school counselors work to ensure that kids know that they do belong in the school, that they do contribute to other's learning, and they do have a future worth fighting for. Professional school counselors make this happen, every day, and they won't stop as long as they have a school that needs them. I dedicate this book, and my undying respect and admiration, to these courageous professionals.

Second, I would like to gratefully acknowledge the support of my family, and the support of my colleague, dear friend, and co-editor, Dr. Matthew Lemberger-Truelove, without whom this book would not exist. C.T.D.

Foremost, I dedicate this work to my family, particularly my wife Tamiko and children Naarah and Atom. I also extend my gratitude to each of the authors who contributed to this book and the school counselors who inspired their ideas. Finally, I thank my mentor, co-editor, and dear friend, Colette. M.E.L.T.

CONTENTS

PREFACE

Collectively, we, Colette and Matthew, have taught theories of counseling for more than 40 years. We have talked numerous times about our concerns: we discuss how narrow our teaching of theories can be, and how those who wish to work with children are left on their own to "translate" the theories into developmentally appropriate practice. I (CD) tell my students that it will be easier for them to learn the theories using the template of adults (clients at their own developmental level) and that they will learn to adapt those concepts to other developmental levels when they are in the field. However, we are painfully aware that assuming they will "figure it out on their own" is fraught with risk for *mis*-learning—that incorrect assumptions about development or incorrect understanding of theories will result in poorly conceptualized counseling interventions. In our credit-heavy, intense, 2- or 3-year, CACREP-accredited graduate programs, there appears to be no room for another class pertaining to theories, but there is room for another book—this book—to help school counselors and others working with children to translate theory into developmentally appropriate conceptualization.

In general, theories are used to describe a phenomenon for explanatory or predictive purposes. In this way, a theory can assist a person in understanding the qualities of an event or entity and predict if the qualities are likely to manifest in a similar way in the future under similar conditions. Specific to counseling, theories of practice generally include suppositions about human nature, wellness and pathology, motivation and change, and efficacy of intervention. Stated simply, theories of counseling suggest that if a counselor exposes a client to certain practices or conditions, that client will experience different and hopefully improved outcomes. While many of these assumptions related to general counseling theories hold true for school counselors, these education professionals must also consider how each theory is or is not relevant to factors endemic to school environments.

Professional school counselors serve a variety of constituents in incredibly complex and diverse learning environments. While the need for counseling theories specific to school environments is apparent, it is curious that descriptions of such practices are either absent or underdeveloped in the literature and professional training. Instead, as described above, what often occurs is that classical theories of counseling are taught and students and new practitioners are expected to infer the relevance and application. Given the complexity of school environments and the challenges faced by school counselors (students' mental health concerns, violence, self-injury, academic failure, career indecision, and fear, to name a few), it is no wonder that many school counselors quickly disregard formal theory.

In the absence of theory, school counseling is reactionary and appears atheoretical. In reality, the language of the theory gets lost in the practice; the school counselor knows what she or he is doing, but can't name it. This is problematic from a variety of perspectives. Adult stakeholders (parents, teachers, administrators) might not understand theoretical jargon as a counselor explains his or her work, but they *do* understand the counselor's confidence and competence when the counselor is able to articulate why she or he did this intervention or gave that recommendation; the language used by the counselor conveys command of the profession. Theory informs research and best practice, research and best practice inform implementation, and it all educates stakeholders, so that counselors have a professionally relevant answer when asked "Why did you do that?" or "Why do you think that?" Confidence in best practice and competence in delivery all begin with command of the theory that informs clinical/educational choices.

In fact, a source of inspiration for this book was the Evidence Based School Counseling Conference. Highlighting best practice and research, the conference was where discussions emerged among counselor educators about the deficit in resources that provide viable, developmentally appropriate theories, further cementing the theory → research → best practice connection. School counselors participating in the discussion affirmed their desire for a resource that would provide the foundation for this chain.

With this backdrop, as editors, we were inspired to engage in a conversation about theories to bring school counselors into the discussion about what informs our work with students and with other stakeholders. This book is not intended to "remediate" school counselors, as if they were somehow deficient in their understanding of counseling theory. Rather, it is to bring counseling intentionality into focus in the schools, because K-12 students deserve professionals who have a deep understanding and appreciation for the ways that theory informs their programs, their developmental curriculum, and their counseling. This work was inspired by our own professional experiences as educators of graduate students in school counseling, supervising graduate students in the field, consulting with practicing school counselors, reading the literature, and recognizing the need to celebrate and enhance the professional lives of school counselors.

It is also important that we define our position on the use of theory in school counseling work. It is not our intent to promote one theory over another, or one body of theories over other bodies of theories, as "better" or "more applicable." The theories selected for this book are ones that appeal to many school counselors; as new theories evolve, we encourage similar exploration of their application in schools. We also want to highlight that we do not recommend that counselors adopt theoretical eclecticism, as reflected in the statement "I just do what works." What we do recommend, and promote as the purpose of this book, is that school counselors examine each theory to find one that matches how the counselor understands life to be and how change happens— that the theory chosen reflect the counselor's beliefs. Then, using that theory, the counselor can build a counseling practice with students and the school counseling program with a solid foundation.

The ASCA National Model provides a theoretical frame related to what school counselors are expected to do, not what they are limited to, and the chapters in this text offer various theoretical perspectives on how school counselors attend to the academic, career, and personal/social development of all students. However, it is important to note that, while ASCA offers the National Model as a template of understanding what school counselors do, the Model does not dictate the rationale, form, or shape of programs and services. The authors who contributed to this book do not assume that the reader has implemented the National Model, and so a number of the authors chose to address their theory without explicitly addressing the National Model. We supported this choice to allow the authors full freedom to explore all the ways that counseling theory breathes life into school counseling practice.

As editors, we wanted to highlight experts in each of the theories found herein, as opposed to our interpretations of each of these complex systems. Each author was specifically recruited to contribute to this book because she or he had demonstrated command of the theory. Each author brought her or his unique perspective based on practice and publications about the theory, and we are grateful for this contribution. In this book, each chapter follows a flexible structure designed so that the readers might compare and contrast the theories, but it simultaneously affords the authors the flexibility to best represent his or her respective theory. Each chapter begins with an overview of the history and development of the theory and how it contributes to the development of the student, then provides an overview of how the theory applies to young children (elementary level) and adolescents (middle and high school).

We start with a section on the context of school counseling, providing the foundation on the role of theory, school counseling history, and conceptual frameworks, as well as the organizational, institutional, and political challenges that confront the school counseling profession. Then the largest section of the book includes six theories (person-centered, Adlerian, cognitive-behavioral, reality therapy, existential, and solution-focused) taken from classical counseling theories and applied to school contexts. Next, three meta-theories are presented, including strengths-based school counseling, ecological school counseling, and advocating student-within-environment approach to counseling. Finally, a school-counseling-specific supervision theory is presented, so that school counseling supervisors who use the book to help new counselor-trainees refine their understanding of theory will also find their work supported through a new model of supervision.

As a final note, one of the chapter authors sent his chapter to a master's level student for feedback, and received this reply. While it might be long, it demonstrates how school counselor trainees yearn for a way to make theories relevant to their practice:

> I'm not sure how fast published work circulates among the counseling community, but I hope it is fast enough to get this chapter out there, so some real conversations about existentialism as a tool for the youth can begin. . . . I couldn't help but think about how cool it could be if a bunch of school counselors linked up in the teacher's lounge to talk about how anxiety is the dizziness of life, and how freedom is ominous, which is why some of the seniors aren't attentive in AP English.
>
> As I was reading, I was glad that you were honest in the sense that you acknowledged that existentialism is *heavy*. When people read words like aloneness, death, meaninglessness, and freedom, it all sounds so bleak lined up in a sentence, but it's relevant. In . . . class, we learned about Frankl and I remember thinking to myself, "So as an existential counselor, I need to let students know that we are born alone, die alone, and besides brief moments in our lives, we live alone?" Obviously, I was being dramatic, but it is important to acknowledge that because of existentialism's *heaviness*, one could be hesitant to integrate existentialism in a school setting. With that being said, a chapter like yours is very much needed; when all of the *heaviness* is broken down intricately and applied to address students' issues, it is obvious that existentialism does as it name implies: addresses *existence*, which in and of itself is something that all people, especially adolescent students, often worry about.
>
> In all of the classes I've taken in this program so far, holism is stressed, and you applied this holism to existentialism, which in a way, provides validity;

it suggests that although existentialism is dismissive of formal techniques, it is still capable of helping students in every aspect of life. And, just when I thought that section couldn't get any better, you provided examples of interventions, and if I was not a fan of existentialism before, that would have been the section that swayed me because it all came full circle: history, candid conversation on the negative viewpoints on existentialism, how the concepts relate specifically to students, how existentialism is holistic, and interventions that can be utilized in school. So awesome! —Ryan Roche (used with permission)

We are excited about this book and the promise it offers school counselors. We are committed to the discussion of how theories inform research and practice, so that school counselors are in conversations about how to improve school counseling programs. We believe that this book will become the foundation of school counseling training, and we welcome readers' ideas about ways to improve the conversation.

ACKNOWLEDGMENTS

This book is the culmination of the work of many people, and we extend our deepest gratitude to the authors who contributed to this book. Specifically, the authors and contributors include the following:

Patrick Akos
Thomas W. Baskin
Hannah Bowers
Erika R.N. Cameron
Thomas Anthony Chávez
Colette T. Dollarhide
Kevin Duquette
Brianne L. France
Kristopher M. Goodrich
Trish Hatch
Brian Hutchison
Kara P. Ieva
Kimberly M. Jayne
Matthew E. Lemberger-Truelove
Melissa Luke
Melissa Mariani
E. (Erin) C. M. Mason
H. George McMahon
Clare Merlin-Knoblich
John J. Murphy
Chris Slaten
Hayley L. Stulmaker
Anya Woronzoff Verriden
Robert E. Wubbolding
Brett Zyromski

ABOUT THE AUTHORS

Patrick Akos, Ph.D., has professional experience as a teacher and school and college counselor that informs his work as a Professor in the School of Education at the University of North Carolina at Chapel Hill. Patrick's research and practice are grounded in strengths-based school counseling. The strengths framework is based in humanistic traditions and is empirically supported by contemporary scholarship (findings on positive youth development and improved noncognitive factors). His main focus is navigating transitions across the lifespan. For example, normative school transitions (e.g., moving from elementary to middle school) involve the developmental intensity and asynchrony of early adolescence, cultural identity development, and stage–environment fit in multiple contexts. Similarly, college and career transitions depend on talents, meaning-making, agency, and opportunity structures. Dr. Akos is a National Certified Counselor and School Counselor, Approved Clinical Supervisor, and Licensed Professional Counselor in North Carolina, as well as a licensed secondary and middle grades teacher and K-12 school counselor in North Carolina.

Thomas W. Baskin, Ph.D., is an Associate Professor of Counseling Psychology at the University of Wisconsin–Milwaukee. He received his B.S. in economic development and technology from the University of California, Davis; his M.S. in both school and community counseling from California State University, East Bay; and his Ph.D. in counseling psychology from the University of Wisconsin–Madison. His research interests include how belongingness relates to academic achievement for K-12 students in multicultural schools and how angry students can benefit from learning to forgive. He also uses meta-analysis to investigate the efficacy of psychotherapy.

Hannah Bowers, Ph.D., is an Assistant Professor at Florida Atlantic University. Dr. Bowers has been working with children and families for the past decade, both as a marriage and family therapist and as a school counselor. Her work focuses on investigating school counseling programs and interventions that are aligned with the ASCA National Model, that advocate for the school counseling profession, and that engage the entirety of the school system. Dr. Bowers examines how such interventions affect social-emotional learning constructs and cognitive abilities. Dr. Bowers also serves as the Associate Editor of the *Journal of Humanistic Counseling*.

Erika R. N. Cameron, Ph.D., is an Associate Professor in the Department of Counseling and Marital and Family Therapy at the University of San Diego. She holds a bachelor's degree in graphic design from Bradley University, a master's degree in counseling from the University of Hawaii–Manoa, and a doctorate in counselor education from the University of Missouri–St. Louis. She has previously worked as a professional school counselor at the elementary, middle, and high school levels in both Hawaii and Missouri. Her scholarly interests include school counselor professional development, qualitative research methods, international school counseling, individual psychology, and interventions for children of military families.

Thomas A. Chávez, Ph.D., is an Assistant Professor of Counselor Education at the University of New Mexico (UNM). He received his B.A. in psychology and an M.A. in counselor education at UNM, and he completed his Ph.D. at the University of Wisconsin–Madison. He has taught courses in school counseling, child and adolescent counseling, professional orientation/ethics, and multiculturalism in the helping professions. He has served communities in Albuquerque, New York, and Wisconsin, focusing on work with youth and families of culturally diverse backgrounds. Specific services have included providing therapeutic recreation programming in after-school programs, school counseling, community-clinic behavioral health consultation, adolescent depression intervention research, adolescent substance use and risky sexual behavior intervention research, and intensive therapy in children psychiatric centers and high-security juvenile justice settings. He has been trained in interpersonal process and motivational interviewing models. He also is a member of the American Psychological Association, National Latino Psychological Association, and American Counseling Association and attends their conferences. Finally, Dr. Chávez has particular interest in bridging traditional/indigenous practices and mainstream counseling.

Colette T. Dollarhide, Ed.D., is a Professor of Counselor Education at The Ohio State University and de facto school counseling coordinator, and she has been a counselor educator since earning her Ed.D. from the University of Nevada, Reno, in 1995. Her main teaching and research focus has been leadership, supervision, school counseling, pedagogy, professional identity, and social justice. She has co-authored two textbooks on school counseling (one book is

in its third edition), and she has written journal articles and presented exten-
sively. She has served as President of the National Association for Humanistic
Counseling and President of the Ohio Association for Counselor Education and
Supervision, and she is the co-founder and president of the Ohio Counselors
for Social Justice. She was the editor of the *Journal of Humanistic Counseling*
(JHC) for 3 years, and she has served on editorial boards of the *Journal of
Counseling and Development* (JCD), the *Journal of Counselor Education and
Supervision* (CES), and the *Journal for Humanistic Counseling* (JHC). She is
the co-editor of a special issue on leadership in *Professional School Counseling*
(PSC). She has won two prestigious national awards in research: the Counselor
Education Research Award from the ACES in 2015, and the Outstanding
Counselor Education and Supervision Article Award, also from ACES in 2011.
She was awarded the Professional Teaching Award from NCACES in 2017 and
the Counselor Educator of the Year from OSCA in 2017. In addition, she is a
Nationally Certified Counselor, currently holds her LPC with supervisor en-
dorsement in Ohio, and is a nationally Approved Clinical Supervisor.

Kevin Duquette is a doctoral candidate in counselor education and supervision at The Pennsylvania State University. His research interests include school
counselor role, school counselors' use of large-scale interventions, and RAMP
designated schools. He is a former middle school counselor and Teach For
America corps member. In his spare time, he enjoys playing guitar and running
obstacle course races.

Brianne L. France is a graduate student and research assistant in school counseling at the University of San Diego. She holds a bachelor's degree in psychology and sociology from the University of Wisconsin–Stevens Point. She
has worked previously both as a substitute teacher and in a mental health institute in Madison, Wisconsin. Currently, she is fulfilling an internship with
the counseling department at O'Farrell High School in San Diego, California.
Her research interests include emotional intelligence in schools, students in
the juvenile court system, and the role of school counselors as mental health
professionals.

Kristopher M. Goodrich, Ph.D., is an Associate Professor of Counselor
Education at the University of New Mexico, where he has taught since 2010.
He completed his graduate education in the CACREP-accredited counseling
program at Syracuse University. Dr. Goodrich has written 44 peer-reviewed
journal articles, co-authored or co-edited three books, and has contributed 18
pieces to other publications. He is the current editor of the *Journal for Specialists
in Group Work*. Dr. Goodrich is also a past president of the Association for
Lesbian, Gay, Bisexual, and Transgender Issues in Counseling (2015–2016), and

the immediate past president of the Rocky Mountain Association for Counselor Education and Supervision (RMACES).

Trish Hatch, Ph.D., is a Professor at San Diego State University (SDSU), where she served as Director of the School Counseling Program from 2004 until 2015. Dr. Hatch is the best-selling author of four books on school counseling, and she has over 50 publications and has presented over 100 times at professional conferences. Dr. Hatch is the Founder and Executive Director of the Center for Excellence in School Counseling and Leadership (CESCaL) in the College of Education at SDSU and is President and CEO of Hatching Results® LLC. Since 2007, she has trained thousands of school counselors and administrators in hundreds of school districts on the use of data to create effective evidence-based school counseling programs that promote equity and access to rigorous educational opportunities for all students. In addition, she has successfully co-authored 13 elementary and secondary school counseling (ESSC) grants that awarded over $16 million in federal funds to school districts. Dr. Hatch is an advocate, advisor, and national leader. She has served on multiple state and national school counseling research summit steering committees, she was one of five original panel members for the National Panel for Evidenced-Based School Counseling Practices, and she currently serves on the Advisory Council for the National Evidence-Based School Counseling Conference and as a national expert consultant on school counseling for The White House, U.S. Department of Education, The Education Trust, and the College Board. A former school counselor, high school administrator, and central office administrator who oversaw 72 school counselors in 32 high-needs schools, Dr. Hatch has received multiple state and national school counseling awards, including National Administrator of the Year from ASCA, the Mary Gehrke Lifetime Achievement Award from ASCA, the Excellence in Education Award from NACA, and the inaugural California Association of School Counselors' School Counselor Educator of the Year (2016) award.

Brian Hutchison, Ph.D., is an Associate Professor at New Jersey City University. Dr. Hutchison is the President of the Asia Pacific Career Development Association (APCDA), Founding President of the Missouri Career Development Association (MoCDA), Treasurer of the National Career Development Association (NCDA), and Editor of the *Asia Pacific Career Development Journal*. Dr. Hutchison's scholarship can be broadly described as focused in two primary counseling domains, school counseling and career coaching/counseling. These broad themes are infused into three primary scholarship areas: international issues in career/school counseling, career theory and practice integration, and counselor training/education broadly defined. To this end, he has written more than four dozen publications pertaining to school and career counseling theory, international career development, social justice and cross-cultural communication, and specific counseling interventions. Recent publications include peer-reviewed articles in *Professional School Counseling, Journal of Counseling & Development, Equity & Excellence in Education*, and *Career Development Quarterly* and textbook chapters in more than a dozen books published by professional organization presses. Dr. Hutchison is the founder of the St. Louis Cultural Competence Institute and an active advocate for intergroup contact and empathy after Michael Brown Jr.'s death in Ferguson, MO, in August 2014. For this work, Dr. Hutchison received the 2014–15 Social Justice Advocacy Award from the Association of Humanistic Counseling.

Kara P. Ieva, Ph.D., is currently an Associate Professor in the Counseling in Educational Settings program at Rowan University. Her areas of research interest include counseling children and adolescent of underserved populations regarding college and career readiness and group counseling and leadership. Dr. Ieva has held leadership positions in the Association of Specialists in Group Work (ASGW), the New Jersey School Counselor Association (NJSCA), and the New Jersey Association for Counselor Educators and Supervision (NJACES). She is also on the editorial review board for *Professional School Counselor Journal*, published by the American School Counselor Association (ASCA). She was the recipient of the Research Article of the Year Award (2011) from the American Counseling Association (ACA), the North Atlantic Region of Counselor Education and Supervision (NARACES) Social Justice Award (2014), and the NARACES Emerging Leader Award (2012). Further, she was the principal investigator and project director for the Rowan University Aim High Science and Technology Academies (grant-funded; $998,259), which aided first-generation and low-income college students in access and preparation for postsecondary education in STEM. This grant resulted in her serving as Director of Student Services for the Rowan University STEAM Academy. She currently serves as a co-PI on a grant from the Forman S. Acton Educational Foundation ($959,627) to evaluate funded college access programs.

Kimberly M. Jayne, Ph.D., is an Assistant Professor of Counselor Education and the school counseling program coordinator at Portland State University. Her scholarship is focused on the effectiveness of play therapy for children and families affected by poverty and trauma and on humanistic counseling interventions for children and families in school and clinical settings. Kimberly is a past Associate Editor for the *Journal of Humanistic Counseling* and serves on the editorial board of the *Journal of Child and Adolescent Counseling*.

Matthew E. Lemberger-Truelove, Ph.D., is a Professor of Counselor Education at the University of North Texas. He graduated with his doctoral degree in counselor education from the University of South Carolina, and he has served as a counselor educator for 12 years. Prior to his employment in academia, he worked as an elementary school counselor, a high school counselor, and a community-based counselor. He is currently the Editor of the *Journal of Counseling and Development*, past-Editor of the *Journal of Humanistic Counseling*, Associate Editor of the *Journal of Individual Psychology*, and Senior Associate Editor of the *Journal of Child and Adolescent Counseling*. Dr. Lemberger-Truelove's scholarly work includes empirical research, funded projects, and theoretical writing, which has resulted in over 40 peer-review journal articles, more than $1.2 million in grant or contract funding, and many national and regional conference presentations. His empirical work pertains to evidence-based counseling practice with children and adolescents. He is especially interested in culturally responsive interventions that support children and families from challenging economic environments. Dr. Lemberger-Truelove has published multiple empirical articles in counseling's flagship journal, the *Journal of Counseling and Development*, including a recent intervention piece that was highlighted in the extremely competitive and noteworthy CASEL Guide (see http://www.casel. org). In addition to his empirical work, he has contributed to theory in the areas of humanistic counseling, social justice, and counseling research practices.

Melissa Luke, Ph.D., is a Dean's Professor in the Department of Counseling and Human Services at Syracuse University, where she also coordinates the doctoral program in counseling and counselor education and the master's program in school counseling. She is a Nationally Certified Counselor (NCC), an Approved Clinical Supervisor (ACS), and a Licensed Mental Health Counselor (LMHC) in the State of New York. Dr. Luke is a member of the American Counseling Association (ACA), the Association for Specialists in Group Work (ASGW), and Counselors for Social Justice (CSJ). She is a member of, and currently serving as a research trustee in, the Association for Lesbian, Gay, Bisexual, and Transgender Issues in Counseling (ALGBTIC), and she is President-Elect of the Association for Counselor Education and Supervision (ACES). Dr. Luke is also a member of Chi Sigma Iota and serves as the Editor of the *Journal of Counselor Leadership and Advocacy*. Having 15 years of experience in the P-12 educational context, Dr. Luke focuses her scholarship specifically on school counselors, and she has published extensively in the area of counselor supervision and group work. Dr. Luke also focuses on counselor preparation and practice to more effectively respond to the needs of underserved persons, particularly LGBTIQ+ youth. Toward that end, Dr. Luke is involved in a number of interdisciplinary research projects, including the design and implementation of training simulations that use actors as standardized school stakeholders (administrators, teachers, students, family members), the professional identity development and ethical decision-making of school counselors across global settings, and the role of mentorship in leadership and research development for counselors-in-training.

Melissa Mariani, Ph.D., is an Assistant Professor in the Department of Counselor Education at Florida Atlantic University. Her research interests include evaluating the effectiveness of evidence-based school counseling interventions, specifically those focused on improving students' prosocial skills, fostering a positive classroom climate, and preventing bullying. Dr. Mariani is co-author of the book *Facilitating Evidence-Based, Data-Driven School Counseling: A Manual for Practice* (Corwin, 2016). In 2011, she was awarded Florida School Counselor of the Year for PK-8 and was recently honored as University Scholar of the Year at the Assistant Level. Dr. Mariani is passionate about professional service and currently sits on national, state, and local advisory councils. She has held leadership positions in the Florida School Counselor Association (FSCA), serves on several editorial review boards for professional counseling journals, and is a national trainer for the Student Success Skills (SSS) curriculum.

E. C. M. Mason, Ph.D., is an Assistant Professor in the School Counseling (Master's) and Counselor Education and Practice (Doctoral) programs at Georgia State University (GSU) in Atlanta. She has published in scholarly journals and texts, and her research agenda focuses on professional identity, action research, innovation, and technology. She has also had national and international opportunities to present on many of these topics. Currently, Dr. Mason serves as one of the co-chairs of the School Counseling Interest Network of ACES and as an associate editor of the *Professional School Counseling* journal, and she is a research fellow with the Ronald H. Fredrickson Center for School Counseling Outcome Research and Evaluation. Before joining the faculty at GSU, Dr. Mason was Associate Professor at DePaul University in Chicago, where she served in department and college leadership roles, and also as President of the Illinois School Counselor Association in 2012–2013. Dr. Mason spent the earlier part of her career as a practicing school counselor, working for 13 years in urban, suburban, and rural settings. She has provided district- and state-level trainings on comprehensive school counseling programs, RAMP, and technology, and she has been the keynote speaker for several state school counseling conferences. Given her interest in technology's influence on the field, Dr. Mason particularly enjoys connecting and learning with those in the profession through social media, and in 2011 she co-founded the now widely used hashtag for school counselors on Twitter, #scchat. Along with her colleagues Dr. Stuart Chen-Hayes and Dr. Melissa Ockerman, she is also the co-author of the 2013 book, *101 Solutions for School Counselors and Leaders in Challenging Times*.

H. George McMahon, Ph.D., is an Assistant Professor in the Counseling and Human Development Department at The University of Georgia. He has been a counselor educator since 2005, focusing on preparing future school counselors and school counselor educators and developing innovative models of school counseling and school counselor preparation. Dr. McMahon developed The Ecological School Counseling Model, and has published research in the areas of school counseling professional identity, multiculturalism and social justice, and group work. Currently, Dr. McMahon is researching the distribution of school counseling innovations to high-need, low-resources school districts and communities. He has served on the editorial board of the *Journal for Specialists in Group Work* and as Associate Editor for *Professional School Counseling* since 2014. Dr. McMahon is a fellow with the Ronald H. Fredrickson Center for School Counseling Outcome Research and Evaluation and is the founder and co-coordinator of the Innovative School Counseling Research Network. Dr. McMahon earned his Ph.D. from The University of Georgia and his M.Ed. from The University of Virginia, and he has worked as a school counselor in New Orleans, LA.

Clare Merlin-Knoblich, Ph.D., is an Assistant Professor in the Department of Counseling at the University of North Carolina (UNC) at Charlotte. She is the current director of UNC Charlotte's post-masters certificate in school counseling, and she teaches master's-level school counseling courses, such as Advocacy and Leadership in Professional School Counseling and Consultation in School Counseling. Dr. Merlin-Knoblich enjoys researching school counselors and multicultural education, including how school counselors can reduce prejudice and create equal opportunities for success for all K-12 students. Her research has been published in the *Journal of School Counseling, The Professional Counselor*, and *The Clinical Supervisor*.

John J. Murphy, Ph.D., is a Licensed Psychologist and Professor of Psychology and Counseling at the University of Central Arkansas and an internationally recognized practitioner, author, and trainer of client-directed, strengths-based practices with young people and schools. His books have been translated into multiple languages, and he received the American School Counselor Association (ASCA) Writer of the Year Award for the widely used text, *Solution-Focused Counseling in Schools*, now in its third edition. Dr. Murphy's work is featured in the *New York Times* best seller *Switch* and the popular DVD training series, *Child Therapy with the Experts*. In addition to his private practice in counseling and consultation, Dr. Murphy is a Consultant/Trainer for the North American Chinese Psychological Association (NACPA), a former finalist for NASP School Psychologist of the Year, and Project Director with the Heart & Soul of Change Project, an international research and advocacy group that promotes respectful, client-directed services for marginalized persons of all ages and circumstances. He is a highly sought-after keynote, workshop, and webinar presenter who has trained thousands of mental health professionals and school personnel throughout the United States and Europe, Scandinavia, China, Canada, New Zealand, and elsewhere. Dr. Murphy's lively training workshops are consistently rated as practical, informative, and inspiring. Information about Dr. Murphy's work and training opportunities is available at www.drjohnmurphy.com.

Chris Slaten, Ph.D., is an Assistant Professor in the Department of Educational, School, and Counseling Psychology at the University of Missouri–Columbia. Dr. Slaten researches the construct of belonging and how it impacts career and academic outcomes for youth and college students, particularly students who have been marginalized by the educational system. Dr. Slaten's passion for this line of research has led to 20 peer-reviewed publications, 25 national presentations, an international keynote address (China), national press recognition (*Wall Street Journal*), and several invited lectures in 6 years in academia. Furthermore, Dr. Slaten's scholarly work has led to publications focusing largely on advocating for school counselors to conduct more mental health services in K-12 settings, specifically related to counseling interventions that have a strong emphasis on marginalized youth and social justice initiatives.

Hayley L. Stulmaker, Ph.D., is currently a director of a nonprofit agency that helps teachers develop social and emotional skills to relate to students in the classroom. Prior to holding this position, she was a professor of counselor education. Dr. Stulmaker has worked in various school settings (public, private, and charter), in addition to different age/grade levels within the schools. She has a passion for developing children and specializes in play therapy. She has published and presented on the topic of play therapy and working with children and teachers in schools throughout her career.

Anya Woronzoff Verriden, Ph.D., works as a psychological assistant at Rogers Behavioral Health in Brown Deer, Wisconsin, on a partial hospitalization unit specializing in DBT with adolescents. Her research interests include belongingness in children and adolescents, STEM interests in underrepresented populations, trauma-informed care for children and adolescents, and identity development. Her background includes working as both a teacher and a school counselor in urban schools in Boston, Houston, and Milwaukee. Dr. Verriden obtained her Ed.M. from Harvard University in risk and prevention with a specialization in school counselingin 2008, and her Ph.D. in educational psychology with a specialization in counseling psychology in 2017.

Robert E. Wubbolding, Ed.D., is a psychologist and is Professor Emeritus at Xavier University, as well as Director of the Center for Reality Therapy in Cincinnati, Ohio. He has taught choice theory/reality therapy from Korea to Kuwait and from Singapore to Slovenia. His professional experience includes work as a high school counselor, elementary school counselor, halfway-house counselor for ex-offenders, consultant to the drug and alcohol abuse programs of the U.S. Army and Air Force, and private practitioner. He has written over 150 articles, chapters in textbooks, and 17 books, including the most comprehensive books on the topic: *Reality Therapy for the 21st Century* (Brunner Routledge), *Reality Therapy: Theories of Psychotherapy Series* (American Psychological Association), and *Reality Therapy and Self-Evaluation: The Key to Client Change* (American Counseling Association). He is a member of the American Psychological Association, American Counseling Association, Ohio Psychological Association, and many other professional groups. In October 2005, he received the award of Outstanding Graduate for the 1970s decade from the University of Cincinnati Counseling Department.

Brett Zyromski, Ph.D., is an Assistant Professor in the Department of Educational Studies at The Ohio State University. His scholarship focuses on the impact of evidence-based interventions in school counseling, evidence-based school counselor education, and evaluation in school counseling. Dr. Zyromski is co-author of *Facilitating Evidence-Based, Data-Driven School Counseling: A Manual for Practice*. He is also co-founder and co-chair of the national Evidence-Based School Counseling Conference. Dr. Zyromski has published over a dozen articles related to school counseling issues, has delivered over 65 international, national, regional, and local presentations, and has served as keynote speaker at numerous state conferences. Dr. Zyromski is also involved with the American School Counselor Association (ASCA) as a Lead RAMP Reviewer (Recognized ASCA Model Program), and he has also served as a trainer of the ASCA National Model for the American School Counselor Association. He has helped over 20 schools successfully earn RAMP over the last 5 years. Dr. Zyromski has served as project manager for $5,541,223 worth of federal and state grants. As a result of these efforts, five Elementary and Secondary School Counseling Grants have been received by Campbell County Schools, Erlanger-Elsmere Independent Schools, and Northern Kentucky Cooperative for Educational Services, which added over 20 additional school counselors to the Northern Kentucky region.

PART ONE

The Context of School Counseling

1

The Context of Professional School Counseling

The Need for Theory

COLETTE T. DOLLARHIDE AND
MATTHEW E. LEMBERGER-TRUELOVE

Schools have a heavy responsibility for educating our youth. Whether fostering cooperative, competitive, or individualistic learning (Johnson & Johnson, 1994), schools present students with learning opportunities in both content and form. Not only will students have learning opportunities in reading, social studies, math, and science, but also they will learn about time management, life management, relationships (with family, peers, and authority figures), managing their learning, and their place in society. Students will learn about themselves and others, and they will explore who they are and what their future holds, individually and collectively. For a narrow demographic segment of society—namely European American, cisgender, typically developing students from the middle and upper classes—school is designed to enhance their social and political capital (Lareau, 2011). For others, however, education may be more challenging than supportive.

Students of diversity—whose identities include racial, cultural, gender, and sexual identity; sexual orientation; cognitive, physical, psychological, and emotional abilities and challenges; faith tradition; economic security, including housing-secure and/or food-secure; family configuration; and other forms of diversity—do not always find schools to be welcoming, affirming places (Kozol, 2005). In fact, for diverse students, schools may be places that replicate colonial processes of marginalization, criminalization, and silencing (Emdin, 2016), a pattern that is also experienced by school counselors of diversity (Dollarhide et al., 2014). Students of racial/ethnic diversity will be the majority in American schools' population in 2020 (United States Census Bureau, 2015), and with other diverse identities factored into that projection, it is reasonable to conjecture that majority status has already been achieved. This means schools must change and must become equitable, just, and welcoming for all students (Advancement Project, 2010; Shields, 2013; Teaching Tolerance, 2014).

Currently, the dominant discourse about students of diversity is a deficit narrative: students are at risk (of failure, dropping out, becoming addicted, etc.) and come from broken or neglectful homes, with absent, uncaring, or dysfunctional caregivers. McWhirter, McWhirter, McWhirter, and McWhirter (2017) examined the social, economic, and family conditions in which students are situated and designed a continuum to help professionals assess students on the prevention–intervention continuum. In the analysis, they explored school factors that contribute to successful students and directly confronted the issues of social capital in schools, neighborhoods, and communities. If the only model of success in schools is the behavior and academic/social attainment of White, cisgender, normally developing middle- and upper-class children, then professional school counselors will become instruments of exclusion and oppression, since children of racial, cultural, economic, developmental, and identity diversity will not be valued for who they are and what they bring to the learning conversations for all persons in the school.

Knowing the reality of life in modern society is essential for school counselors to address nonacademic barriers to learning that manifest within the school. School counselors must be informed about the history and context of racism, misogyny, homophobia, transphobia, ableism, linguicism, and classism, among a host of marginalizing perspectives, and the systemic tools by which children and families of diversity are othered, including oppression, microaggressions, stereotype threat, exclusion, and victim blaming (Goodman & West-Olatunji, 2010). School counselors must know about trauma, poverty, addiction, homelessness, violence, and ways that children and families survive and thrive in the face of great challenges. Being educated about these issues and educating others in the school serve both to mitigate some of the oppressive structures that students must navigate on a daily basis and to provide support for students, families, and colleagues who identify as diverse (Dollarhide et al., 2014; Goodman & West-Olatunji, 2010). In this way, the deficit narrative surrounding families and children of diversity can be transformed into a narrative of resilience, hope, and empowerment.

Professional school counselors are integral to moving schools toward greater inclusivity and justice, and a useful construct for this transformation of the school environment is *community*. A learning community is one that values honest and caring engagement about ideas and relationships (Palmer, 1998). It is a collection of people in a space that is characterized by respect, civility, intellectual inquiry, and collaboration (Dollarhide & Saginak, 2017). The efficacy of

community in education is confirmed by educational research: high expectations for student success; collegial relationships; collaborative planning; a sense
of community, belonging, and safety; fair discipline; community support; and
high social capital (network of care) are all research-grounded indices of highly
effective educational settings (McWhirter et al., 2017). As school counselors
work toward social justice and community, they are transforming schools into
learning spaces where all voices are valued.

While social justice is not explicit in establishing community in schools,
the school counseling profession has infused social justice into its professional mission. In documents like the American School Counselor Association
(ASCA) *The ASCA National Model* (2012), the *The ASCA Mindsets & Behaviors
for Student Success* (2014), and the *Framework for Safe and Successful Schools*
(Cowan, Vaillancourt, Rossen, & Pollitt, 2013), school counselors are positioned
as providers of critical educational perspectives to foster development for
all students, and, to accomplish this, school counselors must be leaders and
advocates. A comprehensive school counseling program is the vehicle by which
school counselors can structure programs to facilitate holistic development for
all members of the school community: students, families, teachers, and staff
(Dollarhide & Saginak, 2017). Such programs are designed to provide for the
academic, career, and personal/social development of all students, using leadership, counseling, advocacy, and collaboration to bring about systemic change
(ASCA, 2012).

THE ASCA NATIONAL MODEL

Examination of *The ASCA National Model* (2012) provides grounding in the
professional perspectives for school counseling. The National Model outlines
how systemic change will evolve as school counselors work to facilitate the academic, career, and personal-social development of all students. To do this,
professional school counselors lead, advocate, and collaborate with students,
parents, teachers, administrators, and others to address individual and systemic
barriers to learning. There are four interlocking elements of the Model that capture an overall picture of what school counselors do:

1. School counselors create a solid *foundation* grounded in the values,
   beliefs, ethics, and vision of the profession of school counseling, the
   school, and the district, and from those foundations, they design
   goals that are informed by data collected on the levels of success of
   students.
2. School counselors design a *delivery system* for direct student
   service that provides counseling, prevention/intervention learning

opportunities, and collaborative planning for students' educational and occupational futures.

3. School counselors implement a *management system* that consists of agreements with administrators, input from all stakeholders, data about the school, students, and the program, and whole-school planning for lessons and closing-the-gap activities.

4. School counselors maintain an *accountability system* that facilitates data analysis and decision-making relative to the school, individual students, and the program as a whole. Outputs from the analyses are then used to guide future decision-making, closing the loop to determine programmatic goals for the coming year.

Because the tasks involved in the National Model's *foundation, management,* and *accountability* elements consist of effective management activities, the work can be conceptualized as a matter of extent—to what extent does the school counselor meet the standards of the National Model? To what extent are the mission, vision, and beliefs in place? To what extent does the school counselor maintain the management of the program and collect data on the numbers and efficacy of the services offered? To what extent does the counselor collect data on the students and their progress, and then to what extent do the results of analysis of that data impact programmatic goals for the coming year? Most school counselors do not consistently employ a theory of counseling to accomplish these activities. Rather, for many counselors, leadership theory and organizational strategies inform these efforts.

In contrast, the delivery system of the model, which outlines the direct services that the school counselor offers to the members of the school community, is a direct reflection of the counseling theory of the practitioner. Counseling theory may be used to organize other elements of the National Model (*foundation, management,* and *accountability*), but that depends on the nature of the theory. For example, while there is no "Adlerian" way of collecting and analyzing data, there is an Adlerian way to provide individual and group counseling. In contrast, counselors who hold an environmental or ecological view of students and schools may find environmental and ecological theories are very useful for conceptualizing an entire school counseling program. As a coherent system of organizing professional school counseling services, the National Model provides an overview of what needs to be done, but it does not provide the underlying why and how. The answers to the questions Why? and How? come from the counselor's theoretical orientation, not from the National Model.

THE NEED FOR THEORY

There is an important distinction between models and theories. Models are organizing structures that enumerate or outline what needs to be done, while theories offer insights into why and how things are done. A few examples will help illustrate this. In education, multiple models exist to help teachers and administrators manage student learning and behaviors, such as Response to Intervention (also known as RTI; available at http://www.rtinetwork.org/ learn/ what/whatisrti) and Positive Behavior Intervention and Support (also known as PBIS; available at https://www.pbis.org/). Models like RTI and PBIS are designed to structure educators' thinking about support for student learning in high-accountability environments like schools. Models for educational reform arise frequently in the literature (and seem to wane quickly as well); it is important for school counselors to be informed about these models so that they can be a part of conversations with building or district leadership about the impact the models might have on the nonacademic barriers to learning and about the potentially oppressive structures that might disenfranchise vulnerable students.

Models of School Counseling

Similarly, there are multiple models of comprehensive school counseling. Those that predate the National Model include the Developmental Guidance and Counseling model (Myrick, 2003), the Comprehensive Guidance Program model (Gysbers, Hughey, Starr, & Lapan, 1992), the Essential Services Model (Brown & Trusty, 2005), and the Strategic Comprehensive Model (Brown & Trusty, 2005). These models outline professional school counseling services and programs based on school needs and student development. However, variations exist in the models in terms of the conceptualization of the school counselor's role and the school counselor's delivery of direct service. Furthermore, the school counselor's role relative to advocacy and social justice is not articulated, since the models predate the Transforming School Counseling Initiative from the Education Trust (https://edtrust.org/).

Currently, the National Model is the model that the school counseling profession uses to define our role in schools. This model is the skeleton of our work; it provides structure. To add more definition to that structure, one model that was developed specifically to fit within the National Model is the Domains/Activities/Partners Model (DAP Model) developed by Dollarhide and Saginak (2017). Consistent with the National Model, the domains of the DAP Model address areas of development for all students, namely academic, career, and personal/social development. Activities in the DAP Model are also consistent with the National Model and include leadership activities (leadership, advocacy, collaboration, and systemic change found in the themes of the National Model), management activities (necessary for foundation, management, and accountability found in the elements of the National Model), counseling activities (counseling, crisis response, appraisal, and advisement found in the direct services of the delivery system of the National Model), educating activities (found in the core curriculum of the delivery system of the National Model), and consulting activities (consultation and referrals, found in the indirect services of the delivery system of the National Model). The partners of the DAP Model include students, families, colleagues in the school, and colleagues outside the school. The interactions among all the elements highlight the comprehensive nature of school counseling, in that all the domains, activities, and partners are mapped according to the needs of the school as outlined in the National Model.

Such large-scale models inform how services are structured and organized, but they are not detailed enough to fully populate school counseling programs. If the National Model is the skeleton, then curricular programming models provide the muscle. The programming models provide specific activities for each component of the school counseling program. For example, there are various curricular models that address suicide assessment from which school counselors can design crisis interventions, such as IS PATH WARM? from the American Association of Suicidology (available from http://www.suicidology.org/resources/warning-signs) and SLAP (Granello & Granello, 2007). There are also various curricular programs and models that can be used to address holistic student development, such as Developmental Assets and Developmental Relationships (available from http://www.search-institute.org/research/developmental-assets). There are programming models that can support career development programs for kindergarten through graduation, such as Career Clusters (available from https://careertech.org/career-clusters) and the eight components of college and career readiness (available from https://professionals.collegeboard.org/guidance/counseling/culture). In addition, there are models that support student learning, self-efficacy, and outcomes efficacy, such as Student Success Skills (available from http://studentsuccessskills.com/). Finally, there are models for student empowerment, such as Ruling Our eXperiences, a girl's empowerment group (ROX; available from https://rulingourexperiences.com/). These and many other excellent curricular programming models provide school counselors with programs to address specific needs in their schools, with interventions at each level: individual, classroom, small group, and whole school.

Theories of School Counseling

Models are necessary, but they are not sufficient. While they are excellent resources, models do not answer the questions Why? and How? To continue the metaphor, if the National Model provides the skeleton for your program and the curricular models provide the muscle, then to bring a program to life, it needs a soul, the why of what you do. You need a theory to integrate all the program components into a conceptual whole. Theory grounds the design of your program within a consistent philosophy about schools, the nature of students, and the process of development. For example, if you are naturally drawn to cognitive psychological theories, you might see the role of schools as the foundation of intellectual growth and career development, and school counselors as the facilitators of academic and career maturation, who implement programs like Career Clusters to teach academic and career decision-making. If you are naturally drawn to theories that deconstruct dynamics of power and oppression, such as feminist theory, you might conceptualize schools as instruments of systemic oppression and see your role in the school to be an advocate who helps students navigate power dynamics throughout life—for example, by implementing programs like ROX to facilitate and teach student empowerment.

Your theory, then, reflects your assumptions about people—how they develop; how they learn about life, themselves, and others; how they manage relationships with themselves and others; and how they encounter, react to, and manage change in their lives. These core assumptions allow you to breathe life into the National Model and guide your selection of other models to flesh out your program. Your theory forms the foundation of your work with students individually and in small groups; you will apply your theory as you design your classroom management strategies, as you select lessons to present to students in the classroom developmental curriculum, and as you engage in leadership with students. As an extension of your way of working, your theory will inform your leadership, advocacy, consultation, and collaboration behaviors. For example, consider the different leadership styles you might see in a task-focused, cognitive-oriented leader versus an affiliation-focused, affect-oriented leader. Such stylistic distinctions manifest in subtle ways for every unique theory in every aspect of the work of a school counselor.

As a result, now is the time to consider your theory and to reflect on how that theory would be used in your school counseling program. Consider the answers to the following questions:

1. What is the nature of human beings? Are we primarily feeling beings
   (affect), thinking beings (cognition), acting beings (behavior),
   or beings molded by context and relationships? Rank these four

constructs (affect, cognition, behavior, and context) from most important to least, from your personal perspective.

2. If you have trouble answering the first question, reflect on a recent life change you have made. This can help you to think about your personal perspective on the nature of human beings. When you made a life change, which construct was the first step for you, the second, etc.? Think about what had to happen for you to make the decision to change:
   a. Did you feel it was the right decision? (affect)
   b. Did you make a pros and cons list to decide? (cognition)
   c. Did you just act first, then decide based on that action? (behavior)
   d. Did you include all your significant others in your consideration of your decision? (context)

3. Now think about the age group of students with whom you wish to work (pre-K, elementary school, middle school, and high school). What ranking would you give each construct (affect, cognition, behavior, or context) for that age group? Use your knowledge of human development as you engage in the ranking process.

4. Reflect on how consistent your natural "theory" is with the style of the students you want to serve. To what extent will you be challenged to meet students where they are?

5. While all theories reflect all of the four constructs to some extent, each theory taps into one construct as its core, or starting place. For example, the cognitive-behavioral approach is highly cognitive, person-centered theory emphasizes affect, solution-focused theory centers on behavior, and ecological theory is highly contextual. Which theories focus on the construct(s) you naturally favor?

6. As you read about each theory in this book, envision yourself using that theory and assess its "goodness of fit" for your natural style as well as the student population you hope to serve.

Theory can also provide school counselors with mechanisms for evaluating outcomes pertaining to their practice. A theory of counseling is different from a theory that describes a static phenomenon, in that counseling theory relates to a therapeutic process designed to contribute to predictable changes in a student's experience. If a counselor adheres to the delivery of a counseling theory, our original questions transmute from why and how we choose to support students in a certain way to why and how those choices resulted in change. Theory also provides the counselor with potential points of evaluation, not limited to inquiries pertaining to the effectiveness of certain theory-informed techniques or student outcomes, such as changes in learning or social behaviors.

Theories of school counseling practice have a number of important uses for practitioners. For some novice school counselors, theory can stoke the counselor's thinking about students, school environments, and the helping process. For more seasoned professionals, theories can deepen practice, especially as one begins to employ techniques in a more personal and useful manner.

This book is designed to serve you as a professional school counselor. Each chapter was written by experts in that theory who are also experts in school counseling, and each chapter is unique in format and content. It is our hope that you will find yourself in these chapters and that you will find a theory or theories that will inspire you to breathe life into your comprehensive school counseling program.

REFERENCES

American School Counselor Association (ASCA). (2012). *The ASCA National Model: A framework for school counseling programs* (3rd ed.). Alexandria, VA: American School Counselor Association.

American School Counselor Association (ASCA). (2014). *The ASCA Mindsets & Behaviors for Student Success: K-12 college- and career-readiness standards for every student.* Alexandria, VA: American School Counselor Association. Retrieved from https://www. schoolcounselor.org/school-counselors-members/about-asca/mindsets-behaviors

Advancement Project. (2010). *Test, punish, and push out: How "zero tolerance" and high stakes testing funnel youth in the school-to-prison pipeline.* Washington, DC: Advancement Project.

Brown, D., & Trusty, J. (2005). *Designing and leading comprehensive school counseling programs: Promoting student competence and meeting student needs.* Belmont, CA: Brooks/Cole.

Cowan, K. C., Vaillancourt, K., Rossen, E., & Pollitt, K. (2013). *A framework for safe and successful schools [Brief].* Bethesda, MD: National Association of School Psychologists.

Dollarhide, C. T., Bowen, N., Baker, C., Kassoy, F., Mayes, R., & Baughman, A. (2014). Exploring the work experiences of school counselors of color. *Professional School Counseling, 17,* 52–62.

Dollarhide, C. T., & Saginak, K. A. (2017). *Comprehensive school counseling programs: K-12 delivery systems in action* (3rd ed.). Boston, MA: Pearson.

Emdin, C. (2016). *For White folks who teach in the hood. . . And the rest of y'all too. Reality pedagogy and urban education.* Boston, MA: Beacon Press.

Goodman, R. D., & West-Olatunji, C. A. (2010). Educational hegemony, traumatic stress, and African American and Latino American students. *Journal of Multicultural Counseling and Development, 38,* 176–186.

Granello, D. H., & Granello, P. (2007). *Suicide: An essential guide for helping professionals and counselors.* Boston, MA: Pearson.

Gysbers, N. C., Hughey, K. F., Starr, M., & Lapan, R. T. (1992). Improving school guidance programs: A framework for program, personnel, and results evaluation. *Journal of Counseling & Development, 70*(5), 565–570.

Johnson, D. W., & Johnson, R. T. (1994). *Learning together and alone: Cooperative, competitive, and individualistic learning* (4th ed.). Boston, MA: Allyn & Bacon.

Kozol, J. (2005). *The shame of the nation: The restoration of apartheid schooling in America.* New York, NY: Broadway Paperbacks.

Lareau, A. (2011). *Unequal childhoods: Class, race, and family life* (2nd ed.). Berkeley, CA: University of California Press.

McWhirter, J. J., McWhirter, B. T., McWhirter, E. H., & McWhirter, A. C. (2017). *At risk youth: A comprehensive response for counselors, teachers, psychologists, and human service professionals* (6th ed.). Boston, MA: Cengage Learning.

Myrick, R. D. (2003). *Developmental guidance and counseling: A practical approach* (4th ed.). Minneapolis, MN: Educational Media Corp.

Palmer, P. (1998). *The courage to teach: Exploring the inner landscape of a teacher's life.* San Francisco, CA: Jossey-Bass.

Shields, C. M. (2013). *Transformative leadership in education: Equitable change in an uncertain and complex world.* New York, NY: Routledge.

Teaching Tolerance. (2014). *Anti-bias framework.* Southern Poverty Law Center, Montgomery, AL: Author. Available from http://www.tolerance.org/social-justice-standards

United States Census Bureau. (2015). *Projections of the size and composition of the U.S. population: 2014 to 2060.* Available from https://www.census.gov/library/publications/2015/demo/p25-1143.html

2

General History and Conceptual Frameworks of School Counseling

CHRIS SLATEN, ANYA WORONZOFF VERRIDEN, AND THOMAS W. BASKIN

The profession of school counseling has evolved over the years, generally in a manner that relates to changes in society. Rapid industrial growth, swelling city populations, social reform and protest, and factory employment were prevalent at the turn of the 20th century and in the Industrial Revolution when the profession began. At this time, for no additional pay and with little structure, teachers were often placed in the position of vocational counselors and were given a list of responsibilities to accomplish in addition to their assigned teaching duties (Gysbers & Henderson, 2001). As the conceptualization of the school counseling profession expanded, it became apparent that school counselors were privy to students' mental health needs in addition to vocational concerns (Baskin & Slaten, 2014). As a result, throughout its history, school counseling has had a continually evolving role, including educator, staff support, administrator, scheduler, and testing coordinator. This means that the counselor has been charged with the responsibility for filling multiple professional gaps in pre-K–12 schools, a situation that has led to counselor burnout and an inability to address the emotional needs of students (Baskin & Slaten, 2014; Dahir, 2009; Foster, Young, & Herman, 2005). The ASCA National Model (ASCA, 2012) has redefined the role of the school counselor, but remnants of the old expectations remain in the minds of many administrators, teachers, and parents.

A BRIEF HISTORY OF SCHOOL COUNSELING

Initially, vocational guidance was the cornerstone of the school counseling movement, which had its origin in the work of Frank Parsons, who founded the Boston Vocational Bureau in 1909 and emphasized the importance of assisting youth. The root of Parsons' philosophy was to help youth choose a vocation via "scientific" means. For Parsons, this meant that the youth and the counselor worked toward three major goals: first, understanding the youth; second, understanding the vocational options available; and third, using logic and insight to direct the student to a productive career trajectory. After the posthumous publication of Parsons' seminal book, *Choosing a Vocation,* the city of Boston and the state of Massachusetts chose to incorporate vocational counselors into all pre-K–12 schools (Baskin & Slaten, 2014). Parsons' reach was broad, and in just a few years, more than 900 high schools in the United States had some component of vocational guidance within the school (Geisler, 1990).

Parsons' influence meant that more and more career and vocational programming was integrated into academic curricula. This systematic development came to be known as "the services model," which was organized around six major services for which school counselors were responsible: orientation, assessment, information, counseling, placement, and follow-up. The services model proved to be problematic from its inception because the model prescribed an extensive series of tasks, but school staff were not given a parallel increase in time and resources to accomplish the tasks. At that time, counselors were often teachers, who struggled to manage their educator responsibilities in addition to newly assigned counseling duties (Gysbers, 1990).

At the same time that Parsons pioneered the idea of vocational guidance, Jesse B. Davis became known as the "first school counselor" through his efforts to implement a systematic guidance program in Michigan public schools (Pope, 2009). Furthermore, Davis's work helped to advance the concept of vocational guidance, and he established the foundations for the National Vocational Guidance Association. Davis explored and expanded upon the concept of vocational guidance in his seminal book, *Vocational and Moral Guidance* (1914), which was widely read and served as a strong foundational resource that helped to further solidify the profession of school counseling.

At that time, the primary role of vocational counselors was to assist students in preparing for the work world. However, even when vocational and career guidance was the counselor's main purpose, debate emerged over the best way to perform this duty. As the profession began to define itself during the 1930s and 1940s, school administrators heavily determined the professional responsibilities of the school counselor (Cinotti, 2014; Gysbers & Henderson, 2006).

The publication of two works by Carl Rogers—*Counseling and Psychotherapy* (1942) and *Client-Centered Therapy* (1951)—moved the profession toward a more person-centered approach, emphasizing one-on-one support and personal growth. In 1953, the fifth division of the American Personnel and Guidance Association was established to meet the needs of the developing profession (Wittmer, 2000). Reflecting this shift in professional discourse, an emphasis on personal counseling expanded vocational guidance to include academic counseling.

In 1957, the Russians' launch of the first space satellite caused fear in many Americans, which resulted in a transformation of American education, with a new focus on science and technology. One direct result was the hurried reorganization of school counseling at the middle and high school levels (Wittmer, 2000). The National Defense Education Act (NDEA), passed in 1958, aided in the transformation, and the opportunity for school counselors to be hired in large numbers in schools across the country led to major growth in the profession. As a result, school counseling began to gain national recognition as a profession in the schools. The NDEA called for professional school counselors to be trained and placed in high schools across the country, primarily for testing purposes, to identify exceptional students and to encourage them to pursue careers in the hard sciences (Baskin & Slaten, 2014; Herr, 2003; Wittmer, 2000). Standardized testing was emphasized, in the belief that students with math and science aptitude could be recognized early and their education could be developed to meet the needs of a global market. Societal shifts also led to the Elementary and Secondary Education Act of 1965 (ESEA), which established funding for guidance and counseling in the schools to aid students in facing challenges due to rising unemployment, lack of civil rights, and poverty. NDEA and ESEA greatly increased employment for professional school counselors across the country and placed the profession on a national platform (Baskin & Slaten, 2014). At this time, the number of school counselors across the nation tripled, the teacher-counselor position prevalent at the beginning of the century was eliminated, and full-time counselors were hired. At the same time, school counselors became part of pupil personnel services, which often also included a school psychologist, a social worker, a nurse or health officer, and an attendance officer (Cinotti, 2014; Wittmer, 2000).

School counseling of the 1970s was redefined into a comprehensive, developmental program (Baskin & Slaten, 2014; Cinotti, 2014; Gysbers & Henderson, 2006). The redefinition endeavored to develop comprehensive approaches consisting of goals and objectives, activities, interventions, and evaluative measures. School counseling was defined in terms of developmentally appropriate, measurable student outcomes (Cinotti, 2014; Gysbers & Henderson, 2006). However, environmental and economic factors slowed the adoption of this new concept. Due to economic and environmental changes, the 1970s were marked by decreasing student enrollment and budgetary reductions, which led to reduction of counselor positions (Cinotti, 2014; Lambie & Williamson, 2004). As a result, counselors' roles and identities shifted to more administrative tasks and responsibilities in an effort to create more visibility and to attain a perception of the school counselor role as being necessary (Cinotti 2014). The added duties were often related to noncounseling school roles (e.g., scheduling, recess duty, clerical duties) and did not align with the current responsibilities of the counselors within the schools (Baskin & Slaten, 2014).

Comprehensive Developmental Guidance Programs (CDGPs)

The pupil personnel services models of the 1960s and 1970s offered services but lacked a defined and systematic approach, which resulted in the constant assignment of other duties to school counselors. The concept of comprehensive programming was created in response to this problem and focused on the program, rather than the position (Baskin & Slaten, 2014; Gysbers & Henderson, 2001, 2006). In other words, it was important for the school counseling profession to define the role of school counseling programmatically rather than to locate the role within one replaceable person. In 1983, the National Commission on Excellence in Education published *A Nation at Risk*, a report examining the quality of education in the United States and prompting a move toward educational reform that focused on testing and accountability (Lambie & Williamson, 2004). Standardized testing coordination duties were assigned to the counselor, in addition to previous administrative duties that had already been assigned, such as record keeping and scheduling. As a result, the concept of CDGPs gained traction in the 1980s and 1990s due to its emphasis on accountability and evaluation of practice (Cinotti, 2014; Gysbers & Henderson, 2006).

The CDGP described by Gysbers and Henderson (2000, 2001) involved developing a school counseling model that utilized "life career development," defined as "self-development over a person's life span through the integration of roles, settings, and events in a person's life" (Baskin & Slaten, 2014, p. 78). Essentially, the belief was that the model should focus on program development in a school setting. The CDGP is implemented in the school in four different domains: guidance curriculum, individual planning, responsive services, and system support (Basin & Slaten, 2014; Gysbers & Henderson, 2001). The first domain, guidance curriculum, encompassed core standards, activities, and interventions. This usually included classroom-level activities and prevention revolving around social/emotional, academic, and career-related information. The second domain, individual planning, encouraged planning and implementation of activities and interventions that are designed to aid in growth in designated areas of student development: academic, personal/social, and career development (ASCA, 2003; Cinotti, 2014). Practically, this meant the school counselor met with every student to ascertain and facilitate the student's academic, personal, and career goals. The third domain, responsive services, involved activities and services associated with student crises or student immediate needs, including suicidal ideation, grief/loss, conflict mediation, and child abuse and neglect. The fourth domain, system support, offered a process of systematic planning, designing, implementing, and evaluating (Gysbers & Henderson, 2006). Gysbers and Henderson (2006) also included a fifth domain, leadership, as school counselors must work toward systemic change to deliver student competency-based results.

Ideally, CDGPs were best executed with prevention in mind, were based on national and state standards, included multiple stakeholders, and were driven by student and school-level data and competencies (Gysbers & Henderson, 2000). Despite engagement in these models, the lack of decisive guidelines for the roles and responsibilities of school counselors was still an issue. To address this need, the American School Counselor Association (ASCA) developed the National Model, a framework for comprehensive school counseling that has become a widely accepted model and is the model most utilized across the country (Dahir, Burnham, & Stone, 2009).

The ASCA National Model

In 2003, ASCA utilized information from multiple sources (e.g., Bowers & Colonna, 2001; Gysbers & Henderson, 2001; The Education Trust "Transforming School Counseling Initiative") to create the National Model (ASCA, 2003), which resulted in guidelines and standards for school counselors on a national level (Baskin & Slaten, 2014). Since then, the model has undergone three revisions, the most recent in 2012. The aim of the National Model has been to integrate CDGPs (Dahir, Burnham, & Stone, 2009) into the academic mission of pre-K–12 schools, with the intent of ensuring that school counselors were incorporated into the mission of the school and were seen as a necessity in the school.

The National Model also consists of four quadrants that were developed to create and maintain effective comprehensive programming. The four quadrants are *foundation*, which includes the philosophy and mission of the program; *delivery system*, which focuses on proactive and responsive services; *management*, which addresses resources; and *accountability*, which incorporates results-based data and intervention outcomes to meet both long- and short-term goals (ASCA, 2003, 2005, 2012). The model further encourages accountability by supporting the collection and examination of data about the efficacy/

effectiveness of the work that school counselors do (Baskin & Slaten, 2012; Kaffenberger & Davis, 2009). The ASCA National Model emphasizes the school counselors' roles in leadership, advocacy, collaboration, and systemic change. Additionally, the standards of the National Model emphasize the educational nature of school counseling roles, encouraging classroom interventions and parent/student/counselor conferences (Baskin & Slaten, 2014).

A primary criticism of the National Model has been the major time commitment required for school counselors to develop and to implement curricula for classroom-based interventions (Baskin & Slaten, 2014). Baskin and Slaten (2014) argued that research reports written by practicing school counselors and published in ASCA's flagship journal have shown the effectiveness of school-based small groups in improving self-esteem (Schellenberg & Grothaus, 2009), in increasing positive behaviors (Sherrod, Getch, & Ziomek-Daigle, 2009), and in reducing loneliness (Bostick & Anderson, 2009). However, the ASCA National Model dictates that school counselors are not mental health therapists (ASCA, 2012, p. 86) and instead encourages more education-based approaches to working with students. In addition, considering a social justice perspective, Galassi and Akos (2004) contended that the ASCA National Model does not address marginalized youth and multicultural awareness.

Recently, ASCA has augmented the National Model with *The ASCA Mindsets & Behaviors for Student Success* (2014). The *Mindsets & Behaviors* are well grounded in empirical research. They include the development of self-management skills, the value of a sense of belonging within the school environment, understanding lifelong learning and long-term career success, and having a positive attitude toward work and learning. Thus, the *ASCA Mindsets & Behaviors* mesh extraordinarily well with the contextual perspective of school counseling. The contextual perspective directs school counselors to be rooted in counseling and psychotherapy and to apply them to the school context. The contextual model works well in the domain of schools and augments the ASCA National Model (Baskin & Slaten, 2014).

CONTEXTUAL SCHOOL COUNSELING (CSC)

CSC (Baskin & Slaten, 2014) aims specifically is not another theoretical orientation for school counselors, but highlights the essence of school counseling in such a way that it clarifies the key elements needed for any effective program. It is a framework developed to utilize counseling and to design activities within the school environment. Given the unique role of the school counselor that is emphasized by CSC, the primary client for the counselor is a combination of both academic student and therapeutic client. Since a school counselor meets with the individual in order to address a multitude of needs and over many different modalities, neither *student* nor *therapeutic client* truly encompasses the relationship between the school counselor and the individual. As a result, when the CSC perspective is discussed, the term *student/client* is used (Baskin & Slaten, 2014).

CSC highlights Frank and Frank's (1991) four major common factors in counseling, with the belief that, if school counselors are aware of and are able to use the common factors within a K-12 school environment, they will be operating with a congruent core philosophy that will benefit all student/clients, including vulnerable and diverse populations (Baskin & Slaten, 2014). The four factors are: confiding counseling relationship, a healing setting, a rationale, and active participation in a procedure.

Confiding Counseling Relationship

A confiding counseling relationship emphasizes the helping role of the school counselor, which Baskin and Slaten (2014, p. 83) described as an "emotionally charged, confiding relationship, with a helper (commonly with the participation of a group)." The counselor provides a psychologically safe environment and also highlights the need for group interventions. Emotions, as emphasized in the contextual model, are inextricably linked to how student/clients view, perform, value, and interact with the educational mission of the school. Thus there is a need for school counselors who are trained to support the emotions of student/clients in the schools. School counselors can serve as immediate identifiers of the emotional needs of student/clients within a school setting. Their training renders them uniquely able to assist student/clients with emotional issues that may become barriers to their academic success.

School counselors can create an environment where confidentiality, support, and a confiding relationship are at the forefront of their relationships with the student/clients they serve. The counselors' helping role may contrast with the roles of many teachers and administrators, because counselors can create a more emotionally positive school environment. Student counseling groups can have a major impact in the therapeutic process and in creating a therapeutic environment where experiences can be shared and allies can be found (Baskin & Slaten, 2014; Frank & Frank, 1991; Yalom, 2000).

A Healing Setting

The affirmation of student/clients' individuality by the school counselor is a critical part of CSC and allows counselors a unique opportunity to create a healing setting where student/clients are heard and taken seriously. Frank and Frank (1991) use the term *healing* to emphasize the instillation of hope and positive motivation, and they place healing in sharp contrast to demoralization. School counselors can achieve healing by increasing support in a school environment (Baskin & Slaten, 2014).

A Rationale

In CSC, school counselors utilize foundational knowledge to create rationales, or counseling conceptualizations, for addressing the challenges of their student/clients by using a strengths-based approach, which moves away from pathology. Frank and Frank (1991) emphasized that a rationale or counseling conceptualization provides a reasonable explanation for symptoms and then provides a procedure for resolving them. As a result, a CSC-informed, strengths-based rationale can encourage and promote the development and growth of strengths that are unique to each student/client (Baskin & Slaten, 2014).

Active Participation in a Procedure

Frank and Frank (1991) emphasized the importance of a procedure or ritual that requires active participation as a way of restoring health. In CSC, school counselors have the ability to implement a variety of interventions with the specific needs of student/clients in their schools in mind. CSC includes activities relevant to the school environment, where personal, social, academic, and career concerns are vital for a student/client. Goals can be broad but are student/client- and school-appropriate and can include racial and cultural priorities, specific personal issues, or family values (Baskin & Slaten, 2014). The interventions are implemented with the overall goal of increasing motivation.

TRAINING PROFESSIONAL SCHOOL COUNSELORS

Slaten and Baskin (2014) provided a framework for training professional school counselors based on CSC. The approach provides a theoretical framework that includes the importance of context in how school counseling is conceptualized. The framework included a competency-based approached and emphasized five main areas: relational, systems, science, application, and professionalism.

Relational

The relational cluster of the Contextual Counseling Professional Training Program (CCPTP) complements the CSC framework area of confiding relationship. This emphasizes the need for school counselors to develop and maintain supportive relationships with student/clients and their families through unconditional positive regard (Slaten & Baskin, 2014). Imel and Wampold (2008) emphasized that the therapeutic relationship is the most important factor that contributes to successful counseling outcomes. Relationship skills are a vital area of competency for school counselors who are trained through CSC. CSC emphasizes that school counselors should be focused on supporting and emphasizing the strengths of student/clients in multiple domains, including academic, career, and social/emotional issues. School counselors are positioned to be involved with student/clients in multiple settings (e.g., interventions, groups, individual encounters), which differ from the settings used by traditional psychotherapists (Slaten & Baskin, 2014).

Systems

Similar to a healing setting, the systems area highlights that navigating large systems can result in student/clients' discomfort. School counselors can contribute to the overall sense of belonging of K-12 student/clients and can provide a feeling of safety in the school setting, through schoolwide interventions (Slaten & Baskin, 2014). School counselors must also work to understand the multicultural needs of their student/clients and develop skills as advocates. School counselors must have effective communication and interpersonal skills for dealing with other adult non-mental-health professionals in a school setting. School counselors may have more access to their student/client throughout a given week, but they may be challenged to meet for shorter amounts of time multiple times a week. Additionally, they may see a student/client in multiple settings, such as a group or classroom intervention. This aspect of school counseling has implications for defining school counseling as a unique way of counseling.

Science

Research that relates to practice can help school counselors develop a basis of knowledge. Slaten and Baskin (2014) emphasized that it is important that school counselors be exposed to scientific knowledge that informs their future practice as professional school counselors. School counselors must be able to understand research activity and how it relates to the therapeutic relationship and the school setting.

Application

The principle utilized from CSC in the application area of training competency is the "procedure," which emphasizes conceptualization and treatment via counseling interventions. This includes the utilization of skills like empathy, reflection, unconditional positive regard, and open-ended questions, which are emphasized in a counselor training program. School counselors are given the unique responsibility of developing these skills with children in mind. As a result, the ability to establish rapport with children and to create a working therapeutic alliance is imperative. From a CSC perspective, this includes being informed about empirical findings in addition to having knowledge of primary and secondary interventions that can be delivered across multiple domains (Slaten & Baskin, 2014).

Professionalism

Ethical issues specifically related to youth should be emphasized in a training program. As highlighted by CSC, school counselors function in a complex school system that often involves ethical dilemmas that require consultation with the ethical codes of multiple professional organizations (e.g., American Counseling Association and ASCA). In addition, the ethical issue of confidentiality is complicated because parents have the right to access their child's mental health records. Thus, ethical principles are essential for school counseling, but they often have unique complications within a school context and require additional training and education to navigate (Slaten & Baskin, 2014).

CSC demonstrates that the core of professional school counseling includes establishing strong supportive relationships with student/clients, an emphasis on students as clients, and being congruent with the school environment. CSC, based in the common factors of contextual psychotherapy and appropriately applied within the K-12 setting, will benefit student/clients across a variety of domains. The contextual approach is consistent with current empirical research and can supplement any other school counseling model or theoretical orientation. These different theoretical approaches will be presented in upcoming chapters.

REFERENCES

American School Counselor Association (ASCA). (2003). *The ASCA National Model: A framework for school counseling programs.* Alexandria, VA: American School Counselor Association.

American School Counselor Association (ASCA). (2005). *The ASCA National Model: A framework for school counseling programs* (2nd ed.). Alexandria, VA: American School Counselor Association.

American School Counselor Association (ASCA). (2012). *The ASCA National Model: A framework for school counseling programs* (3rd ed.). Alexandria, VA: American School Counselor Association.

American School Counselor Association (ASCA). (2014). *Mindsets & Behaviors for Student Success: K-12 college- and career-readiness standards for every student.* Alexandria, VA: American School Counselor Association.

Baskin, T. W., & Slaten, C. D. (2014). Contextual school counseling approach: Linking contextual psychotherapy with the school environment. *The Counseling Psychologist, 42*(1), 73–96.

Bostick, D., & Anderson, R. (2009). Evaluating a small-group counseling program: A model for program planning and improvement in the elementary setting. *Professional School Counseling, 12*, 428–433.

Cinotti, D. (2014). Competing professional identity models in school counseling: A historical perspective and commentary. *The Professional Counselor, 4*(5), 417–425.

Dahir, C. A. (2009). School counseling in the 21st century: Where lies the future? *Journal of Counseling & Development, 87*, 3–5.

Davis, J.B. (1914). *Vocational and moral guidance.* Boston, MA: Ginn.

Foster, L. H., Young, J. S., & Hermann, M. (2005). The work activities of professional school counselors: Are the national standards being addressed? *Professional School Counseling, 8*, 313–321.

Frank, J. D., & Frank, J. B. (1991). *Persuasion and healing: A comparative study of psychotherapy* (3rd ed.). Baltimore, MD: Johns Hopkins University Press.

Imel, Z., & Wampold, B. (2008). The importance of treatment and the science of common actors in psychotherapy. In S. D. Brown & R. W. Lent (Eds.), *Handbook of counseling psychology* (4th ed., pp. 249–262). Hoboken, NJ: John Wiley.

Galassi, J. P., & Akos, P. (2004). Developmental advocacy: Twenty-first century school counseling. *Journal of Counseling & Development, 82*, 146–157.

Geisler, J. S. (1990). *A history of the Michigan Association for Counseling and Development: The silver anniversary.* St. Johns, MI: The Association.

Gysbers, N. C. (1990). *Comprehensive guidance programs that work.* Ann Arbor, MI: ERIC Counseling and Personnel Services Clearinghouse.

Gysbers, N. C., & Henderson, P. (2000). *Developing and managing your school guidance and counseling program* (3rd ed.). Alexandria, VA: American Counseling Association.

Gysbers, N. C., & Henderson, P. (2001). Comprehensive guidance and counseling programs: A rich history and a bright future. *Professional School Counseling, 4*(4), 246–256.

Gysbers, N. C., & Henderson, P. (2006). *Developing & managing your school guidance and counseling program* (4th ed.). Alexandria, VA: American Counseling Association.

Herr, E. L. (2003). The future of career counseling as an instrument of public policy [Special issue: Career counseling in the next decade]. *The Career Development Quarterly, 52*, 8–17.

Lambie, G. W., & Williamson, L. L. (2004). The challenge to change from guidance counseling to professional school counseling: A historical proposition. *Professional School Counseling, 8*, 124–131.

Pope, M. (2009). Jesse Buttrick Davis (1871–1955): Pioneer of vocational guidance in the schools. *Career Development Quarterly, 57*, 248–258.

Schellenberg, R., & Grothaus, T. (2009). Promoting cultural responsiveness and closing the achievement gap with standard blending. *Professional School Counseling, 12*, 440–449.

Sherrod, M. D., Getch, Y. Q., & Ziomek-Daigle, J. (2009). The impact of positive behavior support to decrease discipline referrals with elementary students. *Professional School Counseling, 12*, 421–424.

Slaten, C. D., & Baskin, T. W. (2014). Contextual School Counseling: A framework for training with implications for curriculum, supervision, practice, and future research. *The Counseling Psychologist, 42*, 97–123.

Wittmer, J. (2000). *Managing your school counseling program: K-12 developmental strategies* (2nd ed). Minneapolis, MN: Educational Media Corporation.

Yalom, I. D. (2000). *The theory and practice of group psychotherapy* (4th ed.). New York, NY: Basic Books.

3

Organizational, Institutional, and Political Challenges and Responsibilities in Professional School Counseling

TRISH HATCH

INTRODUCING THEORIES OF ORGANIZATIONAL, INSTITUTIONAL, AND POLITICAL LEGITIMACY

The quest for political legitimacy is an attempt to accumulate the support necessary for a profession to obtain the resources, authority, rights, and responsibilities of a rightful profession. Although the school counseling profession has struggled throughout history to secure a legitimate position as being integral to the educational mission of schools (Hatch, 2002, 2008), more recently the profession has received a boost in legitimacy through increased national attention from the Obama Administration and the Reach Higher Initiative (https://obamawhitehouse.archives.gov/reach-higher). Widely publicized events, such as announcement of the American School Counselor Association (ASCA) School Counselor of the Year (ASCA, 2016) and the initiation of the School Ambassador program at the U.S. Department of Education (Ujifusa, 2016), have increased national awareness of the important and vital role of school counseling in education. Positive press on the vital role that school counselors play in supporting students' academic achievement, college/career readiness, and social emotional development has increased considerably.

Presidential elections often shift the narrative in education, and the extent to which each new leader will affect progress toward previous goals is not known ahead of time. Given that school counseling is a relatively young profession that continues to grow, efforts must be made to guard against losing ground that has been gained. The profession is more likely to maintain its position and to be seen as a legitimate profession if those within it understand theories that form the foundation of professional legitimacy. This chapter describes organizational theory, institutional theory, and political theory, examines the profession through the lens of each theory, discusses how implementing evidenced-based practices and the ASCA National Model aligns with each theory, and suggests specific actions school counseling professionals can take to improve their programs, student outcomes, and the profession of school counseling.

Organizational Theory

> We have consistently been impressed with the dedication and hard work of virtually all of the individuals with whom we have been involved. And yet, we are concerned that a great deal of energy, enthusiasm and re-sources are being expended in ineffective ways.
>
> *(Center for Higher Education Policy Analysis, n.d., p. 18)*

Organizational theory is the study of control, prediction, and explanation in an effort to improve how effective and efficient an organization is in accomplishing its goals and achieving the results (outcomes) the organization aims to produce. In the 1890s, Max Weber, a German sociologist and an early proponent of scientific management, held that rationalizing an organization with precise sets of instructions and time–motion studies would lead to increased productivity, efficiency, and profitability. Weber believed that organizations develop formal structures that contribute to the efficiency with which their goals are pursued. Formal structures were therefore instruments of goal attainment and could be changed or modified to improve employee performance, ensuring participants behaved in calculated ways to achieve the desired objective within a centrally controlled, hierarchically structured, and rationally managed bureaucracy (Ogawa, 1992; Taylor, 1911; Weber, 1947). Further, organizational theory ensured that participants in the organization would behave in efficient ways calculated to achieve the desired objectives (Scott, 1992).

Historically, school counseling programs were not seen as having a "fixed division of labor; hierarchy of offices, and a set of general rules that governs the profession" (Scott, 1992, p. 40). Few programs operated with clear program definition or clear priorities (Gysbers, 2010; Hart & Jacobi, 1992; Olson, 1979). Students received very different prevention and intervention services from school counselors in one district than in another, or from one school counselor to another within the same school. Subsequently, school counseling programs have been perceived to have little to no organizational efficiency.

Rowan and Miskel (1988) theorized that organizational efficiency is often the main determinant of organizational survival. Internal efficiency is the ratio of inputs to outputs, or the amount of energy used for the amount of work performed. Organizations perceived as internally efficient would survive and often grow, whereas those perceived as inefficient would often be eliminated or reorganized. When applied to school counseling programs, organizational efficiency means ensuring that school counselors perform activities in such a way that they achieve the desired educational objectives. School counseling programs have been perceived as lacking internal efficiency (Fitch, Newby, Ballestero, & Marshall, 2001). Although some school counseling programs lack the empirical data needed to conclude that functioning in one way is more productive or produces better results than in another, measuring performance is necessary for the profession's survival (Hartline & Cobia, 2012; Hatch, 2008; Young & Kaffenberger, 2011). Creating formal structures for internal efficiency in the organization of a school means that school counselors utilize their time efficiently and effectively and measure the impact of their work to ensure goal attainment (student outcomes).

For example, say you want to create a widget. You would go through trial and error with different types of machinery and materials until the production of the widget was consistent, predictable, and cost efficient. The formula would be written down in a manual and everyone would know that this is the "recipe" for widget creation. However, if each worker or factory used varying materials or machinery, the widgets they produced would look different. Further, if the organizational manual for how to create the widget was not written, or was written but was not consistently implemented, then widgets within the same factory would likely appear different. Of course, we know that students are not widgets; they are individuals. However, what if we apply the widget metaphor and ask: What should every student know and be able to do as a result of the school counseling program?

Despite the introduction of the ASCA National Model (2002, 2012), many school counseling programs are still incredibly varied from site to site and district to district, so that there is little consistency or predictability in programs and services. Thus the organizational goals of effectiveness and internal efficiency are often not observable. Students receive very different curricula from the school counseling department in one district than in another, or from one school counselor to another within the same school. Goals and objectives may or may not exist, may be unlinked to data-driven needs, or may or may not be evaluated for effectiveness (Hatch, 2002). All too often, programs maintain the status quo of doing things the way they have always been done. Many do not measure the impact of their activities and do not know whether they are achieving the desired outcomes of the organization. For schools, the outcomes are focused on improving student knowledge, attitudes, skills, and behaviors that lead to academic achievement and success, primarily defined as eligibility for postsecondary options. When evidence of contributions to the efficiency and effectiveness of the organizational machine of school are lacking, administrators may decide to eliminate positions or shift responsibilities to support areas demonstrating more efficiency within the educational system.

Organizationally, program evaluation leading to program improvement resolves the professional challenge of organizational inefficiency. By measuring what works and what does not work, and then determining how to improve activities within their programs, school counselors create organizational efficiency leading to program effectiveness. Many school counseling programs adopt components of the ASCA National Model to support improved internal efficiency. Data about programmatic results collected by school counselors are used for program improvement. From an organizational theory perspective, when administrators receive evidence of how the work of the school counselors supports the capacity of schools to attain important educational goals, they value the contributions, see the program as integral, are more reluctant to lose counselors during budget cutbacks, and are less likely to assign counselors duties that detract from their professional work.

Institutional Theory

> In one sense, the entire history of public school guidance and counseling is a chronicle of individuals and movements attempting to gain acceptance by the gatekeepers of the existing educational order.
>
> *(Aubrey, 1986)*

Institutional theory focuses on an organization's effort to institutionalize certain structural elements and processes that establish rules, policies, and procedures (Ogawa, 1992, 1994). Organizations gain institutional legitimacy "by conforming to relevant norms, values, and technical lore institutionalized in society" (Rowan & Miskel, 1988, p. 363). Meyer and Rowan (1977) argued that modern societies have many institutionalized rules that are used in the creation and expansion of formal organizations. Many of these rules are rationalized myths that originate and are sustained through public opinion, the educational system, laws, and various media (for example, myths include retention works, online learning is less effective, class size reduction improves achievement, and homework is necessary for learning). As a result, many of the environmental forces acting on organizations are based on social and cultural pressures to conform to a given structural form. Schools are organizations that respond to these pressures. Policies are created that reflect established procedures—the way we've always done it.

Institutional theory can be discussed in two ways: operationally and socially. Operational legitimacy exists when structural elements, such as standards, policies, and procedures are in place that specifically delineate norms and routines. Social legitimacy exists when organizational members are contributing to the cultural pressures that lead to the creation of structural elements, such as job descriptions or evaluation tools. When members are involved in decision-making and are part of influencing the policymaking team, they are considered socially legitimate. Schools are a social milieu where both actual results and the perception of value to the organization affect resource distribution. Many informal institutional rules (e.g., who participates in leadership meetings, or who serves on interview panels) are not challenged because they derive from public opinion and contain cultural and social pressures to conform to a given structural operational legitimacy. Many school districts lack job descriptions for school counselors, appropriate evaluation tools, policies and procedures manuals, and/or language specifying school counselor-to-student ratios in budget documents. This lack of structural inclusion in district policies is an example of the profession's need for additional social legitimacy from an institutional theory perspective. Social legitimacy is present when school counselors are an indispensable part of the policymaking team responsible for the decision-making process of creating these structures. If school counselors are seen as indispensable to the organization, it will be evident by their inclusion in the important conversations and in the structural elements mentioned above. Thus, social legitimacy will lead to operational legitimacy and resolve the theoretical challenge.

Once school counselors earn social legitimacy as policy actors, they are more likely to be included in the process of decision-making. Subsequently, school counselors can contribute to the operational institutionalization of the structural elements and processes of establishing new policies and procedures that support the appropriate role of the school counselor. When visiting a school site where school counselors have institutional legitimacy, one will find artifacts, such as brochures, pamphlets, school handbooks, accreditation reports, and other similar materials, on display for parents and other interested community members, illustrating the important responsibilities of the professional school counselors and their vital role in the educational system. Statewide laws and education codes and policies will also reflect the essential role and appropriate ratios for school counselors.

Political Theory

> They listen to speeches and read articles by guidance leaders and are in-
> spired by the high-level nature of the work counselors should be doing.
> Then the cold reality of the tasks their administrator assigns them and the
> comparison is quite traumatic.
>
> *(Stewart, 1965, p. 17)*

Politics, as defined by Wirt and Kirst (2001, p. 4), is a "form of social conflict rooted in group differences over values about the use of public resources to meet private needs." Political decisions often hinge on the difference between two important weighted components: value versus resources. When a program is highly valued, it is said to have "social capital," and resources are more likely to be allocated year to year. However, when a program is not valued, it is more likely at risk. Each year, school districts must determine which programs to fund and which ones to cut from the budget. Schools must determine which demands they will meet, and which they will not. These decisions are made with consideration of the belief in a concept or action as the "right thing to do." School counselors operate best within the school system by anticipating and responding, just as others do, to the "various demands from school constituencies that have been organized to seek their share of values allocation from the school system" (Wirt & Kirst, 1997, p. 59).

The essence of any political act is the struggle of private groups to secure the authoritative support of government for their values (Wirst & Kirst, 1997). The quest for social capital by school counselors is an attempt to leverage the support necessary to obtain the resources, authority, rights, and responsibilities as a legitimate profession. This is a typical political move for groups or individuals, such as school counselors, who may see themselves as separate entities within the school organization. For many years, school counselors referred to themselves as being outsiders in school leadership and governance, and they were often directed by administrators to perform tasks that they viewed as not their responsibility (Stewart, 1965, p. 17). Over 40 years ago, Stewart noted comments from school counselors about being frustrated that they had no time to perform individual counseling due to clerical responsibilities and other duties. Unfortunately, little has changed for far too many school counselors. In a nationwide survey of school counselors, administratively assigned noncounseling activities was among the top concerns mentioned by school counselors (Hatch, 2002).

Schools are also political systems where some individuals have more power and influence than others in determining how finite resources are distributed and in establishing the institution's policies, procedures, structures, and routines. To resolve the challenge, school counselors must be integrated leaders at school sites, within school districts, in their regions, in their state, and in our nation. School counselors who garner social capital by increasing their value so that is it worth their resource will be more likely to benefit when local control decision-making models are in place.

It is important to show that the value of the program is worth the resource. As school counselors demonstrate efficiency, their programs' increased value will spur greater legitimacy and result in positive changes in the school counseling profession.

Theory Alignment to the ASCA Model

In 1997, ASCA created National Standards, a set of 122 standards and competencies in three domain areas: academic, career, and personal/social (Campbell & Dahir, 1997). The standards were designed to guide school counselors in what students should know and be able to do as a result of the school counseling program. In 2002, the ASCA National Model was drafted to provide a blueprint for building certain essential components with the comprehensive school counseling program. Driven by data, accountability, and standards, the model supported counseling programs in using a data-driven model for decision-making and in identifying the knowledge, attitudes, and skills all students would acquire as a result of participating in school counseling programs. An ASCA Model program promotes equity and access to rigorous educational experiences for all students and is designed to ensure, through the utilization of the assessments and tools, that the programs and services are delivered in a systematic fashion.

ASCA asserts that it created the ASCA National Standards and National Model to align with the educational reform movement and to link the work of school counselors with the academic mission of schools (ASCA, 2005; Bowers, Hatch, & Schwallie-Guiddis, 2001; Campbell & Dahir, 1997; Hatch & Bowers, 2002). As the co-author of the original versions of the ASCA National Model (2002, 2003, 2005), I believe the Model also addresses three theoretical issues that have historically plagued the profession of school counseling (organizational inefficiency and ineffectiveness, institutional illegitimacy both socially and operationally, and the lack of political social capital).

Organizationally, ASCA originally pushed for both National Standards and a National Model to assist schools in the creation and evaluation of a comprehensive school counseling program. In 1979, Olson complained that the lack of planning, accountability, and evaluation in school counseling programs had resulted in fragmented and inconsistent services for students. Many school counselors did not have access to a common or approved list of programs, services, or curriculum, and no unified structure existed to evaluate the school counseling program's efficiency. Counselors performed what was sometimes referred to as random acts of guidance. Otwell and Mullis claimed, "As counselors recognize legitimate challenges from the public at large for accountability in schools, they must find ways to demonstrate that counseling programs are essential elements of the educational process and contribute to improved academic achievement" (1997, p. 343). They charged that school counselors must show how their program contributes to the school's internal efficiency.

To address this lack of consistency in the profession, the ASCA National Standards (Campbell & Dahir, 1997) and the ASCA National Model (2002, 2003, 2005) were created. The National Model was strategically developed to improve the organizational efficiency of the profession by focusing on the results of the school counseling program. The National Model uses program evaluation as a central component of the school counseling program. Program evaluation derives its questions and concerns from the school's policies and programs; it is the process of drawing conclusions about the value of an activity or program. Program evaluation is linked to organizational theory as it measures and reports if an organization is accomplishing the goals the organization intends to produce (Weiss, 1998; Hatch, 2014a, 2014b).

Institutional theory explains that entrepreneurs work to institutionalize operational and structural elements, which organizations may adopt to gain social legitimacy rather than to enhance technical efficiency (Ogawa, 1994). The authors of the ASCA National Standards, Campbell and Dahir (1997), were entrepreneurs and acted as policy actors contributing to the cultural pressure that led to the creation of cultural structures. ASCA sought to gain operational legitimacy during the standards movement by creating their own "standards." The adoption of standards was perceived to be a useful addition to local school operations, and standards became widespread. In the same way, ASCA, as a professional organization, set out to promote the structural elements followed by the institutionalization of rules, roles, standards, and structures and created the ASCA National Model to better serve the interests of the school counseling profession. Furthering these structural requirements, ASCA created position statements, role descriptions, and evaluation tools that all reflected the National Model. ASCA used its motto, "One Vision, One Voice," as a national policy actor in leadership of the school counseling profession. More recently, *The ASCA Mindsets & Behaviors for Student Success: K-12 college- and career-readiness standards for every student* were released as the next generation of the ASCA National Standards (ASCA, 2015). Finally, ASCA awards a RAMP (Recognized ASCA Model Program) to schools and districts implementing the specific elements outlined in the National Model (ASCA, 2017).

Political clout is acquired through the garnering of social capital and plays an important role in determining the funding level and the role and function of school counselors. Many stakeholders in education are vying for a limited allocation of resources. Thus, it is critical for school counselors and school counselor leaders to operate within the system the same way a politician operates—by anticipating and nullifying the "competing demands from school constituencies that have been organized to seek their share of valued allocations from the school system" (Wirt & Kirst, 1997, p. 59).

Pat Martin, a leading national figure in school counseling, often states that school counselors must be at the "big table" if they are going to make an impact (serve as policy actors). In May 2014, a group of national leaders, including this author, visited the Obama White House and sat at the biggest of all tables to advocate for the inclusion of school counseling in the President's College Opportunity Agenda (January 16, 2014). The meeting stemmed from a growing concern that school counselors were not included during the roll-out of the College Opportunity Agenda. Instead, the language included teacher advisors and college access partners. Since language specifically identifying counselors as central to this work was lacking, one might argue counselors were not perceived as "institutionally legitimate."

The meeting was successful, and the Obama Administration agreed to begin the work of including school counseling language in the vernacular on improving college and career readiness. Since that time, great strides have been seen in operational and social legitimacy. After the May 2014 meeting, First Lady Michelle Obama spoke at the ASCA conference in support of the vital role school counselors play in college and career readiness, stating:

> School counseling should not be an extra or a luxury just for school systems that can afford it. School counseling is a necessity to ensure that all our young people get the education they need to succeed in today's economy.

Following this, two National Convenings were held (at Harvard and San Diego State University) to support school counselors' central role in the college and career readiness movement (Hatch & Owen, 2015; Savitz-Romer & Liu, 2014). The National Consortium for School Counselors and Postsecondary Success (NCSCPS) was then formed to continue to support the work of the Reach Higher Initiative (ncscps.org). Led by Michelle Obama, the initiative provided a platform for collective efforts to increase advocacy for the profession of school counseling (The First Lady's Reach Higher Initiative, n.d.). In collaboration with the Obama Administration, additional convenings were organized by NCSCPS members to support improvements and revisions in state and national policy, practice, research, and credentialing in school counseling

(Brown et al., 2016). Aligning the profession of school counseling with the White House initiative produced increased social legitimacy for the profession of school counseling (The President and First Lady's Call to Action on College Opportunity, n.d.). It contributed to operational and structural changes with the inclusion of school counseling language in the Every Student Succeeds Act (ESSA) (https://www.schoolcounselor.org/school-counselors-members/legislative-affairs). The initiation of the School Ambassador Fellows program at the U.S. Department of Education (DOE; Ujifusa, 2016) is another example of increased social legitimacy. School counselor ambassadors will serve as policy actors within the DOE and will contribute to increased awareness of the school counselors' appropriate role and function within education (see https://www2.ed.gov/programs/schoolfellowship/index.html). School counselors are eligible for this program. Finally, the school counseling profession received a strong social legitimacy boost through increased national attention when the Obama Administration honored the ASCA School Counselor of the Year at the White House (ASCA, 2016).

While national political valuing of school counseling as a profession was vastly improved during the Obama Administration, each new election brings political shifts. Each shift (locally, statewide, or nationally) requires that school counselors continue to demonstrate to their constituents that their value is indeed worth their resource. This requires school counselors to ensure that they are paying attention to the social legitimacy and political clout needed for the school counseling profession at the site level, district level, and state level. At the school site, school counselors must be valued by the administration to protect the sovereignty of their programs and to prevent the addition of quasi-administrative responsibilities to their workload when limited school resources are distributed. At the district level, school counseling social capital is necessary to ensure that the governing board views the program as essential. This means ensuring counselors regularly present results to board members, that leaders of school counseling's central offices are present in meetings with other leadership teams and are part of all reform movements. At the state level, the political clout of school counseling programs must rise to protect proper funding and role definition when state representatives receive pressure from various actions groups attempting to initiate school reform. Professional counselors and associations must proactively demonstrate how counseling programs support student achievement and ensure that reform is not enacted at the expense of counseling programs. This requires a concerted effort on the part of school counselors to address the professional challenges within the three theoretical constructs presented in this chapter. Table 3.1 summarizes these professional challenges.

A CALL TO ACTION FOR CHANGE IN SCHOOL COUNSELING

Organizational challenges can be addressed at all levels (K-12) by focusing on program evaluation and program improvement. This focus means asking questions like: What is the most efficient and effective use of a school counselor's time when teaching bullying prevention? What are the evidence-based programs that address student organizational skills? What is the most efficient way to help students understand graduation requirements? How should these learning topics be presented? Is it more efficient to see each student one on one, or in small groups? Are these topics best presented in a classroom session? Measuring results of school counseling activities (core curriculum, small-group interventions, etc.) will provide important feedback on what works, what does not work, and what to do differently next time. When school counselors collect process, perception, and outcomes data, they can determine the extent to which the lesson or group experience has contributed to improved learning or a shift in student behavior. Improving efficiency requires rethinking how activities are conducted and which steps take the least amount of limited time for the greatest amount of impact. In this way, school counselors will continue to refine their programs both developmentally and instructionally to become more efficient in meeting their program goals and objectives.

Some middle or high school counselors meet with each student individually to develop the student's individual learning plan (also referred to by some as a 4- or 6-year plan). If the school counselor is teaching the content of these plans, as well as graduation requirements, college requirements, and other items during each one-on-one session, this could take up a significant amount of time. However, if pretest and posttest assessments indicate that delivering core curriculum in classroom lessons is equally effective for teaching ninth grade students graduation requirements and can be accomplished in a shorter amount of time than is used in one-on-one sessions, then making this programmatic change will save time that can be spent providing other services to students.

Case Study #1, Ashley's Story

In Ashley's district, elementary school counselors are not required; the district provides counselors only at the middle and high school levels. Ashley is a new elementary school counselor hired after the faculty advocated utilizing site discretionary resources to fund a full-time counselor. Unlike the contracts for counselors at middle and high school, Ashley's contract does not contain a ratio. As a school counselor on soft funding, Ashley is keenly aware that she has no employment guarantees. She will have to earn her contract renewal. She

Table 3.1. THE PROFESSIONAL CHALLENGES OF SCHOOL COUNSELING: ORGANIZATIONAL, INSTITUTIONAL, AND POLITICAL

Theoretical Construct	Professional Challenge Facing the School Counseling Profession	How is the Challenge Manifested?	How Can the Challenge be Addressed?	Desired Outcome
Organizational	Lack of Effectiveness (predictive, desired, and intended goals and outcomes are met)	Do not measure impact of activities and do not know whether they work or not.	Evaluate the program	Measure results. Know what works and what does not work-conscious reflective practice.
	Lack of Internal efficiency (greatest output for least energy and resource)	Status quo, inefficiency, random acts of school counseling	Program improvement	Do more of what works, less of what does not. Program refinement; alignment with educational goals. Time efficiency.

Institutional	**Lack of Operational legitimacy** (structural elements in place)	Lack of structural elements that would serve to institutionalize (rules, norms, routines, policies, procedures, etc.). Unaware of ASCA Mindsets or National Model.	• **Educate on ASCA standards and model programs** • **Program consistency**	Indispensability. Influence policy actors to create institutionalization of structural elements, laws, policies, handbooks, routines, and procedures. reflecting appropriate role of school counselor Job descriptions, evaluation tools,
	Lack of Social legitimacy (serve as decision-making participants contributing to cultural pressures that lead to structural elements)	Not involved in site leadership, no legitimate voice in programs or policies	• **Becoming involved in decision-making** • **Systems change** • **Student advocacy**	Becoming a policy actor Influencing policy actors by contributing to the cultural pressure that lead to the creation of structures Partner with school leadership for systems change
Political	• **Value versus resource** • **Social capital** • **Political clout**	Reduction in force Undervaluing profession Increase in non-school counseling responsibility	• **Reporting program results** • **Marketing**	Seen as integral Valued Performing school counseling activities

begins to strategize through the lens of organizational, institutional, and political theories.

Organizationally, Ashley gathers baseline benchmark school climate and discipline data, and she begins delivering and evaluating her curriculum lessons
and providing both group and individual counseling interventions. She aligns
her lessons and activities to the ASCA Mindsets & Behaviors (2015), shares
her alignment with staff, collects data and adjusts her program based on this
data, and improves her practice. When one of her third grade classroom lessons
doesn't produce the assessed impact (on knowledge, attitudes, and skills) she
desires, Ashley revises the lesson, redelivers the curriculum, and finds improved
results. When her 20-minute 8-week group intervention provided for students
in two fourth grade classes and held at the students' lunch time are less effective
than the 30-minute 6-week groups held for students in two other fourth grade
classes during instructional time, she advocates to hold all groups during instructional time (on a rotating schedule so as not to interrupt the same content
area each week).

When Ashley's individual counseling schedule fills with multiple playground
and classroom referrals from fifth grade classes, Ashley collaborates with a supportive teacher to pilot a two-part lesson on conflict resolution in one fifth grade
classroom. When playground referrals in that class are reduced, she advocates
for the same lessons in all fifth grade classrooms, thus reducing her one-on-
one counseling load. By measuring the impact of her activities and learning
what does and does not work, Ashley becomes more efficient and effective. Her
internal efficiency (greatest output for least amount of energy and resource)
impacts her effectiveness (predictive, desired, and intended goals and outcomes
are met). Random acts of individual intervention are replaced with thoughtful-
ness, time efficiency, increased structure, and program improvement.

Institutionally, Ashley begins to create indispensability. Teachers wonder how
they ever managed without her as a school counselor. In an effort to create a program where there was none, Ashley creates schoolwide action plans, calendars,
and other structural elements, which she contributes to her evolving elementary school counseling program handbook (ASCA, 2012). She knows that operationally, rules, norms, policies, routines, and procedures improve institutional
legitimacy. As she improves her outcomes, teachers and administrators begin to
include her as a policy actor when decisions are made. When the school begins
its adoption of Positive Behavior Intervention and Support (PBIS), Ashley
becomes a central actor contributing to the cultural pressures and structures
that support an implementation where the counselor is a partner in the leadership and systemic change (ASCA, 2012). As she becomes involved in decision-
making, Ashley utilizes her agency to advocate for youth behavior risk surveys,
conflict-management programs, consistent discipline referral mechanisms in
classrooms, and the differentiation between minor and major offenses on the

playground. Her voice is legitimate and her leadership is integral. She has become socially legitimate.

Politically, Ashley regularly communicates program results and student outcomes to her faculty, administrators, and the school community of stakeholders. They experience her and her work as integral to the overall academic program for student success. Marketing her impact ensures everyone knows that her "value is worth the resource." Ashley's principal is impressed with the students' improvements and, valuing her expertise and professionalism, he only rarely assigns her a nonschool counseling task. Ashley has earned both political and social clout among the faculty, which results in her reappointment the following year.

Reflection: Do you know anyone with a similar story? Can you envision yourself following Ashley's example? Why or why not?

Case Study #2: Carlos' Challenge

Activity: Carlos is frustrated. He works so hard as a school counselor: Every day he comes in early and stays late, and he always responds to teacher and parent requests. Carlos has been to ASCA trainings and wishes he had time to use data and accountability, but the revolving door of referrals never stops. Lately, his principal has also added testing to his plate. How will he ever get through all his referrals when he has to organize testing? The last straw comes when he learns there was a committee meeting he wasn't invited to and now every seventh grader will need to take a new math sequence. Why wasn't he included in this meeting? After all, he's actually a former math teacher!

Reflection: What issues does Carlos face? Thinking through the lens of each theory, what professional challenges is Carlos facing? How might he address these challenges?

Case Study #3, Administrator Issues

The superintendent of a rural high school sought improvements in her school counseling program. An external evaluator visited the site to review facilities and counselor practices and to provide suggestions for improvements. Studying the site through the lens of organizational, institutional, and political theory revealed many challenges.

Organizationally, school counselors were unable to share any data on results of their program. They were not measuring impact on any activity. Counselors did not provide core curriculum, data-driven interventions, or other activities. Counselors admitted they spent most of their time performing "random acts of school counseling." The newest counselor confided that the "experienced counselors" didn't appreciate that they had a new counselor because it was making them "work harder." They preferred to maintain the status quo and to provide responsive services to students on an "as needed basis," as they had always done.

Operationally, there was no school counselor handbook, no brochure, no website presence, no current job description, and no evaluation tool or policy indicating the agreed-upon counselor role. Since structural elements were lacking, tradition and custom ran the program (and most of the traditions and customs were kept inside the heads, and not on the computers, of the school counselors). The counselors stated they didn't really know about, nor did they believe they needed to adopt, the ASCA model. In terms of social legitimacy, counselors complained they were not involved in leadership or decision-making at the site. Politically, they were most concerned that they were at risk of being reorganized, because they had heard a threat of reassignment and the possibility of hiring "new" counselors. Additionally, they complained they were asked to organize and deliver testing materials and to undertake other noncounseling responsibilities. Feeling "attacked" by administration for resisting noncounseling activities, and believing the union would not support counselors' positions during union negotiation, counselors did not feel valued or integral to the school.

Reflection: The school counselors in this program clearly lacked organizational efficiency and effectiveness, operational legitimacy, social legitimacy, and social and political clout. As you think about the challenges these counselors face, what recommendations would you have?

During the next year, opportunities were provided for counselors to attend trainings and to collaborate in creating new program policies and practices. At the end of the year, recognizing little shift in services for students, the superintendent "reassigned" the counselors and hired all new ones. Within 2 years, the new team, hired with clear expectations for measuring results, became both efficient and effective in delivering core curriculum and in providing data-driven interventions. As policy actors, the new school counselors participated in leadership team meetings promoting a social justice approach to access and opportunity for rigorous coursework for all students. In year three, the graduation rates and college readiness rates were so improved that school district leaders chose to add additional counselors. The new lead counselor was called on to tell the district's story at state conferences, and the district won a state-level award from the school board association for improved college opportunity outcomes for students.

New Duties: Marketing and Advocating for the Profession

Increasingly, school district governing board members who allocate funds to counselors want to know that counselors are assisting in the effort to improve the academic success of students. As schools move toward a local-control market economy where limited budgets require cost–benefit analyses that may affect programs and services, decisions will be made regarding nonmandated programs. Results of activities within school counseling programs shared effectively with the school and community can impact the profession both politically and institutionally. School counselors will earn social capital by making presentations to school boards that share the outcomes-based contributions of their activities as integral to student achievement. As they are increasingly valued, they will be less likely to receive a reduction in force and less likely to be asked to perform nonschool counseling activities. Reporting results will leverage school counselors' increased social legitimacy as they promote their indispensability as partners in student achievement (Carey, Dimmitt, & Hatch, 2007).

School counselors are encouraged to demonstrate their program's institutional legitimacy by ensuring the school counselor page is easy to find on the school website and that it shares program roles and outcomes. When inviting school board members and other political constituents to their site, counselors are encouraged to ensure vital physical and other program-defining artifacts are on display. A message of legitimacy is sent when the counseling office is called the "School Counseling Department," as opposed to the message of illegitimacy conveyed by calling the office "Attendance," as was recently seen on a campus visit. Legitimate programs have professionally prepared materials (such as action plans, calendars, results reports, newsletters, brochures, etc.) on display for any stakeholder to learn what school counselors do, the difference they make, when they are available, and how to contact them. Offices of counselors display copies (or a poster) of the ASCA National Model and framed certificates from recently attended professional development courses on evidence-based practices.

Table 3.2 lists indicators of legitimacy for school counselors through the lenses of organizational, institutional, and political theories.

CONCLUSION

When measuring the impact of school counseling programs, it is important to acknowledge that counselors can't measure everything they do. Some activities (e.g., crisis response) are difficult to measure and others (intensive interventions with students who self-mutilate, for example) may take years. However, there are certainly activities of school counselors, such as teaching curriculum lessons or running small data-driven group interventions, that can and should be measured. Nor is it expected that school counselors can attend every leadership meeting on campus. Being deliberate and thoughtful about

Table 3.2. CONSIDERATIONS FOR SCHOOL COUNSELORS IN EACH THEORETICAL
DOMAIN AREA

Organizational Theory *(School counselors . . .)*
Have planned curriculum delivered consistently year to year
Use their time efficiently
Use data to drive decisions and to measure outcomes
Write action plans with goals and plans for evaluation
Measure the impact of their activities
Discuss ways to become more efficient and effective
Are held accountable for measuring the impact of their interventions
Are involved in a continually reflective process
Use results for program improvement
Have clearly defined goals, objectives, and outcomes
Have clearly defined job descriptions
Have an evaluation tool specific to their work
Have clearly defined roles and responsibilities

Institutional Theory *Operational legitimacy (School counselors . . .)*
Have job descriptions that reflect their accurate role
Have evaluation tools that reflect their appropriate role
Are written into district policies and practices
Have caseloads that are determined by school policy
Are written into the budget with program goals, objectives, and expected outcomes
Have a program manual or handbook describing program implementation guidelines
Have pamphlets and brochures that clearly delineate roles
Are included on calendar of schoolwide activities
Have a prominent place on school's website that markets program
Have prominent labeling as the Counseling Department

Social legitimacy (School counselors . . .)
Are integral to the school's academic mission
Are an integral part of the site instructional team
Are an integral part of the school leadership team
Are viewed as leaders within the school and district
Are included in decision-making within the school
Serve on decision-making teams
Are student advocates
Are partners in systemic change
Have the support of teachers in the school

Political Theory *(School counselors. . . .)*
Have the support of administration
Share results of programs and activities at staff meetings
Share results of programs and activities at school board meetings

Table 3.2. CONTINUED

Have a website that is informative about the program to staff and parents
Market/share program activities at staff meetings
Market/share program activities in school newsletters
Market/share program activities on school website
Do not perform noncounseling duties (clerical, class coverage, test counting)
Are not at risk of losing their jobs due to budget limitations

the political and social necessity is strategic on the school counselor's part and will serve the school counseling program well. For example, meetings on prerequisite curriculum revisions or creating new discipline policies are examples of meetings where attendance (or lack thereof) would be noticed and send a clear message that the counselors are, or are not, integral to important systemic change issues in the school.

Determining which activities will be measured is an important decision that is best made through the lens of aligning with other academic goals within the school. Caution is recommended in selecting impact data to measure, to ensure it aligns with the site's goals and is central to the schools' mission. Finally, it's important to remember that school counseling is both an art and a science. While measuring impact and collecting results are vital to sustainability, paying attention to the "art" of counseling and the instincts of the school counselors who are implementing content will serve the program well in a balanced approach.

Reflection Moment

Imagine that the organization called "school" needs to test its students and therefore requires testing materials to be counted and collected. These are absolute priorities in the organization that must be accomplished. The organizational leader needs to find someone who can be counted on to do this important and necessary work. It is reasonable to assume the leader will scan the available human resources to determine which employees, if their current duties were reassigned, would be most able to take on this task with the least amount of disruption to the organization. If it is perceived that the testing needs outweigh the contributions that would otherwise be afforded the organization by the school counselor, then it is reasonable that the counselor is selected for these tasks. If, on the other hand, the school counselor is performing duties that are actively contributing to accomplishing the goals of the organization, so that lack of task completion would negatively affect the organization, then the leader will most likely look elsewhere.

1. What would you say if the principal came to you to assign this duty to you? How would you present your case, using concepts from this chapter, to support your contention that someone else should undertake the task?
2. Can you think of a time when you (or your site supervisor) were asked to perform a nonschool counseling activity to support the organizational "system" of school? What was your reaction? How did you respond?
3. What types of school counseling activities are you performing that align with the goals of the organization? What data have you collected and shared that show how your activities contribute to meeting the school's goals? With whom have you shared the data? Did it make a difference? Explain.

Application

Imagine the school principal is considering a new attendance or discipline policy (K–8) or a new academic policy, such as eliminating prerequisites to take AP courses (grades 9 to 12).

- What activities might the school counselor who was operating from an organizationally efficient and effective mindset be involved in to influence the policy decision, as compared to one who was not?
- How might a school counselor who had earned operational and social legitimacy contribute to the policy conversation, as compared to one who had not?
- What activities might a school counselor who had garnered social capital participate in, as compared to a school counselor who had not?

REFERENCES

American School Counselor Association. (2003). *ASCA National Model: A framework for school counseling programs.* Alexandria, VA: American School Counselor Association.
American School Counselor Association. (2005). *ASCA National Model: A framework for school counseling programs* (2nd ed.) Alexandria, VA: American School Counselor Association.
American School Counselor Association. (2012). *ASCA National Model: A framework for school counseling programs* (3rd ed.). Alexandria, VA: American School Counselor Association.

American School Counselor Association. (2014). *Mindsets & Behaviors for Student Success: K-12 college- and career-readiness standards for every student.* Alexandria, VA: American School Counselor Association.

American School Counselor Association. (2016, September, 21). https://www. schoolcounselor.org/asca/media/asca/Press%20releases/2017-SCOY-Finalists-Press-Release-(ASCA).pdf

American School Counselor Association. (n.d.). Recognized ASCA Model Program (RAMP). Available from https://www.schoolcounselor.org/school-counselors-members/recognized-asca-model-program-(ramp)

Aubrey, R. F. (1986). Excellence, school reform and counselors. *Counseling and Human Development, 19,* 1–10.

Bowers, J., Hatch, T., & Schwallie-Guiddis, P. (2001). The brain storm. *School Counselor, 39*(1), 16–19.

Bowers, J. L., & Hatch, P. A. (2002). *The national model for school counseling programs.* Alexandria, VA: American School Counselor Association.

Brown, J., Hatch, T., Holcomb-McCoy, C., Martin, P., McLeod, J., Owen, L., & Savitz-Romer, M. (2016). The state of school counseling: Revisiting the path forward. Washington, DC: National Consortium for School Counseling and Postsecondary Success.

Campbell, C. A., & Dahir, C. A. (1997). *Sharing the vision: The national standards for school counseling programs.* Alexandria, VA: American School Counselor Association.

Carey, J., Dimmitt, C., & Hatch, T. (2007). *Evidence based school counseling: Making a difference with data driven practices.* Thousand Oaks, CA: Corwin Press.

Center for Higher Education Policy Analysis, Rossier School of Education. (n.d.). *Making the grade in college prep: A guide for improving college preparation programs.* Available from http://www.usc.edu/dept/chepa/pdf/makinggrade.pdf

Fitch, T., Newby, E., Ballestero, V., & Marshall, J. L. (2001). Counselor preparation: Future school administrators' perceptions of the school counselor's role. *Counselor Education and Supervision, 41*(2), 89.

Gysbers, N. (2010). *Remembering the past, shaping the future: School counseling principles.* Alexandria, VA: American School Counselor Association.

Hart, P., & Jacobi, M. (1992). *From gatekeeper to advocate: Transforming the role of the school counselor.* New York, NY: College Examination Entrance Board.

Hartline, J., & Cobia, D. (2012). School counselors: Closing achievement gaps and writing results reports. *Professional School Counseling, 16*(1), 71–79.

Hatch, T. (2002). *The ASCA national standards for school counseling programs: A source of legitimacy or reform?* (Doctoral dissertation, University of California, Riverside). *Dissertation Abstracts International, 63,* 2798.

Hatch, T. (2008). Professional challenges in school counseling: Organizational, institutional and political. *Journal of School Counseling, 6*(22), n22.

Hatch, T. (2014a). *The use of data in school counseling: Hatching results for students, programs and the professions.* Thousand Oaks, CA: Corwin Press.

Hatch, T. (2014b). School counselors using data in college and career readiness. In National Association for College Admission Counseling (Ed.), *NACAC's fundamentals of college admission counseling* (4th ed.). Arlington, VA: National Association for College Admission Counseling.

Hatch, T., & Bowers, J. (2002). The block to build on. *ASCA School Counselor, 39*(5), 12–17.

Hatch, T., & Owen, L. (2015). *Strengthening school counseling and college advising: San Diego State University White House post convening report.* Available from http://cescal.org/special-projects/white-house-convening/

Meyer, J. W., & Rowan, B. (1977). Institutional organizations: Formal structure as myth and ceremony. *American Journal of Sociology, 83,* 340–363.

Olson, L. (1979). *Lost in the shuffle: A report on the guidance system in California secondary schools.* Santa Barbara, CA: Citizens Policy Center.

Ogawa, R. T. (1992). Institutional theory and examining leadership in schools. *International Journal of Educational Management, 6*(3), 14–21.

Ogawa, R. T. (1994). The institutional sources of educational reform: The case of site based management. *American Educational Research Journal, 31,* 519–548.

Otwell, P., & Mullis, F. (1997). Academic achievement and counselor accountability. *Elementary School Guidance and Counseling, 37,* 343–348.

Rowan, B., & Miskel, C. G. (1988). Institutional theory and the study of educational organizations. In J. Murphy & K. Seashore Louis (Eds.), *Handbook of research on educational administration* (2nd ed., pp. 359–384). San Francisco, CA: Jossey-Bass.

Savitz-Romer, M., & Liu, P. (2014). Counseling and college completion: The road ahead. Cambridge, MA: Harvard White House Convening Report. https://www.gse.harvard.edu/Counselingand-College-Completion

Scott, W. R. (1992). *Organizations: Rational, natural, and open systems.* Englewood Cliffs, NJ: Prentice-Hall.

Stewart, C. C. (1965). A bill of rights for school counselors. In J. Adams (Ed.), *Counseling and guidance: A summary review* (pp. 16–20). New York, NY: MacMillan.

The First Lady's Reach Higher Initiative. (n.d.). Available from https://obamawhitehouse.archives.gov/reach-higher

The President and First Lady's Call to Action on College Opportunity. (n.d.). Available from https://obamawhitehouse.archives.gov/the-press-office/2014/01/16/fact-sheet-president-and-first

The National Consortium of School Counseling and Postsecondary Success (NCSCPS) http://www.ncscps.org/

Ujifusa, A. (2016). *Education dept. expands ambassador program to school counselors.* Available from http://blogs.edweek.org/edweek/campaign-k 12/2016/10/education_dept_expands_ambassador_school_counselors.html

Weiss, C. (1998). *Evaluation: Methods for studying programs and practices.* Englewood Cliffs, NJ: Prentice-Hall.

Wirt, F. M., & Kirst, M. W. (1997). *The political dynamics of American education.* Berkeley, CA: McCutchan Publishing.

Wirt, F. M., & Kirst, M. W. (2001). *The political dynamics of American education* (2nd ed.). Berkeley, CA: McCutchan Publishing.

Young, A., & Kaffenberger, C. (2011). The beliefs and practices of school counselors who use data to implement comprehensive school counseling programs. *Professional School Counseling, 15*(2), 67–76.

PART TWO

Classical Theories of School Counseling

4

Person-Centered School Counseling

KIMBERLY M. JAYNE AND HAYLEY L. STULMAKER

Relationships are the context for change and growth in person-centered school counseling. Fundamental to this approach is the person of the school counselor and the counselor's embodiment of a philosophy about life as a whole. In this way, person-centered school counseling is an invitation to become a person in the world who seeks to live wholly and genuinely in relationships that allow others to be, and to become, fully themselves. The person-centered school counselor intentionally develops relationships with students, families, administrators, teachers, staff, and community partners to promote a powerful way of being and relating in the world to promote growth, change, and healing.

The epistemological foundation for a person-centered approach to school counseling is found in Carl Rogers' (1959) comprehensive theory of development and growth presented in his 19 propositions and his six necessary and sufficient conditions for change. Carl Rogers began his psychological career working with children and adolescents (Rogers, 1961), and his philosophy extended far beyond the reaches of counseling and psychotherapy to all relationships and environments intended to facilitate growth and development. When implementing person-centered school counseling, it is important to have a thorough understanding of this developmental theory and facilitative process. Together, they have a powerful ability to change not only individuals but also entire classrooms, schools, and larger educational systems (Rogers, 1977).

FOUNDATION AND EPISTEMOLOGY
OF PERSON-CENTERED THEORY

According to Rogers (1951), the individual is the center of a constantly changing world of experience and responds to the phenomenological reality as an organized whole. From birth, the child has one basic actualizing tendency or drive to move toward growth. The actualizing tendency is expressed through goal-directed behavior. Behavior is the child's best effort at meeting needs and seeking growth. Behavior is accompanied and facilitated by emotion and is best understood from the child's internal frame of reference. Most behavior is consistent with the self-concept, but some behavior may be brought about by needs and experiences that are not accurately symbolized in the self-structure (Rogers, 1951).

As the child engages with the environment, a part of the experience is integrated into the child's self-understanding. This self-structure is based on unique perceptions of experiences and the personal values attached to those experiences. Values are experienced directly by the individual or introjected from others as if they were experienced directly. In childhood specifically, values of parents, caregivers, and other significant relations may be adopted as the child's own. Additionally, as children experience conditional positive regard—being loved, accepted, and valued only when they meet the expectations or conditions of another person—they develop conditions of worth. A child believes that he or she is only valuable or acceptable if he or she behaves, thinks, or feels in ways that are pleasing or acceptable to important others.

Experiences are symbolized and organized into the self-concept. For some young students, experiences are ignored because they have no perceived relationship to the self-concept or they are denied and distorted because they are inconsistent with the beliefs about the self-concept. Denial of one's experiences leads to psychological maladjustment, whereas integration of one's experiences into the self-concept leads to growth and well-being. Experiences that are inconsistent with the self-concept may be perceived as a threat. Under threat, the self-concept becomes more rigid in order to protect and maintain itself. In the absence of threat, and in the presence of real understanding and acceptance, the structure of the self can be revised to integrate one's experiences. When all experiences are accurately symbolized in the self-structure through the organismic valuing process (one's moment-by-moment awareness of what best supports one's growth and development), persons become more understanding and accepting of self and others and move toward growth, maturity, and self-actualization.

THEORY OF CHANGE

Taking what we know of the person-centered approach and applying it to the school counseling environment can be very powerful. Imagine thinking about all persons in a school through a person-centered perspective. Immense changes to the school culture could occur through truly valuing, understanding, and connecting with each individual. When valuing, understanding, and connecting occur, all students can live up to their full potential, succeeding academically, socially, emotionally, and congruently developing into their best selves; faculty and staff members can perform their job duties to the best of their abilities; and parents are engaged and eager to work with the school for their students' success. These outcomes are made possible by the self-actualizing tendency, the innate drive that all humans have toward growth and development that is termed the organismic valuing process (Rogers, 1951). People are able to operate from their organismic valuing process when they are in relationships where they feel understood and accepted for who they are. If certain relationship conditions are provided, people will utilize their organismic valuing process to move toward self-actualization, functioning at their highest level.

Tapping into people's organismic valuing process is best achieved through relationships that are characterized by Rogers' (1957) six necessary and sufficient conditions for change. The first condition is that two persons, the counselor and the student, are in contact with one another. The second condition is that the student is in a state of incongruence or anxiety, resulting from a rigid self-structure. The third condition is that the counselor is congruent, real, genuine, and integrated in the relationship with the student. The fourth condition is that the counselor experiences and conveys unconditional positive regard, which is a deep valuing and acceptance of the whole person of the student. The counselor truly prizes the student as he or she is, regardless of behavior or other imposed conditions. The fifth condition is that the counselor experiences and conveys empathic understanding of the student's experience, self-structure, and internal frame of reference. The counselor attempts to truly understand and enter into what the student's world is like, as if it were the counselor's own world. The sixth condition is that the student perceives and experiences the counselor's congruence, empathic understanding, and unconditional positive regard. As long as these conditions are met, students will experience an environment free of threat to their self-structure and will be able to accurately integrate their experiences, grow, and become more congruent and integrated—more fully themselves.

Experiencing these relationship characteristics helps people develop to their full potential, while others who do not experience these conditions tend to experience conditions of worth within relationships, reasons why they are not worthy or good enough to be valued and accepted in the relationship (Rogers, 1951, 1959). All relationships, especially in early experiences, help people develop their self-concept, the way they view their entire sense of being and relate to the world (Rogers, 1959). People's self-concepts can shift due to new experiences of the six necessary and sufficient conditions throughout the lifespan, providing school counselors with a unique opportunity to utilize the school system to best facilitate growth and development of everyone involved.

Every student, teacher, parent, and staff member in the school has a self-concept based on previous relationships. Some of these relationships have developed in a way that is growth promoting for the individuals, but some have thwarted the individuals' optimal development process. The process of navigating a person-centered approach in schools can be challenging, because some personnel may be more primed to engage in supportive relationships, while others might need more time, attention, and creativity to develop secure relationships. However, all of these key personnel come together in a school to create an environment full of new relationships that can be opportunities for growth and change. This provides a perfect opportunity for school counselors to redefine the way that everyone involved in the school interacts and relates to one another to help provide more facilitative relationships.

Using a person-centered approach to school counseling can provide an extremely nurturing and unique perspective to the entire school environment. The goal of the person-centered school counseling program is to help create an environment in the school where students (and essentially everyone else within the school community) experience understanding, acceptance, and authenticity. Although students are ultimately the main focus of the school counseling program, the person-centered approach to school counseling focuses on the whole environment of the school to produce the most facilitative and consistent conditions for students across the school. To do so involves creating relationships among the adults who are involved in the school, as well as among the students. This might manifest as staff meeting groups where everyone is able to share what feels important to him or her and is met with understanding and acceptance from the school counselor and each other, following some instruction or norms around the group process. Conducting similar groups with parents and potentially joining parents and staff together can continue to build this cohesion. These groups can then be used in classroom environments among adults and students to further promote these relationships. The environment helps students move toward growth, learning, and constructive behavioral change.

When students experience environments free of threat, characterized by understanding, acceptance, and authenticity, they are able to move toward growth, learning, and constructive behavioral change (Rogers, 1959). They are able to integrate new experiences into their self-structure, to adapt freely to their environment, and to respond dynamically and constructively to themselves and others. The relationships that students experience throughout their education are the primary context for their learning and growth. To truly implement the person-centered approach to school counseling, it is important to understand children within their developmental and cultural contexts and worldviews in order to engage in facilitative relationships with them.

Theory of Change Applied to Young Children

A person-centered approach with young students includes a deep understanding of, and respect for, their developmental and cultural processes and capacities. Because of the emphasis on relationships as facilitative for growth, it is important to consider how young students best engage in relationships. Young children look to others as they develop in their self-concept (Rogers, 1951). These relationships are crucial and can be challenging if adults are not aware of the developmental status of students.

Young children have different developmental processes than adults. They have language and cognitive capacities that mimic those of adults; however, they are more naturally expressive through play and behaviors (Landreth, 2012). Play is a huge component of students' success because it is a means for them to grow, learn, and communicate (Landreth, 2012). Young children experience, understand, and express themselves more naturally through play or their behaviors. When trying to understand students and engage in relationships with them, it is best to do so through understanding their play or behaviors.

To illustrate how this works, let's look at a 6-year-old student, Omari. Omari is a boy in first grade who is causing disruptions in his classroom. Every time his teacher tries to get through a math lesson, Omari begins to talk to other students in the room, acts like the "class clown," or fumbles around in his desk. His teacher has tried to correct him multiple times through many positive reinforcement and punishment strategies, but nothing seems to work. Omari's behavior tends to escalate when the class is assigned math work independently: he rips up his work, runs around the classroom, and ultimately acts out in a physically aggressive manner. As a result of these behaviors, Omari has lost recess, has had to sit out during music, art, and P.E., has been assigned extra homework, and has had extra tutoring. However, nothing seems to be helping Omari, and he has been labeled a troublemaker throughout the school.

From this example, it seems like Omari is being defiant and trying to cause disruptions on purpose if his behavior is taken at face value. However, if you are attuned to him, it seems like his only struggles are around math. Math has always been difficult for Omari, and he seems to have internalized negative experiences of math into his self-concept. Therefore, as math tasks arise, he rejects the experience to try to keep his sense of self intact. When he is forced to perform math tasks, his self-structure is threatened, causing him anxiety. Omari's behaviors are his way of communicating his discomfort and anxiety with the subject matter, even though it seems like he is confident and being disruptive on purpose. As his teacher continues to focus on the behaviors, she seems to be missing what he is really communicating, reinforcing a negative self-concept and a conditional relationship based on good behavior. Based on this pattern, Omari will most likely experience challenges throughout his educational career.

When children experience obstacles to growth and development, from a person-centered perspective, it is a shift in environment that is essential to supporting health and wellness. In Omari's case, he needs an environment that will be more understanding and accepting of his anxiety around his math performance so he can integrate this experience in a way that allows him to take in more learning around math content without resistance from his self-structure.

When young children experience environments like classrooms or the counselor's office where they feel they are understood, valued, and engaged in a real and genuine relationship, they are able to access their innate capacity to grow, develop, and learn. For Omari, this would mean an adult truly sees his behavior as a means for him to communicate his anxiety around math. When an adult can respond empathically and with unconditional positive regard to Omari's experience of the anxiety, rather than to the behaviors that result from the feelings, he will be able to identify with the anxiety and move beyond it. Otherwise, he will continue to operate from his anxiety and will probably escalate in his behaviors because he wants to be understood and to escape his discomfort.

Finding ways to understand young students through their perspective is crucial in implementing a person-centered approach. Children communicate differently than adults, creating a need to be attuned to them in other ways. Young students need more opportunities to communicate through play-based and nonverbal activities in order to avoid behaviorally based communications that tend to be disruptive. Creating an environment that promotes children's natural way of communicating through play is an important step in being able to provide this approach effectively. Beyond the need to understand children, the theory of the person-centered approach continues to operate similarly across developmental levels.

REFLECTION MOMENT

Think about your early educational experiences as a young child. Remember what it felt like to learn how to be a student. Remember what your school or learning environment looked like. What pictures and words and colors were on the walls? Remember the smells of books, pencils, modeling clay, or the cafeteria. What it felt like to walk through the door. Think about the relationships you had with your teacher(s), principal, school counselor, and other students. Focus on the relationships that positively affected your learning and experience in school. Make a list of the defining characteristics of those relationships.

Theory of Change Applied to Adolescents

Like young children, adolescents thrive when they feel understood and valued as they are. Young children need adults to come to their level to feel understood, as do adolescents. Adolescents have better-developed capabilities, but they do have unique developmental concerns. They place a large importance on their independence and peer group during this stage of development (Ames, Ilg, & Baker, 1989). Therefore, in a person-centered approach, adolescents need to form relationships through feeling understood and valued, and need freedom to collaborate in their learning environment.

Adolescent students tend to feel constantly misunderstood, specifically by adults (Ames et al., 1989). They desperately seek approval and acceptance from their peers, because adults are not the central players in their lives and they feel like their peers can really understand them. They turn to their peers to continue developing their self-structure and may experiment with different behaviors that might contradict their former self-structure. Adults are still important to adolescents, but their peers increase exponentially in importance in developing their sense of self.

To help adolescents develop in their self-actualization, they need to engage in relationships where they feel valued, accepted, and understood. In adolescence, peers provide this acceptance and understanding more easily than adults; however, it is possible for adults to continue to provide these experiences for adolescent students. Adults can display understanding by providing more independence and collaboration in the school environment. Adults can provide the students with more opportunities for taking on responsibility and making choices, such as allowing them to choose to write a paper or create a slideshow presentation for certain projects. Students will feel more valued and accepted when they are allowed the opportunity to personalize their environment and learning. For example, students may benefit from being able to choose topics to explore that meet goals for skill or content mastery, to decorate or to design learning spaces, and to provide mentorship and leadership for other students. This change may require administrators and teachers to share more control with students. As they allow students to lead and direct their own learning, administrators demonstrate that student's experiences and values matter, increasing student motivation and engagement.

Additionally, taking the time to develop genuine relationships with adolescent students is hugely important in their success. As students advance through the educational system, their contact with adults in the school becomes more limited and is shared with more students in each class. For students to be successful, they need to feel they are cared for and understood, meaning that teachers and administrators need to take time to build relationships that are focused on getting to know the students beyond learning and behavior outcomes. School counselors work to build collaborative relationships with teachers and administrators that are characterized by the core conditions and to give their person-centered attitudes and skills away through teacher and staff training, support, and classroom interventions. Adolescents will quickly see through an adult's agenda to see the true motivation. From a person-centered perspective, it is critical for adults to accept and to relate to students fully, because teachers, administrators, and counselors understand that successful behavioral and academic outcomes will ultimately be achieved when students experience this kind of relationship.

With this developmental knowledge, applying a person-centered approach to adolescent counseling in the schools presents multiple opportunities for learning about relationships. Working systemically within the school can help adolescents not only feel valued and accepted by the school counselor, but also by teachers and peers (an especially important group for adolescents) to create a facilitative context for learning and growth. Creating experiences where teachers and peers are also providing understanding and accepting relationships with each other can help promote healthy development for adolescents.

REFLECTION MOMENT

1. Consider yourself as an adolescent learner. What obstacles did you experience to your learning? To your growth? To your behavior? What shut down your learning or ability/desire to behave? Take a few minutes and write down the answers to those questions.
2. Consider the important relationships you experienced as an adolescent in middle school and then in high school. What relationships were most genuine in your adolescence? In which relationship did you feel most genuine, your most open and real self?

PERSON-CENTERED APPROACH OPERATIONALIZED IN SCHOOLS

A person-centered approach to school counseling is holistic, systemic, and developmentally responsive in all aspects of its implementation. In addition to preventative strategies (such as core curriculum delivery; educational and resource programs to meet needs of students, parents, and the community; and individual, group, and crisis interventions), person-centered school counseling is fundamentally about affecting school culture, the learning environment, and relationships among all members of the school community. Cultural shifts based on the core conditions occur at the individual and small-group level within the school environment. Small groups of teachers can begin to feel more understood and accepted by the school counselor, leading to their ability to provide these conditions for students. Students, in turn, can begin to tap into their organismic valuing process through their relationships with their teachers and counselors. All of these changes, although they may seem incremental, can contribute to an overall shift in the school environment over time. A contemporary approach to person-centered school counseling includes adoption of a person-centered philosophy and practice by all major stakeholders in the school environment. If the school counselor adopts a person-centered approach on his/her own, however, other adults in the building may follow the school counselor's example, thereby improving relationships throughout the school.

Elementary

Person-centered school counseling at the elementary level involves seeking opportunities to promote relationships characteristic of Rogers' six necessary and sufficient conditions for change individually and systemically (Jayne & Ray, 2016). Because of the developmental level of young students, incorporating play-based interventions is extremely important to promote growth. Furthermore, intentionally affecting the systems and stakeholders that interact in schools, including teachers and parents, can help facilitate a shift in environment that may enhance the potential for all students. School counselors can utilize a person-centered approach in individual relationships across the school and systemically across families, classrooms, and community partnerships to develop and implement a comprehensive school counseling program, inclusive of all necessary aspects of school counseling.

Direct Services. Intervening individually with students who are demonstrating difficulties is fairly simple using a person-centered approach. Child-centered play therapy (CCPT) is a developmentally responsive intervention, adapted from Rogers' theory of change for children (Axline, 1969; Landreth, 2012). Additionally, CCPT has a strong evidence base supporting its use and effectiveness with children (Lin & Bratton, 2015; Ray, Armstrong, Balkin, & Jayne, 2015). CCPT can be facilitated by the school counselor with children who are identified as needing responsive services. The goal of CCPT is to develop a relationship with children characterized by the six necessary and sufficient conditions for change using children's natural language of play. Toys and materials are selected and set up purposefully to facilitate expression of a wide range of experiences for students. Landreth (2012) provided a full list of the toys that may be included to in a playroom and included how to create a mobile play kit when dedicated play space is limited.

The school counselor uses specific child-centered nonverbal and verbal responses, including eye contact, leaning toward the child, open body language, congruent tone of voice, congruent facial affect, reflections of nonverbal behavior, reflections of content, reflections of feeling, returning responsibility, esteem-building, and therapeutic limit-setting, to communicate empathy, acceptance, and authenticity to help students develop their self-structure in a way that allows them to operate as their fully functioning selves (Landreth, 2012; Ray, 2011). Ray (2011) provided helpful guidelines for how an elementary school counselor can develop a CCPT program to serve students, including advocating and communicating with teachers, administrators, and parents; accessing space and materials in a school environment; and managing assessment, referrals, and delivery of CCPT utilizing a waitlist procedure appropriate for the school setting.

Furthermore, group CCPT may be used to facilitate relationships among children. This modality is similar to individual CCPT, except that the emphasis is less on the relationship between the child and the counselor and more on facilitating interactions between the two or three students participating in group play therapy (Sweeney, Baggerly, & Ray, 2014). Group play therapy can be useful for school counselors to help promote a collaborative learning environment among students and to increase the direct contact between the school counselor and more students. Through individual and group play therapy, students may engage in facilitative relationships with the school counselor to promote growth and change.

School counseling core curriculum. CCPT is an excellent modality to use with students; however, resources are often limited in schools and responsive services may be applied to only a select few students. Therefore, implementing a school counseling core curriculum founded on person-centered principles can impact the school on a grander scale. Lessons that are used schoolwide can be a way to reach more students and build a greater community environment. More specifically, school counseling core curriculum lessons focused on empathy building, social and emotional competencies, and reflective listening skills will best promote a facilitative and safe environment for students. The following curricula have goals and approaches similar to those of a person-centered program, but they were not developed explicitly as a person-centered or child-centered curriculum. Person-centered school counselors are encouraged to utilize and develop curricula that support the philosophy and core conditions central to person-centered school counseling.

The 4Rs program (reading, writing, respect, and resolution) is class session curriculum broken up by grade. The curriculum is designed for teachers to teach weekly lessons (for a total of 35 periods) using children's literature as a starting point. The goal of the lessons is to develop caring and responsible behavior among students. Some of the topics covered in the 4Rs include building community, understanding and handling feelings, listening, cooperation, and dealing with diversity.

MindUP™ is another option for guidance curriculum that has 15 sessions included. The curriculum uses neuroscience concepts and mindfulness to help students learn self-regulation, perspective taking, empathy, and problem-solving skills. Additionally, MindUP™ can help teachers more accurately perceive their students and improves communication between teachers and students.

Last, RULER (Recognizing emotions in self and others, Understanding the causes and consequences of emotions, Labeling emotions accurately, Expressing emotions appropriately, Regulating emotions effectively) is split between 16 general lessons with daily implementation activities and 75 feeling word lessons. RULER is geared toward developing students' emotional intelligence. The focus of RULER is on helping students understand and regulate their emotions while simultaneously developing empathy for others.

In addition to delivering core curriculum that is consistent with a person-centered philosophy, the school counselor also seeks to present core curriculum utilizing child-centered skills and in a manner that is consistent with promoting empathic, accepting, and genuine relationships in the classroom. Classroom management skills and pedagogy are consistent with providing a facilitative environment in which the core conditions are modeled by the school counselor and experienced by the students. For example, when calling on students to participate or answer questions, the school counselor will use reflective listening and set limits in a manner that communicates fundamental trust and valuing of the children and provides an opportunity for the children to develop and express their capacity for self-direction and self-control. Opportunities for self-directed learning and collaboration are central to delivering core curriculum in a person-centered school counseling program.

Individual student planning. Person-centered theory operates on the principle that when people are in optimal environments, they will maximize their potential from their own inner resources. Therefore, in developing individual student planning, it is important to provide opportunities for self-directed learning within a supportive structure. The school counselor needs to possess knowledge regarding various educational and career paths and to work toward facilitating students' exploration of learning goals and careers that are meaningful to them. An example of this may be setting up a career fair that provides different opportunities for children to learn in different ways, such as having reading material on different careers, providing an experiential component to various careers where students can try out skills that are similar to different professions, and having people who currently are working in different professions come to interact with students. When this structure is set up, students can be free to gravitate toward careers that are meaningful and to learn about them in a way that is most supportive of their learning process. Additionally, the school counselor seeks to follow students' leads as they individually or collectively express interest in specific topics, learning or behavioral goals, and careers. The person-centered school counselor then provides opportunity for activities, play, classroom instruction, and relationships that support the students' self-directed learning and growth. For example, if a student or group of students show interest in airplanes, the school counselor may encourage a teacher to allow them to research, to create art, to integrate math, reading, or other subject matter into that area of interest, to incorporate metaphors from that area into dialogue and learning, and also to share their interest with other students.

Indirect student services. Because of the great emphasis placed on the context of the student within person-centered school counseling, working with teachers and parents is a central part of the approach. The school counselor can use various models to educate parents and teachers about person-centered attitudes and skills and to promote this way of engaging throughout the school and even home environments.

Child–Parent Relationship Therapy (CPRT; Landreth & Bratton, 2006) is a 10-session approach to teaching person-centered skills and attitudes to parents. CPRT combines a process-oriented group with a teaching and supervision component to effectively help parents learn and experience these types of relationships with their children. Parents are taught CCPT skills and conduct weekly 30-minute play times with their child to help strengthen their relationship. The school counselor can facilitate these groups with parents to help broaden their reach among students in the school. Additionally, if parents support the school counselor's goals for creating person-centered facilitative relationships, the school culture is more likely to change.

Like CPRT, Relationship Enhancement for Learner and Teacher (RELATe; Ray, Muro, & Schumann, 2004) is a model created for elementary school teachers to develop facilitative relationships with their students. RELATe is a condensed version of CPRT, lasting 7 hours and consisting of role-plays, lectures, demonstrations, live practicing with students, and handouts and worksheets. Teachers select a student to have individual play sessions in which they can practice their relationship-building skills. The teachers consult with the school counselor to continue improving their ability to communicate empathy, unconditional positive regard, and congruence within their individual play sessions and to generalize these skills and attitudes to many of their interactions with all of their students. Ultimately, teachers are able to gain new perspectives on their students, which helps them respond more empathically and effectively during all situations in the classroom.

Combining child-centered play therapy, core curriculum consistent with a person-centered philosophy, self-directed learning in classrooms and the counseling office, and person-centered skills for parents and teachers can create an ideal person-centered approach to elementary school counseling. Students as individuals, small groups, and entire classrooms can experience a warm, understanding, and supporting environment through these services. Additionally, including parents and teachers to continue this level of contact through relationships can lead to a school environment that helps promote learning and growth systemically.

Middle School

Person-centered school counseling at the middle and elementary levels share many similarities. Like young children, adolescents thrive when they feel understood and valued and are given the freedom and opportunity to collaborate with adults in their education and learning environment. The middle school counselor continues to focus on developing empathic, genuine, and accepting relationships with all stakeholders in the school in a manner that honors the developmental needs of students and affects systemic change. Whereas the elementary school counselor typically spends more time in the classroom and in providing direct responsive services to students, the middle school counselor begins to engage in more individual student planning. Additionally, the middle school counselor incorporates more prevention and intervention strategies that are focused on promoting positive peer interactions and relationships, given the ever-increasing importance of peer relationships in social world of the adolescent.

Direct Services. As students enter middle school and begin to straddle the worlds of childhood and adulthood, interventions often include elements of play, activity, and talk. Activity therapy, sandtray, and expressive art activities may be utilized with middle school students individually or in small groups to facilitate relationship development and communication between counselor and students, and to convey acceptance of the students at this unique time in their development. In activity therapy, the counselor provides materials similar to those used in play therapy that are appropriate and engaging for middle school students. Toys and materials are intentionally selected to support the development of a strong relationship between the counselor and student and to facilitate the child's expression and creativity. Items that may be utilized in activity therapy with adolescents include woodworking, sewing, a wide range of craft and art materials, simple cooking or baking supplies, puppets, building toys, dart board or small basketball hoop, tabletop foosball or air hockey, a deck of cards, and/or Jenga.

In sandtray, sand and miniatures are utilized to provide a means of expression and communication. Sandtray can be used in individual and small groups to allow students to explore and to express themselves nonverbally and verbally. Through sandtray, children are provided a plate or tray of sand, then they are allowed to choose from miniatures and to place the miniatures in the sand to create a "scene." Recommended categories of miniatures include people, animals, buildings, vehicles, vegetation, fences/walls, natural items, fantasy, household items, and landscaping items (Homeyer & Sweeney, 2016). A variety of prompts may be utilized to support middle schooler's use of sandtray, but the primary goal is to provide a context where the students' developmental needs and means of communication are valued and supported and the student experiences an authentic, empathic, and accepting relationship with the counselor.

Similarly, expressive art is a modality that allows middle school students to integrate their need for nonverbal and verbal expression. Art can be used by adolescents to visually communicate feelings and experiences that are difficult to explain with words. Many adolescents enjoy using art materials and, when given the opportunity, naturally employ art to express themselves. Expressive arts may be utilized in individual and small-group counseling to facilitate relationships that promote growth. The school counselor responds to the middle school students as they express themselves verbally and nonverbally, carefully attending to their range of experiences and communication.

School Counseling Core Curriculum. 4Rs, MindUP, and RULER all provide curricula that can be utilized beyond elementary school through eighth grade. Additionally, the middle school counselor often supports teachers in delivering school counseling core curriculum in their classes as it relates to their classroom processes and subject matter. The person-centered counselor engages teachers and administrators utilizing the core conditions and models how to provide facilitative environments for students.

Individual Student Planning. At the middle school level, individual student planning shares many similarities to planning in elementary school; however, there is often an increasing emphasis on career and college readiness and academic achievement. It is critical for the person-centered school counselor to balance the demands and expectations of the educational system with the needs and development of the individual student. The goal is to understand the student's goals, to support those goals, and to advocate for understanding and support from key stakeholders in the student's life. The person-centered school counselor believes that all students want to grow and have the capacity for growth, and the counselor seeks to assess and alter how the environment supports or obstructs their growth.

Indirect Services. Child–Parent Relationship Therapy (CPRT) and RELATe may also be used and adapted for young adolescents. Through these programs, parents, teachers, administrators, and/or school volunteers learn person-centered attitudes and skills and then utilize them to connect with the child during a weekly one-on-one, 30-minute age-appropriate activity, such as cooking together, creating or building something, or outdoor or physical activities. The goal is to spend time together doing an activity that is of interest to the child, that is not overly structured, and that is not focused on a specific outcome.

In addition to utilizing child-centered training and education models for parents and teachers, person-centered consultation with parents and teachers continues to be critical in middle school. The objectives of person-centered consultation (Stulmaker & Jayne, 2017) are:

- To provide the core conditions of empathic understanding, unconditional positive regard, and congruence to the parent
- To support the parent's understanding of the child's behavior and internal frame of reference
- To help the parent experience greater empathy for, and acceptance of, the child
- To promote systemic change in the child's environment

In consultation, the person-centered school counselor actively seeks to convey unconditional positive regard, genuineness, and empathy to promote growth within the parent, teacher, and other adult stakeholders. As the parent and teacher experience the core conditions with the school counselor, they will become more capable of accessing and demonstrating these attitudes in their interactions with the student. This allows the growth-promoting environment to extend beyond the school counselor's office and creates systemic change in the learning environment for students.

EXAMPLE: PERSON-CENTERED SANDTRAY THERAPY

Sophie comes to the counseling office to see the school counselor because she and her best friend, Paige, had a fight during lunch. Sophie is visibly upset and has been crying. She sits down in a chair in the counseling office. She has a math test next period.

COUNSELOR: Hi, Sophie. Looks like things are a bit rough for you right now.

SOPHIE: [Teary.] I can't go back to class. Everyone is staring at me and Paige just keeps laughing at me.

COUNSELOR: Mmm. You're embarrassed to cry in front of everyone and it sounds like you and Paige are not getting along right now.

Counselor uses empathic responding to convey understanding and acceptance of Sophie's experience.

SOPHIE: She took my notebook and showed it to everyone at lunch. I have private stuff in there that I don't want everyone to see. It's not their business. [Sophie starts sifting sand through her fingers in the sand tray on the school counselor's table.]

COUNSELOR: You feel betrayed and angry.

Counselor reflects Sophie's feelings to facilitate self-understanding and convey empathy.

SOPHIE: I don't know why she always does stuff like that. She's supposed to be my best friend.

COUNSELOR: That's not how you want your best friend to treat you.

Counselor makes a reflection of the deeper significance of this experience in order to convey to Sophie that the counselor is fully aware and is open to Sophie's experience.

Sophie continues to sift and smooth the sand. Glances towards the shelf of miniatures.

COUNSELOR: You're welcome to use any of the miniatures on the shelf, too, if you want.

Counselor is attentive to Sophie's verbal and nonverbal communication. Sensitive to her interest in using the sand, the counselor provides understanding and support for the natural direction Sophie's expression of herself.

Sophie stands up and starts looking at different figurines. She chooses a shark, a puppy, a purple flower, a stone wall, and several blue stones. Using the stones, she makes a circle and puts the shark in the middle, she puts the puppy dog near the edge of the circle and then picks it up and places it behind the wall. Sophie adds purple flower, ladybugs, and butterflies around the periphery. Counselor attends to Sophie as she creates a scene in the sand. Sophie becomes more calm and is no longer as angry or tearful as she creates her sandtray. Sophie pauses after adding more butterflies.

COUNSELOR: It looks like you've added lots of different things. We only have a few minutes before you need to get back for fifth period. Can you tell me about what you made?

Counselor provides structure for Sophie by providing a reminder of the limit on the time they have to spend together. Counselor allows Sophie to share about her creation and the counselor is careful not to impose an agenda or interpretation on Sophie's sandtray. Sophie sits back down. She begins by pointing out and labeling all the miniatures she's added.

SOPHIE: Here are some flowers, and butterflies, because I think they're pretty. . . .
    And this is a shark in the water. And the puppy is over here.
COUNSELOR: Behind the wall.

Counselor clarifies to check for understanding and convey engaged attention to Sophie's description and experience.

SOPHIE: Yeah. The puppy wants to get near the water but it's too dangerous with the shark.
COUNSELOR: So the puppy wants to swim and play in the water, but is afraid of the shark.
SOPHIE: It's safer behind the wall.
COUNSELOR: Safer to hide where the shark can't get him. The puppy wants to feel safe.
SOPHIE: The puppy wants to swim and not get eaten.
COUNSELOR: It wants to be in the water and be safe, but doesn't feel like it will be, because the shark is there.
SOPHIE: Yeah. You know, sharks just circle and circle around, they don't stop swimming. So there's nowhere to hide or go in the water.
COUNSELOR: Mmm. Shark-infested waters. Yikes. [Pause.] It's hard for the puppy to feel like he either has to swim with sharks where it's dangerous or hide alone behind the wall. Looking at them, I feel some fear and sadness.
SOPHIE: It's not fair.
COUNSELOR: Oh, and there's some anger too.

Sophie reaches into the sandtray and squishes the shark with her fingers, burying it under the sand.

COUNSELOR: There it goes.
SOPHIE: Now it can't bite anyone.
COUNSELOR: You got rid of the shark.

Depending on time, the counselor may draw parallels between Sophie's sandtray and her own experiences at school. However, the person-centered school counselor values and trusts Sophie's ability to express her thoughts and feelings nonverbally, through the symbols and sandtray she has created. The counselor begins by relating genuinely with Sophie and following the student's natural direction. The school counselor seeks to communicate empathy and understanding of Sophie's experience in the way Sophie naturally communicates it. The counselor also understands that Sophie may experience a greater sense of control and agency through her sandtray than she feels in her peer relationships at this time. The counselor provides structure and safety, by attending to the time Sophie is in her office, and allows Sophie to move toward a more calm and regulated state before returning to class. Depending on Sophie's needs and future social interactions, the counselor may follow up with Sophie in the following days or weeks.

High School

As in elementary and middle school, high school counseling from a person-centered perspective is focused primarily on a philosophy and belief system that is expressed through the person of the counselor and the counselor's relationships with all members of the school community. Each encounter is an opportunity for empathy, genuineness, and unconditional regard, as well as engaging students as growing persons in dynamic processes of becoming their full selves.

Direct Services. Activity therapy, expressive art, and sandtray may all be utilized with high school students, but many older adolescents increasingly utilize verbal communication in their interactions with the school counselor. Group interventions are key to responsive services at the high school level because they allow the person-centered counselor to utilize peers as agents of change and support and to access more students in need of responsive services. In addition to responding to students experiencing challenges and crises individually and in groups, counselors can also offer high school students a modified CPRT mentorship program, in which the students are taught person-centered attitudes and skills and build relationships with middle or elementary school students (mentees) with whom they have regular play or activity interactions. The high school students benefit from experiencing and practicing how to build strong relationships which are characterized by empathy, acceptance, and perspective-taking. In this way, high school students learn how to provide a relationship and context that supports the growth of younger students. A CPRT mentorship program allows counselors to collaborate across developmental levels to support the needs of students as they transition through elementary, middle, and high school.

School Counseling Core Curriculum. High school counselors typically have few opportunities to deliver core curriculum, but they often provide classroom support related to college and career preparation. The person-centered high school counselor utilizes opportunities in the classroom or at assemblies to build relationships with, and among, students and teachers, and to help students explore topics and developmental tasks, such as taking the SAT, applying for jobs, or learning study skills, within the context of an environment that facilitates growth. The high school counselor models and utilizes person-centered attitudes and skills in the classroom.

Individual Student Planning. Individual student planning is the high school counselor's primary medium for direct interaction with students. While the focus of individual student planning is often student performance, academic and/or behavioral outcomes, planning and support toward graduation, and college and career readiness, the person-centered school counselor approaches these tasks and interactions with a deep valuing of the student and trust in the student's innate ability to grow and develop. The counselor maintains the primary goal of providing an environment for the student in which growth and self-direction are possible. Regardless of the concern or task at hand, student check-ins always focus on establishing an authentic relationship with the student as a whole person and communicating regard and empathy to the student. Additionally, the counselor collaborates with the student to understand needs and goals within and beyond the school setting.

The person-centered counselor recognizes that all other tasks are secondary to, and supported by, the core conditions. Even in a brief 10- or 15-minute interaction with students, the person-centered school counselor considers the following questions: Am I showing students I care about them as a whole person? Am I showing students that I understand and value them exactly as they are in this moment? Am I showing students that I trust in their ability to grow in the ways they need to? Am I being real in my interaction with students?

Indirect Services. In addition to providing training and education that teaches person-centered skills and attitudes to parents, teachers, and administrators, the counselor uses parent and teacher consultation as a key opportunity to create systemic change. Especially as adolescents move closer to adulthood and gain increasing independence, it is important to include and collaborate with the adolescents in consultation. In person-centered consultation, the high school counselor seeks to develop strong relationships with the students and other consultees and to facilitate constructive relationships among all members of the consultation team. Goals are developed collaboratively, honoring the student's experience and perspective and promoting true empathy and under-standing among all participants.

Example of Individual Student Planning

Marcus, a gender nonconforming student who identifies as nonbinary and prefers the pronouns they/them, is called to the school counselor's office be-cause Marcus has received multiple zeroes on homework in algebra and lan-guage arts classes. The school counselor is asked to track and support all students with failing grades at multiple times throughout the term. The school counselor has had only brief interactions with Marcus previously to help Marcus make schedule changes and forecast career plans. The school coun-selor is aware that Marcus transferred to this high school at the beginning of junior year, 3 months earlier, and does not seem to have many friends at school.

Marcus enters the school counselor's office and sits down.

COUNSELOR: Hi, Marcus. I'm glad to see you.

Marcus nods and appears solemn.

COUNSELOR: So, you may have an idea why I called you here today, and you may even be wondering if you're in trouble or something because most students don't really love being called to the office.

Marcus makes more eye contact with counselor.

COUNSELOR: I was made aware that you have had several missing assignments in algebra and language arts.

The counselor wants to establish trust with Marcus and to be congruent in the relationship by quickly acknowledging Marcus' unease at being called to the counselor's office and the initiating reason.

Marcus nods his head again and looks away at a poster on the wall.

COUNSELOR: So that's the "official" reason why I was able to pull you out of class, but what I'm really hoping is that we can actually spend our time today getting to know each other better. We haven't had a chance to spend much time together since you started here.

Marcus appears to relax a little bit and returns eye contact, but starts shaking his leg up and down.

COUNSELOR: [Points to some pens and paper on the corner of his desk.] Maybe you'd like to start by making a list of the top 10 most interesting things about yourself.

The counselor quickly focuses on building a relationship with Marcus and strives to demonstrate empathy and acceptance, while understanding that Marcus will only be open to the counselor and able to grow and learn in an environment where he feels understood, valued, and accepted.

Marcus smiles briefly and then rolls his eyes.

COUNSELOR: Ah. Or you can use the pens and markers to doodle if you prefer. I'm curious what you think of it here, since you started a few months ago.

MARCUS: It's okay, I guess.

COUNSELOR: I'm guessing, some parts feel more or less okay than others.

MARCUS: I don't know. It's different.

COUNSELOR: Mmm. Different. Good different? Bad different?

MARCUS: I don't know. I guess I like some of the teachers here.

COUNSELOR: Yeah. I noticed your grades are Bs and Cs in your other classes. Maybe those teachers or subjects are easier to connect with.

MARCUS: [Appearing more anxious.] Uh. Yeah. They're not as hard, I guess.

COUNSELOR: Oh, looks like that worried you a bit. Me bringing up grades again. . . . I wanted to be honest that I looked at your student record before you came into the office and that I know your grades in your other classes.

Marcus nods his head in understanding.

COUNSELOR: So, you were saying that maybe those classes are not as hard or maybe those teachers are easier to connect with.

MARCUS: I guess so. Some teachers get me. Some teachers don't.

COUNSELOR: Mmm. Yeah. And it makes sense to me that maybe you're wondering if I am going to "get you" or not since you don't really know me yet.

MARCUS: [Looks away again.] Yeah. I guess.

COUNSELOR: I promise I'm not trying to make this the most awkward conversation ever. [Smiles.]

Marcus makes eye contact again, and smirks.

COUNSELOR: I'm guessing that it is the same with other students. Some get you. Some don't.

MARCUS: Yeah. I'm not like every other kid here.

COUNSELOR: And maybe you enjoy being different in some ways, take pride in it even, but it can also be hard. Isolating.

MARCUS: Sometimes.

COUNSELOR: Just being new here can be tough. And I'd like to try to see if we could make things a little better for you.

Marcus shrugs.

COUNSELOR: You're not convinced that's possible.

MARCUS: I don't know.

COUNSELOR: Okay. Well, I'd like to talk more about it, if that works for you. If we could check in once a week for a few weeks.

MARCUS: Okay.

COUNSELOR: Cool. I will take that "OK" and run with it. [Smiles.]

Marcus smiles briefly.

COUNSELOR: I also want to see if maybe there's a few things we can do to help you out in math and language arts. See if maybe your teachers would be willing to give you some extra time to make up your missing assignments.

Marcus shrugs.

COUNSELOR: Is it okay with you if I check in with them before we meet next week?

MARCUS: Sure, I guess.

The counselor continues by scheduling a time to meet with Marcus for a 10- to 15-minute check-in the following week. Through this interaction, the counselor actively worked to convey empathy and understanding for Marcus. The goal was to allow Marcus to experience the counselor's empathy and acceptance of Marcus as a whole person, not simply a student who is experiencing barriers and missing assignments. While the counselor is committed to supporting Marcus' academic, social, personal, and career development, the counselor understands and believes that Marcus will only be able to achieve success and growth in these domains if Marcus experiences an environment free of threat and characterized by the core conditions. Throughout the interaction, the counselor sought to understand Marcus' experience and to provide unconditional acceptance of Marcus' missing grades and willingness or unwillingness to communicate openly to the counselor.

LIMITATIONS

Further research and development of effective person-centered preventions and interventions are needed to support person-centered school counseling. While Rogers considered person-centered philosophy applicable to all relationships and contexts and focused much of his own work on learning and education from a person-centered perspective, more work needs to be done by contemporary person-centered researchers and practitioners to continue to develop and to explore the effectiveness of person-centered interventions in schools, including person-centered core curriculum, responsive services, individual student planning, and consultation.

Application of person-centered theory with the high caseload of a modern-day school counselor and with the demand for brief interventions is often cited as a limitation of a person-centered approach to school counseling. However, it is important to understand that person-centered school counseling is truly about a "way of being" for the school counselor as he or she interacts in the educational environment and with students, teachers, administrators, parents/guardians, and the community. Additionally, person-centered interventions can be effectively facilitated in brief and short-term applications. For example, CCPT can effectively be provided in 20 to 30 minutes, and sandtray, expressive arts, play, and activity therapy can be skillfully and creatively utilized in 5- to 30-minute interactions with students.

To have maximum impact, commitment and implementation beyond the comprehensive school counseling program and the school counselor is ideal. However, person-centered school counseling can improve relationships in the building through modeling growth-producing ways of relating and interacting. Person-centered school counseling is fundamentally a belief system about how children and adults best grow and learn, and it is a commitment to creating an optimal environment that facilitates growth. Many educational environments are established and administered on principles that are in direct opposition to a person-centered philosophy and approach. While some may consider the incongruence between a person-centered approach and modern education an overwhelming or impossible challenge, the necessity for person-centered practice and principles in schools and school counseling is even more critical to support the growth and learning of students today. The belief that each relationship and interaction has the potential to be individually and systemically transformative is fundamental to person-centered school counseling.

Application

1. Make a list of the characteristics and skills that you consider essential for a person-centered school counselor. After completing the list, consider what you would need to continue to develop each of those essential characteristics and skills.
2. Write a mission and/or vision statement for your person-centered school counseling program. How would you communicate person-centered principles and philosophy through the mission and vision statement for your comprehensive school counseling program?
3. Create an outline or annual plan for a person-centered counseling program for the age level (elementary, middle, or high school) you plan on working with or currently work with as a school counselor. What services and programs are you going to provide for your school community based on a person-centered perspective? How would a person-centered approach affect your annual calendar and your use of time as a school counselor? What would be your 1-, 3-, and 5-year plan for integrating a person-centered philosophy throughout your school?

RESOURCES FOR FURTHER LEARNING

BOOKS AND ARTICLES

Fabelo, T., Thompson, M. D., Plotkin, M., Carmichael, D., Marchbanks, M. P. III, & Booth E. A. (2011). *Breaking schools' rules: A statewide study of how school discipline relates to students' success and juvenile justice involvement.* New York, NY: Council of State Governments Justice Center; Public Policy Research Institute of Texas A&M University.

Homeyer, L., & Sweeney, D. (2016). *Sandtrapy therapy: A practical manual.* New York, NY: Routledge.

Landreth, G. L., & Bratton, S. C. (2006). *Child parent relationship therapy (CPRT): A 10-session filial therapy model.* New York, NY: Routledge.

Lin, D., & Bratton, S. (2015). A meta-analytic review of child-centered play therapy approaches. *Journal of Counseling & Development, 93,* 45–58.

Morrison, M. O., & Helker, W. P. (2010). Child–teacher relationship training. In A. Drewes & C. Schaefer (Eds.), *School-based play therapy* (pp.73–88). Hoboken, NJ: John Wiley & Sons.

Ray, D. C. (2011). *Advanced play therapy: Essential conditions, knowledge, and skills for child practice.* New York, NY: Routledge.

Ray, D. C. (Ed.). (2016). *A therapist's guide to child development: The extraordinarily normal years.* New York, NY: Routledge.

Ray, D., Armstrong, S., Balkin, R., & Jayne, K. (2015). Child centered play therapy in the schools: Review and meta-analysis. *Psychology in the Schools, 52*, 107–123.
Rogers, C., & Freiberg, H. J. (1994). *Freedom to learn*. New York, NY: Pearson.
Sweeney, D., Baggerly, J., & Ray, D. C. (2014). *Group play therapy*. New York, NY: Routledge.

WEBSITES

Center for Play Therapy, University of North Texas: http://cpt.unt.edu/
Evidence-based Child Therapy: http://evidencebasedchildtherapy.com/

REFERENCES

Ames, L. B., Ilg, F. L, & Baker, S. M. (1989). Your ten- to fourteen-year-old. New York, NY: Dell Publishing.
Axline, V. (1969). *Play therapy*. New York, NY: Ballantine.
Homeyer, L., & Sweeney, D. (2016). Sandtrapy therapy: A practical manual. New York, NY: Routledge.
Jayne, K. M., & Ray, D. C. (2016). Child-centered play therapy as a comprehensive school counseling approach in schools: Directions for research and practice. *Person-Centered & Experiential Psychotherapies, 15*(1), 5–18.
Landreth, G. (2012). *Play therapy: The art of the relationship* (3rd ed.). New York, NY: Routledge.
Landreth, G. L., & Bratton, S. (2006). *Child-parent relationship therapy: A 10-session filial therapy model*. New York, NY: Brunner-Routledge.
Lin, D., & Bratton, S. (2015). A meta-analytic review of child-centered play therapy approaches. *Journal of Counseling & Development, 93*, 45–58.
Ray, D. C. (2011). *Advanced play therapy: Essential conditions, knowledge, and skills for child practice*. New York, NY: Routledge.
Ray, D., Armstrong, S., Balkin, R., & Jayne, K. (2015). Child centered play therapy in the schools: Review and meta-analysis. *Psychology in the Schools, 52*, 107–123.
Ray, D., Muro, J., & Schumann, B. (2004). Implementing play therapy in the schools: Lessons learned. *International Journal of Play Therapy, 13*, 79–100.
Rogers, C. (1951). *Client-centered therapy: Its current practice, implications and theory*. London, England: Constable and Company.
Rogers, C. R. (1957). The necessary and sufficient conditions of therapeutic personality change. In H. Kirschenbaum & V. L. Henderson (Eds.), *The Carl Rogers reader* (pp. 219–235). New York, NY: Houghton Mifflin. (Reprinted from *Journal of Consulting Psychology, 21*(2), 95–103.)
Rogers, C. R. (1959). A theory of therapy, personality and interpersonal relationships, as developed in the client-centered framework. In S. Koch (Ed.), *Psychology: A study of science* (Vol. 3, pp. 184–256). New York, NY: McGraw Hill.
Rogers, C. (1961). *On becoming a person: A therapist's view of psychotherapy*. Boston, MA: Houghton Mifflin.
Rogers, C. R. (1977). *Carl Rogers on personal power: Inner strength and its revolutionary impact*. New York, NY: Delacorte Press.

Stulmaker, H. L., & Jayne, K. M. (2017). Child-centered play therapy parent consultation model: Clinical implementation and implications. *Journal of Child & Adolescent
Counseling,* 4(1), 3–19.
Sweeney, D. S., Baggerly, J., & Ray, D. C. (2014). *Group play therapy: A dynamic approach.* New York, NY: Routledge.

5

Adlerian School Counseling

ERIKA R. N. CAMERON, KARA P. IEVA, AND BRIANNE L. FRANCE

The aim of this chapter is to provide a foundation for a school counselor to use Adlerian theory, otherwise known as individual psychology. Adlerian theory was first applied to education in a child guidance clinic at the Volksheim, Vienna's Institute for Adult Education, in 1914 (Bottome, 1939; Orgler, 1963). Early applications of the theory have extended into contemporary comprehensive school counseling programs (Brown & Trusty, 2005; Pryor & Tollerud, 1999). Over the 20th century, Adlerian theory and related principles for practice contributed to school counseling in several ways (as cited in Lemberger & Nash, 2008), including structured programs in school curriculum (Dreikurs, 1968), parenting programs (Dinkmeyer, McKay, & Dinkmeyer, 1997), models for consultation (Dinkmeyer, Carlson, & Dinkmeyer, 1994), school counseling programs (Dinkmeyer, Pew, & Dinkmeyer, 1979; Nicoll, 1994), and supervision in schools (Lemberger & Dollarhide, 2006). Additionally, many of the core tenets of Adler's theory translate into practices critical to working with students, including focus on the uniqueness of the individual, social embeddedness, and striving toward goals (Sweeney, 1998), which are discussed in the following sections.

FOUNDATION AND EPISTEMOLOGY OF INDIVIDUAL PSYCHOLOGY

Individual psychology is a holistic, phenomenological, socially oriented, and teleological (goal-directed) approach to understanding and working with people. Individual psychology has been associated with other theories of counseling practice, not limited to cognitive, constructivist, existential-humanistic, psychodynamic, and systemic perspectives (Carlson, 2017). The epistemological basis of individual psychology emphasizes the proactive, form-giving, and fictional nature of human cognition and its role in constructing the "realities" that persons know and to which they respond. Individual psychology asserts that humans construct, manufacture, or narrate their ways of viewing and experiencing the world. It is an optimistic, positive psychological theory affirming that humans are not determined by heredity or environment. Rather, they are creative, proactive, meaning-making beings, with the ability to choose and to be responsible for their choices.

Adler's ideas have been applied to education ever since individual psychology was first introduced to professional school counselors. Adler held the believed that people are goal-oriented and social beings (Adler, 1927, 1930, 1980). He believed that each person is born with the capacity to develop his or her so-cial interest and is trying to belong and to fit socially in the world (Carlson, Watts, & Maniacci, 2006). Social interest is a person's ability to interact coop-eratively with people that leads to a healthy society. In this way, people develop a sense of belonging and tend to contribute to others in the society. While a person is born with social interest, it must be nurtured and developed. How an individual engages and develops social interest shapes his or her person-ality. Because schools are often a second home for children and adolescents, a student's personality could be molded not only by parental upbringing but also by the way the student is connected and supported in his or her school life.

The implementation of a comprehensive school counseling program can support students through important developmental periods. School counselors are trained to provide education, prevention and intervention activities, which are integrated into all aspects of children's lives, especially the development of their personality, social relationships, and academic and career trajectory. The principles of Adler's theory can help school counselors to conceptualize the de-velopmental needs of students, to set goals to meet those needs, and to support students in their development.

For the purposes of applying individual psychology to school counseling specifically, the theory is called Adlerian school counseling throughout the remainder of the chapter. Below are some key concepts from individual psy-chology that are important for the application of Adler's ideas to school counseling.

Holism

When Adler developed the term *individual psychology* (in German, *Individualpsychologie*), his intent was to emphasize that the individual was an indivisible whole. Adler believed that, to understand a person and his or her behaviors, one must consider all aspects of the individual's life, or what he referred to as holism (Milliren & Clemmer, 2006). Holism includes the assertion that every person is unique and greater than the sum of one's parts. An Adlerian school counselor looks at a student as a "whole person." The counselor explores the student's world from a holistic perspective by assessing and understanding the biological (e.g., disabilities and physical health), psychological (e.g., personality, goals, logic), and social factors (e.g., family, peers, feelings of connectedness) that apply to the student.

Encouragement

Encouragement is both a principle and a technique that pervades all of Adlerian counseling; however, it is particularly important when working with children. Adlerian counselors believe that an individual's presenting problem stems from discouragement (i.e., lack of motivation or lack of belief in one's ability to change), and that, without encouragement, the individual cannot envision the possibility of being well (Dreikurs, 1967). Discouragement from family members, parents, peers, and society can lower one's self-esteem and self-worth, causing feelings of inferiority. Adlerian counselors can use encouragement as a foundation for the process of therapeutic change (Main & Boughner, 2011; Watts & Pietrzak, 2000), to increase the student's courage in facing the difficulties in life, in perceiving the world as an inviting place, and in risking being wrong (Carlson et al., 2006). In contrast, a discouraged person does not take risks to grow as a person.

Encouragement can also serve as a technique to initiate change. It is a process of focusing on a person's resources and calling attention to positive attributes in order to build a person's self-esteem, self-concept, and self-worth (Dinkmeyer, McKay, & Dinkmeyer, 2008). A school counselor should help the student to develop courage and hope and to take action by engaging in the community and serving others (Ansbacher & Ansbacher, 1956). School counselors have to be able to see students' strengths and to believe in students' ability to change.

Adler asserted that encouragement is necessary for the student's healthy self-image. Confident students are able to handle whatever obstacles lie ahead of them (Carlson et al., 2006). Often, a pampered, overprotected, and physically ill student lacks self-esteem, because overprotective and overly helpful adults unconsciously send the message that they will do everything for the student, because the student does not have the ability to do anything for him- or herself. Students become what they are encouraged to become (Dinkmeyer & Dreikurs, 2000). School counselors can use encouragement when they express faith and belief in their students. The encouraging school counselor:

- Values the student as he or she is
- Demonstrates faith in the student

- Tries to build a positive self-concept in the student
- Gives the student recognition for his or her efforts
- Concentrates on the strengths and assets of the student

Private Logic

Adlerian school counselors strive to understand the world from the individual's point of view. Adlerians look at the the unique way that each individual perceives the world. The reasoning that individuals use to justify their style of life (defined below) is known as private logic. Individual psychology holds that each person creates her or his own reality and that any experience can have a variety of possible interpretations based on how the individual chooses to view the situation (Carlson et al., 2006). One's private logic is comprised of ideas developed in early childhood that may or may not be appropriate to later life. As children develop, their ideas about right and wrong are based on their subjective personal experience. For example, if a student witnesses domestic abuse between their parents early in life and consequently comes to believe that love is expressed in anger and physical abuse, that belief constitutes faulty logic. Another example of private logic is when children and adolescents learn that, in order to get attention, they must act out in negative ways. The private logic behind children's attention-seeking behavior is the belief that they are not important and need others to notice them in order to be somebody. If the only time they are noticed by others is when they misbehave, then misbehavior becomes their style of seeking attention and their faulty logic is cemented. Even if the attention they receive is painful, for most children, any kind of attention is better than no attention at all.

For Adlerian school counselors, private logic is used to understand a student's perception of past events and how the student's interpretation of early events has a continuing influence on the student's life. Often, school counselors participate in completing a Functional Behavioral Assessment (FBA) for a student of concern. The FBA is a comprehensive and individualized strategy to identify the purpose or function of a student's problem behavior(s). In addition, an FBA is used to develop and implement a plan to modify variables that maintain the problem behavior and to teach appropriate replacement behaviors using positive interventions (Watson & Steege, 2003). This behavorial intervention uses the same insights into behavior as Adler's faulty logic.

The Style of Life

The Adlerian concept of personality is called the style of life or lifestyle. The style of life is unique to each person. It consists of an individual's basic convictions, choices, and values that influence decisions and behaviors (Ansbacher & Ansbacher, 1956; Mosak & Maniacci, 1999; Shulman & Mosak, 1988; Stein & Edwards, 1998). The style of life is learned from social interactions that occur in the early years of life and is fixed at 5 or 6 years of age (Ansbacher & Ansbacher, 1956). As a result, it becomes the guiding framework for all later behaviors. One's style of life can be influenced by family, peers, school personnel, neighbors, community, and culture, such as movies, books, and music (Powers & Griffith, 1987). It is important to note that, for many children, the first significant contact with an adult other than their parents occurs when they start school. School experiences have a major influence on a student's style of life outside of the family (Lemberger & Krauss, 2013). The style of life helps a student to navigate and to make sense of life and to develop habits (Carlson et al., 2006). Adlerians have proposed that there are several types of style of life (Ansbacher & Ansbacher, 1956; Mosak & Di Pietro, 2006). Adler described four basic styles of life; they are shown in Table 5.1, along with the coping strategies used by students with each type.

It is important to note that no two people have the same lifestyle and nobody fits completely into only one of the types. In addition, Adler was generally opposed to rigid classification of people, stating that he proposed four styles of life solely for teaching purposes; he also cautioned counselors to avoid the mistake of assigning people to mutually exclusive categories.

Table 5.1. Types of Style of Life

Style of Life	Description of Coping Behavior
Ruling	The student has minimal social interests in others (peers, adults, family, etc.) and needs to be the boss.
Getting	The student is dependent on, and expects things from, others. Student shows little initiative and social interest. The student is happy as long as he or she gets what he or she wants.
Avoiding	The student has minimal social interests or concern for others and avoids difficulties in order to prevent any possibility of failure.
Socially Useful	The student cooperates with others and copes with problems in the best interests of others.

Adapted from Mosak & Di Pietro (2006).

REFLECTION MOMENT

Adler pointedly mentioned that he discouraged counselors from typecasting an individual into a particular lifestyle type. What do you think Adler's reasoning for this was? Reflect on your school environment. How are students identified within your school? What are the advantages and disadvantages of categorizing students?

Basic Mistakes and Core Fears

Basic mistakes are the self-defeating attitudes and beliefs of an individual's style of life that often reflect avoidance or withdrawal from others, excessive self-interest, or the desire for power. Mosak (2005) lists five common basic mistakes.

1. Overgeneralization ("Everyone in school hates me.")
2. False or impossible goals ("I must be perfect in order for people to love me.")
3. Misperceptions of life and life's demands ("Girls are not good at math and science.")
4. Denial of one's basic worth. ("I'm getting a D, what's the point in trying?")
5. Faulty values ("I must be captain of the football team, regardless of who gets hurt in the process.")

Along with outlining basic mistakes, Adlerian theory has also identified and addressed an individual's core fears. Table 5.2 describes the most common core fears and their counseling implications (Dinkmeyer & Sperry, 2000; Shulman, 1973).

Social Interest

Adler believed that human beings are social beings who want to belong and to find a place in society (Ansbacher & Ansbacher, 1956). "Social interest" is a loose translation of the German term *Gemeinschaftsgefühl*, which, when broken down into its parts, explains Adler's concept of social interest. *Gemein* is "a community of equals," *schafts* is "to create or maintain," and *gefühl* is "social feeling." Taken together, Gemeinschaftsgefühl means a community of equals creating and maintaining social feelings and interests; that is, people working together as equals to better themselves as individuals and as a community. Social interest is an empathic bond that people feel for each other,

Table 5.2. COMMON CORE FEARS

Core Fear	Description	Counseling Implication
Being imperfect	A student fears that he or she is a fraud or an imposter.	Support students in become aware of the fear and develop the "courage to be imperfect."
Being vulnerable	A student fears that others will discover what he or she does not know and will reject her or him.	Create a safe space where students can honestly share how they think and feel. Students will learn and practice to be authentic and honest without the fear of being rejected.
Disapproval	A student fears that he or she will experience the disapproval of others.	Help students to realize that it is impossible to please everyone and there are other students who also want to be loved or appreciated.

a sense of belonging and participating with others for the common good (Ansbacher, 1992).

Social interest is conceptually similar to the modern concept of school connectedness (Blum, 2005). School connectedness, according to Blum (2005), is characterized in three areas:

1. High academic standards with teacher support
2. Positive and respectful relationships between adults and students
3. Physically and emotionally safe environment

When students reported higher levels of connectedness, they also had higher levels of academic achievement, experienced lower levels of school violence and bullying, had less participation in antisocial and risky behaviors, and had higher graduation rates (Blum, 2005). Similarly, in a school, social interest for a student would be defined as the student's experience of belonging and how this might manifest in the goals of the individual student (Oberst, 2009). Counselors can assist students to acquire and develop a healthy social interest (e.g., helping children to belong, feel valued, develop positive self-worth, and not feel discouraged).

Compensation for Inferiority and Superiority

Adler believed that all humans are born inferior (Watts, 2012). In infancy, infants are helpless and dependent upon on adult caregivers. As a result, the infant develops feelings of inferiority relative to the larger, stronger people around him or her. While these feelings of inferiority are inescapable during infancy, Adler believed that they are necessary in helping an individual develop the motivation to strive and grow. An individual's growth results from compensation, from the attempts to overcome real or imagined inferiorities. Humans are driven by the need to overcome this sense of inferiority and to strive for increasingly higher levels of development. As a result, inferiority feelings are a motivating force in behavior and not a sign of weakness or abnormality.

Adler believed that a child's inability to overcome feelings of inferiority would lead to the development of an inferiority complex (Watts, 2012). He believed that the inferiority complex was derived from three sources in childhood: organic inferiority, spoiling, and neglect.

ORGANIC INFERIORITY

It was Adler's belief that physical disabilities influenced the shaping of a person's personality, because of the person's need to compensate for the disability. He believed that an individual's effort to overcome their weaknesses could result in a variety of accomplishments (e.g., athletic, artistic, social). For example, Stephen Hawking was diagnosed with ALS when he was 21 years old and became one of the world's leading physicists. If the effort to overcome a disability or weakness failed, Adler believed that an inferiority complex could develop.

SPOILING

Spoiled children get every need met with little denied, are the center of attention in the home, and believe that they are most important person in every situation. When spoiled children start school, they realized that they are no longer the focus of attention and often they have a hard time with the transition, because they are unprepared to share the focus. Often they are impatient with peers, lack empathy, and find it difficult to adjust for others. As they face these challenges, spoiled children begin to believe that they possess a personal deficiency. Adler posited that this belief develops into an inferiority complex.

NEGLECT

A neglected child grows up with a lack of love and security and often is unwanted and rejected by parents and caregivers. As a result, the child develops feelings of worthlessness or even anger and distrust of others. These feelings result in feelings of inadequacy that lead to an inferiority complex.

STRIVING FOR SUPERIORITY

Superiority is the ultimate goal toward which an individual strives (Ansbacher & Ansbacher, 1979). Striving for superiority is the drive for personal perfection rather than an attempt to be better than others (Watts, 2012). The word *perfection* is derived from a Latin word meaning to complete or to finish. Thus, Adler suggested that we strive for superiority in an effort to perfect ourselves, to make ourselves complete or whole. This innate goal, the drive toward wholeness or completion, is oriented toward the future. It is important to note that Adler held that striving for superiority requires a great deal of energy and effort that is manifested both by the individual and by society. Most individuals are social beings who strive for superiority not only as individuals but also as members of a group. Adler believed that individuals and society are interrelated and interdependent. People must function constructively with others for the good of all and to have a positive impact on the community.

According to individual psychology, children work to understand their world and to be competent within it. Along the way, children will experience feelings of competence and connection. They will also experience feelings of inferiority and disconnection. These feelings could be supported or compounded by the family and school atmosphere in which the child lives. For instance, if a child is raised in an authoritarian home, a child may never develop the ability to be independent, which could make him or her feel insecure in peer relationships in school. Professional school counselors using Adlerian techniques and interventions can help children and adolescents to overcome their insecurities by learning to work with others, to work for the common good of the community (e.g., classroom), and to master tasks. Utilizing Adlerian counseling techniques can help students gain insight into themselves by learning to live effectively in school and other social settings (Daniels, 1998).

REFLECTION MOMENT

Adler stated that individuals can overcome insecurities by learning to work with others, to work for the common good of the community, and to master tasks. Reflect on your counseling approach. How do you help students overcome insecurities? How might your comprehensive school counseling program help support student competence and connection?

Goals and Belonging

A key principle of individual psychology is that all behavior is goal directed. People are constantly striving to reach goals and to fulfill a need. Adler believed that people were ultimately striving for significance and belonging, but how people achieve that goal varies. For instance, even when a child is misbehaving, her or his behavior is fulfilling one of four possible goals: attention, power, revenge, or inadequacy. A child with a goal of attention believes: "I belong only when I am being noticed." Therefore, she or he will behave in both positive and negative ways to get noticed by others. A child who has a goal of power believes: "I belong only when I am the boss." Therefore, she or he will behave in ways that challenge others, such as arguing or defiance. A child with a goal of revenge feels hurt and tries to hurt back in order to even the score: "I belong only when I hurt others as I feel hurt." A child with a goal of inadequacy feels worthless and wants others to view her or him as incapable: "Others shouldn't expect anything of me." Many professionals do not understand children's goal-directed motivation and try in vain to change children's behavior; in this way, they actually unknowingly strengthen the problem. Table 5.3 lists goals of misbehavior and provides examples of typical adult reactions and responses that perpetuate the problem. In addition, the table gives corrective responses that can be used to assist in changing the child's misbehavior.

The basic ingredient to successful counseling is the relationship. All the techniques and quick fixes in the world cannot be effective outside of a close emotional bond between adults and children. Thus, the questions we must ask when a child chronically misbehaves is, "How can I improve my relationship with him?" and "What mistaken goal is he pursuing?" Because punishment is rarely the answer to a student's problem behavior, the question to be avoided is, "What punishment can I use to make her stop this behavior?"

LET'S PRACTICE
Melanie gets out of her seat and annoys other students during your classroom guidance lesson. When you tell her to sit down, she smiles at you and takes her seat. Fifteen minutes later, she is out of her seat again.

1. What is the probable goal of her misbehavior?
2. How does she make you feel?
3. How does she react to you?

Escobar didn't hand in his homework again this week. When you asked him why, he looked down and said, "What's the use?"

1. What is the probable goal of his misbehavior?
2. How does he make you feel?
3. How does he react to you?

Table 5.3. GOALS OF MISBEHAVIOR

Goal (and faulty belief)	Student Behavior and Actions	Adult Reaction and Behavior	Corrective Response
Attention ("I belong when I am noticed.")	Acting out; overly dramatic; faking an illness. Needs constant validation. Needs to be center of attention. Acts super-busy so that people will be amazed that he or she is are able to complete tasks.	Annoyed. Frustrated. Bargains with child to behave. Focuses on child only when he or she is misbehaving.	Adult should ignore the child's misbehavior and provide attention when the child is not trying to get it— "Catch them being good."
Power ("If I defy adults or authority, I matter.")	Starts arguments. Refuses to obey. Throws tantrums. Lies. Talks back to adults. Wants everything his or her way.	Angry. Provoked. Feels that authority is threatened. Engages in power struggle with child. Takes away individual privileges.	Adult should withdraw from power struggle, provide opportunities for responsibility, and offer choices. take away privileges from the group.
Revenge ("I belong when others feel my hurt.")	Similar to power. Wants to do what they want without anyone getting in the way. Does not care about consequences. Feeling attacked justifies a counter strike.	Feelings of hurt rather than irritation.	Adult should avoid punishment, encourage and recognize student's individual talents, assist the student in making amends, and provide or schedule one-on-one attention to the student.
Inadequacy ("I am helpless and unable, so I'll convince others not to expect anything of me.")	Says and believes he can't do anything. Has low expectations of self.	Feeling sorry. Hopeless. Overly helps the child. Has low expectations of the child.	Adults should find the potential in the student and provide him or her with opportunities to succeed and to be patient. Adults should train the child to be successful and to build on his or her interests. Adults should not give up on the child.

Adapted from Dreikurs (1972).

Family Constellation and Birth Order

One of Adler's most important contributions to psychology was recognizing that birth order had an influence on the development of one's personality (Eckstein & Kaufman, 2012; Stewart, 2012). In addition, birth order occurs within the family constellation, a family system consisting of individuals operating in relation to other individuals in the system (Griffith & Powers, 2007).

Adler believed that sibling position is a critical variable to consider (Ansbacher & Ansbacher, 1956) and that, despite siblings' being raised by the same parents, living in the same house, and attending the same schools, they will experience and interpret life in completely different ways based on their birth order and interactions with others. While ordinal position (actual order of birth) provides context, Adlerians focus on the psychological position, which is the role the child adopts to interact with others (Shulman & Mosak, 1988). Adler posited five psychological birth-order positions: oldest born, second born, middle child, youngest born, and only child (Eckstein et al., 2010).

Oldest-born children tend to prefer to do things independently, like to be in charge, and are often analytical, detailed, and perfectionist. As a result of losing their parents' undivided attention with the advent of siblings, the eldest child tends to do what is right and to be a people pleaser. The oldest born tend to have the highest rate of academic success and are motivated high achievers (Shulman & Mosak, 1977).

Second-born children grow up having to share attention with their elder sibling but have an example to follow. As a result, the second child is the most likely to be better adjusted to life in general than children in other birth orders. Second borns tend to be the peacemakers in their families, but they are competitive with their older siblings. They often become rebels or try to outdo everyone (Shulman & Mosak, 1977).

Middle children are sandwiched between older and younger siblings, and they often develop a competitive nature. They tend to be the most diplomatic and flexible members of the family and are often eager for parental praise. However, they often have a harder time fitting in (Shulman & Mosak, 1977).

Youngest-born children tend to be dependent and selfish, because they are used to others providing and caring for them. In contrast, they are often the life of the party, crave stimulation, and are comfortable entertaining others. Because they are always following in elder siblings' footsteps, they often feel far behind and desire to prove they are not babies. This drive can make them very ambitious and rebellious (Shulman & Mosak, 1977).

Only children tend to be spoiled, like the youngest born, but they are used to getting their way. Often they are perfectionist and have lofty goals. For a young only child, beginning school can be a particularly difficult transition, because the child is used to being the focus in the family. Only children are often viewed as very mature for their age, because they are comfortable in adult situations and conversations (Shulman & Mosak, 1977).

Birth order allows the Adlerian therapist to make some generalizations about individuals, but it is the individual who ultimately determines how he or she views the position in the family. Other family position factors (Manaster & Corsini, 1982; Shulman & Mosak, 1977) can be found in Table 5.4.

Clearly, cultural considerations are important when looking at one's family constellation. Across cultures, the definitions of family and family roles based on gender and age vary widely (McGoldrick, Giordano, & Garcia-Preto, 2005). Adlerian counselors should take steps to define the family constellation based on the client's one's concept of family and community. This is especially important in understanding modern family types, such as blended, step, and chosen families.

REFLECTION MOMENT

When working with a student, how important is it for you to assess the ramifications of her or his birth order? How might you consider using birth order in prescreening for group counseling?

THEORY OF CHANGE

The previous section introduced Adlerian concepts that are essential to individual psychology. In this section, we address how to apply those concepts to facilitate change in students and we explain the Adlerian stages of counseling.

Most Adlerian school counselors view students in distress as discouraged individuals and favor using a growth model that emphasizes their strengths. As a result, the focus in counseling is on the student's health and well-being and on prevention of issues rather than remediation. The counseling process is focused on teaching, providing information, and offering encouragement (Ansbacher & Ansbacher, 1956). As stated earlier, encouragement is an essential intervention in individual psychology. The counselor's ability to encourage the individual helps her or him to develop courage, to address mistaken goals and faulty logic, and to change beliefs. The encouraging counselor assesses the individual's style of life, goals, and beliefs. When a full understanding is developed, change happens through re-education (Corey, 2009).

Adler described the school as the place to educate, and not merely give instruction to, a child (as cited in Ansbacher & Ansbacher, 1956, p. 399). Thus, the school is seen as more than a place; instead, it is "enticing the child, as it

Table 5.4. FAMILY POSITION CONSIDERATIONS

Family Factors	Implications
Age differences among siblings	Closer together, the more competitive; further apart, the less influence.
Large families	It is possible to have more than one "family."
Extra-family competitors	Families become complicated by remarriage, adoption, and their extended families.
Gender differences	Having all boys or all girls, or having only one boy or girl in a large family, can affect the family. Having transgender siblings could also apply here.
Death and survivorship	Children are affected by the death of a sibling.
Special siblings	When one child is exceptional (e.g., athlete, scholar, mentally or physically challenged), everyone else is affected.
Roles available	Socioeconomic or cultural traditions may limit available roles.
Social views	Physical appearance (e.g., skin color, body type) and level of overall attractiveness favor some children and limit others.
Parental prejudice	Parents have favorites.
Parents as models	Parents intentionally or unintentionally guide their children through their own personalities and preferences.

were, from one fruitful pasture to another" (p. 400). In this manner, a school represents an incubator of possible experiences that influence the student's developing skills and preferences. The goals of Adlerian school counseling include helping students to overcome feelings of inferiority, nurturing social interests, identifying mistaken goals, changing faulty assumptions, and encouraging students to become contributing members of society (Mosak, 1995). In order to achieve these goals, school counselors can utilize the four stages of Adlerian counseling (Ansbacher & Ansbacher, 1956; Kottman, 2003; Manaster & Corsini 1982) for individual student planning.

Stage One: Establishing the Relationship

Working with students is based on a sense of deep caring, involvement, and friendship. Adlerian school counselors' initial focus should be on the student, not the problem. The counselor starts by helping the student become aware of his or her assets and strengths, rather than focusing on the student's deficits and liabilities. The school counselor develops a positive relationship with the student by listening, responding, demonstrating respect for students' capacity to understand purpose and seek change, and exhibiting faith, hope, and caring. Once trust and a therapeutic alliance have been developed between the school counselor and student, the school counselor can move forward in the counseling process.

REFLECTION MOMENT

Take a moment to consider your current counseling approach with students. Are there current practices you use that align with stage one? How do you think these methods of establishing a relationship would work in your school?

Stage Two: Analysis and Assessment

Next, the school counselor conducts a comprehensive assessment of the student's functioning, style of life, and goals. This occurs through a combination of approaches like the lifestyle assessment, reviewing early recollections, and a clinical interview. The school counselor gathers information about how the student seeks to belong in the social world of family, school, and friends. As much as possible in the context of school counseling, Adlerian counselors utilize a lifestyle assessment that obtains family background, belief systems, cultural heritage, educational level, personal goals, early memories, and other facets of the client's life. In addition, the counselor can gather information about a student from the cumulative file, health records, student information system, teacher interviews, observations, and parent meetings. When meeting with the student, the school counselor can ask the student the following questions:

- "What was it like for you growing up?" "What roles did you play in your family?" (Family constellation.)
- "To whom are you closest?" "What is most satisfying to you about your friendships?" (Social relationships.)
- "How do you feel about who you are and the ways you have developed?" (Sense of self.)

REFLECTION MOMENT

Being able to understand the cultural values, norms, and relationships in a student's family is important to being able to appreciate and to recognize each student's individual needs and to structure your counseling techniques according to that student. How do you think you can utilize lifestyle assessments in your counseling program? How do you think these techniques would differ when working with students of different age groups (i.e., students in elementary, middle, or high school or students in higher education)?

Stage Three: Encourage Insight

In the third stage, the Adlerian counselor interprets the findings of the assessment in order to promote insight for the individual. A school counselor can take an active role in the assessment and interpretation and can work with the student to see how the results help her or him make sense of her or his style of life, as well as how the student is pursuing her or his goals. Adlerians will pay particular attention to basic mistakes in the lifestyle and in exploring how the basic mistakes contribute to a student's presenting concern, and then how a student can make changes in her or his approach to life to be more successful. The school counselor helps students to develop a new orientation to life, one that is more fully functioning. In the third stage of therapy, Adlerian counselors are inclined to explore students' self-defeating thinking patterns that contribute to distorted perceptions (Carlson et al., 2006; Mosak & Maniacci, 1999).

Stage Four: Re-Education and Reorientation

Once the student develops insight into her or his problems, the focus of counseling shifts to taking action. A school counselor can give students assignments that involve thinking, feeling, and responding in a different fashion. For instance, if a student has test anxiety, the school counselor could instruct the student how to practice mindfulness activities and assign the student the task of implementing mindfulness practice when feeling anxious.

ADLERIAN SCHOOL COUNSELING OPERATIONALIZED

Adlerian school counselors use a number of techniques in working with their students in various levels of schools. This section provides brief explanations of 10 Adlerian techniques (acting "as if," asking the question, brainstorming, catching oneself, classroom meetings, hypothesis interpretation, push button technique, spitting in the student's soup, task setting, and vertical arrow) that can be utilized by a school counselor and that can be adapted to the age and developmental level of the student. It is important to note that Adlerian school counselors maintain that time limits must be set with students. Sessions with children usually last for 30 minutes, but they can be as brief as 15 minutes. When nearing the end of the session, school counselors should not bring up any new material. Instead, the student summarizes the counseling time together (Slavik & King, 2007). If the school counselor wants to assign the student homework, that should be done near the end of a session before the summary.

Acting "as if" is utilized when a school counselor asks the student to begin acting as if she or he is already the person she or he would like to be, possessing certain qualities she or he lacks, or to try on new behaviors or roles. The "as if" technique is based on the belief that students must change their behaviors to elicit different responses from others. Examples of questions that may elicit the "as if" mindset could be:

- If you were the person you wanted to be, what would be different about you?
- If your situation somehow started to improve or to feel better, what types of things would you be doing differently?
- If you were never late to class again, how do you imagine school would be different?

The goal is to encourage the student to imagine and to select ideas or behaviors that are within reach and to begin to put them into practice.

Asking "the question" is a method of questioning that a school counselor uses to aid the student in envisioning how the future will be different when the problem is no longer present. Also, this may help to establish goals.

COUNSELOR: "Imagine you wake up tomorrow and a miracle happened over-night, and your test taking fears are gone. What things would have had to have changed for this to occur?"

With this question, the school counselor elicits the student's feelings of inferiority when she challenges the student to consider the influence of fears related to taking a test.

STUDENT: "I really don't know, I guess I would have to feel confident that I will do okay. I guess I would have to believe that I prepared enough."

COUNSELOR: "You're saying that you'd have to first invest the effort in preparing for the test and then believe that that same effort will lead to more desirable performance on the test."

In this statement, the school counselor is influenced by Adler's concept of teleology, as illustrated by connecting the client's beliefs about how preparing for the test might add to her confidence. Also, this statement is a subtle example of encouragement by reflecting the student's courage in attempting difficult or uncertain behaviors.

Brainstorming is helping the student to identify mistakes in thinking. The school counselor would help the student brainstorm alternative beliefs and convictions. For example, in place of "I never get what I want," a student might substitute "Sometimes I get what I want." The latter conviction promotes healthy development.

Catching oneself permits students to become aware of their self-destructive behaviors or thoughts without feeling guilty about them. For instance, when trying to change nonfunctional behavior, some students may revert back to their old behavior out of sheer habit. Students are told to "catch themselves" when they are just about ready to revert back to their old ways and to substitute the new behavior. If the student yells at his classmate for taking the book he wanted, he catches himself in the angry mode and chooses a different response. The goal is to help students change maladaptive old habits.

Classroom meetings allow students to practice democratic principles and to develop empathy and group cohesion. For instance, a student who is acting inappropriately in class (e.g., consistently teasing other students) can be a problem for the whole class, and the solution to the problem grows most naturally out of the helpful involvement of all class members (Dreikurs, 1972, p. 78). The teacher facilitates group discussion, helps the students to understand themselves, and helps students to change their concept of themselves and others, which will eventually change their motivations from hostile to cooperative living (Dreikurs, 1972, p. 79). Nelsen, Lott, and Glenn (2013) have developed a list of eight building blocks for an effective classroom meeting. They are:

1. Form a circle
2. Practice compliments and appreciation
3. Create an agenda
4. Develop communication skills
5. Learn about separate realities
6. Recognize the four purposes of behavior
7. Practice role playing and brainstorming
8. Focus on nonpunitive solutions

Hypothesis interpretation is used to convey to the student that more than one explanation for behavior exists and that the school counselor wants to check out his or her own hunches to see if they are on the mark. The school counselor would use phrases like: "Could it be that . . . ," "I have a guess that . . . ," or "Is it possible that . . .?" The school counselor would also be looking for an "ah-ha" moment in the student's expression (recognition reflex) or for a quick glance of disapproval in reaction to the interpretation, responses that indicate the counselor should continue or move in a different direction.

"Spitting in the student's soup" is a technique that helps students to interpret the goals of a behavior in order to facilitate change. Students are led to recognition of possible behavioral intentions of which they may have been unaware. The school counselor can help the student realize the payoff for the behavior (e.g., acting out in math class in order to avoid doing the work). The behavior can be stripped of its utility or it can be accentuated.

A student presents to the school counselor stating, "I'm not going to that class anymore. That teacher has something against me and he just wants me to fail anyway so I stopped showing up." Often, the student is expecting that the counselor will try to play into the statement or persuade him to go to class, so the counselor may choose to respond instead with "Well, who is really winning here? If he's got something against you, it sure sounds like you're giving him exactly what he wants, doesn't it?" The student, caught off guard, might respond by saying, "No way, I'm not letting him get to me," to which the counselor may reply, "But if he's trying to get you in trouble, to stop going to class, and to fail, aren't you playing into his hands then? Wouldn't he be disappointed if you decided to show him by doing exactly the opposite of what he expects?"

Task setting is when a school counselor gives homework assignments to students to practice a behavior (see Table 5.5). It can help students to become more comfortable with frightening situations or it can promote students' social interest.

Using *push-button technique* is a visualization activity that school counselor can use to help students exercise inner control over their feelings by controlling their thoughts. This technique seeks to interrupt a symptom or behavior and to help students become aware of their role in maintaining, or even creating,

Table 5.5. TASK SETTING

Situation	Example Homework
Student is has difficulty making and keeping friends.	Identify what having and being a good friend looks like before the next meeting.
Student would like to be more involved at school.	Find three to five possible activities, sports, clubs, or events to look into joining next quarter.
Student has identified disorganization as the root of missing assignments.	Brainstorm one way to keep track of assignments for the end of the week.

their unpleasant feelings (Carlson et al., 2006; Mosak & Maniacci, 1998). School counselors should give the following directions to the student:

1. Close your eyes and recall a pleasant memory (a time when you felt happy, loved, successful, etc.). Focus on as much specific detail as possible and strongly focus on the positive feelings generated by the memory. Stay with those feelings. After you have relived the memory and experienced the positive feelings, lift your index finger to indicate you are finished.
2. Clear that memory from your mind. Now, close your eyes and recall an unpleasant memory (a time when you felt sad, unloved, unsuccessful, etc.). As in #1, focus on as much specific detail as possible and strongly focus on the unpleasant feelings created by the memory. Stay with the feelings. Again, lift your index finger when you have finished recalling the memory and the accompanying feelings.
3. Clear that memory from you mind. Now, recall the first, positive memory or, if you prefer, retrieve another pleasant memory. Again, recall the memory in specific detail and focus on the positive feelings. After you have relived the pleasant memory and positive feelings, raise your index finger and open your eyes.

After the third visualization, the school counselor processes the exercise with the student. The counselor can begin by asking the student to share what he or she learned from the exercise. Typically, students are able to make the connection between beliefs and feelings. If they are unable to make this connection, the school counselor should help them understand that certain thoughts or images usually generate certain types of feelings. The school counselor can empower students to be in control of their thoughts and feelings and to be able to shift from unpleasant to pleasant thoughts.

Vertical arrow is a process school counselors can use to help students identify, understand, and contradict self-defeating behaviors. The process is used to move through the cognitive layers to where the core beliefs reside. As a result, it brings a student's beliefs into awareness. The process of using the vertical arrow is found in Table 5.6.

LIMITATIONS OF THE APPROACH

Research on Adler's basic concepts, such as birth order, earliest childhood memories, and social interest, has been extensive and mixed, but little empirical research has been conducted on the effectiveness of Adlerian therapy with either adults or children (Grawe, Donati, & Bernaver, 1998; Weisz, Weiss, Han,

Table 5.6. VERTICAL ARROW STEPS FOR SCHOOL COUNSELORS

Vertical Arrow Steps	Example of Questions to Obtain Meanings about the Situation
Step 1. Invite the student to tell his or her story about the presenting problem.	Student: If I don't study harder, I may blow the exam.
Step 2. Ask for a recent specific occurrence of the problem.	Counselor: If this were true, what would it mean to you or about you? Why would it be upsetting to you?
Step 3. Ask the client to relate his or her experience of the situation. • "How did you experience the situation?" "What was it like for you?" • "Were there any disturbing feelings and/or behaviors?	Student: If I blow the exam, I may fail the course. Counselor: And if you failed, why would that be upsetting to you? What would it mean to you or about you? Student: That would mean I was a failure and people would think less of me.
Step 4. Ask the client to share the "meanings" of the situation. • "What did the situation mean for you or about you?" • "What thoughts and images crossed your mind?" • "What did you say to or about yourself?"	

Granger, & Morton, 1995). Because Adler failed to systematize his theory, it is not easily understood or easily recognized in school counseling. While Adlerian therapy has influenced concepts and interventions in education (e.g., Functional Behavioral Assessments, Positive Psychology, Growth Mindset, etc.), it is not organized, well defined, or systemic. Another limitation of the approach is that school counselors would need to spend a lot of time collecting large amounts of family and lifestyle information to understand a student fully. While this is ideal, the average caseload of school counselors is 471:1, and they would not have the time needed to do thorough family and lifestyle assessments. Last, Adlerian therapy tends to be most effective with individuals who are highly verbal and intelligent; therefore, students who do not possess these skills or are English Language Learners might experience limited success.

CONCLUSION

Adlerian school counseling is a positive approach that provides encouragement to students. It is a theoretical approach that allows school counselors to adapt its interventions to students from diverse backgrounds with various behavioral, academic, social, and emotional issues. School counselors using Adlerian theory are able to empower students to control their own fate and to evaluate the specific causes of their behavior. This theoretical approach allows the counselor to focus on the total wellness of students of any age and developmental background. Last, individual psychology allows the school counselor to analyze and assess the student's lifestyle, family history, and logic in order to ascertain what the student's strengths, areas of growth, and goals are, as well as to assist students in developing into successful adults.

SUGGESTED READINGS AND RESOURCES

READINGS

Adler, A., & Wolfe, W. B. (1982). *The pattern of life*. Chicago, IL: Alfred Adler Institute of Chicago.

Dreikurs, R. (1983). *Social equality: The challenge of today*. Chicago, IL: Alfred Adler Institute of Chicago.

Dreikurs, R. (1989). *Fundamentals of Adlerian psychology*. Chicago, IL: Alfred Adler Institute of Chicago.

Dreikurs, R. (1973). *Psychodynamics, psychotherapy, and counseling: Collected papers of Rudolf Dreikurs, M.D.* Chicago, IL: Alfred Adler Institute of Chicago.

Dreikurs, R., & Dreikurs, S. (2009). *Child guidance and education: Collected papers*. North Charleston, SC: BookSurge Publishing.

Dreikurs, R., & Goldman, M. (1961). *ABCs of guiding the child*. Chicago, IL: Alfred Adler Institute of Chicago.

Dreikurs, R., Shulman, B. H., & Mosak, H. H. (1984). *Multiple psychotherapy: The use of two therapists with one patient*. Chicago, IL: Alfred Adler Institute of Chicago.

Dreikurs, S. T. (2009). *Cows can be purple*. Chicago, IL: Alfred Adler Institute of Chicago.

Dreikurs Ferguson, E. (2009). *Adlerian theory: An introduction*. North Charleston, SC: BookSurge Publishing.

Kottman, T. (1995). The king of rock and roll: An application of Adlerian play therapy. In T. Kottman & C. Shaefer, *Play therapy in action: A casebook for practitioners* (pp. 133–167). Northvale, NJ: Aronson.

Kottman, T. (1999). Integrating the crucial Cs into Adlerian play therapy. *The Journal of Individual Psychology, 55*(3), 288–297.

Kottman, T., & Meany-Walen, K. (2016). *Partners in play: An Adlerian approach to play therapy* (3rd ed.). Alexandria, VA: American Counseling Association.

Kottman, T. T., & Warlick, J. (1989). Adlerian play therapy: Practical considerations. *Individual Psychology, 45*(4), 433–446.

Linden, G. W., & McAbee, N. L. (1995). *Achi Yotam: A memorial booklet*. Chicago, IL: Alfred Adler Institute of Chicago.

Mosak, H. H., & Cucher, L. M. (1980). *A child's guide to parent rearing*. Chicago, IL: Alfred Adler Institute of Chicago.

Shulman, B. H. (1984). *Essays in schizophrenia*. Chicago, IL: Alfred Adler Institute of Chicago.

Snow, M. S., Buckley, M. R., & Williams, S. C. (1999). Case study using Adlerian play therapy. *The Journal of Individual Psychology, 55*(3), 288–297.

Van Der Smissen, G. (1998, Spring). Adlerian play therapy. *Virginia Association for Play Therapy Newsletter, 1*(2). Available from http://vapt.cisat.jmu.edu/v1n2p1.htm

Resources

Adlerian Play Therapy. Adlerian play therapy uses the concepts of individual psychology while using toys, art, and play material to communicate with children under the age of 10 (Kottman, 2001). An example of Adlerian play therapy sessions can be found at the end of the chapter. More information is available from http://www.encouragementzone.com/

Positive Discipline book series. Positive Discipline is a program designed to teach young people to become responsible, respectful, and resourceful members of their communities by teaching social and life skills (Positive Discipline, 2016). More information is available from https://www.positivediscipline.com/

Student Success Skills (SSS). SSS is a school counseling intervention that supports student academic achievement by helping students develop the necessary skills for success (Brigman & Campbell, 2003). SSS focuses on teaching cognitive, metacognitive, self-management, and social skills, building positive attitudes, and creating a caring classroom environment (Lemberger & Clemens, 2012; Villares, Lemberger, Brigman, & Webb, 2011). More information is available from http://studentsuccessskills.com/

Systemic Training for Effective Parenting (STEP) book series. STEP is a parenting guide that shows parents how they can become more knowledgeable, confident, and successful in relating to their children. The guide discusses misbehavior, communication, encouragement, natural and logical consequences, family meetings, and drug and alcohol abuse prevention. More information is available from http://www.steppublishers.com/

REFERENCES

Adler, A. (1927). *The practice and theory of individual psychology.* New York, NY: Harcourt Brace.

Adler, A. (1930). Individual psychology. In C. Murchison (Ed.), *Psychologies of 1930* (pp. 395–405). Worcester, MA: Clark University Press.

Adler, A. (1980). *What life should mean to you.* New York: Perigee. (Originally published in 1931.)

Ansbacher, H. L. (1992). Alfred Adler's concept of community feeling and of social interest and the relevance of community feeling for old age. *Individual Psychology: Journal of Adlerian Theory, Research & Practice, 48,* 402–412.

Ansbacher, H. L., & Ansbacher, R. (Eds). (1956). *The individual psychology of Alfred Adler.* New York, NY: Basic Books.

Ansbacher, H. L., & Ansbacher, R. R. (1979). *Superiority and social interest.* New York, NY: W. W. Norton.

Blum, R. (2005). A case for school connectedness. *Educational Leadership, 62*(7), 16–20.

Bottome, P. (1939). *Alfred Adler: Apostle of freedom.* London, England: Faber & Faber.

Brown, D., & Trusty, J. (2005). *Designing & leading comprehensive school counseling programs: Promoting student competence & meeting student needs*. Belmont, CA: Thomson Brooks/Cole.

Carlson, J. (2017). Introduction to the neo-Adlerian approaches to psychotherapy [Special issue, Part 1]. *The Journal of Individual Psychology, 73*(2), 92–94.

Carlson, J., Watts, R. E., & Maniacci, M. (2006). *Adlerian therapy: Theory and practice*. Washington, DC: American Psychological Association.

Corey, G. (2009). *Theory and practice of counseling and psychotherapy*. Belmont, CA: Brooks/Cole.

Daniels, V. I. (1998). How to manage disruptive behaviour in inclusive classrooms. *Teaching Exceptional Children, 30*(4), 26–31.

Dinkmeyer, D., & Dreikurs, R. (2000). *Encouraging children to learn*. New York, NY: Brunner Routledge.

Dinkmeyer, D. C., Jr., Carlson, J., & Dinkmeyer, D. C., Sr. (1994). *Consultation: School mental health professionals as consultants*. Muncie, IN: Accelerated Development.

Dinkmeyer, D. C, Sr., McKay, G., & Dinkmeyer, D., Jr. (1997). *Systematic training for effective parenting*. Circle Pines, MN: American Guidance Services Publishing.

Dinkmeyer, D. C., Sr., McKay, G. D., & Dinkmeyer, D. C., Jr. (2008). *The parent's handbook*. Circle Pines, MN: American Guidance Service.

Dinkmeyer, D. C, Sr., Pew, W. L., & Dinkmeyer, D. C, Jr. (1979). *Adlerian counseling and psychotherapy*. Monterey, CA: Brooks/Cole.

Dinkmeyer, D. C., Jr., & Sperry, L. (2000). *Counseling and psychotherapy: An integrated, individual psychology approach* (3rd ed.). Upper Saddle River, NJ: Merrill/Prentice Hall.

Dreikurs, R. (1967). *Psychodynamics, psychotherapy, and counseling*. Chicago, IL: Alfred Adler Institute.

Dreikurs, R. (1968). *Psychology in the classroom: A manual for teachers*. New York, NY: Harper & Row.

Dreikurs, R. (1972). *Coping with children's misbehaviour*. New York, NY: Hawthorne.

Eckstein, D., Aycock, K. J., Sperber, M. A., McDonald, J., Van Wiesner, V. I., Watts, R. E., & Ginsburg, P. (2010). A review of 200 birth-order studies: Lifestyle characteristics. *The Journal of Individual Psychology, 66*, 408–434.

Eckstein, D., & Kaufman, J. A. (2012). The role of birth order in personality: An enduring intellectual legacy of Alfred Adler. *The Journal of Individual Psychology, 68*, 60–61.

Grawe, L., Donati, R., & Bernauer, F. (1998). *Psychotherapy in transition*. Seattle, WA: Hogrefe & Huber.

Griffith, J., & Powers, R. L. (2007). *The lexicon of Adlerian psychology* (2nd ed.). Port Townsend, WA: Adlerian Psychology Associates.

Kottman, T. (2001). Adlerian play therapy. *International Journal of Play Therapy, 10*, 1–12.

Kottman, T. (2003). *Partners in play: An Adlerian approach to play therapy* (2nd ed.). Alexandria, VA: American Counseling Association.

Lemberger, M. E., & Clemens, E. V. (2012). Connectedness and self-regulation as constructs of the Student Success Skills program in inner-city African American elementary school students. *Journal of Counseling & Development, 90*(4), 450–458.

Lemberger, M. E., & Dollarhide, C. T. (2006). Encouraging the supervisee's style of counseling: An Adlerian model for counseling supervision. *The Journal of Individual Psychology, 62*(2), 106–125.

Lemberger, M. E., & Krauss, S. (2013). Individual psychology and factors associated with the development of elementary and secondary school students. *The Journal of Individual Psychology, 69*(1), 84–91.

Lemberger, M. E., & Nash, E. R. (2008). School counselors and the influence of Adler: Individual psychology since the advent of the ASCA National Model. *Journal of Individual Psychology, 64*(4), 386–402.

Main, F. O., & Boughner, S. R. (2011). Encouragement and actionable hope: The source of Adler's clinical agency. *The Journal of Individual Psychology, 67*, 269–291.

Manaster, G. J. & Corsini, R. J. (1982). *Individual psychology.* Itasca, IL: F. E. Peacock.

McGoldrick, M., Giordano, J., & Garcia-Preto, N. (2005). Overview: Ethnicity and family therapy. In M. McGoldrick, J. Giordano, & N. Garcia-Preto (Eds.), *Ethnicity and family therapy* (3rd ed., pp. 1–40). New York, NY: Guilford Press.

Milliren, A. P., & Clemmer, F. (2006). Introduction to Adlerian psychology: Basic principles and methodology. In S. Slavik & J. D. Carlson (Eds.), *Readings in the theory of individual psychology* (pp. 17–32). New York, NY: Routledge.

Mosak, H. (1995). Adlerian psychotherapy. In R. J. Corsini & D. Wedding (Eds.), *Current psychotherapies* (5th ed., pp. 51–94). Itasca, IL: F. E. Peacock.

Mosak, H. H. (2005). Adlerian psychotherapy. In R. J. Corsini & D. Wedding (Eds.), *Current psychotherapies* (pp.52–95). Belmont, CA: Brooks/Cole-Thomson Learning.

Mosak, H. H., & Di Pietro, R. (2006). *Early recollections: Interpretative method and application.* New York, NY: Routledge.

Mosak, H. H., & Maniacci, M. P. (1998). *Tactics in counseling and psychotherapy.* Itasca, IL: F. E. Peacock.

Mosak, H. H., & Maniacci, M. P. (1999). *A primer of Adlerian psychology: The analytic–behavioral–cognitive psychology of Alfred Adler.* Philadelphia, PA: Taylor & Francis.

Nelsen, J., Lott, L., & Glenn, H. S. (2013). *Positive discipline in the classroom: Developing mutual respect, cooperation, and responsibility in your classroom* (4th ed.). New York, NY: Three Rivers Press.

Nicoll, W. G. (1994). Developing effective classroom guidance programs: An integrative framework. *School Counselor, 41*(5), 360–364.

Nicoll, W. G. (1996). School lifestyle, social interest, and educational reform. *The Journal of Individual Psychology, 52*(2), 130–149.

Oberst, U. (2009). Educating for social responsibility. *The Journal of Individual Psychology, 65*(4), 397–411.

Orgler, H. (1963). *Alfred Adler, the man and his work: Triumph over the inferiority complex.* New York, NY: Liveright Publishing.

Positive Discipline. (2016). *Positive discipline.* Retrieved from https://www.positivediscipline.com/

Powers, R. L., & Griffith, J. (1987). *Understanding lifestyle: The psycho-clarity process.* Port Townsend, WA: Adlerian Psychology Associates.

Pryor, D. B., & Tollerud, T. R. (1999). Applications of Adlerian principles in school settings. *Professional School Counseling, 2*, 299–304.

Shulman, B. H. (1973). *Contributions to individual psychology.* Chicago, IL: Alfred Adler Institute.

Shulman, B. H., & Mosak, H. H. (1977). Birth order and ordinal position: Two Adlerian views. *Journal of Individual Psychology, 33,* 114–121.

Shulman, B. H., & Mosak, H. H. (1988). *Manual for life style assessment.* Muncie, IN: Accelerated Development.

Slavik, S., & King, R. (2007). Adlerian therapeutic strategy. *Canadian Journal of Adlerian Psychology, 37*(1), 3–16.

Stein, H. T., & Edwards, M. E. (1998). Alfred Adler: Classical theory and practice. In P. Marcus & A. Rosenberg (Eds.), *Psychoanalytic versions of the human condition: Philosophies of life and their impact on practice* (pp. 64–93). New York, NY: New York University Press.

Stewart, A. E. (2012). Issues in birth order research methodology: Perspectives from individual psychology. *The Journal of Individual Psychology, 68,* 75–106.

Sweeney, T. J. (1998). *Adlerian counseling: A practitioner's approach* (4th ed.). Muncie, IN: Accelerated Development.

Watson, T. S., & Steege, M. W. (2003). *The Guilford practical intervention in the schools series. Conducting school-based functional behavioral assessments: A practitioner's guide.* New York, NY: Guilford Press.

Watts, R. E. (2012). On the origin of the striving for superiority and of social interest (1933). In J. D. Carlson & M. Maniacci (Eds.), *Alfred Adler revisited* (pp. 41–46). New York, NY: Routledge.

Watts, R. E., & Pietrzak, D. (2000). Adlerian "encouragement" and the therapeutic process of solution-focused brief therapy. *Journal of Counseling & Development, 78,* 442–447. http://dx.doi.org/10.1002/j.1556-6676.2000.tb01927.x

Weisz, J. R., Weiss, B., Han, S. S., Granger, D. A., & Morton, T. (1995). Effects of psychotherapy with children and adolescents revisited: A meta-analysis of treatment outcome studies. *Psychological Bulletin, 117,* 450–468.

6

Cognitive-Behavioral Therapy in the Schools

MELISSA MARIANI AND BRETT ZYROMSKI

Cognitive-behavioral theory or therapy (CBT) is an umbrella term used to describe a group of related empirical approaches to psychotherapy, including rational emotive behavior therapy (REBT), cognitive therapy (CT), behavior therapy (BT), rational behavior therapy (RBT), and stress inoculation therapy (SIT). Emerging in the early 1940s out of a need for brief, effective treatments for war veterans who were experiencing high levels of anxiety and depression, CBT was embraced by scientists, psychologists, and patients alike. The theory is grounded in the belief that people are ultimately in control of their own thoughts, feelings, and behaviors and that these three components are interrelated, affecting one another on a continuous basis. Prior to CBT's inception, the general school of psychological thought was that human beings were passive receptacles, victims of whatever experiences and fate awaited them. With CBT, people were challenged and empowered to take action to consciously improve their conditions, an approach that was very different from the approaches of Freudian psychoanalysis and psychodynamic theory. Interest in CBT continued into the late 1960s as mental health professionals began to investigate further how thinking could affect feelings and behaviors (Beck Institute, n.d.). While CBT is presently regarded as one of the most empirically supported therapeutic approaches (Butler, Chapman, Forman, & Beck, 2006; Hofmann et al., 2012), it is important to note that several of the techniques it employs have roots in other theories.

REFLECTION MOMENT

Think about how your own thoughts affect your feelings. Imagine you are driving along and someone in another car cuts quickly in front of you in your lane. How might your emotional and physical response differ, depending on your thoughts? For example, if you think, "Wow, that person is in a hurry, I hope they safely get to where they are going!" how might your emotions and physical response differ from your responses if you think, "Wow, that person is dangerous and rude and I hate it when people are rude!"

FOUNDATION AND EPISTEMOLOGY OF CBT

Behavioral Theory

Many philosophical principles of CBT were taken from other theories, including behavioral theory, cognitive theory, social learning theory, and attribution theory. From behavioral theory, attributed primarily to the work of the Russian physiologist Ivan Pavlov and the American psychologists John B. Watson (regarded as "the father of behaviorism") and B. F. Skinner, CBT incorporates the general principles of learning and reinforcement (Baum, 2004; Skinner, 1938, 1965; Watson, 1913, 1924). Changes in behavior occur as human beings learn to replace problematic behaviors with more appropriate ones. Learning is shaped through the processes of classical (also termed "respondent") and operant conditioning, whereby antecedents (stimuli) are presented that then lead to a particular behavior and consequence (i.e., A [antecedent] + B [behavior] = C [consequence]). Variations in behavior and resulting consequences can be manipulated by the introduction of neutral stimuli, reinforcement, or punishment, which can either strengthen or weaken certain behaviors. Thus, all actions can be affected, encouraged, or discouraged.

Pavlov is best known for his experiments testing the saliva response in dogs that were presented with various stimuli; he is credited with first investigating the process of classical conditioning and defining both conditioned and unconditioned responses in the early 1900s (Pavlov, 1955), concepts that were later developed by Watson. Watson's *Behaviorism* (1924) is viewed as the foundational text of behavioral theory. In it, he argued that all that can be measured is what one can directly observe (overt behaviors); cognitions, although acknowledged by behaviorists, are considered covert processes. Watson further emphasized that the presentation of various stimuli either increases or decreases the likelihood that an organism will exhibit certain observable behaviors. Skinner then expanded on this principle. In particular, Skinner investigated operant conditioning patterns and further developed the concepts of positive reinforcement and punishment, two central constructs in CBT. Skinner's *The Behavior of Organisms* (1938) summarized the basic tenets of applied behavior analysis.

REFLECTION MOMENT

Consider the difference between extinguishing behavior versus replacing behavior patterns with more appropriate behavior patterns. Have you ever attempted to stop a bad habit? For example, something as seemingly innocuous as biting fingernails can be incredibly difficult to stop. However, if a person chews gum or something crunchy (e.g., carrots or nuts) when feeling the urge to bite his or her fingernails, the behavior can be more easily replaced. Think about a time when you attempted to extinguish a behavior or you attempted to replace a behavior with a more appropriate option. What did that feel like? What worked and what didn't work for you?

Though behaviorists recognize that learning is an internal process, they contend that it cannot truly be realized until it is demonstrated in overt behavior. In counseling, the counselor and student work together to develop realistic goals based on objective, measureable outcomes (behaviors). Progress is then determined by what can be directly seen or observed. These principles are applied in CBT practice when the counselor calls on the student to challenge old, maladaptive behavior patterns and to institute new, more appropriate habits (Baum, 2004).

Cognitive Theory

CBT also incorporates principles from cognitive theory (CT), which is based on Jean Piaget's groundbreaking studies of children (Piaget, 1932, 1936, 1945, 1957). CT suggests that a structural framework exists for human developmental thought and that all future learning and knowledge are based on this framework. Children grow, change, and mature as a result of their environmental experiences, continuously constructing and understanding the world around them, shifting and modifying their perceptions accordingly. Cognitive activity affects behavior and behavior change can be realized by amending one's thoughts (Dobson & Dozois, 2001). Three basic components comprise CT: schemas, which are building blocks of knowledge related to aspects of the world; adaptation processes—equilibrium, assimilation, and/or accommodation—which assist youngsters in successfully navigating and transitioning from one stage to the next; and stages of development, which are universal stages of cognitive development that must be navigated in a predictable order (McLeod, 2015). Although CBT does not adhere to the fixed structure that Piaget's stages do, it does support the critical importance of thought processes, personal interpretations, perspectives, and views and how they affect one's behavior. While healthy, constructive thinking contributes to productive action, faulty thought patterns can lead to problematic actions and negative habits (Meichenbaum, 1977). To change negative behavior, school counselors challenge students to modify negative, automatic thought patterns and to replace them with more appropriate, positive ones. Later developers of CT, including psychologists Albert Ellis (Ellis & MacLaren, 2005) and Aaron Beck (Beck Institute, n.d.), expanded these constructs, adding in cognition's resulting effect on behavior.

Social Learning Theory and Social Cognitive Theory

Elements of social learning theory are echoed in CBT as well. Its founder, Albert Bandura (1976), suggested that all learning takes place in a social context and that people incorporate new behaviors by observing, modeling, imitating, or being directly taught by others in their environment. Without human interaction, learning is absent, therefore the presence and distinct influence of key people promotes or discourages appropriate and/or inappropriate behaviors (Kendall, 2011). Social cognitive theory expands on the idea of modeling by suggesting behavior is focused on achieving particular goals, and as a result, behavior becomes self-regulated over time (Ormrod, 2008). In the school context, students can be driven by goals, such as increasing their friendships or intimate relationships with peers, achieving a high grade point average or a high score on a test, or some other athletic, social, or academic goal. The goals direct behavior. Also, according to social learning theory, since human interaction is required for learning to take place, responsibility is placed on students to acknowledge, address, and involve those within their social circle in the counseling process in order to make progress. Though each individual person is ultimately responsible for him- or herself, the environment and its influences, positive or negative, can impact that person's growth and ability to move forward in life.

Although Bandura's writings are more reflective of behavioral principles than cognitive ones, the value of cognitions in social learning theory should not be dismissed. Social learning therapists (Tollefson, 2000) continually note how an individual's thoughts and expectations about a situation's outcome can predict his or her behavior. How a student interprets and perceives reinforcers and punishers in the classroom or school environment, for example, can undoubtedly influence his or her actions. Bandura also contended that self-efficacy develops through the successful navigation, experience, and mastery of social situations. Success breeds confidence and leads to a greater likelihood of continuing behaviors. If students experience success in the classroom, they become comfortable, confident, and more willing to exert effort; however, if they are unsuccessful or, worse yet, if they fail, they will likely avoid that context, as is evidenced by increased truancy and drop-out rates. Surrounding environments are critical in terms of working with children and adolescent populations, because both are distinctly affected by the societal, cultural, familial, and school context within which they live. Furthermore, youngsters are limited in their capacity to change their environments, so good or bad, the consequences of early self-efficacy (and unhealthy environments) can be lasting.

REFLECTION MOMENT

Think about the social, cultural, familial, and school context within which you grew up. Think about one way in which you learned something that you then applied to your own behavior, through observing the environment in which you lived. For example, I (Zyromski) have three siblings. I remember watching my eldest sister navigate relationships with her peers, even when she was in elementary school and I had yet to enter kindergarten, and choosing how I would interact with some of my peers based on what I watched her do.

Attribution Theory

The theory of attribution, another theory contributing to CBT, attempts to explain how people attribute the causes and effects of their behavior. Individuals typically interpret precipitating events and subsequent results to either external factors (perceived to be beyond their control) or internal factors (perceived to be within their control). Gestalt psychologist Fritz Heider (1958) is credited with initiating the work that led to this theory. Heider believed that people attempt to make sense of the social world and often mistakenly make cause and effect connections between events and actions even when there might be no direct link. When people make these external or internal attributions, which are often errors in judgment, their resulting behaviors can be either positive or negative (see Table 6.1). Attribution theory has critical implications for CBT, namely, a student's level of awareness and acceptance at the onset of counseling of personal ownership of his or her thoughts, emotions, and actions can greatly affect the course and success of treatment. Will a student acknowledge personal qualities that might help or hinder the counseling process, or will the student be "stuck" in blaming outside forces? On the other side, will students internalize or take on problems that are more likely caused by external factors beyond their control (e.g., family situations, socioeconomic status)?

Table 6.1. ATTRIBUTION THEORY

Attributions	Description	Examples
External	Situational factors Environmental factors	Natural disasters, illnesses, accidents, crimes (*negative*) Awards, rewards, prizes, luck (*positive*)
Internal	Personality traits Characteristics Attributes	Pessimism, meanness, cruelty, selfishness, laziness (*negative*) Optimism, smartness, kindness, selflessness, hard work (*positive*)

REFLECTION MOMENT

Consider some of your own life experiences, both negative and positive. In those experiences, what attributions (external or internal) did you make about why the situations occurred and who or what was responsible for the situations? In what way(s) does attribution theory explain your interpretation of life events?

History and Developers of CBT

Aaron T. Beck is often credited with pioneering CBT in the 1960s while he was studying to be a psychiatrist at the University of Pennsylvania. In researching the effectiveness of psychoanalysis in treating depression, Beck was surprised to find that the psychoanalytic approach had limited effectiveness (Beck, Rush, Shaw, & Emery, 1979). Rather, he observed that depressed patients suffered from negative "automatic thoughts" about themselves, the world, and/or their futures. These thought patterns seemed to be contributors to their resulting feelings and actions. Beck then hypothesized that if he worked with patients to challenge unhealthy thought patterns and to replace them with more realistic, healthy cognitions, then their symptoms (emotional, psychological, and behavioral) might improve. His approach proved effective and CBT has since been used to treat a wide variety of psychiatric disorders and psychological maladies. Furthermore, CBT is one of the most widely studied and supported therapeutic treatments to date (Butler et al., 2006; Hofmann et al., 2012).

Independent of Beck yet nearly simultaneously, Albert Ellis began formulating rational emotive behavior therapy (REBT), which was first termed rational therapy and later rational-emotive therapy (RET), another approach in the general category of CBT (Ellis, 1980). Essentially, REBT can be summarized by the acronym ABCDE (Dryden & Ellis, 2001), as articulated in Figure 6.1. *A* represents an event that activates irrational thinking in an individual; *B* stands for beliefs, which are both irrational and illogical; *C* is the emotional and behavioral consequences of the irrational/illogical thoughts; *D* is for disputing, which represents the therapist or counselor's role in challenging students to confront their problematic thought patterns; and, finally, representing how students must choose, *E* stands for more effective emotional, behavioral, and cognitive functioning. While CBT emphasizes how cognitions affect behavior, REBT emphasizes how cognitions affect emotions, which in turn affect behavior. Emotions/feelings, therefore, are viewed as intermediate variables in the process.

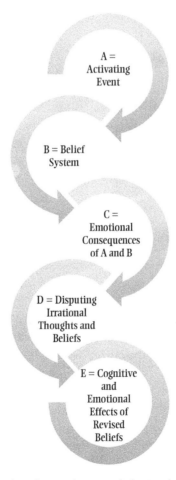

Figure 6.1. ABCDE principles of rational emotive behavior therapy.

Ellis's theory emphasizes the interaction between thoughts, feelings, and actions, all of which play key roles in affecting a person's emotional and physical health and wellness. The counselor–student relationship is critical in initiating recognition of irrational thoughts and facilitating change. Without confronting their irrational thought processes, students will continue in a negative spiral, unable to see the errors in their own judgments. Contrary to other therapeutic approaches (which work to foster mutual respect, caring, and acceptance), an REBT school counselor operates in a more directive, challenging manner, pushing the students in directions they might not be ready or willing to go.

Beck and Ellis argued that irrational thoughts contribute to maladaptive behavior patterns; however, neither contended that negative thought patterns alone caused psychopathology (Hersen & Gross, 2008), and both acknowledged the salience of environmental stressors and genetics. Yet CBT has been used effectively to counteract many psychological, emotional, and behavioral disturbances. What is it, then, that contributes to its high level of effectiveness?

REFLECTION MOMENT

Think about how environmental factors might compound stress and mental distress. Think about when you were in your graduate program. How did environmental stressors (e.g., family expectations, time commitments, financial issues) affect your thought patterns? How might environmental factors, such as those experienced by underrepresented populations or people living in poverty, create additional psychological and emotional burdens for students?

CBT THEORY OF CHANGE

CBT rests on a theory of change that suggests that an individual's feelings, thoughts, and behaviors all influence one another, and that each is affected equally by one's beliefs. When a person's core beliefs about themselves, others, and their future is negative, their emotions, cognitions, and actions reflect the negativity. For example, Johnny, a middle school student who is struggling to fit in socially, might look in the mirror and think "I'm ugly. Who would ever date me with all this acne?" (negative cognitions) and as a result feel lonely and sad (negative emotions) and shy away from talking to someone he might be romantically interested in (negative actions). His retreating behavior could send a nonverbal message to others that Johnny likes to be alone, so the others keep their distance (negative reactions of others), although Johnny may actually be craving some connection. In this example, it is clear how Johnny's beliefs reflect

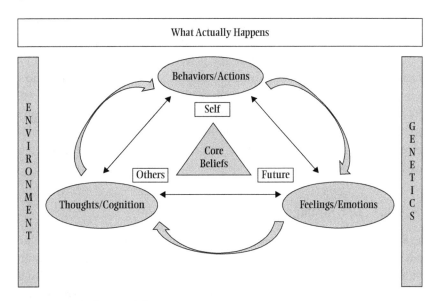

Figure 6.2. CBT theory of change.

in his emotions and subsequent actions, which in turn effect how others in his environment react to him.

A visual model of this theory of change is shown in Figure 6.2. CBT is considered a directive, problem-focused, action-oriented approach to psychotherapy. In order to reach a state of homeostasis, or balance, and to move toward greater health and wellness, students must become aware of this interaction. On the one hand, destructive thinking patterns, feelings of hopelessness, loss, despair, and unproductive behaviors can contribute to an increased likelihood of relationship woes and life struggles. On the other hand, productive beliefs contribute to healthy feelings and thoughts, resulting in positive behavior change.

CBT Delivery, Strategies, and Techniques

CBT was developed for use with adult populations, although it has been effectively implemented with youth as well (Hofmann et al., 2012). CBT can be incorporated in a range of formats, including individual counseling (Weisz et al., 2012), small-group counseling (Bernstein, Layne, Egan, & Tennison, 2005; Durlak, Weissberg, Quintana, & Perez, 2004; Manassis et al., 2010), family counseling (Bernstein et al., 2005), and even classroom-based lessons (Miller, Laye-Gindhu, Bennett, Liu, & Gold, 2011; Stallard et al., 2014). Most commonly, CBT techniques are integrated into one-on-one sessions between a counselor and student. When CBT is delivered in this format, students can receive individualized counseling (Weisz et al., 2012). In these more intimate situations, personalized attention can be placed on issues specific to that particular student's life. Typical individual sessions last anywhere from 20 to 60 minutes each, depending upon the age of the student; a student and counselor usually meet on a weekly basis to review therapeutic goals and progress. The number of sessions varies depending upon the severity of the problem, the receptivity of the student, and the student's willingness to make necessary changes for his or her betterment.

The A, B, C, D, E Strategy

The REBT A, B, C, D, and E intervention is a way for school counselors to help students realize how problems develop and can help students replace irrational or unhelpful thoughts. It can also lead to goal setting. The following discussion builds from the example provided by Thompson and Henderson (2007) for using the REBT approach and applying the A, B, C, D, and E strategy with students.

A. Represents the activating event: "I failed the exam."
B. How the student evaluates the event: An irrational message might be, "I failed; therefore, I am a total failure as a person." A rational message might be, "I failed, which is inconvenient and uncomfortable, but that's it. I need to study more effectively." As previously mentioned, how a student attributes success or failure is critical in CBT. The awareness of how much of failure and success can be attributed to external or internal attributes can directly affect rational or irrational messages.
C. Represents the consequences or feelings from the self-message at the B stage above: The irrational message might lead to feelings of frustration. The rational message might not feel comfortable but the feelings won't inhibit success on the next test.
D. Represents the disputing arguments the student can use to attack the irrational message expressed in the B stage: School counselors can help students identify and create disputing arguments against negative self-messages.
E. Represents answers to questions regarding the rationality of the self-messages of the B stage.

With the student, a school counselor can use the A, B, C, D, and E cycle to delve into pertinent issues, and the CBT counselor makes use of open-ended questions designed to elicit further information from the student and to place him or her in the "driver's seat." Together, goals and an action plan are discussed and developed (and refined later, if need be). During this process, students are actively exploring their self-efficacy expectations (Bandura, 1977), or their beliefs about whether they are capable of performing the required behaviors, as well as their outcome expectations, which reflects their belief that the behavior will lead to an outcome. The school counselor can help the student explore and express his or her beliefs about how certain behaviors might lead to specific outcomes. As the A, B, C, D, and E cycle is used, the students' self-efficacy expectations and outcome expectations will become clear and the school counselor will have the opportunity to dispute irrational thoughts and messages through cognitive restructuring. Mood/ temperature checks, scaling questions, role-play, ongoing feedback, encouragement, and support are employed. A feedback loop is suggested as well, whereby students are taught to self-monitor their cognitions, emotions, and actions and to report to the therapist about them. In doing so, patterns are noted and addressed. Students are also given homework, a hallmark of the CBT approach, in order to extend and apply what is learned in counseling to real-life situations.

CBT OPERATIONALIZED IN SCHOOLS

School counselors need to consider how CBT implementation in schools can be delivered. Traditionally, CBT is delivered on an individualized, case-by-case basis; however, cognitive-behavioral techniques and strategies might also be employed in small-group sessions and classroom guidance lessons. Similarly, families might be involved in CBT-based interventions. (A review of CBT-based small- and large-group programs that can be utilized by school-based professionals is offered in Table 6.2 "Evidence-based CBT Programs").

Recent research efforts have been devoted to assessing the extent to which CBT can be implemented effectively in schools and can result in positive outcomes for students (Bernstein et al., 2005; Chui et al., 2013; Fazzio-Griffith & Ballard, 2014; Flanagan, Allen, & Henry, 2010; Flanagan, Allen, & Levine, 2015; Ginsburg & Drake, 2002; Manassis et al., 2010; Masia, Warner, Fisher, Shrout, Rathor, & Klein, 2007; Miller et al., 2011). Yet, much more research is needed to demonstrate the benefits of the CBT approach in educational settings (Bernstein et al., 2005; Ginsburg & Drake, 2002; Masia et al., 2007; Weisz, Jensen, & McLeod, 2005).

Table 6.2. CBT EVIDENCE-BASED PROGRAMS

Name	Resource	Synopsis
Adolescent Coping with Depression	Clarke, Lewinsohn, Hops, & Grossen (1990a). Clarke, Lewinsohn, Hops, & Grossen (1990b). Lewinsohn, Clarke, Hops, & Andrews (1990).	Cognitive-behavioral group intervention that targets: • Discomfort and anxiety • Irrational/negative thoughts • Poor social skills • Limited experiences of pleasant activities The intervention is composed of 16 2-hour sessions conducted over an 8-week period. Target population: 13- to 17-year-old students.
Coping Cat	Kendall (1994). Kendall & Hedtke (2006a). Kendall & Hedtke (2006b).	A treatment program for children with anxiety. The program has four coordinated components: • Recognizing and understanding emotional and physical reactions to anxiety • Clarifying thoughts and feelings in anxious situations • Developing plans for effective coping • Evaluating performance and giving self-reinforcement Weekly 50-minute sessions for 16 weeks. Target population: Children ages 7 to 13 suffering from anxiety or social disorders.
Coping Power Program	Lochman & Wells (2003). Lochman, Wells, & Lenhart (2008). Wells, Lochman, & Lenhart (2008).	Focuses on children and adolescents at risk for antisocial behavior. The program focuses on: • Social cognition • Self-regulation • Peer relationships • Positive parental involvement It is designed to be implemented with the child and parent components as interwoven interventions. The child component has 34 group sessions. The parent component has 16 sessions. Target population: Children 8 to 14 years old.

Table 6.2. Continued

Name	Resource	Synopsis
Student Success Skills	http://studentsuccessskills.com/ Brigman, Campbell, & Webb (2010). Brigman, Lane, & Lane (2008). Brigman & Peluso (2009). Brigman & Webb (2007). Brigman & Webb (2010).	Multiple publications (Mariani, Villares, Wirth, & Brigman, 2014; Mariani, Webb, Villares, & Brigman, 2015; Villares, Frain, Brigman, Webb, & Peluso, 2012; Zyromski, Mariani, Kim, Lee, & Carey, 2017) also report that SSS helps students enhance: • Cognitive factors (memory and learning strategies) • Attitudinal skills (optimism and self-efficacy) • Self-regulatory and metacognitive skills (managing attention, anxiety, motivation, and anger) • Behavioral strategies (goal setting and progress monitoring) • Social skills It is delivered in a 5-week classroom guidance component with an 8-week small-group counseling component for students identified as needing additional reinforcement of concepts and skills. A parent component exists as well. Target populations: K–First grade: *Ready to Learn* curriculum Second–third grade: *Ready for Success* curriculum Fourth–twelfth grades: *Student Success Skills* curriculum

REFLECTION MOMENT

Participation in extracurricular activities, such as sports or clubs, has gained popularity in our culture. Think about the ways that children and adolescents respond to success or failure in these activities. How does their reaction reflect their thoughts about their experiences? How might school counselors use their students' participation in these activities as concrete learning opportunities to practice beneficial cognitive thought patterns?

Application of CBT with Children

Children dealing with a broad range of diagnoses and challenges, including anxiety, fear, disruptive behaviors, academic and social skill problems, family issues, eating and sleeping disorders, anger, obsessive-compulsive and perfectionist tendencies, communication difficulties, and bullying, can benefit from CBT. Positive outcomes for children receiving CBT intervention have been clearly evidenced in the literature (Cartwright-Hatton, Roberts, Chitsabeasan, Fothergill, & Harrington, 2004; Chiu et al., 2013; Fazzio-Griffith & Ballard, 2014; James, Soler, & Weatherall, 2008; Knell, 2009; Lösel & Beelmann, 2003; Manassis et al., 2010; Miller et al., 2011; Özabaci, 2011; Silvermann, Pina, & Viswesvaran, 2008; Van der Oord, Prins, Oosterlaan, & Emmelkamp, 2008). Specifically, James, Soler, and Weatherall (2008) reported large effect sizes when CBT was employed to treat childhood anxiety disorders. Benefits have also been evidenced when CBT techniques were applied with children suffering from obsessive-compulsive behaviors (Guggisberg, 2005; Phillips, 2003). Researchers have compared CBT efficacy to no treatment, to other therapeutic approaches, and to medicinal treatments; findings indicated that children who received CBT demonstrated significantly better outcomes (Guggisberg, 2005; Phillips, 2003). Studies have focused on comparing CBT to other psychosocial treatments, as well as on comparing CBT to, and CBT in conjunction with, medicinal treatments. CBT consistently evidences significant outcomes for participating youth. In addition, CBT has been found to be cost effective and to have fewer side effects than other treatments (Haby, Tonge, Littlefield, Carter, & Vos, 2004).

As counselors apply CBT interventions with children, they should pay special attention to ensure the interventions are developmentally appropriate (Arora at al., 2015; Grave & Blissett, 2004; Reinecke, Dattilio, & Freeman, 2003a; Stone, 2007). The counselor using CBT approaches to work with children and adolescents will take into consideration genetic influences on development, as well as environmental factors, cultural contexts, and the interaction among core beliefs and thoughts, emotions, and behaviors. As Figure 6.2 shows, the interrelation between contexts of the environment with thoughts, behaviors, and emotions results in constant interaction and influence between contexts. In other words, it is important to understand how a child's culture, learning environment, learning history at school, cognitive structures, and behavioral history interact with the presenting problem (Friedberg & McClure, 2002). In addition to these considerations, practitioners should ensure that CBT intervention with children is adapted to use simple, concrete examples, is highly active, is structured, uses interactive and visual devices (such as experiential learning strategies), and includes frequent practice (Arora et al., 2015; Reinecke, Dattilio, & Freeman, 2003b). Using traditional CBT approaches combined with play therapy strategies may allow younger children to benefit from the strategic structure of CBT while providing interactive, developmentally appropriate strategies to deliver the intervention.

CBT Developmental Examples with Children

School counselors who utilize CBT can employ strategies like bibliotherapy, constructive play, and puppets. These approaches can be helpful with younger children in kindergarten or first grade and can by aligned specifically with CBT by helping students cognitively replace irrational or unhelpful thoughts. Imagine a student who is afraid to come to school; the school counselor could first use bibliotherapy to help identify which parts of school are scary to the student and to normalize the experience. The student could then work with the school counselor to create her own book about her fears and attempts to overcome those fears when coming to school. The school counselor could then have the student use a puppet to share how it feels to be scared. The school counselor and student could create a list of coping self-messages for the puppet to practice when it is scared. Eventually, the student could begin practicing the statements to help her as she comes to school and feels scared.

CBT interventions with children can be delivered at the Tier One (classroom guidance), Tier Two (small-group counseling), or Tier Three (individual counseling) levels. Two examples of Tier One interventions that apply CBT tenets are the PATHS curriculum (Kusche & Greenberg, 1994) and the Student Success Skills curriculum (Brigman & Webb, 2010). Both curricula are designed to be delivered in the classroom setting. Both apply tenets of CBT to help students increase their self-direction, self-management, and interpersonal skills, among others. Clearly, each program uses different interventions and delivery mechanisms to accomplish its outcomes, and practitioners should research both to determine which would best meet the needs of their particular populations.

Tier Two CBT interventions might be delivered using a small-group curriculum, such as Coping Cat (Kendall & Hedtke, 2006), I Can Problem Solve (Shure, 1992), or others (see Table 6.2 for others), or the small group might be a structured group not based on a specific curriculum. A school counselor building a CBT small-group intervention would first examine the results of the needs assessments or other data indicating a need for small-group intervention. Then, the school counselor would build the small-group intervention to meet the needs of the students. For example, if the needs assessments revealed that students were expressing the need for anxiety management, a small group could help children identify symptoms of anxiety, help students apply CBT interventions to manage the anxiety, and employ practice using role-play. The Coping Cat (Kendall & Hedtke, 2006) curriculum serves as an excellent resource for building a CBT small-group intervention. The CBT concepts and skills are sequentially introduced in each session, building from basic to more advanced skills. For example, Kendall and Hedtke (2006) introduced a four-step plan for coping with anxiety. The FEAR plan includes the following steps: (a) Feeling frightened, (b) Expecting bad things to happen, (c) Attitudes and actions that can help, and (d) Results and rewards. The FEAR plan represents several important components of CBT, such as helping children identify overgeneralizations, thought distortions, catastrophizing, and absolutes (such as shoulds, musts, always, oughts, and nevers). The process might also help identify fortune telling that students are engaging in regarding how anxiety might affect their future. Fortune telling occurs when a student predicts the future, usually with negative outcomes, without considering the chances of that outcome's actually happening or realistically considering alternate outcomes. Interventions the FEAR plan include role-playing, thought replacement, challenging cognitive distortions, and practice.

In Tier Three, school counselors have a variety of resources available that provide significant depth and breadth for working with children in individual counseling sessions using CBT (Creed, Reisweber, & Beck, 2011; Friedberg & McClure, 2015; Kendall, 2011; Reinecke, Dattilio, & Freeman, 2003b). Readers can refer to these resources for specific suggestions for applying CBT in individual settings with children struggling with specific issues, such as anger management, attention deficit hyperactivity disorder, depression, eating disorders, family problems, posttraumatic stress disorder, and self-harming behaviors, among others. Details are beyond the scope of this chapter, but a brief overview of using CBT with children in schools, followed by a synopsis of using CBT with adolescents in schools, is offered below.

As children interact with the world around them, they interpret their experiences as positive, negative, or neutral (Friedberg & McClure, 2015). The way in which the child interprets the interaction of the contexts in his environment directly influences his thoughts, emotions, and behavioral functioning. For example, a 7-year-old who wakes up to help take care of his baby brother because his mother is working three jobs and needs help in the morning may or may not have physiological problems (lack of sleep, headaches, stomach aches), a disturbed mood (anxiety), behavioral problems (passivity, withdrawal), and cognitive symptoms (overwhelmed). How the child constructs meaning and interacts with his environment will shape his mental and emotional functioning (Friedberg & McClure). If the child interprets his experience with distorted thoughts, it may lead to exaggerated behaviors. It is these behaviors that often result in a child's being referred to, or seeking out, help (Stewart, Christner, & Freeman, 2007).

As the counselor moves forward with helping the student, he or she will gather information regarding the presenting problem. Again, it is vital that the counselor understand the problem within the interaction of the variables illustrated in Figure 6.2. Friedberg and McClure (2015) suggested formulating an understanding of the child's behavioral, cognitive, emotional, and physiological realities before proceeding. These realities must be understood within environmental and genetic factors, such as family systems, social systems, school systems, and other cultural contexts. Although working with children in a school setting is often subject to time constraints, it is important to take the time to understand objective and subjective data regarding the presenting problem (Reinecke, Dattilio, & Freeman, 2003a). Once the data and the child's reality have been collected, a case conceptualization can be developed, leading to a treatment plan.

As the counselor works to understand the child's cognitions and behaviors, understanding the child's schema, his or her basic beliefs (which have been shaped by the child's life events), is vital (Friedberg & McClure, 2015). Stewart, Christner, and Freeman (2007) offered a list of eleven common cognitive distortions occurring in children and adolescents, including dichotomous thinking, overgeneralization, mind reading, emotional reasoning, disqualifying the positive, catastrophizing, personalization, should statements, comparing, selective abstraction, and labeling. As the counselor works with the child, specific interventions are used to address the underlying beliefs that may lead to a cognitive distortion experienced by the child. These cognitive and behavioral interventions should be developmentally appropriate for the student and can be reinforced by homework.

DETECTING IRRATIONAL BELIEFS AND CHALLENGING THEM—AN EXAMPLE

School counselors can ask open-ended questions to uncover irrational beliefs, and then the counselor can dispute and challenge them.

School Counselor: So tell me more about how you feel about your grade on the math test.

Student: Well, I failed the math test. I totally bombed it. I think I got worse than an F. I will never get better than an F on a math test. I'll be lucky to pass fourth grade.

In this statement, the student overgeneralizes and then catastrophizes. The overgeneralization occurs in the student's statement that he will never get better than an F on a math test. The catastrophizing occurs when the student says he will be lucky to pass fourth grade. The school counselor can dispute and challenge both irrational beliefs.

School Counselor: So, because you got an F on this one math test you will get an F on every math test you ever take in the future?
The school counselor could continue:
You've told me you have fair grades in reading and a B+ in science. Yet, you will be lucky to pass fourth grade?

The goal is to help the student identify irrational beliefs, then to formulate alternate self-messages, and then to apply and practice the new messages.

Friedberg and McClure (2015) suggested that each session consist of a check-in with the child, a review of homework, the setting of an agenda, work, a homework assignment, and then a feedback loop. It is important to remember that working with children in session will require creativity on the part of the counselor. For example, a school counselor could use puppet play to help the student express thoughts and feelings. The counselor might offer hand puppets that the child can use to represent family members. Puppet play provides the opportunity for the student to express cognitive thought processes about life events. The school counselor can enact typical family scenes while being aware of ways the students is expressing underlying beliefs that may lead to one of the cognitive distortions mentioned previously. Other play therapy approaches, such as games, stories, workbooks, interactive activities, and experiential exercises, can be used to engage the child in the therapeutic process and are encouraged.

REFLECTION MOMENT

Think back to your own learning experiences. In what ways do you learn best? What is your learning style? What learning styles have you seen in others? How would you make an analogy between learning styles and ways a child or adolescent best experiences counseling interventions?

Application of CBT with Adolescents

Research has suggested that cognitive-behavioral interventions produce increases in school attendance and reductions in anxiety, fear, depression, and other behaviors that lead to students' refusal to attend school (Pina, Zerr, Gonzalez, & Ortiz, 2009). For example, a seven-session small-group intervention with 16 high school students greatly reduced the students' assessed scores for anxiety and depression and produced a significant increase in the students' belief in self (Melnyk, Kelly, & Lusk, 2014). Additional studies examining the impact of CBT interventions in school settings with adolescents are needed. As previously mentioned, counselors should pay special attention to developmental issues when working with children and adolescents (Arora at al., 2015; Grave & Blissett, 2004; Reinecke, Dattilio, & Freeman, 2003b; Stone, 2007). Adolescents experience a tremendous amount of change, including transitions from childhood to adulthood, as well as other biological, psychological, and social changes (Holmbeck et al., 2011). Adolescents experience the effects of puberty, the effects of relational emphasis from parents to peers, and the effects of increased behavioral autonomy. The counselor must take into effect these contextual issues, as well as cognitive development factors, other environmental factors, other cultural implications, and the interaction among fluctuating beliefs and thoughts, emotions, and behaviors. Figure 6.2 illustrates the complex interaction between contexts in an adolescent's environment, thoughts, behaviors, and emotions, and yet implicit within these categories, but worth mentioning, are developmental processes encumbering the adolescent. As previously mentioned, it is important to understand how a child's culture, learning environment, learning history overall and at that school, cognitive structures, and behavioral history interact with the presenting problem (Friedberg & McClure, 2002). In addition to these considerations, practitioners working with adolescents should consider how changes in biology, social roles, and cognition interact with adolescent experiences of relational intimacy, increased autonomy, evolving sexuality, and developing identity (Holmbeck et al., 2011). A thoughtful practitioner considers the relationship between these factors when working with adolescents. These developmental factors differ significantly from the developmental issues faced by children or adults.

USING POSITIVE SELF-TALK AND POSITIVE REINFORCEMENT—AN EXAMPLE

CBT interventions often pair the practice of positive self-talk by the student with positive reinforcement from the school counselor (Thompson & Henderson, 2007).

School Counselor: So, you were initially quite anxious when your boyfriend didn't text you right back after you texted him to find out plans for last Friday evening?

Student: Yes, but then I remembered my homework and thought about the possible reasons he didn't text right back. I also thought it wasn't the end of the world. He would text at some point. Plus [she laughs], I took a deep breath and practiced my relaxation techniques.

School Counselor: So, you made the situation manageable at that moment! You practiced your anxiety and relaxation techniques to keep you in the moment and you identified ways to cope with the stress of not hearing right back from your boyfriend. You did it.

What's pertinent to CBT in this interaction is that the student and counselor worked through the management of the stressor and the student's ability to cope with the stressor, and the counselor used reinforcement to encourage practice of the self-statements.

REFLECTION MOMENT

Consider how developmental changes, such as puberty, affect how adolescents think. How might developmental changes, when combined with the changing dynamic of interpersonal contexts of adolescence, affect the cognitive functioning of an adolescent?

LIMITATIONS OF CBT

Although there are obvious benefits to employing CBT with students of any age, the approach does have limitations. For one, CBT requires a conscious commitment from the student; without the proper level of readiness, willingness, and motivation, this type of therapy can fail. Coupled with this consideration comes the understanding that CBT can be a time-consuming and labor-intensive process. Both student and counselor need to be patient and to remain focused on the agreed-upon goals. Next, CBT is not suitable for everyone; specifically, it may not be right for students with complex mental health problems or severe learning needs, because the techniques used in CBT require the student to demonstrate understanding of his or her current problem, acknowledge his or her own thoughts, feelings, and behaviors, and confront thoughts, feelings, and behaviors that may be the most uncomfortable or difficult. In working through this process, students suffering from certain disorders may experience increased anxiety and/or increased negative symptoms, putting them at risk for getting worse instead of improving. Furthermore, much of CBT focuses on what individuals themselves have control over and can do to improve their current situation. However, often individuals do not have control over the other people, systems, and/or situations that are negatively affecting their lives the most (e.g., a child may be subjected to physical and emotional abuse at home). Finally, another limitation of CBT is that it relies heavily on the relationship and connection between counselor and student, and this connection must be adequately established and maintained. Many factors can affect the counselor–student relationship and it can be difficult to control for all of them.

SUGGESTED READINGS

BOOKS

Creed, T. A., Reisweber, J., & Beck, A. T. (2011). *Cognitive therapy for adolescents in school settings.* New York, NY: Guilford Press.

Friedberg, R. D., & McClure, J. M. (2015). *Clinical practice of cognitive therapy with children and adolescents: The nuts and bolts* (2nd ed.). New York, NY: Guilford Press.

Friedberg, R. D., McClure, J. M., & Garcia, J. H. (2009). *Cognitive therapy techniques for children and adolescents: Tools for enhancing practice.* New York, NY: Guilford Press.

Kendall, P. C. (2011). *Child and adolescent therapy: Cognitive-behavioral procedures* (4th ed.). New York, NY: Guilford Press.

Kendall, P. C., & Hedtke, K. A. (2006). *Coping Cat workbook* (2nd ed.). Ardmore, PA: Workbook Publishing.

Mennuti, R. B., Christner, R. W., & Freeman, A. (2012). *Cognitive-behavioral interventions in educational settings: A handbook for practice* (2nd ed.). New York, NY: Routledge.

Vernon, A. (2009). *What works when with children and adolescents: A handbook of counseling techniques.* Champaign, IL: Research Press.

WEBSITES

- Centers for Disease Control and Prevention, Division of Adolescent School Health (CDC/DASH): http://www.cdc.gov/healthyyouth/
- Collaborative for Academic, Social and Emotional Learning (CASEL): http://www.casel.org/guide/
- Ronald H. Fredrickson Center for School Counseling Outcome Research and Evaluation (CSCORE)—Resources for School Counselors page: http://www.umass.edu/schoolcounseling/resources-for-counselors.php
- SAMHSA National Registry of Evidence-based Programs and Practices: http://www.nrepp.samhsa.gov/
- What Works Clearinghouse: www.whatworks.ed.gov/

REFERENCES

Arora, P., Pössel, P., Barnard, A. D., Terjesen, M., Lai, B. S., Ehrlich, C. J., ... Gogos, A. K. (2015). Cognitive interventions. In R. Flanagan, J. L. Stewart, & A. Freeman (Eds.), *Cognitive and behavioral interventions in the schools: Integrating theory and research into practice.* New York, NY: Springer.

Bandura, A. (1976). *Social learning theory.* Upper Saddle River, NJ: Prentice-Hall.

Bandura, A. (1977). *Self-efficacy: The exercise of control.* New York, NY: W.H. Freeman.

Baum, W. M. (2004). Understanding behaviorism: Behavior, culture, and evolution (2nd ed.). Hoboken, NJ: Wiley-Blackwell.

Beck Institute. (n.d.). *History of Dr. Aaron Beck*. Available from https://owl.english.purdue.edu/owl/resource/560/10/

Beck, A. T., Rush, A. J., Shaw, B. F., & Emery, G. (1979). *Cognitive therapy of depression*. New York, NY: Guilford Press.

Bernstein, G. A., Layne, A. E., Egan, E. A., & Tennison, D. M. (2005). School-based interventions for anxious children. *Journal of the American Academy of Child and Adolescent Psychiatry, 44*, 1118–1127.

Brigman, G., Campbell, C., & Webb, L. (2010). *Student success skills: Group counseling manual* (3rd ed.). Boca Raton, FL: Atlantic Education Consultants.

Brigman, G., Lane, D., & Lane, D. (2008). *Ready to learn* (2nd ed.). Boca Raton, FL: Atlantic Education Consultants.

Brigman, G., & Peluso, P. (2009). *Parent success skills*. Boca Raton, FL: Atlantic Education Consultants.

Brigman, G., & Webb, L. (2007). *Ready for success skills: Classroom manual*. Boca Raton, FL: Atlantic Education Consultants.

Brigman, G., & Webb, L. (2010). *Student success skills: Classroom manual* (3rd ed.). Boca Raton, FL: Atlantic Education Consultants.

Butler, A. C., Chapman, J. E., Forman, E. M., & Beck, A. T. (2006). An empirical status of cognitive-behavioral therapy: A review of meta-analyses. *Clinical Psychology Review, 26*(1), 17–31.

Cartwright-Hatton, S., Roberts, C., Chitsabesan, P., Fothergill, C., & Harrington, R. (2004). Systematic review of the efficacy of cognitive behavioral therapies for childhood and adolescent anxiety disorders. *Journal of Clinical Psychology, 43*, 421–436.

Christner, R. W., Stewart, J. L., & Freeman, A. (Eds.). (2007). *Handbook of cognitive-behavior group therapy with children and adolescents*. New York, NY: Routledge.

Chiu, A. W., Langer, D. A., McLeod, B. D., Har, K., Drahota, A., Galla, B. M., . . . Wood, J. J. (2013). Effectiveness of modular CBT for child anxiety in elementary schools. *School Psychology Quarterly, 28*(2), 141–153.

Clarke, G., Lewinsohn, P., Hops, H., & Grossen, B. (1990a). Leader's manual for adolescent groups: Adolescent Coping With Depression course. Available from http://www.kpchr.org/public/acwd/CWDA_manual.pdf

Clarke, G., Lewinsohn, P., Hops, H., & Grossen, B. (1990b). Student workbook: Adolescent Coping With Depression course. Available from http://www.kpchr.org/public/acwd/CWDA_workbook.pdf

Creed, T. A., Reisweber, J., & Beck, A. T. (2011). *Cognitive therapy for adolescents in school settings*. New York, NY: Guilford Press.

Dobson, K. S., & Dozois, D. J. (2001). Historical and philosophical bases of cognitive- behavioral therapies. In K. S. Dobson (Ed.), *Handbook of cognitive-behavioral therapies* (2nd ed., pp. 3–38). New York, NY: Guilford Press.

Dryden, W., & Ellis, A. (2001). Rational emotive behavioral therapy. In K. S. Dobson (Ed.), *Handbook of cognitive-behavioral therapies* (2nd ed., pp. 295–348). New York, NY: Guilford Press.

Durlak, J. A., Weissberg, R. P., Quintana, E., & Perez, F. (2004). Primary prevention: Involving schools and communities in youth health promotion. In L. A. Jason, C. B. Keys, Y. Suarez-Balcazar, R. R. Taylor, & M. I. Davis. (Eds.), *Participatory community research: Theories and methods in action* (pp. 73–86). Washington, DC: American Psychological Association.

Ellis, A., & MacLaren, C. (2005). *Rational emotive behavior therapy: A therapist's guide* (2nd ed.). Oakland, CA: Impact Publishers.

Fazzio-Griffith, L. J., & Ballard, M. B. (2014). Cognitive behavioral play therapy techniques in school-based group counseling: Assisting students in the development of social skills. *Vistas Online, 18*, 1–14. Available from www.counseling.org/knowledge-center/vistas.

Flanagan, R., Allen, K., & Henry, D. J. (2010). The impact of anger management treatment and rational emotive behavior therapy in a public school setting on social skills, anger management, and depression. *Journal of Rational-Emotive & Cognitive Behavior Therapy, 28*, 87–99.

Flanagan, R., Allen, K., & Levine, E. (Eds). (2015). *Cognitive and behavioral interventions in the schools: Integrating theory and research into practice.* New York, NY: Springer.

Friedberg, R. D., & McClure, J. M. (2002). *Clinical practice of cognitive therapy with children and adolescents.* New York, NY: Guilford Press.

Ginsburg, G. S., & Drake, K. L. (2002). School-based treatment for anxious African-American adolescents: A controlled pilot study. *Journal of the American Academy of Child and Adolescent Psychiatry, 41*, 768–775.

Grave, J., & Blissett, J. (2004). Is cognitive behavior therapy developmentally appropriate for young children? A critical review of the evidence. *Clinical Psychology Review, 24*(4), 399–420.

Guggisberg, K. W. (2005). *Methodological review and meta-analysis of treatments for child and adolescent obsessive-compulsive disorder.* Salt Lake City, UT: University of Utah.

Haby, M. M., Tonge, B., Littlefield, L., Carter, R., & Vos, T. (2004). Cost-effectiveness of cognitive behavioural therapy and selective serotonin reuptake inhibitors for major depression in children and adolescents. *The Australian and New Zealand Journal of Psychiatry, 38*, 579–591.

Heider, F. (1958). *The psychology of interpersonal relations.* New York, NY: Wiley.

Hersen, M., & Gross, A. M. (2008). *Handbook of clinical psychology: Children and adolescents* (Vol. 2). Hoboken, NJ: John Wiley & Sons.

Hofmann, S. G., Asnaani, A., Imke, J. J., Vonk, M. A., Sawyer, A. T., & Fang, A. (2012). The efficacy of cognitive behavioral therapy: A review of meta-analyses. *Cognitive Therapy Research, 36*(5), 427–440.

Holmbeck, G. N., O'Mahar, K., Abad, M., Colder, C., & Updegrove, A. (2011). Cognitive-behavioral therapy with adolescents: Guides from developmental psychology. In P.C. Kendall (Ed.), *Child and adolescent therapy: Cognitive-behavioral procedures* (4th ed.). New York, NY: Guilford Press.

James, A., Soler, A., & Weatherall, R. (2008). Cognitive behavioral therapy for anxiety disorders in children and adolescents. *Cochrane Database of Systemic Reviews, 4*, CD004690.

Kendall, P. C. (1994). Treating anxiety disorders in children: Results of a randomized clinical trial. *Journal of Consulting and Clinical Psychology, 62*, 100–110.

Kendall, P. C. (2011). *Child and adolescent therapy: Cognitive-behavioral procedures* (4th ed.). New York, NY: Guilford Press.

Kendall, P. C., & Hedtke, K. (2006a). *Cognitive-behavioral therapy for anxious children: Therapist manual* (3rd ed.). Ardmore, PA: Workbook Publishing.

Kendall, P. C., & Hedtke, K. A. (2006b). *Coping Cat workbook* (2nd ed.). Ardmore, PA: Workbook Publishing.

Knell, S. M. (2009). *Cognitive-behavioral play therapy*. Northvale, NJ: Jason Aronson.

Kusche, C. A., & Greenberg, M. T. (1994) *The PATHS curriculum*. Seattle, WA: Developmental Research and Programs.

Lewinsohn, P. M., Clarke, G. N., Hops, H., & Andrews, J. (1990). Cognitive-behavioral group treatment of depression in adolescents. *Behavior Therapy, 21*(4), 385–401.

Lochman, J. E., & Wells, K. C. (2003). Effectiveness of the Coping Power Program and of classroom intervention with aggressive children: Outcomes at a 1-year follow-up. *Behavior Therapy, 34*, 493–515.

Lochman, J. E., Wells, K. C., & Lenhart, L. A. (2008). *Coping Power child group program: Facilitator guide*. New York, NY: Oxford University Press.

Lösel, F., & Beelmann, A. (2003). Effects of child skills training in preventing antisocial behavior: A systematic review of randomized evaluations. *Annals of the American Academy of Political and Social Science, 587*, 84–109.

Manassis, K., Wilansky-Traynor, P., Farzan, N., Kleiman, V., Parker, K., & Sanford, M. (2010). The Feelings Club: Randomized controlled evaluation of a school-based CBT for anxious or depressive symptoms. *Depression and Anxiety, 27*, 945–952.

Mariani, M., Villares, E., Wirth, J., & Brigman, G. (2014). An evaluation of the Student Success Skills program on student learning, behavior, and wellness outcomes. *Hellenic Journal of Psychology, 11*, 223–240.

Mariani, M., Webb, L., Villares, E., & Brigman, G. (2015). Effects of Student Success Skills on pro-social and bullying behavior. *The Professional Counselor, 5*(3), 341–353.

Masia Warner, C., Fisher, P. H., Shrout, P. E., Rathor, S., & Klein, R. G. (2007). Treating adolescents with social anxiety disorder in school: An attention control trial. *Journal of Child Psychology and Psychiatry, 48*, 676–686.

McLeod, S. (2015). *Jean Piaget*. Available from http://www.simplypsychology.org/piaget.html

Meichenbaum, D. (1977). *Cognitive-behavior modification*. New York, NY: Plenum Press.

Melnyk, B. M., Kelly, S., & Lusk, P. (2014). Outcomes and feasibility of a manualized cognitive-behavioral skills building intervention: Group COPE for depressed and anxious adolescents in school settings. *Journal of Child and Adolescent Psychiatric Nursing, 27*, 3–13.

Miller, L. D., Laye-Gindhu, A., Bennett, J. L., Liu, Y., & Gold, S. (2011). An effectiveness study of a culturally enriched school-based CBT anxiety prevention program. *Journal of Clinical Child & Adolescent Psychology, 40*(4), 618–629.

Ormrod, J. E. (2008). *Educational psychology: Developing learners* (6th ed.). Upper Saddle River, NJ: Pearson.

Özabaci, N. (2011). Cognitive behavioural therapy for violent behaviour in children and adolescents: A meta-analysis. *Children and Youth Services Review, 33*(10), 1989–1993.

Pavlov, I. P. (1955). *Selected works*. Moscow, Russia: Foreign Languages Publishing House.

Phillips, A. S. (2003). *A meta-analysis of treatments for pediatric obsessive-compulsive disorder*. Manhattan, KS: Kansas State University.

Piaget, J. (1932). *The moral judgment of the child*. London, England: Routledge & Kegan Paul.

Piaget, J. (1936). *Origins of intelligence in the child*. London, England: Routledge & Kegan Paul.

Piaget, J. (1945). *Play, dreams and imitation in childhood*. London, England: Heinemann.

Piaget, J. (1957). *Construction of reality in the child*. London, England: Routledge & Kegan Paul.

Pina, A. A., Zerr, A. A., Gonzalez, N. A., & Ortiz, C. D. (2009). Psychosocial interventions for school refusal behavior in children and adolescents. *Child Development Perspectives, 3*, 11–20.

Reinecke, M. A., Dattilio, F. M., & Freeman, A. (Eds.). (2003a). *Cognitive therapy with children and adolescents: A casebook for clinical practice* (2nd ed.). New York, NY: Guilford Press.

Reinecke, M. A., Dattilio, F. M., & Freeman, A. (2003b). What makes for an effective treatment? In M. A. Reinecke, F. M. Dattilio, & A. Freeman (Eds.), *Cognitive therapy with children and adolescents: A casebook for clinical practice* (2nd ed.). New York, NY: Guilford Press.

Shure, M. B. (1992). *I can problem solve: An interpersonal cognitive problem-solving program for children*. Champaign, IL: Research Press.

Silverman, W. K., Pina, A. A., & Viswesvaran, C. (2008). Evidence-based psychosocial treatments for phobic and anxiety disorders in children and adolescents. *Journal of Clinical Child and Adolescent Psychology, 37*, 105–130.

Skinner, B. F. (1938). *The behavior of organisms: An experimental analysis*. New York, NY: Appleton-Century.

Skinner, B. F. (1965). *Science and human behavior*. New York, NY: Free Press.

Stallard, P., Skryabina, E., Taylor, G., Phillips, R., Daniels, H., Anderson, R., & Simpson, N. (2014). Classroom-based cognitive behaviour therapy (FRIENDS): A cluster randomized controlled trial to prevent anxiety in children through education in schools (PACES). *Lancet Psychiatry, 1*, 185–192.

Stewart, J. L., Christner, R. W., & Freeman, A. (2007). An introduction to cognitive-behavior group therapy with youth. In R.W. Christner, J. L. Stewart, & A. Freeman (Eds.), *Handbook of cognitive-behavior group therapy with children and adolescents*. New York, NY: Routledge.

Stone, M. H. (2007). CBT group treatment with children and adolescents: What makes for effective group therapy. In R. W. Christner, J. L. Stewart, & A. Freeman (Eds.), *Handbook of cognitive-behavior group therapy with children and adolescents*. New York, NY: Routledge.

Thompson, C. L., & Henderson, D. A. (2007). *Counseling children* (7th ed.). Belmont, CA: Thomson Higher Education.

Tollefson, N. (2000). Classroom applications of cognitive theories of motivation. *Educational Psychology Review, 12*(1), 63–83.

Van der Oord, S., Prins, P. J., Oosterlaan, J., & Emmelkamp, P. M. (2008). Efficacy of methylphenidate, psychosocial treatments and their combination in school-aged children with ADHD: A meta-analysis. *Clinical Psychology Review, 28*, 783–800.

Villares, E., Frain, M., Brigman, G., Webb, L., & Peluso, P. (2012). The impact of student success skills on standardized test scores: A meta-analysis. *Counseling Outcome Research and Evaluation, 3*(1), 3–16.

Watson, J. B. (1913). Psychology as the behaviorist views it. *Psychological Review, 20,* 158–178.

Watson, J. B. (1924). *Behaviorism*. Chicago, IL: University of Chicago Press.

Weisz, J. R., Chorpita, B. F., Palinkas, L. A., Palinkas, L. A., Schoenwald, S. K., Miranda, J., . . . The Research Network on Youth Mental Health. (2012). Testing standard and modular designs for psychotherapy treating depressing, anxiety, and conduct problems in youth: A randomized effectiveness trial. *Archives of General Psychiatry, 69,* 274–282.

Weisz, J. R., Jensen, A. L., & McLeod, B. D. (2005). Development and dissemination of child and adolescent psychotherapies: Milestones, methods, and a new development-focused model. In E. D. Hibbs & P. S. Jensen (Eds.), *Psychosocial treatments for child and adolescent disorders: Empirically based strategies for clinical practice* (2nd ed., pp. 9–39). Washington, DC: American Psychological Association.

Wells, K. C., Lochman, J. E., & Lenhart, L. A. (2008). *Coping Power parent group program: Facilitator guide.* New York, NY: Oxford University Press.

Zyromski, B., Mariani, M., Kim, B., Lee, S., & Carey, J. (2017). The impact of Student Success Skills on students' metacognitive functioning in a naturalistic school setting. *The Professional Counselor, 7*(1), 33–44.

7

Counseling for Results

Reality Therapy in Action

ROBERT E. WUBBOLDING

HISTORICAL DEVELOPMENT OF REALITY THERAPY

In the 1960s, when William Glasser began teaching Reality Therapy by giving public lectures in California, educators were among the first groups to greet Reality Therapy enthusiastically. Administrators, classroom teachers, school counselors, and educational specialists found the ideas practical, hands on, and helpful. Many stated, "I can use these ideas tomorrow in my school." They learned that they could communicate with students and help them accept responsibility, rather than arguing and blaming students or allowing students to avoid the consequences of their behavior. The early formulation of Reality Therapy consisted of eight steps (Glasser, 1972) that were later formulated as the WDEP system (Wants, Doing and Direction, Evaluation, Planning). Educators reported, anecdotally, that students took more responsibility for their behavior, caused less trouble in the classroom, and became more interested in class content. Glasser and several members of the Institute for Reality Therapy developed class meetings as a way to involve large groups in learning the principles of Reality Therapy (Glasser, 1968; Glasser & Iverson, 1966). Later, Glasser and others developed a schoolwide organizational application of Choice Theory and Reality Therapy known as the Glasser Quality School (Glasser, 1992).

FOUNDATION AND EPISTEMOLOGY OF REALITY THERAPY

In explaining how the human mind works, theoreticians have used many analogies. The foundational theory for Reality Therapy was originally known as control theory (Glasser, 1981, 1984), which was so named because, in the theory, the human mind was seen to function like a control system for a rocket or a torpedo. The target of the rocket or torpedo's trajectory is programmed into its operating system, and when it deviates from its target, the programming mechanism sends a signal to the aiming device to correct its course. The human mind functions analogously to this control system. Its behavior is purposeful and targeted, and when it receives negative input (i.e., that it has veered off target), it corrects itself. When Glasser adapted control theory to education, therapy, and counseling, he named his adaptation Choice Theory. Making choices and selecting from among alternatives have occupied, and continue to occupy, a central role in Choice Theory (Glasser, 1998, 2011).

Four principles summarize Choice Theory and provide the basis for Reality Therapy:

1. Five human needs serve as the bedrock of Choice Theory. These motivators are universal, multicultural, genetic, and undeniable. Human beings attempt to satisfy their needs via all the behaviors they generate. The first need is universal: all people are born with the need for belonging, love, or connectedness with other people. The second need is for inner control or power, for people to be in charge of their lives. The third need is freedom or independence, allowing people to choose among alternatives. The fourth need, for fun, enjoying life and learning (absent from many classrooms), is often a significant influence in the learning environment of the school. The fifth need, both general and universal, is for survival or self-preservation, which is a physiological drive. School counselors need to be especially cognizant of deficits in physiological need satisfaction among students.

   As students grow, they interact with the world around them and develop specific pictures or images related to the satisfaction of each of their needs. The collection of these pictures or wants is called the quality world. Everything in this inner world of wants (or mental picture album) has value and represents ideal expectations for the individual. Practitioners of Reality Therapy are conscious of the importance of becoming part of the student's quality world, in that the student believes that the school counselor can be of assistance. Students explicitly or implicitly come to believe that a particular school counselor can and will help them. Students therefore feel a connection or a sense of belonging with the school counselor.

2. An inner state of balance exists when people perceive that a specific want or several wants have been achieved. In contrast, when a human being's wants are not satisfied, it is as if a mental scale is out of balance.

Thus, a discrepancy or a gap between the desire and the fulfillment of the desire is the proximate cause of behavior. A teacher wants an orderly classroom but observes out-of-control behavior on the part of a student. The variance between the teacher's want and reality prompts the teacher to take action. The action includes self-talk, "I need to correct this child's behavior," or "I'm not going to let this child get away with this behavior." Sometimes, very intense emotions accompany actions and self-talk: the emotions can range from anger, frustration, and resentment to hopefulness and enthusiasm.

3. Actions, self-talk, and emotions make up "total behavior," which is purposeful and targeted. In the language of Choice Theory, actions are explicit choices. Human beings have the most control over their actions and less direct control over thinking and emotions. Though many choices appear to others to be aimless and capricious, the person who directs behavior toward the outside world can, with counseling, at least become aware of the purpose of their behavior.

4. All that human beings can know is what they perceive. Perceptions result from the person's interaction with the world around them. In all cases, behaviors provide opportunities for students to self-evaluate or to ask themselves, "Is what I'm doing helping me get what I want?" When counselors help students evaluate their behaviors, they are implementing the most important component in the constellation of Reality Therapy interventions. From the point of view of Choice Theory, our perceptions of the world often disagree with the perceptions of other people, resulting in contrasting interpretations of the same external facts or information.

The perceptual system functions as if it has three filters, as depicted in Figure 7.1. Information passes through the first filter, known as low-level perception or the total knowledge filter. The perceiver simply labels the information and does not make an approving or disapproving judgment about it. No value is placed on the perception. A teacher observes a student and says, "This is a child," or "This is a student." At the middle level of perception, we see a connection or a relationship between the incoming information and an already existing perception. For example, upon seeing a child, the teacher perceives "my student in my class." The high level of perception, also known as the valuing filter, involves a judgment made by the perceiver: "My student in my class is an excellent student." In summary, the information is first labeled, then it is connected with other perceptions, and finally it receives a value.

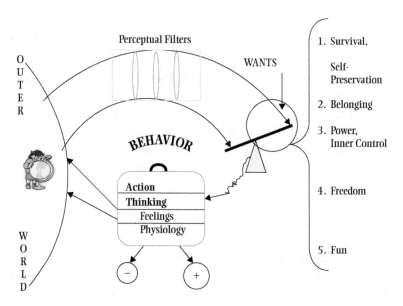

Figure 7.1. A Reality Therapy portrait of how the brain works.
Adapted by Robert E. Wubboldine from a diagram in *How the Brain Works*
(Glasser, 2005).

The practical value of this understanding of the perceptual system is that using Reality Therapy helps some individuals modify their level of perception. If they make judgments, especially harsh judgments, about every bit of information, they are often unhappy. On the other hand, if they are apathetic and don't care about school, they seem to view education with the attitude, "I don't care. It's only school. It makes no difference to me." In the latter case, the counselor using Reality Therapy attempts to assist such students to raise their levels of perception and to develop a positive and productive sense of values. Helping students modify their levels of perception assists them to develop a more flexible and therefore need-satisfying sense of values. Some students modify their values upwardly by abandoning apathy and coming to evaluate the world around them in a more satisfying and often humanitarian way. Students who see everything as a crisis learn to modify their level of perception toward less dire conclusions.

Basic to the teaching of Choice Theory and the use of Reality Therapy is the replacement of toxic behaviors with tonic behaviors. Glasser (2000) proposed that school leaders eliminate the seven deadly habits they use to control the behavior of others: criticizing, bribing, blaming, threatening, nagging, complaining, and rewarding. These ineffective and even harmful behaviors are replaced by the seven caring habits: supporting, encouraging, listening, accepting, trusting, respecting, and negotiating differences. Wubbolding (2007) stated, "These tonics facilitate human relationships that are the *sine qua non* for school improvement. When relationships within a school are internally satisfying to stakeholders, the result is joy, pride, competence, security, and even excitement about the educational process" (p. 254). School counselors can function as key facilitators and trainers in the school for enhancing the school environment by assisting other educators to practice tonic behaviors and reduce toxic behaviors.

THEORY OF CHANGE

Choice Theory explains human motivation and contains substantive ideas that school counselors can teach to faculty, students, and community. It constitutes the theory, the explanation, and the grounding principles for Reality Therapy. The WDEP system is a system for teaching and learning Reality Therapy. It summarizes a wide range of possible counseling interventions to be used by individual school counselors in their own creative manner and applied to students at every developmental level. The WDEP formulation is a pedagogical tool useful for learning Reality Therapy. Utilizing a structure in counseling ensures that counseling is more effective. Also, the school counselor can explain the structure to students and utilize counseling aids, such as a flip chart, to make an informal record of the conversation.

The WDEP system also facilitates the building of human relationships. Effective counseling and teaching are based on the helper's ability to create a safe and friendly environment. Arguing, blaming, and criticizing are obstacles to the healthy relationships needed in schools (Wubbolding, 2015). The next sections offer explanations of each component of the WDEP system, followed by examples of specific dialogues with students in elementary school, middle school, and high school. Several useful acronyms arise in the dialogues and provide a structure for use in counseling and for teaching other professionals.

W: Exploring Wants and Quality World

Helping students describe their quality world serves several purposes. Students conclude that what they want and value is important. This exploration also provides the school counselor with a specific tool for demonstrating positive regard for students. Many students have vague and imprecise pictures of what they want. School counselors asking about students' desires and hopes often hear, "I don't know." Consequently, school counselors assist students in clarifying their wants, and helping them formulate those wants in healthy, positive terms. The importance of assisting students to conduct a thorough examination of their quality worlds (i.e., what they want) can hardly be overemphasized.

Exploring Level of Desirability of their Wants

The exploration of wants sometimes includes helping students determine the level of desirability of their wants. Listed below in descending order of desirability are wants that form a schema for thinking about the quality world of students. The possible categories of wants described below are not intended to be mutually exclusive. There is always overlap in many such psychological categories.

Nonnegotiable demand. The world of wants exists in a prioritized fashion. Some wants or desires are not negotiable. We do not negotiate our desire for oxygen. It is necessary for human life. Some parents elevate what they want from their children to the nonnegotiable level, a process that might be effective with preschool children but would need some variations with adolescents. For example, a curfew might be negotiable with a 17-year-old son or daughter.

Pursued goal. When students establish goals such as "I want to do better in school," or "I would like to pass math class," or "I would like to have a friend," they are expressing a positive trajectory that invites further counselor responses.

Wish. Clients expressing a wish often are willing to exert a minimal amount of effort to satisfy their want. For example, a child who fails to study might tell the school counselor, "I wish I could get good grades." Or a student wishes to be "left alone" might still continuously choose behavior that attracts corrections from the teacher.

Weak whim. A whim often involves a want that is of little importance. A child's decision to wear green socks or blue socks might be a weak whim. The child feels indifferent about the color selection.

Double bind. Some wants are in conflict with each other. A junior high student wants to play soccer but also wants to be in the band or to "hang out with my other friends" who use drugs.

Reluctant, passive acceptance. People often learn to accept what is inevitable and unavoidable. The death of a parent might require a long time to process and to eventually accept, but the reality of the death is not desirable.

Fantasy dream. Students often desire the impossible. Children of divorced parents want their parents to reunite. This is often highly unlikely and yet it is the dream of many children.

For most people, the pictures or wants in the quality world are not equally desirable. Students of any age can be asked questions, such as, "Would you like to be happy here at school?" "Would you like your time spent in your classroom and outside the classroom to be more enjoyable?" "Do you want to have friends who don't get you in trouble and who help you feel good about learning?" School counselors need to make special efforts to help students clarify and define their wants. For example, counselors can ask students to consider other children who seem to be happy. By considering what happy children do, the students can gradually insert the observed positive behaviors into their quality world. Children raised in a substance-abusing family can be very confused about what satisfies their needs. If they are treated inconsistently at home, they can be ambivalent about human relationships (i.e., what pleases or displeases other people). Children with attention deficit disorder are often raised in a family with attention deficit disorder, where inconsistent adult expectations are the norm. Counseling and coaching using the WDEP system can provide a guidebook for establishing a direction and for satisfying children's wants. This occurs when counselors utilize the D, E, and P of the WDEP system.

Exploring Level of Commitment to their Wants

Clarifying and defining wants are important interventions in the exploration of the quality world. Yet, they are only part of the exploration. An added useful process is helping students identify their level of commitment. Wubbolding (2000, 2011) outlined five levels of commitment: (1)" I don't want to be here. I don't care." (2) "I would like to have the outcome but I don't want to make any effort." (3) "I'll try. I might. I could." (4) "I will do my best." (5) "I will do whatever it takes." Whether school counselors are working with individual students, groups of students, families, faculty members, or even community leaders, helping clarify their level of commitment is an effective intervention for bringing about change and improvement. As with other questions and reflections focusing on the quality world, discussing the level of commitment is an excellent way to build and enrich relationships. The key question in defining level of commitment is, "How hard do you want to work in order to achieve your goal or satisfy your desire?"

Exploring "From and For" In Counseling

Another aspect of quality world exploration is shedding light on, and enlarging, the pictures of what students want from and for themselves, their school, their family, their job, their recreational time, their religion, and their higher power, as well as, especially, how they want to benefit from the counseling relationship. A sample statement frequently made by counselors is, "Talk to me about what you want to be different in your life as a result of our conversation here today."

Exploring Perceptions of Locus of Control

Part of the W includes a discussion of students' perceptions, especially their locus of control (LOC), and an exploration of where they perceive their control to be: inside or outside of themselves. Do they believe that they have choices, or do they see themselves as victims oppressed by others? Some school counselors use a simple form with two columns: What can I control? and What can I *not* control? Students are asked to make two lists, and results often resemble such observations as, "What I cannot control is what other people say and do." "I can control only what I do." The specific perceptions of controllable and uncontrollable behaviors expressed by students represent issues characteristic of their developmental levels. In clarifying and distinguishing between the controllable and the uncontrollable, students often conclude that they have more control than previously thought. They come to the insight that, regardless of their current plight, they still retain the ability to choose. Many practitioners see similarities between Reality Therapy and existential therapy. Both systems place emphasis on choosing and on personal responsibility. In discussing existential therapy, Diamond (2016) stated, "We are responsible for actively choosing and defining ourselves" (p. 326).

Effective school counselors using Reality Therapy often communicate indirectly that their mission is to help students achieve the satisfaction of their needs and wants—within reasonable and acceptable boundaries. The main technique for such communication is skillful questioning, as implemented throughout the entire Reality Therapy process. Additionally, by exploring perceptions, goals, level of commitment, and level of desirability, school counselors show respect for students, and the respectful relationship helps the students amplify their wants and the goals that will ultimately facilitate their success. Assisting students to clarify where they see their control and what they have control of opens previously unknown vistas to them and communicates hope.

REFLECTION MOMENT

Spend a few minutes thinking about what you want from your job and career. Emphasize your internal wants, the satisfaction of your needs, and what would be more satisfying to you. Examine your level of commitment. What do you have control over that leads you to change? Keep in mind that working for the welfare of others can have a long-lasting internal payoff (want and need satisfaction) in addition to side benefits. Altruistic behaviors are an effective way to lessen loneliness, anxiety, and stress. Those who are not neophyte counselors also should keep in mind that altruistic behaviors can fend off the effects of aging.

D: Exploring Current Behavior, Doing and Direction

The second major procedure in the Reality Therapy system is a long-standing tradition. In the early days of Reality Therapy, when Glasser (1972) outlined the practice of Reality Therapy, he emphasized the importance of helping clients become aware of their behavior, stating, "No one can work to gain a successful identity or to increase his [sic] success without being aware of his current behavior" (p. 113). The reality therapist accepts the student and does not judge or criticize a student who describes ineffective choices. The D (doing and direction) represents a description of the facts or action choices as seen by the student. The generic questions that help students reflect on and identify their specific current behavioral choices (doing) are, "What are you doing?" "How are you spending your time?" "What exactly happened?" For a more detailed description of possible D interventions, refer to *Reality Therapy and Self-Evaluation: The Key to Client Change* (Wubbolding, 2017).

The behavioral suitcase (see Figure 7.1) is composed of four levels of behaviors, listed here in descending order of the amount of direct control—action, thinking, feelings, and physiology—and symbolizes a major paradox in Choice Theory and Reality Therapy. We are more aware of our feelings, our thinking, and our physiology than we are of our actions. As you read this chapter, perhaps you feel eagerness or fatigue or anxiety about an upcoming test. Your thoughts may be, "I can't wait to practice Reality Therapy!" or "I wonder if this will be on the test." You might be very aware of your physiology. If you have just finished exercising, you might be aware of your limber muscles, or if you missed a meal, you may be aware of a thumping headache. But, ironically, we have more direct and immediate control of our actions. An axiom used in 12-step programs summarizes the D: "You can act your way to a new way of thinking and feeling easier than you can think your way to a new way of acting."

Besides doing, the D component also represents direction. The school counselor can help students explore and describe their overall direction by such interventions as, "Tell me where are you headed if you continue your current actions." Using an inquiry like this one, for example, the school counselor can assist bullies in describing how long they can continue to make choices that take advantage of other students before they get into even more serious trouble.

Although actions are emphasized, school counselors also help students to identify both helpful and ineffective self-talk related to Choice Theory, such as, "I can't," "I can," "No one can tell me what to do," "I'm happier when I live according to reasonable rules," "Even though what I'm doing is not helping, I will continue to do it," or "Because my previous choice was unhelpful, I will now choose a different tactic" (Wubbolding, 2000, 2017).

Discussing the feelings level of the behavioral suitcase (Figure 7.1) occupies a less prominent place in the practice of Reality Therapy than in other counseling systems. Emotions are not ignored, however. As Siegel (2015) said, "Name it to tame it." Clients become aware of their feelings particularly when they are intense and obvious, as is often true of anger, depression, joy, and pride in an accomplishment.

In summary, after describing their actions, self-talk, or feelings, many students develop motivation to change. Skilled school counselors realize that they don't need to "oversell." A sales representative learns that, after the sale is made, quit talking. The same is true for the school counselor. In the next step, the school counselor helps the student to articulate that motivation in terms of self-evaluation.

E: Self-Evaluation, the Prerequisite for Behavioral Change

Student evaluation of current behavior and attainability of wants most often precedes plan formulation. The explicit use of multifaceted self-evaluation interventions sets Reality Therapy apart from other counseling systems. Self-evaluation is so important that it occupies the keystone in the arch of procedures by supporting and linking them to form a unified system of counseling interventions. Without implicit or explicit self-evaluations, the use of procedures remains incomplete and is less effective. When students conduct a thorough and incisive self-assessment with the guidance of an empathic school counselor, they are more likely to make immediate and effective choices. Self-evaluation occurs when the student makes a noncritical and blame-free judgment. It is critical for Reality Therapy school counselors to ask, (1)"What have you been doing?", (2) "What is your evaluation of what you have been doing?, and (3) "What is your plan?". As with other procedures, self-evaluation takes many forms, including the following:

- "Is your overall direction leading you to your destination?" "Is your destination good for you and for others?"
- "Are you directing your behaviors in a manner that brings you closer or further away from the people around you?"
- "When you chose (specific behaviors), did it they help you or hurt you?"
- "When you chose to get into a fight, were your actions against the rules of the school?"
- "Even if your actions were not violations of written rules, do you think they were acceptable, i.e., congruent with the unwritten rules, the expectations of other people?"

- "If you continue to repeat your current self-talk, will it work to your benefit or your harm?"
- "Are your desires and wants realistically attainable?"
- "Will your current level of commitment to your plans get the job done for you?"
- "Is it really true that you have no control over your feeling of happiness or contentment?"
- "How accurate is it that you can't do anything to make your life better?"

Self-evaluation is the *sine qua non* for genuine behavioral change. Internalized and efficacious plans are built on sincere self-reflections. Reality therapists assist students to look in the figurative mirror and describe what they see. With the help of the school counselor, students examine their wants, behaviors, and perceptions without undermining their self-esteem. They do not evaluate themselves as total human beings.

P: Action Plans, a Crucial Component of Reality Therapy

Action plans are common to many counseling systems and are a crucial requirement for the successful use of Reality Therapy. In his work at the Ventura School for Girls, a correctional institution, Glasser stressed the significance of the therapeutic relationship and positive planning, which have always been central to the practice of Reality Therapy (Glasser, 1965).

Wubbolding (2011, 2017) offered the characteristics of an effective plan using the acronym SAMIC(3), as described in the list that follows:

- **Simple**: uncomplicated
- **Attainable**: realistically doable
- **Measurable**: answers questions such as when, with whom, where, how often?
- **Immediate**: implemented as soon as possible
- **Controlled by the planner**: not dependent on outside circumstances or other people
- **Consistent**: performed repeatedly if possible
- **Committed to**: the planner is serious about follow-through

When school counselors help students formulate plans, they communicate hope. Students come to believe that a better life is possible for them. Students of any age and developmental level who perform successful plans receive a payoff, i.e., inner satisfaction that often exceeds their expectations.

In describing effective planning, Arden (2010) described a useful formula for planning: FEED. The planner selects a specific new behavior and *f*ocuses on it. *E*ffort activates the behavioral system. The planner urges continuing the action until it becomes *e*ffortless, and then the client is encouraged to stay in practice by repeating the behavior with *d*etermination. Arden stated, "By being determined, you'll complete the feeding process to rewire your brain" (p. 20).

APPLICATION

In order to imprint the WDEP system in your mind, you should implement at least one of the ideas as soon as possible. You could do this in conversation with a relative or friend by simply inserting questions into your conversation, such as, "What did you do today? Were you happy with the way things went today?" If you have a younger brother or sister, ask them if they were satisfied with their conversations with friends, teachers, or other students. Refer to Chapter 4 in Reality Therapy (Wubbolding, 2011) or www. realitytherapywub.com.

REALITY THERAPY OPERATIONALIZED IN SCHOOLS

Individual Counseling

The specific sample dialogues in this section illustrate the implementation of the WDEP system with elementary school, middle school, and high school students, as well as parents.

Elementary School. Rudy, who is in the fourth grade, has been acting out in his classes for about 2 months and his grades have begun slipping. He previously was a popular student who had many friends. But recently, even though his classmates laugh at his antics, they have begun to avoid him. Several teachers, including the gym teacher and the art teacher, have referred Rudy to the school counselor.

R = Rudy, C = School Counselor
c: Rudy, how is your day going so far?
r: Okay, but I got yelled at again in class.
c: Yelled at! Which teacher was upset with you?
r: The gym teacher. She doesn't like me.
c: How do you know she doesn't like you?
r: She always picks on me. Everybody does things but she yells at me.
c: Let's take a look at today. What did she think you did?

R: I didn't do nothin'.

C: I understand. But what did she say you did?

R: She yelled at me. She told me to quit talking and pay attention to the directions and rules for the volleyball game we were learning to play.

C: Do you enjoy playing volleyball?

R: No, I hate it.

C: But she wants to teach it to you and she thought you were not listening. Is that right?

R: Yeah.

C: Rudy, I have a very important question. You said that you feel frustrated and upset about the way things are going in that class and maybe even other classes. Are you ready for this question?

R: I guess.

C: You say you're frustrated. Sometimes frustration is a good reason to want things to get better. Do you want things to get better for you in that class and in other classes?

R: Yeah, okay.

C: I believe I can help you get rid of some of the frustration and even get along with the teacher better.

R: How?

C: Let's put it this way. Whatever is going on in the class, would you be willing to do something different that would help you?

R: Like what?

C: She thinks you're not listening. Right or wrong, that's what she thinks. If you made a special effort to show her by your actions that you're listening, would that help you or stop you from getting along better with her in the class?

R: Well, I guess it would help.

C: Would you be willing to do that for three gym classes? Could you handle that much?

R: If I wanted to.

C: Do you want her off your back? To leave you alone?

R: Yeah, that's what I want.

C: Why not give it a try for 3 days.

R: Okay, I'll do it.

Commentary: In this session the school counselor does not blame Rudy, but only discusses the differences in perceptions. The school counselor also helps Rudy evaluate what would help him get what he wants. If the dialogue could be continued, the school counselor could help Rudy practice how he would smile, sit in the class, stand in the class, or how he would show that he's listening. The school counselor would help Rudy identify specific actions that will help him.

REFLECTION MOMENT

Think for a moment about the above dialogue and identify one or two interventions that you can use. Are you able to practice any of them in your work? Which one is most useful to you?

Middle School. The principles of Reality Therapy are eminently practical for use in middle school. As middle school students struggle to develop a sense of identity through interpersonal relationships, the need for belonging becomes more prominent and complex. Students develop close peer group relationships that can be very temporary. These often take on a characteristic of competitiveness that deteriorates into bullying. The case below illustrates one way to deal with a middle school student.

Leslie, grade 7, is sent for counseling because the other girls are bullying her. Her parents have called the school counselor and asked for help. They report that Leslie comes home in tears and won't eat supper. She's lost interest in school and says she doesn't have any friends. After especially painful incidents, she refuses to attend school. The other girls call her ugly, skinny, stupid, and tell her "Nobody likes you." The counselor, however, believes that Leslie is above average in intelligence, attractive, and shy. In the past she related well to adults and was well liked by the teachers. They have noticed a change in her behavior. She has become mildly troublesome in class, withdrawn, and uninterested in the class content.

L = Leslie, C = School Counselor

c: Leslie, your parents called and asked me to talk to you because they are very worried about you. They told me about how you are upset more than usual and feel bad about how the other students treat you. I've also checked with several teachers and they, too, are concerned. Everyone wants to help you.

L: I hate this place. Nobody likes me here. They're all mean and nasty.

c: I can tell from what you're saying that you're pretty down in the dumps about school.

L: [Looks down and begins to cry.]

c: This is a good place for you to cry and to be upset. It's okay. No one is going to criticize you for it. When you're ready to speak you can say whatever you want or if you would like to sit here and be quiet for a few minutes, that's okay too.

L: [After 2 minutes of silence.] Why do people hate me?

c: I, for one, do not hate you. I want the best for you. And I will do my best to help you relieve some of your pain. Like I said, you are completely safe in this room. No one will criticize you.

L: [Appearing to be visibly relieved, sits back in the chair and glances at the counselor. Amid her tears she speaks.] I feel a little better.

C: I believe that if we talk once in a while you will feel a lot better. Also, we can figure out together how to deal with this situation that you are facing.

L: I hope so.

C: I'd like to say a few things to you and ask you a few questions. Is that okay?

L: I guess so.

C: Is there anything I should not ask you about?

L: Well . . . no, you can ask me anything.

C: You seem a little hesitant about that. So let me suggest that if I ask you anything that you don't want to talk about, just tell me you don't want to talk about it. I won't ask you anything that's deeply personal anyway. I'm wondering if you would like to make your situation better.

L: Yes, I would.

C: Let's think of your problem like this piece of notebook paper. Imagine that all your problems are on this paper. They are not really part of you. They're kind of outside of you. When you leave here would you like to leave this paper with me here in this office?

L: Yes, I'd like to leave it here and make it go away.

C: I can tell you this. I'll let you hold this paper while we talk. And when you leave, you can hand it to me. This doesn't mean that everything will be perfect. It means that over time you and I and everyone working with you can make things better. [Counselor hands the notebook paper to Leslie.]

L: I can give this back to you when I leave?

C: Absolutely. I don't want you walking out of this office with it. Tell me. Would you like to *do* something to improve your situation?

L: I wish those other kids would leave me alone.

C: I wish they would too. And if they were sitting here, I would have a few things to say to them. In the meantime, tell me about the last time they talked nasty to you.

L: Yesterday, they followed me down the hall laughing at me. They said my clothes were stupid and so was I. They call me "scraggy."

C: What did you say to them?

L: I didn't say anything. I just ran away and started crying.

C: Now, Leslie, I have a very important question and I'd like you to think about the answer. If you run away from them, does that help solve the problem and does it help you feel better?

L: No, it doesn't do either.

C: So the next time they do this, is there something different you could do?

L: I don't know what to do.

c: We'll try to figure it out. But let me ask you this and I'd like you to answer now and think about it for a day or so. Would you like me to call the girls in and have a talk with them? I would not tell them what you said. I would only tell them that it is well known that they have publicly bullied other students. You notice I said students plural. They might ask me, "Have you talked to Leslie?" My answer would be. "It makes no difference who I talked to. I'm talking to you right now because you have a reputation for causing trouble and whether it's true or not, I want to help you reclaim a good reputation. Because I believe you are hurting yourselves."

Commentary: The dialogue above is not intended to demonstrate how to solve the problem. Its purpose is to present several counseling interventions to illustrate specific Reality Therapy procedural comments and to exemplify Choice Theory applied to a widespread middle school problem.

Leslie feels powerless and victimized. The school counselor attempts to help her lessen these feelings by presenting to her the choice *not* to discuss topics that she might select. The school counselor helps Leslie externalize her problem by making it tangible like a piece of paper. The school counselor hopes Leslie can feel a slight surge of power and control. Leslie also feels empowered when she realizes she can take the problem with her or leave it with the school counselor. Subtly, but clearly and without criticism, the conversation moves from her victimhood to empowerment with the question, "Would you like to do something to improve your situation?" School counselors using Reality Therapy communicate in an indirect way that clients have within them at least a fraction of inner control that they can bring forth and expand to confront their external forces of aggression and oppression.

Frequently, school counselors attempt to prevent problems rather than merely helping students solve problems. This school counselor could approach the bullies to discuss their behavior and how it is helping or hurting them or the people around them. The school counselor could also lead classroom meetings that focus on peer relationships. During such meetings, students could discuss the nature of friendship, what nurtures and what hinders friendships (bullying), and how to include new students or diverse students in their peer groups. Many issues relate to school achievement and peer relationships. In the case of Leslie, the focus is on peer relationships.

REFLECTION MOMENT

Identify how the counselor helps Leslie to conduct a self-evaluation. Describe the overall context for the self-evaluation question. Is it empathic? Does it encourage excuses? Does it blame the victim? How does it express hope and empowerment? Which idea expressed in the dialogue is most useful to you?

Application: Discuss with a colleague the above dialogue as well as the questions listed under the reflection moment. How would you intervene differently with Leslie that suits you own personal style? Justify your answers.

Suggested Readings: Chapter 9, *Reality Therapy for the 21st Century,* (Wubbolding, 2000); Chapter 4, *Reality Therapy* (Wubbolding, 2011); Chapter 4, *Reality Therapy and Self-Evaluation, Key to Client Change* (Wubbolding, 2017).

High School: The WDEP system of Reality Therapy applies to high school, defined here as grades 9 through 12. Socioeconomic, family, ethnic, and many other differences need to be considered.

Selina, who is Chinese, is 17 and has nearly finished her third year of high school. The school counselor recently was hired late in the school year and knows little about the students, including Selina, except that she is very popular with other students. Selina is a self-referral.

S = Selina, C = School Counselor

c: Good morning, Selina. I'm the new counselor here and I understand you want to talk to me. I'm just wondering what you were thinking about as you walked in the door to this office.

s: Good morning, thank you for seeing me. I wanted to talk to you about my future.

c: We can certainly talk about that. But first tell me a little about the present. I'd be interested in hearing about what's going on around here at school with you and even about your family if you want to tell me.

s: My grades are okay. But the teachers expect me to be a superior student. One of them even said, "You're Chinese, how come you're not first in your class?"

c: Wow! Carrying expectations like that is quite a load. Do you know your class ranking?

s: Yes, I'm a little above the middle, about the 60th percentile.

c: I don't see anything wrong with that. That sounds pretty good to me. Are you happy with the effort you're making?

s: I feel like I'm doing the best I can. I study hard.

c: Tell me a little about your family. I have not met them yet.

s: My mother works in a department store and my father is an executive with a company that makes computer chips. I have three brothers who are older than I am. One is in a PhD program and the other two are in college.

c: What do your parents think about how you're doing here in school?

s: They don't say too much, but I believe my father is like the teacher who said I ought to be first in my class. They also say that I have become very Westernized.

c: What do they mean by that?

s: They say I've become like every other American teenager. I like to hang out with my friends and go on dates.

c: Do they try to stop you from doing those things?

s: No, they pretty much recognize that I am now a U.S. citizen and act like one. I don't do any drugs or alcohol. I enjoy socializing and I'm even vice-president of my class. My classmates accept me even though I look a little different than many of them.

c: It sounds to me like your parents are not putting a lot of pressure on you to be a traditional Chinese student. Of course, to be honest, it's hard to define what a "traditional Chinese student" is supposed to be. It seems to me that I could help you be yourself and be what you want to be. This could be balanced and reconciled with what your parents expect of you. What have your parents said about you lately?

s: They said they were proud of me when I was elected vice-president of the class and now am on student council. They don't say a lot about being proud of me for my grades. But I can tell what they think.

c: And what do they think?

s: They think I should do a lot better.

c: Just to satisfy my curiosity, do you think that as your counselor, I believe you should do better?

s: You probably think I could be much higher on the top honor roll.

c: I appreciate your candid response. It's not exactly what I expected. But actually, I believe that there's more to high school than being at the top. And yet I hope that belief does not get me in trouble with the parents in this school. You stated that you're making a genuine effort in your classes. I think that's something to be proud of.

s: So you're not going to pressure me to do better?

c: Would that help?

s: [Appears to be reluctant to answer the question.]

c: It seems to me from the way you act right now and the expression on your face, that it might not help.

s: [Speaks softly.] You're right. I don't think that would help me.

c: So I'm not going to do anything to pressure you because it appears to me that school is going very well for you even though you might feel pressure from others. But you did have something on your mind that prompted you to seek out a counselor.

s: Yes. For many years I have taken ballet lessons. And I would like to pursue ballet as a career when I graduate. The ballet teachers say that I am especially talented. But my parents don't think that dancing offers a long-term or high-paying career.

c: Are you committed to following this dream?

s: I would like to give it a try.

c: So you're faced with what is called a dilemma. On one hand, you want to pursue a very well-defined career. On the other hand, your parents would like you to pursue something in some field that pays higher salaries and is a long-range career.

s: Yes, I will be faced with these two choices.

c: Your parents have ideas about your future and yet they seem to have been supportive of you for many years. They have even paid for your ballet classes. How do they feel about your determination?

s: They are very proud of the fact that I am a social person and that I have stuck with the ballet classes when many students my age drop out of extracurricular activities after a short time.

c: It sounds like they are parents who want the best for you and that they don't say "No" to your interests.

s: Yes, overall my parents are supportive.

c: And yet you are faced with the decision: to go in the direction that you are vitally interested in or to follow a direction similar to what your brothers have followed.

Commentary: The school counselor attempts to strike a balance between the individuality of Selina and the well-intentioned expectations of teachers and parents. Selina does not fit the stereotype that Chinese students are academically superior to their peers. The school counselor attempts to help her evaluate her behaviors not merely on the basis of what she wants but on the basis of what she and her parents want for her. In many families, self-evaluation needs to be broadened to include the expectations of others, in this case the parents.

REFLECTION MOMENT

Examine your own thoughts, feelings, and attitudes about counseling a person whose ethnicity differs from your own. Could you counsel Selina without any feelings of inadequacy or would you feel perfectly adequate to work with her? What are the advantages of feeling inadequate, and what are the pitfalls of feeling adequate in using Reality Therapy cross-culturally? How would you consult with Selina's parents? What would be the goals of such a consulting session? In discussing the above questions, keep in mind the importance of the general atmosphere within the school. Selina is widely accepted by her peers. But in many schools, acceptance is an area requiring intervention by the school counselor in order to ensure that students who are more quiet and withdrawn have the opportunity to develop friendships. From the point of view of Choice Theory and Reality Therapy, satisfying the need for belonging with peers is central to student development. It also contributes to the prevention of subsequent problems, some of which can be quite serious.

Suggested Readings: Chapter 6, Cross-cultural applications. *Reality Therapy and Self-Evaluation: Key to Client Change* (Wubbolding, 2017).

Group Counseling

Reality Therapy provides a flexible structure for counseling groups that can be utilized at all levels from elementary school through college and even graduate school. Corey (2016) described four stages of group development. Below are possible interventions that counselors can use to handle several issues and tasks of each stage.

Inclusion in the group is a major task in the initial stage of group counseling. You might consider the following interventions for facilitating the group members' sense of inclusion:

- You came with expectations. What do you want to accomplish in these group sessions?
- What do other people, i.e., those who sent you, want from you?
- What do you want from your teachers, your parents, the other students, the school, etc.?

The second stage of group development, the transition stage, includes dealing with conflict and resistance. Reality Therapy interventions focus on such tools as:

- Pointing out that interpersonal conflict is a strength of the group. It indicates that the group is developing and that group members are listening to each other.
- Using the paradoxical technique of reframing when clients seem to resist. For instance, when a client refuses to talk, the counselor can respond that it is perfectly normal and healthy to remain silent.
- When clients demonstrate conflict, such as criticism of another member, the reality therapist asks a third person to make a similar statement in a kinder and more considerate way.

The third stage of group development, the working stage, involves building cohesion, getting a commitment to change, and cognitive restructuring. The reality therapist is cognizant of the following:

- Cohesion is more than inclusion. The school counselor helps students express that they need each other by such interventions as, "Tell us, who in the group do you believe can help you?"
- Challenging group members in their desire to change. "Do you really want to change?"
- Cognitive restructuring, which in Reality Therapy means helping students self-evaluate. "Is your current behavior or manner of communicating helping you and the people in this group or hurting them?"

The fourth stage of group development, consolidation and termination, includes dealing with feelings of separation, completing unfinished business, and carrying the learning further. Applications of the WDEP system include:

- Giving members an opportunity to describe their own strengths and those of other group members.
- Formulating short-term and long-term plans and identifying obstacles to the fulfillment of plans.
- Providing time for answering such questions as, "Is there anything else on your mind that you can address in the group?" "What do you want to hear from other group members, including me, the school counselor?"

In summary, school counselors skilled in Reality Therapy have available a wide range of counseling techniques and skills summarized in the four letters that they teach to students, staff, and other stakeholders. Each letter of the WDEP system represents a variety of possible interventions that can be adapted to every level of school and to virtually every culture represented in the school system. Research studies have validated its use with juvenile offenders, persons addicted to drugs, individuals with anger issues, and many other problems. School counselors have applied it to international cultures including those from the Middle East, Asia, Africa, East India Australia, Europe, and South America (Wubbolding, 2000, 2011, 2017).

REFLECTION MOMENT

What are your thoughts about the idea that emphasizing human choice is tantamount to blaming the victim? Do you agree or disagree? Using Reality Therapy and Choice Theory, discuss your reactions.

Application: If you are practicing as a school counselor, select a single student or a group of students to use one or more of the components of Reality Therapy. Make a special effort to use Reality Therapy with people who are "different" from you. Keep in mind that difference has multiple meanings related to age, gender, race, ethnicity, value systems, nationality, and many more.

Suggested Readings: Chapters 4, 5, and 15 in *Theory and practice of group counseling* (Corey, 2016); McClung and Hoglund (2013).

Classroom Applications: Class Meetings

Class meetings represent a significant application of Choice Theory and Reality Therapy in the classroom. The role of the school counselor is to teach classroom teachers the rationale for, and the benefit of, class meetings and to demonstrate how to conduct them. Class meetings provide teachers with the opportunity to help students appreciate each other, in that the focus of meetings, especially open-ended meetings, is the expression of opinions. Far from group counseling, class meetings are intellectual discussions. Students develop the art of discussion without "put downs," criticizing, or blaming each other. The meetings also provide an effective vehicle for students to grow in respect for each other and noncritically acknowledge cultural and ethnic differences. Moreover, students enjoy the interactions (fun), feel free to express themselves (freedom), acquire a sense of respect (power), and connect with other students in an intellectual manner (belonging).

School counselors demonstrate class meetings, thereby encouraging classroom teachers to use them for the purpose of helping students satisfy their needs, increase their self-esteem, and appreciate diversity, especially the diversity of ideas. Through class meetings, students learn the validity of many opinions and perceptions. They develop values around the topics discussed. They learn the merit of having intellectual discussions about ideas, a process that supplements and even replaces conversations that all too often focus on belittling the values and character of others. Accomplishing these goals, which are built on altruism, generosity, kindness, and a spirit of healthy concern for self and others, is by no means trivial. Students are bombarded with media images focusing on violence, dominance over others, self-centeredness, and unprincipled rivalry. And yet, Reality Therapy counseling and the use of class meetings have a far-reaching positive and counterbalancing effect. The next sections presents a brief summary of the types of class meetings, their characteristics, and the mechanics of implementation.

Types of Class Meetings. Although there can be overlap between the various types of class meetings, it is useful to understand that there are three kinds of meetings: those focusing on intellectual topics or open-ended meetings, those addressing educational issues, and those focusing on social problem solving (Glasser, 1968). Because of behavioral problems and the desire for more effective classroom management, some teachers and school counselors begin the process of class meetings with a discussion of problems. However, after even a few open-ended meetings, students can quickly proceed to a more direct discussion of social problems. The students first learn something about each other and then they can trust each other. Therefore, it is good to begin the process with open-ended meetings. Another reason is that both leader and students can become more comfortable with verbal interactions in a meeting format. If the topic of the first meeting is classroom disruption, the discussion can rapidly degenerate into a complaining session or one in which students engage in blaming each other, the school, or the faculty. Therefore, school counselors need to instruct both students and teachers that meetings have positive purposes.

From the outset, the school counselor communicates the rationale for, and benefits of, classroom meetings to teachers. Most importantly, the meetings are conducted occasionally, not daily. They are time limited, often lasting only a few minutes. School counselors and teachers need not feel that they are required to significantly alter their schedules. Another purpose for class meetings is to provide school counselors with a venue for teaching students the American School Counselor Association (ASCA) *Mindsets & Behaviors for Student Success*, such as self-management skills and social skills (American School Counselor Association, 2014).

Guidelines for Conducting Meetings. When school counselors conduct class meetings at the invitation of teachers, the school counselor models how to lead the meeting and thus facilitates questioning the students. As teachers learn from the school counselor how to conduct meetings, they quickly become the meeting facilitators and are no longer in need of coaching by the school counselor. Rather, the school counselor becomes a resource for the teacher by providing topics for discussion and added information on the mechanics of class meetings.

- The students are asked, if possible, to sit in a circle. If it is not practical to arrange the chairs in a circle, they sit in such a way that they can see and hear each other which makes communications easier and more natural.

- Initiating class meetings begins by encouraging the students to set rules for the meetings. Most of the time, they formulate four or five guidelines, such as only one person talks at a time, no put downs or criticism, and the right to pass.
- Meetings should be conducted on a regular basis and for a very limited amount of time. Individual classes and teachers determine the frequency of meetings and their length of time. The length of time for the meeting also varies, and the school counselor and teacher need not feel compelled to exhaust a topic. A successful meeting often ends with the students' desiring to continue.
- The best topics for meetings emerge from issues current to each classroom, school, or community or are derived from the ASCA standards. The age level of students influences the selection of topics.
- By focusing on student opinions, leaders avoid correcting answers during the meetings. The purpose of this guideline is the feeling of success and respect gained by students who choose to participate. Asking questions for which there is no correct answer helps the leader resist the urge to correct answers. The leader asks many students for their opinions. For example, when initiating class meetings in elementary school, part of the first meeting might be "What is your favorite color?" The leader encourages many students to express their opinion without criticizing others or being the object of criticism.
- The format for meetings is threefold and is intended to be very flexible: define, personalize, and challenge. In middle school, the topic of a meeting could be friendship. The leader asks the participants, "What is a friend?" Personalizing questions include, "How would you know someone is a friend?" Two kinds of challenge questions are especially useful, "What if?" and "Why?" "What if everyone were your friend?" "How could you find time to spend with everyone?" "Why do people have friends?" The why question is not designed to elicit excuses. It is not a behavioral why, in the sense of asking students why they did not study or why they got into a fight. The why in class meetings focuses on intellectual answers and rational responses, not emotional finger pointing.

School Counselor Involvement in Class Meetings. The role of the counselor is to teach the mechanics of class meetings to classroom teachers and to explain the rationale for, and the possible results and value of, conducting meetings on a regular basis. The counselor can also choose to gather data on behavioral change on the part of the students. Teachers report anecdotally that student behavior improves and interest in curriculum increases. A counselor could measure and record such changes and present them to significant stakeholders, such as school administrators, boards of education, and the community. Moreover, the counselor can explain that class meetings do not imply that the students should be indifferent to searching for correct answers. It is only during the time that students express opinions that the teacher accepts all answers and remains nonjudgmental.

Topics and Initial Questions for Class Meetings. In elementary school, topics for open-ended meetings could be: friendship, classroom rules, respect for each other, fun, or favorite foods. The format to be followed is to define what the topic is, what is the students' personal connection with the topic, and why does it occur? For example, if the topic is rules, questions could be: What is a rule? Why do we have rules? What is your favorite rule? What if there were no rules? An educational meeting might focus on learning styles or studying techniques. A social problem-solving meeting at all levels focuses on conditions, not on individuals. For example: Define promptness. Why do you think promptness is important? What if everything always worked on time and no person would ever be late for anything?

Topics in middle school could be the same as elementary school but geared to students' developmental level. Clothing styles could be addressed in an open-ended meeting. Discussion could focus on what clothing styles are. What styles do students prefer? What if everyone preferred the same style? How do students think clothing stores would deal with their taste in clothing? As in elementary school, educational meetings would focus on learning and serve as effective ways to introduce a new unit. The leader asks questions like: "What do you think . . . is about? What would it take for you to become excited about this topic? What have other students who have studied . . . said about this lesson?" Social problem-solving meetings could focus on appropriate ways to appreciate students who dress differently than the majority. Another meeting might emphasize school uniforms, or balancing school, home, and community activities. In high school, topics can be careers, work, and education after high school. For example, career-centered meetings include: What is a career? If you have a part time job, how could it become a career? How would seeing your job as a career help you contribute to your family and community?

Many of the same topics apply to every level of school, but the specifics of questioning vary according to the school setting, cultural norms, language development, age, and current social customs.

In summary, school counselors intervene in the process of education in a variety of ways. For the most part, they counsel students, and Reality Therapy provides practical tools for dealing with the range of circumstances faced by students: interpersonal relationships with other students, teachers, parents, family, trauma experiences, poverty, community turmoil, and the transitional decisions that all students face, such as advancing to the next grade or moving to a different school building or graduation. Reality Therapy can also be a major tool for consulting with teachers about how to develop a helpful class-room atmosphere, facilitating the improvement of classroom behaviors, and conducting class meetings that serve as effective prevention of student problems. Consequently, class meetings serve as group strategies for enhancing academic development and for facilitating career development, such as planning a successful transition from school to postsecondary education or the world of work. Finally, the skilled school counselor helps students handle their emotions and develop appropriate interpersonal skills (American School Counselor Association, 2014).

REFLECTION MOMENT

Spend a few minutes thinking about topics for class meetings. Consider how you would consult with teachers regarding the initiation of class meetings and regarding teachers' frustration when they feel that they are experiencing failure in leading class meetings.

Application: Brainstorm a list of topics for class meetings and various ways to ask questions that fit the format: define, personalize, and challenge. Use the ASCA *Mindsets & Behaviors* to develop topics.

LIMITATIONS

As is true of most counseling theories, Choice Theory and Reality Therapy have limitations. Choice Theory and Reality Therapy emphasize here-and-now motivation. Therefore, reality therapy does not address past behavior or circumstances. Reality Therapy has also been criticized for de-emphasizing so-cietal limitations imposed on clients and students. Seligman and Reichenberg (2014) stated, "Reality Therapy . . . pays only limited attention to helping people understand and deal with their environments and minimizes the importance of the past in people's development and difficulties. As a result, reality therapists may overlook some of the barriers and experiences that limit people's choices and may focus too much on symptoms" (p. 383). In the author's opinion, Reality Therapy is sometimes taught in a narrow and superficial manner that results in the understandable impression that Reality Therapy is limited in this way, but a thorough, up-to-date, and accurate instruction helps to defeat this objection.

Another limitation worth noting is that Glasser (1998) and Wubbolding (2011, 2017) have always explained Choice Theory and Reality Therapy in language that is easily understood by the reader. However, Wubbolding (2016) stated, "Using down-to-earth language is a double-edged sword. The principles, though understandable and practical, can appear simplistic" (p. 195).

Corey (2017) referred to the minimization of the use of dreams and the unconscious, the validity of transference, and the underestimation of the value of psychotropic drugs as useful tools for counselors.

CONCLUSION

Reality Therapy began in the 1960s and continues to be widely used in educational settings. When Glasser began his public lectures, educators responded with enthusiasm to his statement of the principle that human beings are responsible for their own behavior. In the context of Reality Therapy, students are capable of choosing positive and helpful behaviors to fulfill their five needs, even in the face of an unhappy history and distressing current circumstances.

Counselors at every school level can model and teach the WDEP system in addition to using it as they counsel students. When school counselors implement the principles of Reality Therapy, they put emphasis on current actions rather than on feelings because human beings have more direct control over their actions than their emotions. School counselors do not ignore feelings, however. They show empathy and understanding and assist students in changing their feelings, if appropriate, by changing their action choices. The cases included in this chapter emphasize, but do not exhaust, the possibilities for Reality Therapy applied to a variety of students and clients.

REFERENCES

American School Counselor Association. (2014). *Mindsets & Behaviors for Student Success: K-12 college-and career-readiness standards for every student.* Alexandria, VA: American School Counselor Association.

Arden, J. (2010). *Rewire your brain.* Hoboken, NJ: John Wiley & Sons.

Corey, G. (2016). *Theory and practice of group counseling* (9th ed.). Boston, MA: Cengage Learning.

Corey, G. (2017). *Theory and practice of counseling and psychotherapy* (10th ed.). Boston, MA: Cengage Learning.

Diamond, S. (2016). Existential therapy: Confronting life's ultimate concerns. In H. E. A. Tinsley, S. H. Lease, & N. S. Giffin Wiersma (Eds.), *Contemporary theory and practice in counseling and psychotherapy* (pp. 323–352). Los Angeles, CA: Sage Publications.

Glasser, W. (1965). *Reality Therapy.* New York, NY: Harper & Row.

Glasser, W. (1968). *Schools without failure.* New York, NY: Harper & Row.

Glasser, W. (1972). *The identity society.* New York, NY: Harper & Row.

Glasser, W. (1981). *Stations of the mind.* New York, NY: Harper & Row.

Glasser, W. (1984). *Control theory*. New York, NY: HarperCollins.

Glasser, W. (1992). *The quality school*. New York, NY: HarperCollins.

Glasser, W. (1998). *Choice Theory*. New York, NY: HarperCollins.

Glasser, W. (2000). *Every student can succeed*. Chula Vista, CA: Black Forest Press.

Glasser, W. (2011). *Take charge of your life*. Bloomington, IN: iUniverse.

Glasser, W., & Glasser, C. (2008, Summer). Procedures: The cornerstone of institute training. *The William Glasser Institute Newsletter*. Chatsworth, CA: The William Glasser Institute.

Glasser, W., & Iverson, N. (1966). *Large group counseling: A manual of procedure and practice*. Los Angeles, CA: The Reality Press.

McClung, C., & Hoglund, J. R. (2013). A Glasser Quality School leads to choosing excellence. *International Journal of Choice Theory and Reality Therapy, 32*(2), 54–64.

Seligman, L., & Reichenberg, L. (2014). *Theories of counseling and psychotherapy: Systems, strategies and skills*. Boston, MA: Pearson Education.

Siegel, D. (2015). *Brainstorm*. New York, NY: Tarcher.

Stutey, D., & Wubbolding, R. (2018). Reality Therapy and play therapy: A case example. Manuscript submitted for publication.

Wubbolding, R. (2000). *Reality Therapy for the 21st century*. Philadelphia, PA: Brunner Routledge.

Wubbolding, R. (2007). Glasser Quality School. *Group Dynamics: Theory, Research and Practice, 11*(4), 253–261.

Wubbolding, R. (2011). *Reality Therapy: Theories of psychotherapy series*. Washington, DC: American Psychological Association.

Wubbolding, R. (2015). Reality Therapy and school practice. In R. Witte & G. S. Mosley-Howard (Eds.), *Mental health practice in today's schools* (pp. 169–192). New York, NY: Springer.

Wubbolding, R. (2016). Reality Therapy. In H. E. A. Tinsley, S. H. Lease, & N. S. Giffin Wiersma (Eds.), *Contemporary theory and practice in counseling and psychotherapy* (pp. 173–200). Los Angeles, CA: Sage Publications.

Wubbolding, R. (2017). *Reality Therapy and self-evaluation, the key to client change*. Alexandria, VA: American Counseling Association.

8

School Counseling from an Existential Perspective

BRIAN HUTCHISON AND THOMAS A. CHÁVEZ

Consider three school-age students. Devon is a fourth grader who struggles with focus in school because of persistent nightmares about monsters under the bed. Jesse, a middle schooler, acts out in class in an attempt to get attention from peers who are perceived as part of the "in crowd" of the seventh grade. Junior-year student Toni experiences anxiety from the pressure of making a college choice and is unable to focus in classes or during extracurricular activities.

Experienced school personnel will likely report that these student issues are so common that they might be considered typical. School counselors would most often employ solution-focused, cognitive-behavioral, play, and behavioral therapies to conceptualize each case and to implement a treatment plan (Brown & Trusty, 2005). Despite the commonality of approaches listed, there are other options with which professional school counselors might think about, plan for, and intervene with these and other presenting problems within school counseling practice. This chapter explicates one theoretical option, school counseling from an existential perspective, in the hope that the application of existential thought in school counseling can become a means of deepening the conceptual and interventional framework for counseling practice.

REFLECTION MOMENT

Take a few moments to picture the student described above who represents the grade level you intend to work in. Think about Devon, Jesse, and Toni and imagine what they are like. What are their hobbies? How would you describe their home situation? How might they feel about school? It is good to practice imagining "the whole student" in order to increase empathy and understanding of the student beyond behavioral assessments, IEP files, and other ways that schools document students' lived experiences.

We note that existentialism is often associated with words like *anxiety, death, angst*, and *crisis*, which may discourage a school counselor from considering its utility. Yet there is another side to the proverbial existential coin, and this rich theoretical perspective can be used to frame thinking about problems of existence with a kid-friendly, strengths-based, or positive-focused approach, while still recognizing the rich existential material underneath all presenting phenomena. Despite any preconceived notions, existential theory has great utility for working with young students who are in the midst of making sense of not only themselves and others, but also ambiguous educational choices that are often framed by adults within the context of their future life.

This chapter first lays a foundation of existential philosophy, relating it to practice in the fields of psychology and counseling. Next, existentialism is situated within modern school counseling by providing context and presenting a theory of change. Finally, the chapter provides a detailed description of how to apply existential theory in school settings while differentiating among elementary, middle, and high school settings as well as among the strengths, capacities, and limitations of such an approach. The aim of the chapter is that the school counseling practitioner will find it a comprehensive and useful introduction that will benefit counseling practice "in real time."

FOUNDATION AND EPISTEMOLOGY FOR EXISTENTIALISM

The award-winning biographer and author Sarah Bakewell (2016) painted a vivid picture of the existential philosophers as they interacted with one another in European lecture halls and cafés to create a philosophy that was instrumental in the 20th century movements of humanism, feminism, and liberation psychologies. Existentialism as a philosophy, and as a theory for psychology, grew out of the turmoil surrounding its founders during World War I and then accelerated in its popularity and applicability during and immediately after World War II. This origin story is important because it embeds existential theory and thought in a time when the totality of human existence was thought to be in jeopardy both as an ideal (Western democratic society) and literally (the advent of nuclear war), a possibility that previously had not been considered by the masses. Living on the edge of darkness allowed for an exploration of living in its purest form: glimpsing life from the viewpoint of the liminal space between life and death.

The origins of existential philosophy are attributed to 19th century European proto-existentialist philosophers, such as Søren Kierkegaard and Friedrich Nietzsche, as well as 20th century European existentialist philosophers, such as Edmund Husserl, Georg Wilhelm Hegel, Martin Heidegger, Jean-Paul Sartre, Simone de Beauvoir, Albert Camus, Karl Jaspers, and Maurice Merleau-Ponty (Bakewell, 2016). Although each thinker contributed immensely to existential thought, few subscribed to the label *existentialist,* and it is likely that even fewer anticipated that their ideas would be applied to psychotherapy or school counseling. Instead of providing an exhaustive history of one of the world's most complex philosophies, the discussion here gleans the important concepts of existential philosophy, concentrating on those that have been adopted in the field of counseling. There is one predominant concept from the field of phenomenology through which all others within this philosophy are viewed. Existence as it relates to existentialism can be defined etymologically as "that which stands out, that which 'emerges'. . . a philosophy that emerges out of problems of life" (Koirala, 2011, p. 40).

REFLECTION MOMENT

Create small groups of two or three peers in your class. Do the following:

1. Take 3 or 4 minutes for each group member to silently read the above quote provided by Koirala in the text. Each person should take a moment to write about what might "emerge out of the problems of life."
2. As a small group, share and discuss the ideas generated in the first step. What does a focus on these types of problems suggest about the theory?
3. What problems of life emerge during child and adolescent stages of development?

Philosophers who shared existential concepts did not intend to develop an fully coherent existential philosophy, because they believed that doing so would be contradictory when life itself is not completely coherent. For example, life does not come with a manual with rules that, if one simply follows their prescriptions, guarantee "success" or the most exceptional "good life." The idea of living without a manual may seem counterintuitive in the practice of modern school counseling, a practice where academic benchmarks, curricula-based interventions, and comprehensive guidance approaches are the norm. The concepts described in the following paragraphs in themselves bring about a variety of meanings for each individual, and the path to a life well lived can stem from many propositions, each one just as valid as the next. Nevertheless, Bigelow (1961) delineated six themes or characteristics of existential thought, as follow, along with the authors' reflections of how philosophy may inform counseling:

1. *Existence before essence.* This proposition pertains to the belief that one is a living being (one exists) first and foremost before one makes decisions about what one's life is and how one identifies (one's essence). It is the experiences of living that lead to a definition of what it means to be human. Each individual has unique life experiences and thus is unique in the definition of what it means to be human and have a "good life."

    Application to school context: Students participate in the process of becoming a graduate, yet is only through this process that they begin to learn about themselves as a student and what it means to one day be a graduate. This process of essence creation includes understanding what it means to be themselves as well as what the supporting adults in their lives have taught them about this meaning. Ultimately, it is the students' prerogative to accept or reject what it is to be a student on the pathway to becoming a graduate.

2. *Reason alone is insufficient to deal with the depths of human life.* Existential philosophers hold that a human is a whole being with both subjective and objective truths. Although rational thinking and intellectual reasoning are a critical part of being human, they are not considered perfect. This also means that what is considered "irrational," such as emotion, is not necessarily so. The term *nonrationality* may be much more appropriate, because it emphasizes intuition, the visceral, or "gut sense" over rational observations. Each aspect of being human is believed to be best integrated in making meaning of one's existence. The concepts of absurdity, ambiguity, and contradiction in life are prominent in this characteristic. Therefore, what does not make logical sense is not necessarily inherently false or unreal.

    Application to school context: As school counselors, we are placed in a position of power, especially because we are adults, with greater educational and general life experiences than students. Within this power dynamic, we could define or deem what is real or imaginary, rational or irrational, and true or false. However, any such judgments would be based on the counselor's biases as an adult. For example, it is often heard that children or adolescents can "make mountains out of molehills" or be "overly dramatic" at times. This observation is typically made from the worldview of an adult. However, responding to one's context with behaviors that appear to be overly dramatic may be the most reasonable given the challenges that that child endures in that context. Whether it is objectively true or right is moot. Most important is that the school counselor be open to the subjectivity, the drama and life poetics, despite the child's "unreasonable" reactions. If we are willing to listen, the child's reactions have something important to tell us about the child's lived experience.

3. *Alienation or estrangement.* Bigelow (1961) explained that since the Renaissance period, and increasingly so since the dawn of the Industrial Age, humans have been forced by societal changes to exist at more intellectual or abstract levels. This has resulted in our removing ourselves more and more from human experiences, leaving us in isolation. Furthermore, this has reduced human nature to be explained in mechanistic terms. Therefore, a person experiences a sense of estrangement from one's true self, fellow humans, nature, and culture. Furthermore, lower civic participation, such as engagement in religious or spiritual practices, has further distanced us from each other. These phenomena may be observed even more as technology has rapidly developed (Brynjolfsson & McAfee, 2014).

   Application to school context: Although youth across the globe are connected via the Internet, digital identities may have effects on how they understand their true selves as well as relationships with their peers. Adjusting who exists in one's social circle with the click of a "like" button has deeper existential weight than is often acknowledged (Boyd, 2008; Buckingham, 2006). Students and educators today may live "behind the computer screen" or the Facebook wall that limits nonverbal communication and thus deeper human connection. The term *friend* thus becomes abstract. Also, in the digital world, identity is only partially provided, not allowing the other to fully be known, if at all, despite the context's being labeled "social" media.

4. *Anxiety (Angst).* With the advancement of science and its contribution to great conveniences, there is an associated effect of intensified angst, nervousness, and restlessness. This may be due to grave inventions in recent history that have great potential to completely destroy humanity, such as tools of war and terrorism, initiated with the touch of a button. Humans now live with the possibility of either personal or social annihilation, or both, at any moment. Furthermore, in times of crisis or

dilemma, one must make ethical decisions that take into consideration the well-being of self as well as others, which may at times create great "fear and trembling." It is generally believed by existentialists, however, that anxiety is a fundamental human issue that arises from the contemplation of mortality, meaninglessness, emptiness, guilt, and condemnation (Weems, Costa, Dehon, & Berman, 2004).

Application to school context: Anxiety as a normal human condition can be observed often in the school counseling setting. The anxiety seen may include students' worry about performance, achievement, peer acceptance, and transitions between elementary, middle, and high school as well as from school to postsecondary life. School counselors may be called upon to help students cope with the inevitable anxieties that emerge due to experiences with divorced parents or living in unpredictable, violent neighborhoods. Making sense or meaning of such anxiety-provoking situations becomes critical as students make sense of what role they play in their experience of living.

5. *The encounter with nothingness.* Without robust relationships with our true self and others (and for some existential philosophers, with religious and spiritual entities as well), which are thwarted by aspects of modernity, we encounter a sense of nothingness, or a life without any purpose or meaning. Therefore, life is a void (or empty) when humans lack a sense of connection with self, other, and society.

Application to school context: In a student's life, connection may entail self-understanding, friendships with peers, relationships with educators, and the general pride of being part of a school community. A sense of belonging, as opposed to a marginalized status, thus becomes vital, providing a sense of being "something" or somebody with dignity and worth, instead of a "nobody," a position of being less than human or having a dehumanized existence. Connectedness may become increasingly important for students as they enter adolescence, where social interactions become more complex than those of childhood. Struggles with connectedness contribute to problematic behavior, school problems, and interpersonal interactions (Lee & Robbins, 1995; Schulz & Rubel, 2011). For example, Calabrese (1987) stated that adolescents experience a higher level of alienation because each adolescent interacts in multiple environments, including "disorganized or disruptive families, schools that encourage students to become passive participants in the learning process, and high-pressured pace of life" (p. 929). Educators who promote social engagement along with facilitated meaning-making and collaborative decision-making can help alleviate the sense of dehumanization, alienation, marginalization, or nothingness (Calabrese, 1987; Schulz & Rubel, 2011). It is important to note that encounters with a sense of nothingness or events that may evoke the experience are inevitable throughout life.

6. *Freedom.* One cannot be free without having responsibilities and thus the two concepts are one in the same (DeCarvalho, 1992; May, 1962). In existential philosophy, responsibility has two different implications, again slightly differing between atheist and theist perspectives, wherein the former emphasizes human will, with the latter emphasizes the importance of faith. What is highlighted by theists may be related to the responsibility of fulfilling one's vocation or "calling" as deemed by a greater power more so than deemed internally. Nevertheless, Bigelow (1961) explained that each of the previous five existential characteristics pose a loss of, or threat to, personal freedom or autonomy. It is proposed that, with the abandonment of responsibility for choices as well as deserting commitment to that choice, we forgo our very own freedom. One's sense of freedom, therefore, is intimately linked with one's taking responsibility, such as creating meaning or an active choosing of one's experiences and life endeavors.

   Application to school context: The proposition about freedom can be quite confusing for students because the concept is used in the context of an educational system that imposes broad contingencies or restrictions on students. It is often stated that one of the main goals in formal education is personal and civic responsibility, especially in terms of moral character development (Lickona, 1996a, 1996b). Lickona (2009) proposed that there has been a decline in moral education within school systems and attributed this to the "rise of personalism" in a society that "promotes rights more than responsibility, freedom more than commitment" (p. 9). In addition, freedom may be assumed to be a given, rather than assumed to be a demand for active self-determination. Lickona stated that personalism leads to extreme self-interest, thus dismissing social responsibility or accountability for the well-being of others.

   Suggested video: The authors recommend watching the video of David Foster Wallace's 2005 graduation speech at Kenyon College (https://vimeo.com/188418265). Keeping in mind the six themes previously outlined, identify how each is represented in the video and then consider which theme or themes resonated most strongly for you while you were watching.

Existentialist ideas were a reaction to changes in society. Existentialists observed the process of dehumanization of members of society in the 19th century; the growth of technology, specifically, turned individuals into mechanistic beings without freedom, choice, or a sense of wholeness. Technological development also created the possibility of annihilation by powerful weapons of mass destruction (Halling & Nill, 1995; Heidegger, 1977; Kemp, 1971).

THEORY OF CHANGE

Seminal counseling and psychotherapy theorists and practitioners who have taken the philosophical tenets of existential philosophy as a basis for theories on human behavior, personality, and the counseling process include Otto Rank, Viktor Frankl, Rollo May, and Irvin Yalom (Corey, 2012). Just like existential philosophers, existentially based counselors do not share a common framework, but they do share common themes.

Historical development. When we think about counseling and psychotherapy in general, the first theorist who most often comes to mind is psychoanalyst Sigmund Freud. While Freud did not attribute the origins of his counseling theories to studies in existential philosophy, Halling and Nill (1995) have noted similarities between Freud's thought and the thought of proto-existential philosopher Friedrich Nietzsche, such as Freud's concept of the superego being comparable to Nietzsche's bad conscience (Nietzsche, Kaufmann, Hollingdale, & Nietzsche, 1989).

Nevertheless, Freud's proposed understanding of human behavior was based on, or determined by, biological drives. Early behaviorists, such as B. F. Skinner, followed suit with a deterministic emphasis, focusing only on human responses to environmental stimuli and thus purposely ignoring the internal world of experiences. Cognitivists, such as Aaron Beck, attended to internal processes but focused primarily on distorted thoughts and beliefs and how they affect personality and behavior. Later in the 20th century, humanism emerged as a response to the reductionist perspectives of the previous theories and practices. Psychologists Carl Rogers, Abraham Maslow, and Rollo May promoted the perspective that humans and human behavior could not be reduced to biological functions or simple thoughts alone. Instead, humanistic theorists were more concerned with human potential and the drive toward self-actualization, that is, the need to achieve one's full human capacities and aptitudes (Jones-Smith, 2016). The human will is at the center of existential-humanistic perspectives on personality and behaviors, rather than human illness or pathology, which medical/deficit models high-light. Herein existentialism grew, sharing common roots with humanists, or as philosopher Jean-Paul Sartre (1948) declared, "existentialism is a humanism." The following paragraphs provide a brief description of the thinkers who helped transfer the philosophy of existentialism to the practice of existential psychotherapy.

Viktor Frankl. The work of Viktor Frankl is often referenced with regard to existential counseling, especially his work *Man's Search for Meaning* (1962), which was introduced to the United States in 1959. Schulenberg, Nassif, Hutzell, and Rogina (2008) explained that Frankl's form of counseling, called logotherapy (*logos* = meaning), is based on the idea that the counselor helps clients to develop ways to help themselves through developing meaning from life circumstances. According to Schulenberg et al., Frankl emphasized that humans have a tridimensional ontology, including physical, psychological, and spiritual ways of being in the world. Respectively, these existential dimensions are referred to in German as the *Umwelt, Eigenwelt,* and *Überwelt. Mitwelt,* the fourth dimension also cited by existentialists, is the social or relational aspects of living. Interestingly, Frankl's early work as a physician and therapist was with adolescents; together with the existential-humanistic psychologist Charlotte Bühler, he developed a holistic framework that focused on healthy physical, psychological, and spiritual growth of children and adolescents (DeRobertis, 2006).

Recommended Reading : Victor Frankl's *Man's Search for Meaning.* An open-source copy is available at http://www.fablar.in/yahoo_site_admin/assets/docs/Mans_Search_for_Meaning.78114942.pdf.

Rollo May. Rollo May, sometimes called the "father of American existential psychology" (Bugental, 1996, p. 418), wrote extensively on social and cultural topics, such as beauty and creativity, anxiety, being and existence, love and will, power, freedom, and myth. These topics cannot easily be defined and, therefore, are not readily measurable; nevertheless, they are part of subjective human experience. May developed a theory of stages of development that informs existentially focused school counseling. Children experience a rebellion stage, where they develop motivation to care for themselves, thus developing the associated understanding of responsibility and freedom. This leads to the need to develop independence, wherein making decisions about life becomes critical. By adulthood, life becomes ordinary, as the individual has come to terms with adult responsibilities. However, the adult realizes the burdens of responsibilities, leading to the maintenance of rigid value systems to cope with the unavoidable anxiety of human existence. Finally, in the creative stage, adults have accepted the unavoidability of life's challenges and thus strive to meet their potential through them.

Suggested video: The interview titled *Rollo May: The Human Dilemma (Part One Complete): Thinking Allowed with Jeffrey Mishlove* provides a rich description of how May used existential philosophy in psychotherapy. The video is available at https://www.youtube.com/watch?v=HH-9XkjqYHY.

Irvin Yalom. It is critical to mention at this point the work of Irvin Yalom, American existential psychiatrist, who provided four core themes or existential "givens" that summarize what may commonly be addressed in existential counseling (Yalom, 1980). The givens include death, freedom, isolation, and meaninglessness. Yalom explained that humans of every age are continuously grappling, albeit to various degrees throughout time, with the fear of death and the process of dying. This is in conflict with the desire to be or to exist. Much as discussed previously in the primer of existential philosophy, Yalom also accepted the notion that freedom is intricately linked to responsibility. For Yalom, freedom also has potential to produce anxiety, especially when there is lack of structure in our world. Yalom distinguished three forms of isolation: interpersonal isolation, which is most often thought of as loneliness; intrapersonal isolation, which is a separation between various aspects of self; and existential isolation, the "unbridgeable gap . . . between our awareness of our absolute isolation and our wish to be part of the larger whole" (Yalom, 1980, p. 9).

May and Yalom (2000) believed that humans are constantly seeking meaning in all worldly things. The last given of the human condition, meaninglessness, elucidates the fact that living life does not necessitate that people experience specific meaning in life. We are not provided a handbook for life that defines our own sense of self, the role of others, the world, or what living is all about. Furthermore, individuals are "thrown" into the world of meaninglessness, while in turn intrinsically feeling the responsibility to look for, or to make, meaning. Observable behaviors that demonstrate the search for meaning include the developmental processes of defining values, beliefs, goals, and life purposes. The search can be done alone or can be encouraged by another human being, such as a parent or a school counselor. Regardless of a person's age or developmental level, life comes with many uncertainties that are grappled with only through lived experience. In living this experience, a person enters any developmental stage without a priori, intrinsic knowledge and wisdom to live by. While others may provide guidance, it is only in personal experience and action that patterns are recognized and are ultimately pieced together in a comprehensible way that might lessen existential anxieties produced by questions like "Who am I?," "What is life all about?," "What is the best way to live?," or "What happens after death?"

Suggested Reading: Yalom's *Love's Executioner: & Other Tales of Psychotherapy* is the book I (Brian Hutchison) first read when exploring the idea of becoming a counselor. A description is found at https://www.amazon.com/

Loves-Executioner-Other-Tales-Psychotherapy/dp/0465020119/ref=pd_lpo_
sbs_14_img_0?_encoding=UTF8&psc=1&refRID=4KDBJC59RS0CE8PR3YJJ.
Staring at the Sun is Yalom's most recent book, addressing the issue of death and
death anxiety. A description of the book can be found at https://www.amazon.
com/Staring-Sun-Overcoming-Terror-Death/dp/0470401818.

An existential view of humans and common theoretical assumptions of existential counseling and psychotherapy are well summarized by van Deurzen
(2012), who further elaborated on the ontological dimensions of human existence employed in practice by Frankl and Bühler. Human nature, as understood by the existentialist, means that humans are constantly in an experiential
process and thus require open-mindedness and flexibility. Self is shaped by the
individual's immediate and active relationship with the environment. This im-
mediacy and passing sense of presence contribute to anxiety or sense of angst.
The interaction between self, environment, and experience of anxiety is constantly being evaluated and made sense (or meaning) of. This is a universal
experience among all individuals regardless of age or cultural diversity.

EXISTENTIALISM OPERATIONALIZED IN SCHOOLS

The historic figures of existential theory and psychotherapy did not have school
counseling in mind as they developed their thinking and approach. Yet a review
of the previous section suggests that child and adolescent development were
key aspects of each person's work, and thus school counseling is an apt system
of intervention planning and delivery.

REFLECTION MOMENT

*Take some time (30 to 60 minutes) and reflect upon what you have learned
about existential philosophy and counseling theory thus far. Using paper and
a writing utensil (colored pencils and crayons are our favorites), write or
sketch out your own ideas for using existentialism in your school counseling
practice as you imagine it.*

From early developmental beginnings, we strive to make sense of our self,
others, and the world in general. Each incremental moment of human development brings more sophisticated social, affective, and cognitive tools for
navigating all that we encounter. Our cumulative process of development
contributes to our conceptions of what it means to be an individual and what it
means to be part of a family or a particular group in society. We also try to make
meaning of the various situations and events that comprise our lived experience, including our own understanding of what purpose we have in the greater

universe. With this developmental process comes the requirement for making life choices and accepting personal freedoms and responsibilities, as well as coping with circumstantial limitations, uncertainties, anxieties, and struggles (May & Yalom, 2000; Yalom, 1980).

Parents and other caregivers interact with the child's developmental process of seeking understanding of the world by imparting their worldviews to children and adolescents. Their worldviews include their attitudes, knowledge, and beliefs about identity, relationships, and life circumstances. Upon reaching school age, young people have the worldview imparted by the adults in their life until then. This temporarily serves as a guideline or filter through which they understand new tasks at hand. A child's primary task upon entering school is to create an understanding of the school environment. The school is an environment that is a microcosm of current and future life endeavors, including the living project that it sponsors to help the young student attain educational and future career goals. Attending school entails the establishment of new relationships with teachers and peers and overall expectations of what it means to be not only a student in the school system, but also a participant in larger society. Schooling requires that students develop an awareness of self, other, and society that certainly includes one's own worldview but also retains aspects of their parents' worldviews.

Herein, the school counselor plays a critical role, offering skills, practices, and growth-fostering experiences beyond those accessible by parents and the community in general. Along with inspiring students to acquire general knowledge and skills to move toward greater achievements and providing guidance toward higher education and career goals, the school counselor may also help the student link the student's knowledge, skills, and goals with ideas about who they are, what role others play in their life, and what their experiences in the world mean. Addressing the social, emotional, academic, and higher education/career aspects simultaneously is critical to meet the comprehensive needs of each student.

Conceptualizing the Total School Climate From an Existential Perspective

Schooling, which is affected by larger sociocultural changes, may have adopted the idea that the role of schooling is to produce well-prepared citizens and workers while ignoring the meaning school and work have for the developing child and emerging adult. American society, Kemp (1971) explained, was much slower to accept existential thought than its European counterparts due to Americans' emphasis on positivism, an inclination toward science over philosophy, and preference for action-driven processes over promotion of personal insights or meaning-making. Furthermore, the often criticized "factory model of education" was adopted in American school systems (Banathy, 2001; Leland & Kasten, 2002; Rogoff, Turkanis, & Bartlett, 2001), thus contributing to the need to address existential concerns and the meaning-making process in American education since the 20th century (Feldman, 2007; Greene, 1967, 1988; Koirala, 2011; Magrini, 2012).

The ontological dimensions considered by van Deurzen (2012) intersect within the school environment, leading to a dialectic tension between aspiration and fear, freedom and contingency. The physical dimension (Umwelt) consists of concerns about one's relationship to physical surroundings and bodily functions. In school, students may ponder their own physical agility or limitations in comparison to those of their peers for the first time. The social dimension (Mitwelt) is concerned with relational belongingness versus being rejected. This plays out across the age spectrum as children and adolescents navigate ever-evolving relational dynamics with peers and the adults in their lives. The psychological dimension (Eigenwelt) is the personal world and is concerned with the development of our sense of self and identity within a dialectical process of discovering a personalized value system or giving in to conformity. The spiritual dimension (Überwelt) consists of developing an ideology or philosophy about life, particularly death and dying. Religion or spirituality may become a focus to help address or to make meaning of the uncertainties and absurdities that are encountered. In the school setting, only recently has spirituality been considered a part of helping students develop a sense of purpose in life. Spirituality may be considered in the development of a comprehensive school counseling program to support mental health and adjustment as well as in the development of coping strategies (Sink, 2004; Yeh, Borrero, & Shea, 2011). Finally, the Lebenswelt, or total school climate as it becomes prominent in the child's awareness, represents the seedbed within which students develop in a school system.

Theory of Change that Drives the Existential Approach to School Counseling

Freedom and contingency are the guiding concerns of existential school counseling practice. In discussing Simone de Beauvoir's view on the human condition, Bakewell (2016, p. 226) wrote, "The ambiguous human condition means tirelessly trying to take control of things. We have to do two near-impossible things at once: understand ourselves as limited by circumstances, and yet continue to pursue our projects as though we are truly in control." Freedom, then, is this act of living as if we have control and are the creators of meaning in our lives, while contingency describes the fact that we choose to exercise this freedom within boundaries and constraints, including the finiteness of our individual existence. Being so deeply concerned with freedom and contingency, or the givens of one's existence, including historical context, the body, social relationships, and environments, makes existential theory consequential in understanding one's existence, especially during the critical developmental ages of childhood and adolescence. The dialectic between freedom and contingency, and the process of grappling with these factors, are well situated for thinking about the developmental, moral, and social tasks that children and adolescents perform during school years while striving to understand their freedom and making their own choices.

APPLICATION WITH OTHERS

Meet with a group of your peers who wish to work at the same school level (i.e., elementary, middle, or high school) and discuss the different ways students in that level grapple with freedom versus contingency. Organize your list by the domains of comprehensive guidance: personal/social, career, and academic.

This process is expected to be quite distressing, because constantly choosing within the framework of freedom brings pervasive anxiety (Sartre, 1956) or, as Kierkegaard (1980) stated, "Anxiety is the dizziness of freedom." Kierkegaard expounded upon this idea by describing vertigo as one looks over the edge of a cliff. He argued that it is not the fear of falling that causes vertigo but the distrust that we will not in a moment of impulse throw ourselves off the cliff. Deep knowledge of our own freedom is not unlike this analogy. We are anxious because we always have a sense of our own freedom, yet we do not trust ourselves to embrace it; instead, we might relinquish freedom, resulting in a life of inauthenticity or "bad faith." Childhood and adolescence are the stages of life when we first encounter our sense of freedom and then possibly realize our own capacity to embrace freedom and meaning-making. Theoretically, this is an individual pursuit (Sartre [1948] reminded us that "No authority can relieve you of the burden of freedom") that can only be encouraged by others (i.e., school counselors), but it is a pursuit that we humans are apt to undertake.

Existential school counselors view anxiety as a condition of living, and they identify two types of anxiety: neurotic anxiety and existential anxiety. Another description of the types of anxiety is to call them maladaptive anxiety (neurotic anxiety or an inauthentic response) and adaptive anxiety (existential anxiety or a constructive form resulting from increased awareness of our freedom and responsibility; van Deurzen-Smith, 1990). In a school counseling practice, students with neurotic anxiety often present to the school counselor because of peer conflicts, conflicts with teachers or other adults, changes in focus, performance, or mood, or other concerns that might be viewed as arising due to inauthentic living in the context of the school environment. Existential anxiety, which is positive and adaptive, is present when students are developing greater insight or awareness of themselves as being in the world and making meaning of their being. We envision existential school counselors addressing existential anxiety in individual meetings with students, small-group counseling, classroom guidance lessons, and school systemwide interventions that foster personal awareness and critical consciousness.

Within the broad dialectical framework described in previous paragraphs of this section, Pine (1969) identified three overarching objectives for the existentially driven school counselor to pursue in the delivery of services. The first is to help students develop awareness of their freedoms. Second, the counselor emphasizes and nurtures positive relationships with teachers or other adults and peers in the school context (including the contingencies inherent in this milieu). Finally, the third objective is to assist students in discovering meaning. Each of the three objectives is pursued within the contingencies or boundaries that children and adolescents experience in their lives.

REFLECTION MOMENT

Consider these contingencies and their impact on child and adolescent development:

- Family of origin norms, values, and environmental considerations.
- Community of residence and its sociopolitical history, including access to, or segregation from, societal assets, safety, and security, as well as strength of community identity.
- School culture, expectations, and resources.
- Identity perceptions of ingroups/outgroups based on race, ethnicity, gender identity, sexual identity, religion, ability status, and social class within systems of oppression.

Existential theory does not delineate a set of techniques or mechanisms for change. First and foremost, the counselor maintains the philosophical stance discussed in the previous sections. Using an existential lens, Bugental (1990) identified the following goals for practitioners. Each goal should be addressed using developmentally appropriate language and interventions.

1. Help clients (students) recognize that they are not fully in the present (authentic) while existing in the school environment and that this situation hinders their personal growth and success.

2. Support clients (students) as anxieties arise while normalizing the
    anxieties in context.
3. Promote client (student) change toward greater authenticity.

Vontress, Johnson, and Epps (1999) characterized addressing inauthenticity
in therapy as helping clients with their "stuckness" by focusing on embracing
versus resisting client (student) responsibility to build self-awareness and by
encouraging choice-making within the set of contingencies the client (student)
may be confronting. We believe the broad framework presented here is useful
in planning school counseling practice within elementary, middle, and high
school settings by conceptualizing interventions at the individual, small-group,
classroom guidance, and school system levels.

Practical Applications for Applying Existential Theory
to School Counseling

Imagine Devon, a child of elementary school age, standing alone near a
playground apparatus. While knowing that the bar above his head is meant
for hanging and swinging, Devon is too short to reach the bar. While he is
contemplating this, a group of older (and taller!) children arrive and begin to
tease Devon for not being able to reach the bar. Later that evening, Devon listens
to his parents discuss a famous athlete and how amazing the athlete is due to his
physical abilities and personal effect on fans. The child begins to think about his
perceived lack of athleticism compared to the children who had teased him. He
begins to wonder if those children, too, might have a positive impact on others,
if they are "good" as it seems to be defined by his parents.

This scenario illuminates important facets of existential school counseling.
The playground apparatus is part of the Lebenswelt or background environment that creates the context within which children experience their lives. The
scenario opens with the child contemplating his/her physical limitations (i.e.,
physical contingency) or Umwelt. The older and taller youth represent Mitwelt,
or relational experience, in an interaction that causes the child to reflect on his/
her Eigenwelt, or psychological development, later that evening. It is within
these four existential structures, Umwelt, Eigenwelt, Mitwelt, and Lebenswelt,
that we present practical examples of school counseling work as conceptualized
from an existential perspective. Please note that Überwelt is not included because many schools are cautious about counselor-led interventions of a reli-
gious/spiritual nature.

Elementary Schools. Understanding self in relationship to others, particularly peers, and developing an identity as a student are the novel developmental tasks most often encountered upon entry into the first level of

schooling. Concomitant with these two novel tasks, early elementary school students (grades K–4) will begin to identify feelings in themselves and others, to learn about friendship in the more complex school environment, to identify and begin to solve problems, and to learn about coping with contingencies and unexpected events. Grappling with each of these existential issues will remain present, although it will change with personal development and school context, throughout the school years.

If you have ever watched the famous *Gloria* videos, where a single client named Gloria is videotaped receiving therapy from three prominent psychotherapists (Carl Rogers, Albert Ellis, and Fritz Perls), you might have noted that the presentation of the client is very consistent, whereas the focus of the session changes based on the theoretical orientation and the client content selected by the therapist. The same is true about existential school counseling!

- Student concerns are going to be the same, but an existential school counselor may choose to focus on certain ones more frequently or urgently than others.
- Intervention designs are going to be the same, but an existential school counselor will approach the interventions with different thoughts (existential conceptualizations of concerns, processes, and outcomes), styles (humanistic yet directed toward grappling with freedom and contingency in a developmentally appropriate way), and objectives.

This truth should be kept in mind when reviewing Table 8.1 for examples of existential phenomena and intervention ideas appropriate for the elementary school setting. While the table is not exhaustive, it demonstrates the types of conceptual concerns and interventions an existential school counselor might choose while maintaining the philosophical grounding described in this chapter.

APPLICATION WITH OTHERS

Meet with a group of five or six peers and select an existential phenomenon from the list above (or create your own). Assuming an existential theoretical perspective, create a detailed treatment (for individuals) or lesson plan (for small groups or classroom guidance) addressing your phenomenon of choice. Be sure to provide conceptual information for all of the choices you make when completing this task.

Middle Schools. Jesse, the middle school student introduced at the beginning of this chapter, is entering middle school for the first time. Imagine for a

Table 8.1. THE FOUR EXISTENTIAL WORLDS (UMWELT, EIGENWELT, MITWELT, AND LEBENSWELT) AND THEIR RELATIONSHIP TO COUNSELOR IDENTIFICATION OF ELEMENTARY SCHOOL STUDENT ISSUES AND THEORETICALLY BASED INTERVENTIONS

	Existential Phenomena	Interventions
Umwelt (Physical)	• Body awareness • Orientation to size and physical power, including limitations and boundaries • Gender identity	• Stress breaks from class, including dance breaks during the school day • Social group experiences that include movement interventions • Play therapy, including directed play (with rules, i.e., contingencies) and sand tray therapy (e.g., the sand tray space is a contingent space for creating scenes) • Playground observation and positive behavioral and interpersonal support
Eigenwelt (Psychological)	• Identity as a student • Community membership • Career awareness • Making choices	• Nondirected play therapy for presenting behavioral and mental health concerns • Small groups for existential topics, such as parental divorce, grief, and illness • Classroom guidance addressing what it means to be a student • Classroom or system-level career programs that highlight gender, racial, ethnic, and social class possibility • System program on community, what it means to be a member of a community, using public spaces, and character education interventions
Mitwelt (Relational)	• Teasing • Making friends • Conflict	• Lunch-bunch friendship groups • Bullying prevention interventions • Buddy programs • Peer mediation programs

Table 8.1. CONTINUED

	Existential Phenomena	Interventions
Lebenswelt (Environmental)	• School safety and security • Cultural space in school • School belongingness in the broader culture	• Trauma-informed programs • School resource officer inclusion as a positive force in the school • Representation of student cultural identity in an ongoing manner through school decorations, curriculum, and faculty/administrative inclusion • Creating a global context for the school in a way that situates students, school, and community within the broader context of the world

moment what anxieties might be on Jesse's mind. Older children may have told Jesse about gym class and how it differs from the class in elementary school. Concerns about her body and gender identity (Umwelt) may weigh heavily on Jesse's mind as she wonders how the locker room is constructed (Lebenswelt), particularly questions about how much personal privacy there might be. Jesse's cousin once suggested that the locker room is where teasing by peers (Mitwelt) happens, and Jesse feels very anxious about this due to her questions about gender identity and sexual orientation (Eigenwelt), which remain unanswered due to family religious beliefs (Überwelt).

Orientation of self to peers is a primary aspect of middle school development (Gottfredson, 2005). The existential schema we are using provide few answers to Jesse's dilemma, yet knowing that there is a theoretical map from which a school counselor can conceptualize student experience is helpful when identifying (and normalizing) student experiences as well in planning existentially sensitive interventions. Table 8.2 lists examples of existential phenomena and intervention ideas appropriate for the middle school setting, although the list is not exhaustive.

High Schools. Toni has a problem. Her romantic partner is becoming more and more expressive while making demands of Toni that she does not feel comfortable with, including requests that she dress differently (i.e., more provocatively; Umwelt), "go further" in their intimate relationship (Mitwelt), and sneak away from class so that they can spend time together in the privacy of the old theatre room (Lebenswelt). Toni suspects that this is leading to a request that

Table 8.2. The Four Existential Worlds (Umwelt, Eigenwelt, Mitwelt, and Lebenswelt) and Their Relationship to Counselor Identification of Middle School Student Issues and Theoretically Based Interventions

	Existential Phenomena	Interventions
Umwelt (Physical)	• Body development awareness and care • Gender identity • Sexual orientation	• Self-care kits for students • Evidence-informed human growth and sexual development curriculum • Gay Student Alliance (GSA) • Dating and relationship interventions that are affirmative of sexual minorities
Eigenwelt (Psychological)	• Academic planning • Career development • Competence and self-concept	• Individual counseling services for individual concerns • Individual planning and classroom guidance for academic planning and decision-making • Narrative career development portfolios (on-line, paper) that help students view career development and identity as being authored or constructed • Comprehensive school guidance programming designed for development of self-awareness, multiple identities, goal setting, and decision-making
Mitwelt (Relational)	• Bullying • Conflict • Technology and social media	• Peer mediation programs and interventions • Counselor mediation interventions • Small-group counseling services for relational concerns • Comprehensive guidance interventions focused on social media/cyber bullying

Table 8.2. CONTINUED

	Existential Phenomena	Interventions
Lebenswelt (Environmental)	• Community safety and security • Cultural space in local community • Community belongingness in the broader culture	• Character education programs • Trauma-informed programs • Cross-cultural exchange programs with other schools/ clubs

they not go away to college next year. "And all of this is happening when I am retaking the SATs and have to fill out scholarship applications!" (Eigenwelt).

Yes, high school students have more cognitive tools available to them than they had when they were younger, yet the decisions they face carry equal if not more complexity than the problems of their younger developmental years. Existential school counseling practice meets the complexity of these lived experiences with the richness of thought needed for the tasks at hand. There is no cookie cutter answer to Toni's dilemma; thus, there is no manualized treatment plan or intervention that addresses Toni's concerns. Table 8.3 gives examples of existential phenomena and intervention ideas appropriate for the high school setting; in reviewing the table, imagine how you might be with a student in each situation.

There is a challenge in writing about a theoretical approach to school counseling that eschews techniques and encourages a way of being. Part of the challenge is the authors' own sense of responsibility to write about something that has rarely been written about before. Another aspect is that, in the current historical context, formularized approaches to school counseling are the norm. We encourage readers to concentrate their efforts on understanding the meaning behind practicing existentially versus the other techniques and offer the following questions for you answer for yourself:

1. What work have you done, and do you need to do, along the four dimensions of anxiety about death and living, freedom and responsibility, isolation, and meaning versus meaninglessness?
2. How does the work described in question 1 change your thinking? How does it change what you look for, and at, in your school counseling practice?
3. How does the work described in question 1 change your way of being with people? How does it change your attitudes and behaviors as you work with students in your school counseling practice?

Table 8.3. THE FOUR EXISTENTIAL WORLDS (UMWELT, EIGENWELT, MITWELT, AND LEBENSWELT) AND THEIR RELATIONSHIP TO COUNSELOR IDENTIFICATION OF HIGH SCHOOL STUDENT ISSUES AND THEORETICALLY BASED INTERVENTIONS

	Existential Phenomena	Interventions
Umwelt (Physical)	• Relationships and sex education • Gender identity • Social class and poverty impacts on health and well-being	• Individual sessions where the counselor employs an existential stance of therapeutic intervention • Scientifically based sex and relationship psychoeducation • Gay Student Alliance (GSA) • Small-group therapy using existential theory to address family planning, post-incarceration issues, social class and poverty, and other issues
Eigenwelt (Psychological)	• Academic decision-making • Career decision-making • Identity development and acceptance, including gender, sexual orientation, race/ethnicity, ability/disability, and other givens of existence	• Individual academic and career planning coaching and counseling • Individual assessment and referral for mental health concerns (i.e., neurotic anxiety) • Cultural and ethnic identity small groups and/or clubs
Mitwelt (Relational)	• Dating and relationships • Managing relationships with authority • Technology and social media	• Individual sessions concerning dating and relationships, including healthy romance/friendship • Small groups conducted with an existential framework by principals, community leaders, and other school personnel • Classroom guidance interventions focused on meaning-making and social media
Lebenswelt (Environmental)	• Global safety and security • Cultural space in the world • Personal belongingness in the broader culture	• Democratically governed school programs • Global exchange programs, including study abroad trips, sister-classroom initiatives using technology, and pen pal relationships. The prompts for dialogue can be framed from an existential perspective.

4. How does the work described in question 1 change your way of
   organizing your time? How does it change the way you interact with
   the structural components (e.g., comprehensive guidance, scheduling,
   IEP processes) of your school counseling practice?

The authors found that answering these four essential questions has allowed us
to blossom into the people and school counselors we chose to be.

LIMITATIONS OF THE EXISTENTIAL APPROACH

Practicing as an existential school counselor is an exercise in navigating the
dialectic between freedom and contingency. American society has a complicated history (Kemp, 1971) with existential thought, and U.S. schools are not
typically structured to encourage the exploration of freedom, responsibility,
and meaning-making. This goes for school counselors as well as other school
personnel and students. Constant tension, likely leading to anxiety at times,
between this theory of choice and the expectations of the school environment
are likely. In the best cases, school administration and other counselors remain
open to personal approaches and systems of accountability provide evidence
that existential approaches are equal or superior to more traditional approaches
to school counseling. School counselors themselves will have to provide this
evidence because there are no empirical studies of existential approaches in
schools.

Comprehensive school counseling (e.g., ASCA National Model, 2012) is not
readily amenable to an existential perspective. It is flexible enough that school
counselors can operate within the structures of comprehensive approaches
using existential thinking and conceptualization. This is made somewhat easier
given that there are no explicitly existential techniques, only attitudes that come
from immersing oneself in the existential school of thought. It is our experience
that thinking about comprehensive school counseling existentially eliminates
certain approaches that do not fit the theory but otherwise simply influences
the way the majority of comprehensive school counseling program initiatives
are designed and delivered.

The long-standing critique of existential psychotherapy is that it is overly
individualistic and is not attuned to cultural dynamics when working with
multicultural populations (Lemberger & Lemberger-Truelove, 2016). This
critique seems to us to ignore the effect existential thought has had on feminism (e.g., de Beauvoir's *The Second Sex* is a seminal feminist phenomenological study) and liberation psychology (e.g., Sartre wrote the forward to Franz
Fanon's *Wretched of the Earth*). We agree that its evolution within the field of
psychology has been led by Western, privileged persons, but we see the theory

as highly adaptable within counseling settings if counselors have "done their own work" around issues of privilege and difference. The continuum of freedom versus contingency we present creates ample space to theoretically consider issues of marginalization, oppression, and cultural differences in a useful way.

Finally, existential school counseling (and therapy) is often described as vague, lacking explicit principles, and "technique-less." We view it as rich, complex, guided but not dictated, and highly personalized. The practice of existential school counseling occurs despite the contingencies this choice demands. It requires a belief that there is solace to be found within the hardship of living, if only we seek it together.

CONCLUSION

Authenticity can be described as living life based upon the values and needs of one's inner being, instead of external factors, such as parents or society. In other words, being authentic means making one's own choices or embracing our existential freedom. We would not be the school counselors we wish to be if we had not rejected external factors suggesting that cognitive-behavioral therapy or solution-focused approaches were our only options. That is not to diminish those theoretical perspectives; rather, it is to own the choices we have made and the freedom we have found as counselors in school environments. We wish the same for you: that you freely choose the theory that informs your practice in a way that is meaningful to your work and creates meaning in your life.

REFERENCES

American School Counselor Association. (2012). *ASCA National Model: A framework for school counseling programs* (3rd ed.). Alexandria, VA: American School Counselor Association.

Bakewell, S. (2016). *At the existentialist café: Freedom, being, and apricot cocktails with Jean-Paul Sartre, Simone de Beauvoir, Albert Camus, Martin Heidegger, Karl Jaspers, Edmund Husserl, Maurice Merleau-Ponty and others*. New York: Other Pres.

Banathy, B. H. (2001). We enter the twenty-first century with schooling designed in the nineteenth. *Systems Research and Behavioral Science, 18*(4), 287–290.

Bigelow, G. E. (1961). A primer of existentialism. *College English, 23*(3), 171–178.

Boyd, D. (2008). Why youth (heart) social network sites: The role of networked publics in teenage social life. *MacArthur Foundation series on digital learning–Youth, identity, and digital media volume* (pp. 119–142). Cambridge, MA: MIT Press.

Brown, D., & Trusty, J. (2005). *Designing and leading comprehensive school counseling programs: Promoting student competence and meeting student needs*. Belmont, CA: Brooks/Cole.

Brynjolfsson, E., & McAfee, A. (2014). *The second machine age: Work, progress, and prosperity in a time of brilliant technologies*. New York: W. W. Norton.

Buckingham, D. (2006). Defining digital literacy. What do young people need to know about digital media. *Nordic Journal of Digital Literacy, 4*(1), 263–276.

Bugental, J. F. T. (1996). Rollo May (1909–1994): Obituary. *American Psychologist, 51*(4), 418–419.

Bugental, J. F. (1990). *Intimate journeys: Stories from life-changing therapy*. San Francisco Jossey-Bass.

Calabrese, R. L. (1987). Adolescence: A growth period conducive to alienation. *Adolescence, 22*(88), 929.

Corey, G. (2012). *The art of integrative counseling*. Sydney: Brooks/Cole.

DeCarvalho, R. J. (1992). The humanistic ethics of Rollo May. *Journal of Humanistic Psychology, 32*(1), 7–18.

DeRobertis, E. M. (2006). Charlotte Bühler's existential-humanistic contributions to child and adolescent psychology. *Journal of Humanistic Psychology, 46*(1), 48–76.

Feldman, A. (2007). Teachers, responsibility and action research. *Educational Action Research, 15*(2), 239–252.

Frankl, V. E. (1962). *Man's search for meaning: An introduction to logotherapy,* from death-camp to existentialism (I. Lasch, Trans.). Boston, MA: Beacon Press.

Gottfredson, L. S. (2005). Applying Gottfredson's theory of circumscription and compromise in career guidance and counseling. In S. D. Brown & R. L. Lent (Eds.), *Career development and counseling: Putting theory and research to work* (pp. 71–100). Hoboken, NJ, USA: John Wiley & Sons.

Greene, M. (1967). *Existential encounters for teachers*. New York, NY: Random House.

Greene, M. (1988). *The dialectic of freedom*. New York, NY: Teachers College Press.

Halling, S., & Nill, J. D. (1995). A brief history of existential-phenomenological psychiatry and psychotherapy. *Journal of Phenomenological Psychology, 26*(1), 1–45.

Heidegger, M. (1977). *The question concerning technology, and other essays*. New York, NY: Harper & Row.

Jones-Smith, E. (2016). *Theories of counseling and psychotherapy: An integrative approach.* Thousand Oaks, CA: Sage.

Kemp, C. G. (1971). Existential counseling. *The Counseling Psychologist, 2*(3), 2–30.

Kierkegaard, S. (1980). *The concept of anxiety* (R. Thomte, Trans.). Princeton, NJ: Princeton University Press.

Koirala, M. P. (2011). Existentialism in education. *Academic Voices: A Multidisciplinary Journal, 1*, 39–44.

Lee, R. M., & Robbins, S. B. (1995). Measuring belongingness: The social connectedness and the social assurance Scales. *Journal of Counseling Psychology, 42*(2), 232 - 241.

Leland, C. H., & Kasten, W. C. (2002). Literacy education for the 21st century: It's time to close the factory. *Reading & Writing Quarterly, 18*(1), 5–15.

Lemberger, M. E., & Lemberger-Truelove, T. L. (2016). Bases for a more socially just humanistic praxis. *Journal of Humanistic Psychology, 56*(6), 571–580.

Lickona, T. (1996a). Eleven principles of effective character education. *Journal of Moral Education, 25*(1), 93–100.

Lickona, T. (1996b). Teaching respect and responsibility. *Reclaiming Children and Youth: Journal of Emotional and Behavioral Problems, 5*(3), 143–51.

Lickona, T. (2009). *Educating for character: How our schools can teach respect and re-sponsibility*. New York: Bantam.

Magrini, J. (2012). Phenomenology for educators: Max van Manen and "human sci-ence" research. *Philosophy Scholarship, 32*. Retrieved from http://dc.cod.edu/philosophypub/32

May, R., & Yalom, I. (2000). Existential psychotherapy. *Current Psychotherapies, 6*, 273–302.

May, R. (1962, April). *Freedom and responsibility re-examined*. Paper presented at the 1962 meeting of the American College Personnel Association, Chicago, IL.

Nietzsche, F. W., Kaufmann, W., Hollingdale, R. J., & Nietzsche, F. W. (1989). *On the ge-nealogy of morals*. New York, NY: Vintage Books.

Pine, G. J. (1969). Existential counseling in the schools. *The School Counselor, 16*(3), 174–178.

Rogoff, B., Bartlett, L., & Goodman Turkanis, C. (2001). Lessons about learning as a community. In B. Rogoff, C. G. Turkanis & et al. (Eds.), *Learning together: Children and adults in a school community*. New York: Oxford University Press.

Sartre, J. P. (1948). *Existentialism and humanism*. London: Methuen.

Sartre, J. P. (1956). *Being and nothingness* (H. Barnes, Trans.). New York, NY: Washington Square Press.

Schulenberg, S. E., Hutzell, R. R., Nassif, C., & Rogina, J. M. (2008). Logotherapy for clinical practice. *Psychotherapy: Theory, Research and Practice, 45*(4), 447.

Schulz, L., & Rubel, D. (2011). A phenomenology of alienation in high school: The experiences of five male non-completers. *Professional School Counseling, 14*(5), 286–298.

Sink, C. A. (2004). Spirituality and comprehensive school counseling programs. *Professional School Counseling, 7*(5), 309–317.

van Deurzen, E. (2012). *Existential counselling & psychotherapy in practice*. Thousand Oaks, CA: Sage.

van Deurzen-Smith, E. (1990). Philosophical underpinnings of counselling psychology. *Counselling Psychology Review, 5*(2), 8–12.

Vontress, C., Johnson, J., & Epps, L. (Eds.). (1999). *Cross-cultural counseling: A casebook*. Alexandria, VA: American Counseling Association.

Weems, C. F., Costa, N. M., Dehon, C., & Berman, S. L. (2004). Paul Tillich's theory of existential anxiety: A preliminary conceptual and empirical examination. *Anxiety, Stress & Coping, 17*(4), 383–399.

Yalom, I. D. (1980). *Existential psychotherapy*. New York: Basic Books.

Yeh, C. J., Borrero, N. E., & Shea, M. (2011). Spirituality as a cultural asset for culturally diverse youth in urban schools. *Counseling and Values, 55*(2), 185–198.

9

Solution-Focused School Counseling

JOHN J. MURPHY

The world is full of suffering. It is also full of the overcoming of it.

—HELEN KELLER

Picture your life a year from now as if you were watching scenes from a movie. Would you describe the overall nature of your scenes as positive or negative? Odds are, they were positive because hopefulness seems to be part of our DNA. That's the good news. The bad news is many struggling students enter counseling demoralized by the weight of the problem—as do their teachers, parents, and other caregivers. The burden of a persistent school problem diminishes people's hope, limits their creativity in developing solutions, and reduces their self-efficacy and confidence. As if the problem is not enough to deal with, these added elements compound the challenge and conspire against solutions (Murphy, 2015). Fortunately, we can do something about it.

School counselors and students are offered hope in the form of solution-focused counseling (SFC). SFC is a practical, efficient approach that counteracts the oppressive power of problems by inviting students to envision and describe their desired future and to apply their naturally occurring strengths, successes, and resources to solutions that enhance their desired future. The discussion begins with an overview of SFC's empirical and theoretical foundations, followed by a description of the theory of change that drives SFC in schools. Real-life examples illustrate how to apply SFC with a variety of students, caregivers, and problems. While most of the examples involve students, the processes and techniques of SFC are equally applicable to working with teachers, parents, school administrators, and other stakeholders. Periodic references to the American School Counselor Association (ASCA) National Model for school counseling programs (American School Counselor Association, 2012) are included to demonstrate how SFC supports the model's recommendations and standards.

FOUNDATION AND EPISTEMOLOGY OF SFC

The two main sources of empirical support for SFC in schools—effectiveness studies and common factors research—are described below.

Effectiveness Studies on Solution-Focused Practice

Research has played a key role in the development of solution-focused practice from its origins in the late 1970s to the present day. Guided by a practical question—What works in therapy?—Steve de Shazer, Insoo Kim Berg, and other members of the original Brief Family Therapy Center team in Milwaukee "utilized a research approach that relied on clinical observations and client data to discover which therapeutic techniques would most effectively facilitate behavioral change" (Lipchik, Derks, Lacourt, & Nunnaly, 2012, p. 3). Empirical studies of solution-focused brief therapy (SFBT) and counseling have grown steadily in recent decades to include randomized designs and a variety of outcome measures. In a review of 48 empirical studies and two meta-analyses, Gingerich, Kim, Stams, and MacDonald (2012) found SFBT to be effective with a wide range of clients and challenges, including families, couples, children, adolescents, and school problems. In sum, SFBT works about as well as other approaches but does so in fewer sessions and, therefore, at a lower cost.

Findings from school-based studies provide specific support for the effectiveness of SFC in schools with a variety of students, caregivers, and difficulties, such as disruptive behaviors (Kim & Franklin, 2009), emotional difficulties (Murphy, 2015), attention problems (Cane, 2016), and academic struggles (Franklin, Streeter, Kim, & Tripodi, 2007). The fact that outcome studies of SFC in schools have generally yielded medium effect sizes (Kim, 2008) provides additional support for SFC in schools.

Common Factors and SFC

Students typically enter counseling because parents or teachers seek a change due to concerns about students' personal, behavioral, or social-emotional functioning. The effectiveness of school counselors depends largely on their ability to help people change. Decades of research indicate that successful counseling outcomes result primarily from several common factors of change that operate regardless of the counselor's theoretical orientation or model (Lambert, 2013; Wampold & Imel, 2015). Three of the most researched and powerful common factors are described here.

Client factors. Extensive literature reviews have led researchers to conclude, "The time has come to set the story straight, to spotlight the largest and most neglected factor in treatment outcome: the client" (Bohart & Tallman, 2010, p. 84) and "There is an abundance of data that points to the crucial nature of client contributions to therapy outcome" (Bohart & Wade, 2013, p. 247). Client factors include people's unique strengths, wisdom, successes, cultural heritage, opinions, life experiences, resilience, and social supports.

SFC identifies client factors and explores how clients can use their resources to achieve their goals. For example, upon discovering that clients have displayed a high level of creativity and courage in handling previous difficulties, the counselor would encourage clients to apply these valuable assets to their current challenges and goals. One of the most common ways school counselors incorporate client factors into SFC is to identify and build on "exceptions" to the problem. Exceptions refer to times when the problem is absent or less noticeable. For a student who displays classroom behavior problems at school, the solution-focused school counselor would (a) locate exceptions by examining records and asking the student and teachers about the class in which behavior problems are absent or least frequent, (b) explore conditions that distinguish the exception class from other classes, and (c) replicate exception-related conditions in other classes. Solution-focused school counselors employ client factors by building on exceptions and other student resources. Client factors are there for the asking, and SFC actively seeks out these resources in every conversation with a student, teacher, or parent.

Relationship factors. Relationship factors are the second most powerful element of counseling. This category includes the client's experience of empathy, collaboration, and connection with the counselor. The powerful combination of client and relationship factors led Duncan (2014) to dub them "the heart and soul of change" in counseling.

Establishing and maintaining effective client–counselor relationships is a central focus of SFC. Solution-focused school counselors do this by collaborating with students and caregivers and involving them in every aspect of counseling services. SFC in schools operates on the evidence-based premise that counseling works best when students actively participate in counseling, when they experience a positive relationship with the school counselor, and when the counselor and counseling services address what the student sees as important. The methods in this chapter strengthen relationships by involving students in every aspect of counseling and by applying their strengths and resources to school solutions. These collaborative features of SFC in schools are consistent with the National Model's emphasis on collaboration with students and stakeholders as a cornerstone of effective school counseling services (American School Counselor Association, 2012).

Hope factors. Hope also plays a vital role in counseling, although its influence is relatively less than that of client or relationship factors. Hope consists of people's belief that positive change is possible (expectancy) and that they are capable of changing and improving their lives (self-efficacy). Hope not only benefits clients but also is a key attribute of effective counselors (Wampold & Imel, 2015). Solution-focused theory assumes that every client offers valuable strengths and resources that can help the client resolve problems and reach goals, that clients and others often overlook potentially useful assets, and that small successes, strengths, and other resources will remain unnoticed unless counselors explicitly ask about them. These assumptions prepare counselors to be hopeful from the outset of counseling, which makes it more likely that clients will be hopeful as well.

Solution-focused school counselors instill hope by inviting students to describe their desired future and to apply their unique strengths and resources toward that future. Another way SFC boosts students' hope is to connect school successes to their efforts by asking questions like, "What did you do differently to change your behavior?" and "How did you come up with that idea?" The last thing struggling students need is a reminder of what is wrong with them or missing in them; what they need is a strong dose of hope. SFC in schools addresses this need by focusing on students' strengths and possibilities without denying the pain and frustration of the school problem.

APPLICATION OF COMMON FACTORS

Common factors of change play a large role in the SFC approach described in this chapter. Pair up with a colleague or classmate and discuss three practical ways you can apply common factors in your current or future work with students.

SFC folds the common factors of change into a practical recipe for building school solutions by applying students' strengths and resources, involving them in their care, and focusing on their desired future instead of their problematic past. The combination of effectiveness studies and common factors research provides the impetus for the theory, tasks, and techniques of SFC in schools.

Theoretical Foundations

> You cannot solve a problem with the same kind of thinking that created it.
>
> *—Albert Einstein*

This section includes a summary of key theoretical foundations of SFC in schools. Refer to Murphy (2015) for a more detailed discussion of SFC's theoretical features.

Social Constructionism. The theory of social constructionism maintains that people do not have direct or complete access to objective truth, and that perceptions about oneself and the world are personal constructions shaped less by objective discovery and more by social and linguistic creation (Gergen, 2009). Social constructionism holds that social interactions and dialogues—including those that occur between school counselors and students—significantly affect the students' self-concept and behavior. As Shapiro, Friedberg, and Bardenstein (2006) noted: "The personal meanings and stories that people construct make an important difference to their quality of life experience—for better or worse. Such filters affect the individual's self-concept, . . . understanding of her past, . . . and behavior in the future, because we behave in accordance with what we believe to be possible" (pp. 137–138). For these reasons, SFC encourages school counselors to be mindful and precise in their use of language and questions.

Positive Psychology. The broaden-and-build theory in positive psychology (Frederickson, 2001) proposes that positive emotions elicit and broaden people's solution-building thoughts, actions, and creativity, while negative emotions limit and suppress these assets. Instead of viewing positive emotions as merely an outcome of effective counseling, this theory urges counselors to view positive emotions as a means of change and to use techniques that enhance such emotions (Garland et al., 2010). As Wachtel (2011) pointed out, "The overall vision of most psychotherapy is too one-sidedly focused on the negative" and "it is on . . . strengths that change is built, and failure to see them clearly can make change extremely unlikely" (pp. 168–169). SFC includes many techniques that set the stage for positive emotions by encouraging students to acknowledge and build on their strengths.

Systems Theory. Systems theory views school problems as embedded in and influenced by their social-ecological contexts, rather than as residing strictly within the student. From this perspective, a referral for counseling does not automatically imply there is something lacking or wrong with the student. For example, a school problem may result largely from a poor fit between the student and the teacher. Systems theory encourages school counselors to consider multiple options for building solutions in addition to individual counseling with the student. Consulting with teachers and parents, altering the classroom environment, changing any aspect of the problem pattern, and building on times when the problem is absent are but a few such options that emerge from thinking systemically.

Another systemic concept that influences SFC is the idea that small changes ripple into larger changes. Students and caregivers are more likely to remain hopeful and motivated when they realize one small change can "tip the first domino" and create a chain of positive events.

Cultural Humility. Multicultural theorists have advocated for individualized, collaborative, socially just counseling approaches in which clients are actively involved in developing counseling goals, planning interventions, and making decisions about other important aspects of their services (Sue & Sue, 2016). Ridley (2005) noted that clients of color often "enter counseling feeling powerless" and "gain a sense of empowerment and ownership of the counseling process when they participate in their own goal setting" (p. 107). Eliciting and accommodating students' goals are hallmarks of SFC in schools and of culturally respectful, socially just counseling services (Murphy, 2015).

The term *cultural humility* (Tervalon & Murray-García, 1998) captures the way school counselors relate to students and others in SFC. Culturally humble counselors approach clients with respectful openness, treat them as experts on themselves, and enlist them as vital partners in solution building (Hook, Davis, Owen, Worthington, & Utsey, 2013). SFC puts cultural humility into action by viewing every student as a unique culture of one and every session as a cross-cultural exchange, involving students in every aspect of counseling, and building solutions from students' indigenous strengths and resources.

THEORY OF CHANGE

> We may need to solve problems not by removing the cause but by designing the way forward.
>
> —*Edward de Bono*

Everything we do as counselors evolves from our theories, assumptions, and attitudes about people, problems, and solutions. They guide the questions we ask, the focus of our conversations, and the methods we use to evaluate counseling services. The following assumptions of SFC in schools are adapted from de Shazer et al. (2007) and Murphy (2015).

Assumptions of SFC

If it works, do more; if it doesn't work, try something different. Putting this practical assumption into action is not as easy as it sounds, because people typically focus on correcting what is not working (the problem) instead of building on what is working (the solution), and people often repeat "more of the same" strategies despite their ineffectiveness in promoting change. The first part—doing more of what works—highlights the importance of building on exceptions or "nonproblem times" at school. The second part urges students and counselors to try something different when counseling stalls and things are not improving at school.

Every student has strengths and resources. This assumption encourages school counselors to acknowledge and apply students' wisdom, experiences, successes, and other resources. Struggling students may not think that they have any strengths or resources unless asked about them. For example, the fact that all children and adolescents have solved many different problems in their lives means they already possess useful skills and strategies that might help them address the current school problem. Solution-focused school counselors view struggling students as stuck, not sick, and their struggles as temporary roadblocks, not permanent symptoms of internal pathology. SFC recasts children and adolescents as vital contributors to solutions rather than as passive players in an adults-only version of counseling.

Solutions are more important than problems. In contrast to approaches that spend considerable time diagnosing problems and discussing their history, SFC invites students to envision and describe their desired future. Students welcome the opportunity to discuss what they can do to make things better rather than what they have done to make things worse. Solution-focused counselors are not problem phobic. To avoid problem-related discussions altogether may invalidate the student's struggle. There is a big difference, however, between acknowledging the struggle and conducting extensive analyses of the problem's history and presumed causes. Whereas most approaches assume there is a logical relationship between problems and solutions—and that successful change results from a problem-leading-to-solution sequence—SFC proposes that effective solutions may have little or nothing to do with the problem, as evidenced in the next assumption.

Change is inevitable; no problem is constant. No matter how constant a school problem seems to those involved, there are always fluctuations in its presence and intensity. In other words, positive changes are inevitable and always happening. Solution-focused counselors thoroughly explore these fluctuations or "exceptions to the problem" with students and others. Students' realization that exceptions coexist with problems increases their hope for the possibility of solutions and their ability to bring them about. After all, the solution is already happening, just not as often as people would prefer.

Small changes lead to larger changes. SFC invites students to take small steps toward their desired future. Every productive action, no matter how small or trivial it may seem, increases the likelihood of other positive actions. The SFC idea that one small change can ripple into a meaningful solution is encouraging to busy school counselors who do not have the luxury of implementing extensive, time-consuming interventions for every problem they encounter.

Dialogue shapes perceptions and possibilities. What we say to students and how we say it strongly affect the way they view themselves and their possibilities (Wachtel, 2011). Social psychology research (Fiske & Taylor, 2008) suggests that students' conversations with school counselors—whether positive or negative—can shape their self-perceptions in ways that match the discussion. For this reason, SFC favors solution talk over problem talk. Whereas problem talk focuses on problem history and diagnosis, solution talk addresses students' goals, resources, and possibilities.

Tasks and Techniques

As evidenced in the preceding assumptions, SFC's theory of change draws from a combination of empirical, theoretical, and pragmatic principles of therapeutic change. These principles drive the following major tasks and techniques of SFC.

Task 1: Building collaborative relationships. When young people are asked what they most need and appreciate from counselors, listening and respect are at the top of their list (Everall & Paulson, 2006; Freake, Barley, & Kent, 2007). The fact that most students enter counseling as "mandated clients" at someone else's urging highlights the importance of adopting a collaborative stance in school-based counseling. The quality of the student–counselor alliance is the best predictor of outcomes, and the student's participation in counseling is the key to a strong alliance. The following techniques strengthen alliances and improve outcomes in SFC.

Adopting the ambassador mindset. Approach every student as a culture of one by displaying the humility, respect, and curiosity a foreign ambassador would show when entering an unfamiliar country or culture. Good ambassadors look, listen, and learn before making assumptions or suggestions. They also validate people's feelings and experiences, which helps people focus on achieving their goals rather than defending their feelings.

Complimenting students. Anything school counselors can do to boost students' hope will improve outcomes, which is why meaningful compliments are an important part of SFC. In contrast to disingenuous or superficial compliments designed to ingratiate oneself to students, meaningful compliments address specific actions and attributes of the student. Compliments invite students to consider larger and more hopeful views of themselves and their possibilities. Solution-focused school counselors often fold compliments into questions. For example, asking a student who complains of being depressed, "How have you managed to cope with this on top of everything else?" or "Where do you find the compassion to be kind to your friends when you're feeling bad?" invites students to embrace a more empowering, expansive self-identity that includes these admirable attributes and abilities.

Solution-focused counselors can compliment a student for attending counseling sessions ("It takes courage to meet like this"), cooperating with the counselor ("I appreciate your patience in answering these questions"), and trying to change ("With all you've been through, where do you find the strength to keep on trying instead of giving up?"). Although meaningful compliments are useful with all students, their impact may be strongest for those who rarely receive them. Some students have had very few compliments throughout their lives, which can diminish hope and result in a "What's the use?" outlook.

APPLICATION

Offering meaningful compliments enhances the student–counselor alliance by acknowledging students' substantive actions and attributes that can help them achieve their goals. To practice the SFC technique of complimenting, select a student with whom you are currently working, or pick a friend/classmate to practice with; construct and deliver a customized, meaningful compliment; and, if appropriate, explore the meaning and impact of the compliment for the person who received it. (What did receiving this compliment mean for you? What impact did it have on your self-image and hope?)

Tailoring counseling to the student. Just as a tailor adjusts a suit to fit the owner, solution-focused counselors customize their approach "one student at a time." This means incorporating students' key words and phrases into the conversation, exploring their theories and opinions, and determining what they want from counseling services. Incorporating students' language validates their perceptions and reinforces the student-centered emphasis of SFC. For example, if the student says, "My teacher gets on my case all the time," the counselor might ask, "What can you do to get your teacher off your case?" Counselors can also explore students' opinions about the problem and possible solutions by asking, "What needs to happen to improve things at school?" and "If you were helping another fifth grader with this, what would you advise them to do?" Students are more likely to accept and implement intervention strategies that incorporate their ideas rather than ideas from other sources. Obtaining feedback from students is another way to ensure customized, student-driven services. The Outcome Rating Scale (Miller & Duncan, 2000) and the Session Rating Scale (Miller, Duncan, & Johnson, 2002)—two client feedback tools that take 1 minute to administer and score—provide ongoing snapshots of students' and caregivers' perceptions of progress and alliance. Collecting formal feedback in this manner can dramatically improve counseling outcomes regardless of one's theoretical orientation or counseling model (Duncan, 2014). These practical, empirically valid tools also support the ASCA National Model's emphasis on data-driven school counseling practices. Refer to Murphy (2015) for additional information about these feedback tools and their use in school counseling.

Task 2: Clarifying the desired future. Solution-focused counselors ask the following types of questions early in the first session to obtain a detailed description of the student's desired future:

- What are your best hopes for counseling?
- If our meetings work well, what will be different a month from now? What will you be doing differently at school? How will your teachers or parents know counseling is working?
- Miracle questions: Suppose a miracle happened tonight while you were sleeping and this problem vanished. How would you be able to tell the miracle happened as you were going through the next day at school? What would your friends and teachers notice that was different?
- Scaling questions: On a scale of 0 to 10, where 1 is where it is now and 10 is where you want it to be when we finish counseling, what will a 1.5 or 2 look like? How will you and others be able to tell you moved up a little?

5-S guideline of effective goals. Solution-focused counselors assist students in developing useful goals or "next steps" to their desired future with attention to five features of effective goals. Murphy (2015) coined the term *5-S guideline* to help counselors remember these features.

Significant. The most important characteristic of a counseling goal is its personal significance to the student. As obvious as this seems, it is easy to forget when working with students who enter counseling because someone else refers them. The following questions promote significant goals that matter to students: "What do you want your life to stand for?" "What are you willing to do differently this week at school to move a little closer to the life you want?"

Specific. SFC encourages concrete, observable goals so that the student and anyone else involved can tell when things are improving. When the student's desired future includes vague terms like "being better" at school, counselors can facilitate a more specific goal by asking, "If I videotaped you being better at school, what would I see you doing differently?" and "What will be happening at school next week to let us know you're on the right track?"

Small. Effective goals are small enough to be attained and challenging enough to inspire action. Questions that help in this regard include the following: "What will be the first tiny sign that things are improving a little at school?" "You rated school as a '2' on the 0 to 10 scale. What would a 2.5 look like?"

Start-based. When asked what they want from counseling, most students state what they do not want: "I don't want to get in trouble all the time" or "I don't want to feel as depressed." When a student uses negative terms, solution-focused counselors ask "instead of" questions that evoke the expression as the presence of something desirable that the student would like to "start" doing, rather than the end or absence of something undesirable: "What will you be doing 'instead of' getting in trouble?" or "What would you rather be doing 'instead of' being depressed?" In addition to being more noticeable and measurable than negatively worded goals, start-based goals are more motivating because they focus students' attention on moving toward what they want (solutions) rather than away from what they do not want (problems).

Self-manageable. Students rarely refer themselves for counseling, so it is understandable that they may initially emphasize what their teachers or others could do differently to make school better ("My teachers need to back off and chill"). These statements, accurate as they may be, set students up for frustration because they require changes over which they have little control. When this occurs in SFC, counselors acknowledge students' perceptions while inviting them to consider the more empowering prospect of what they can do to achieve their desired future: "What have you found helpful in getting your teachers to back off and chill a little?"

REFLECTION MOMENT

One effective way to learn a counseling technique is to apply the technique to yourself and experience it from the client's perspective. Pick a personal concern and ask yourself the following SFC miracle questions: Suppose a miracle happened tonight while you were sleeping and this concern completely vanished. How would you know the miracle happened when you woke up the next day? What would be different? Who would notice and what would they say about the change? What would that be like for you? What small piece of the miracle is already happening, if only just a little?

Task 3: Building on Exceptions and Other Resources. Building solutions from what is "right" with students takes two forms in SFC—building on exceptions and building on other resources.

Building on exceptions. Most students are well aware of their school problems, which is why the strategy of building on exceptions to the problem engages their attention and energy. Exceptions refer to times at school when the problem is absent or less noticeable. Exceptions are mini-solutions that are already happening, although not as often as people would prefer. Building on exceptions is a core SFC technique involving three steps: eliciting exceptions ("Tell me about a time the problem could have happened but did not." "When doesn't the problem happen at school?"), exploring the conditions under which they occur ("How did you make that happen? What was different about your approach that time?"), and expanding their presence at school ("What will it take to do that more often at school?" "How willing are you to try that in another class?"). This strategy epitomizes SFC's emphasis on doing more of what already works.

Many students become more hopeful when they realize they are already doing, and already possess, what it takes to improve their school experience. The strategy of building on exceptions—and SFC in general—encourages struggling students to shift from asking, "How can I be more like other 'better' students?" to "How can I be more like myself during my better moments?"

REFLECTION MOMENT

Select a concern or problem in your life and ask yourself the following questions to identify, explore, and expand on exceptions to the problem. Think of a recent time the problem could have happened but did not happen, or a time it was less noticeable than usual. What was different about that time? How did you approach things differently? Based on the information above, what can you do tomorrow to increase the frequency of exceptions?

Building on other resources. Every student brings valuable resources to counseling, and SFC helps the student identify and apply such resources at school and elsewhere. Resources include students' cultural heritage and life experiences, values, strengths, role models, special interests and talents, and community support systems.

The following example of building on resources involves Dalia, a 9-year-old student referred for classroom behavior problems. According to her teacher, Dalia became easily frustrated and verbally aggressive when she made mistakes or things did not go her way in the classroom.

During the opening moments of the first meeting, the school counselor asked Dalia about her interests and hobbies outside of school. Dalia said she enjoyed soccer and played on a local team. After a few minutes of discussion during which Dalia briefed the counselor about general soccer strategy and rules, they explored similarities between the challenges of school and challenges of soccer. They discussed how both required knowledge, skill, and practice, and how failure was a natural part of learning in soccer and school. The counselor suggested an experiment in which Dalia would approach a school day as she would a soccer game. Dalia agreed to "step onto the field" each day and do her best, knowing that every day—like every soccer game—would involve a fair share of undesired mistakes and events. Dalia improved her classroom behavior over the next month, and her teacher commented several times on the turnaround in her overall attitude and behavior.

Dalia's example captures the collaborative process of building on resources by identifying indigenous, naturally occurring resources in the student's life and incorporating them into school-based action plans. Every student offers a unique set of resources, which is why resource-based interventions are constructed "one student at a time" with no preconceived notions about what they should look like. You will not find these interventions in textbooks or treatment manuals because they are formulated on the spot, based on material supplied by the student—which is precisely why they work so well.

Implementing SFC with Young Children and Adolescents

Although many school counselors have worked as teachers, the idea of engaging a young person's participation in an ongoing conversation or relationship may seem like a daunting task. Basic knowledge of child and adolescent development helps school counselors "meet students where they are" by tailoring SFC to students of all ages and circumstances. The following discussion describes general guidelines and strategies for implementing SFC in ways that accommodate the developmental needs and circumstances of young children and adolescents. Refer to Murphy (2015) for a more detailed discussion of developmental accommodations in SFC with preschool through secondary students.

SFC with Young Children. In addition to a blossoming imagination and fondness for play, children's preschool through intermediate school years are characterized by substantial muscle and motor development, social play, concrete versus abstract language, and psychological differentiation between oneself and others. The following guidelines and techniques, which cut across all the above domains, help counselors connect and communicate with preschool and elementary school-age students when implementing SFC:

- Take a walk around the school instead of sitting in chairs ("walk talks").
- Allow students to stand or walk around the room during the counseling session.

- Ask students to draw a picture of the solution and explain it to you.
- Keep a set of hands-on props in your office, including toys, colored pencils, blocks, beads, drawing paper, puppets, modeling clay, and other age-appropriate materials for young children.
- Use visual aids and manipulatives to supplement questions and comments (hand gestures, drawings, blocks, etc.).
- Conduct conversations while stacking blocks, rolling dice, or tossing a ball.
- Use sentence completion strategies ("I'm really good at . . ." "The person who helps me most when I have a problem is . . .").
- Ask students how their favorite cartoon characters might respond to the school problem.
- Inject fun, playfulness, and healthy mischief into counseling conversations and interventions (invite children to conduct top-secret experiments in which they behave differently and observe changes in the teacher's behavior).
- Invite students to direct and star in a short movie about school or school behavior (*How to Get More Work Done* or *How to Make Friends*).

Among the many benefits of working with young people is that we can exercise our own imagination in tailoring SFC techniques to the developmental needs and preferences of students. For example, instead of using words alone to present the miracle question, counselors can add visual images and metaphors to engage children's imagination and help them envision and describe life without the problem:

- If someone waved a magic wand and made this problem disappear tonight while you were sleeping [counselor mimics a wand], how would you be able to tell things were different at school tomorrow?
- Imagine we are looking into a crystal ball at a time in the future when the problem between you and your teacher is gone. What do you see? What are you and your teacher doing differently?
- Pretend there are two movies about your life. Movie #1 is about your life with the problem, and Movie #2 is about your life without the problem. I already know about Movie #1. Tell me what Movie #2 would look like. Who would be in it? What would they be doing?

SFC accommodates children's language and cognitive development by encouraging small steps toward the desired future (what the student and others want) rather than away from what the student and others do not want. The positive wording of counseling goals in SFC—the presence of a desired solution versus the absence or reduction of the problem—matches the concrete nature of children's language and cognitive abilities. For example, it is much easier for a child to comprehend and notice the concrete "presence" of a desirable event (a positive comment to another student or adult) compared to the abstract "absence" of an undesirable event, thought, or feeling. Similarly, the strategy of building on exceptions is a simple, straightforward concept that makes sense to young children.

SFC with Adolescents. The transition from childhood to adolescence involves significant developmental changes in physical, social, cognitive, and psychological domains. The discussion here focuses on SFC techniques that acknowledge adolescents' abstract thinking abilities, desire or demand for respect from adults, interest in social relationships, ability to consider other people's perspectives, and psychological quest for identity and independence. For example, the following strategies take advantage of middle and secondary students' ability to envision future events and to consider the perspectives of others.

- I already know why your teachers and parents wanted us to talk. I'm curious what you would like to be different in school or life. Can you help me with that?
- If this problem vanished in 2 months, how would your life be different at school and home?
- If our meetings work just the way you want, how will your life be different 3 months from now? What will you have done to make things better at school?
- Who will be the first person besides you to notice when things get a little better at school? How might they react?
- What would Ms. Rodriguez (teacher) do if you walked into class tomorrow and thanked her for being your teacher?
- How willing are you to take one small step this week to move closer to the desired future you just described?

These questions capitalize on adolescents' growing intellectual skills and quest for independence by inviting them to describe what they want in the future and what they are willing to do to get it. Middle and secondary students may have more influence on their school experience than they think. SFC taps into adolescents' growing interest in self-identity and independence by inviting them to view school performance in the larger context of their desired future, to assume responsibility for their role in school struggles and solutions, and to take specific action to improve their school experience.

SFC OPERATIONALIZED IN SCHOOLS

This section highlights several ways in which SFC fits well with schools and school counselors.

SFC is Brief, Clear, and Practical

The practical nature of SFC has strong face validity with students, caregivers, and school counselors. People are more likely to benefit from counseling approaches that are sensible, respectful, and tailored to their goals and preferences (Wampold & Imel, 2015). SFC meets all of these criteria, which explains why it has been effective in schools with students of all ages. The "less talk, more action" nature of SFC appeals to the pragmatic dispositions of students and school counselors. As one of the original brief therapies, SFC accommodates the time constraints and large caseloads of busy school counselors. By approaching every session as the last, SFC acknowledges the practical realities of school counselors and urges them to make the most of every interaction with students. In teaching SFC classes and workshops all over the world, the author consistently hears that SFC's practical emphasis on "doing what works" as efficiently as possible is one of its greatest advantages for schools and school practitioners.

SFC Is Strength-Based, Empowerment-Oriented, and Culturally Responsive

The strength-based, empowerment-oriented nature of SFC grabs students' attention as "something different," rather than more of the same. Struggling students are accustomed to school-based conversations that emphasize what is wrong with them, with little attention to what they are doing well, which might include coping with the problem and preventing it from getting worse. SFC collaborates with students and caregivers to identify strengths and apply them toward solutions. In addition to improving outcomes by focusing on strengths and resources (Gassman & Grawe, 2006), SFC supports the ASCA National Model's emphasis on recognizing strengths and building partnerships with students, teachers, parents, and other stakeholders (American School Counselor Association, 2012).

Building on people's strengths and resources also supports the counseling profession's long-standing commitment to client empowerment, social justice, and culturally responsive counseling services (Murphy, 2015). As a client-directed approach, SFC honors these principles and accommodates students and caregivers from a wide range of cultural backgrounds (Kim, 2014). The diversity of school communities will continue to increase, which is why cultural responsiveness is an essential requirement for any counseling approach in the 21st century. Finally, most school counselors enter the profession to lift students up, especially those who face formidable challenges inside and outside the school building's walls. SFC fits well with the strengths-based, empowerment-driven goal of school counselors and school counseling programs.

SFC is Flexible, Versatile, and Value Added

Since schools are not designed for counseling, school counselors—and school counseling approaches—need to be flexible and versatile in order to be effective. SFC meets these criteria in that school counselors can: (a) apply small, specific components of SFC without conducting full-scale counseling sessions; (b) use SFC "on the fly" whenever and wherever they happen to be with a student or caregiver (lunchroom, hallway, playground, parking lot, etc.); (c) implement SFC with any student and any school difficulty; and (d) apply SFC ideas and methods to other roles and functions, such as parent conferencing, classroom lessons, teacher and parent consultation, small groups, and IEP meetings. The versatile and flexible nature of SFC enables counselors to bring a solution-focused mindset to everything they do in schools.

The value-added aspect of SFC is one of its greatest benefits for school counselors. A value-added technique adds value to whatever it is combined with, making everything else one does with students more effective. Examples of value-added techniques in SFC include collecting feedback, validating people's struggles, building on exceptions and resources, and giving compliments. The beauty of value-added methods is that there are generally no risks to using them. The worst thing that can happen is that the student does not respond and nothing changes—at which point you simply move on and try something else. Even then, value-added strategies can enhance the student–counselor alliance and thereby improve outcomes. SFC techniques can enhance the effectiveness of counseling and counselors regardless of one's theoretical affiliation. For example, any school counselor will be more successful when he or she builds on people's strengths and resources. The bottom line is this: You can use the techniques in this chapter regardless of your theoretical orientation and regardless of whether or not you consider yourself a solution-focused counselor.

SFC in Action with Students and Caregivers

This section illustrates SFC in action with various students and caregivers. Dialogue and commentary are included to provide a personalized perspective of SFC.

Elementary School Example: Jacob, Age 9. Jacob's teachers and school principal referred him for counseling toward the end of his fourth grade year due to concerns that included his talking without permission in class, his refusals to complete academic assignments, and his struggle with peer relationships. When the school counselor contacted Jacob's mother and teachers to clarify the referral, they said the problems had been ongoing all year and had increased during the past month.

The following conversation took place during the counselor's first meeting with Jacob and his mother (Sherese) one week after the end of the school year. Earlier in the session, Jacob said he wanted to do better at school but the teachers and principal made it impossible. The dialogue picks up a few minutes later with the counselor's attempt to build a collaborative relationship and identify an exception.

SCHOOL COUNSELOR (SC): You've been through a lot this year, Jacob, and I'm wondering what helps you hang in there in school instead of giving up?

JACOB: [Pauses for several seconds.] They let us play basketball in the gym sometimes after school, and I guess that helps a little.

SC: Mmm. I've never heard of that. Can you tell me about that?

[The counselor lays the foundation for collaboration by requesting Jacob's help in clarifying prior solution attempts and exceptions to the problem.]

JACOB: On Tuesdays and Thursdays, you can play basketball or volleyball in the gym after school lets out.

Jacob's perception of what enables him to hang in there and cope with school struggles may help in developing subsequent intervention strategies. A few minutes later, the counselor clarifies Jacob's desired future by asking the miracle question.

SC: I've got a strange question for both of you if that's okay. Is that okay? [Jacob and Sherese nod "yes."]

SC: If there was a miracle that happened tonight while you were sleeping and these school problems vanished, just like that, what would be different when Jacob woke up and went to school the next day?

[The miracle question invites Jacob and Sherese to envision and describe life without the problem. In addition to focusing on future possibilities instead of past problems, this question encourages people to describe concrete indicators of progress. These indicators serve as specific goals that help students, caregivers, and school counselors detect progress when it occurs.]

SHERESE: He won't holler and scream. He won't act up and give everybody such a hard time at school. And I won't have to go up there so much to hear what he's done or to take him home.

SC: What else?

SHERESE: He'll start participating in school activities, and his grades will be decent. They don't have to be great grades, just not as many failing grades.

SC: So his grades will be certainly better than . . .?

SHERESE: Like a C average.

SC: Jacob, what else will show you things are better in school after this miracle?

JACOB: [Shrugs.] I don't know.

SC: Sherese, back to your statement of "he won't act up" or "give people a hard time." What will that look like? What will he be doing instead of acting up and giving people a hard time?

The counselor requests a specific, observable description of Sherese's response to the miracle question. The next exchange occurs a few minutes later, after Jacob says he spent a lot of time in the principal's office instead of class.

SC: Which do you like better, being in the office or in class?

JACOB: Class.

SC: Why?

Jacob proceeds to describe several advantages of being in class instead of the principal's office. The next conversation picks up after Jacob says, "School doesn't really bother me." Since this statement differs from his overall negative experience of school, the counselor follows up by exploring what Jacob likes about school.

SC: What is it about school you like?

JACOB: I like math and science.

SC: Math and science. Okay. Which one do you like the best?

JACOB: Math.

SC: What's your favorite thing about math?

[The conversation continues to shift from problem talk (about what Jacob did not want) to solution talk about exceptions and resources that might help him achieve his goal of staying in class more often. The school counselor continues to explore exceptions in the next exchange.]

SC: Jacob, can you think of a day this year that you stayed in class all day and were not sent to the office?

JACOB: Yeah. A lot of days before winter break. I made better grades.

SC: How would you explain that?

JACOB: One of my teachers gave a special award.

SC: What kind of award?

The school counselor learns more about the award and other aspects of this exception, such as what Jacob did differently to improve his grades and to stay in class more often during the month preceding winter break. In addition to exploring the exception, the counselor invites Jacob and Sherese to make a list of anything that might help improve his school behavior. The meeting concludes with compliments to Jacob and Sherese for attending the meeting during the summer (not something all parents and students would do), and for the courage and commitment required to continue trying to improve the school situation.

Grades and discipline records confirmed Jacob's report of better grades and behavior prior to the winter break. At the start of the next school year, the school counselor collaborates with Jacob and his teachers to develop exception-based interventions from what had worked before the winter break of the previous year. Interventions include an adaptation of the special award and Jacob's participation in the after-school basketball program. Jacob is also encouraged to implement other ideas and strategies that reportedly helped him at school. For example, since Jacob found it helpful to remind himself that he did not want to repeat fifth grade, the counselor suggests that he take a few seconds to remind himself of this upon entering school each morning. Jacob significantly improves his school behavior and grades during the first quarter of the new school year. The following exchange occurs about 3 months into the new school year, with the primary purpose of empowering and sustaining Jacob's improvements.

SC: You seem to be on track for your goal of passing to the sixth grade—a lot different than last year. What are you doing differently to make this happen?

[This question seeks to enhance Jacob's self-efficacy and hope by attributing recent school improvements to his efforts, not luck or fate. The question also invites Jacob to reflect on and describe specific actions that helped him improve the quality of his school life.]

JACOB: Well, I'm doing my work without complaining. I'm listening to the teacher. I'm not smarting off like I used to, because it just gets you in trouble. I'm tired of being in trouble.

The counselor and Jacob further explore how he managed to complete school work without complaining, listen to the teacher, and avoid "smarting off" like he used to. They also discuss his plans to continue such efforts. Jacob maintains his academic and behavioral improvements throughout the school year and successfully passes to sixth grade.

Secondary School Example: Dierdre, Age 16. Dierdre, a 10th-grade gifted student in advanced classes, was referred to the school counselor because her grades were considerably lower than her ability level according to her teachers. The following dialogue took place early in the first meeting with Dierdre.

DIERDRE: Everything is going wrong for me right now.
SCHOOL COUNSELOR (SC): I'm sorry to hear that.

Dierdre said she could not concentrate in class, had problems getting along with her mother, and felt depressed about things in general. At one point in the conversation, she said, "Nothing is going right. I don't know what's happening with me. I wish I could just snap out of it." In the ensuing dialogue, the school counselor follows up on this statement and obtains a description of Dierdre's desired future.

SC: What would you be doing differently if you snapped out of it?

[The school counselor incorporates Dierdre's desire to "snap out of it" into a question that invites her to focus on actions that will promote a better future.]

DIERDRE: I'd just be happier. I'd do my school work.
SC: Okay. So you would be happier and doing your school work. That makes sense. If I followed you around with a video camera and filmed you being happier, what other things would I see you doing to indicate you were happier?
DIERDRE: I'd joke around more with my friends, you know. People always tell me I'm funny. But I don't do that anymore.
SC: Do you like it when people tell say you're funny?
DIERDRE: Yes. I like it because I can make them feel better.

[This conversation helped Dierdre translate the abstract goal of "being happier" into a specific, observable indicator of improvement (joking around with friends). Obtaining concrete details applies to several aspects of SFC, such as formulating goals, identifying exceptions and conditions under which they occur, and exploring student resources.]

sc: That's a great skill, Dierdre. You know any good jokes you can tell me?
Dierdre: Not really.
sc: They're not all dirty, are they?
dierdre: [Smiles.] Not all of them. Most of them aren't.
sc: That's impressive. It's impressive you can entertain friends with jokes that are mostly clean. You should write a book about that.
dierdre: [Smiles.] Maybe I will.

[If done respectfully, humor adds some flexibility and playfulness into otherwise grim problem situations.]

At the end of the session, the counselor invited Dierdre to complete the following exception-finding homework exercise, referred to as the "formula first session task" (de Shazer, 1985) in SFC.

sc: I appreciate your meeting with me today. It takes courage to talk about yourself to someone you just met. I feel like I've got a pretty good handle on your concerns, so I'm wondering if you'd be willing to help learn more about what you want to continue in your life. I'd like you to make a list of the things in your life that you want to see continue happening, and we can talk about these things when we meet next week. Are you willing to do that?

[Acknowledging and validating students' struggles are important parts of establishing cooperative relationships in SFC. Rather than challenging Dierdre's perception that "nothing was going right" for her, the school counselor acknowledges her problem ("I feel like I've got a pretty good handle on your concerns") before delivering the exception-finding task. SFC is not problem-phobic; rather, it is a "both/and" approach that acknowledges people's problem-related experiences while inviting them to focus on what is already working and what they want more of in their lives.]

At the start of the next meeting, Dierdre said she hadn't realized how much she had going for her as she shared an extensive list of exceptions and resources that included the following: (a) friends with whom she could talk about anything; (b) two teachers who treated her with respect, and the realization that she needed to work harder in their classes to return the favor; (c) her sense of humor; (d) a recent conversation with her mother in which they both agreed to treat each other better; (e) improved concentration at school; and (f) the acknowledgment that no one achieves complete happiness and a person can still function in the midst of problems and challenges. The counselor and Dierdre explored how she could build on and sustain these strengths, resources, and improvements.

Dierdre raised her grades over the next few weeks and successfully finished the school year. Instead of challenging or otherwise invalidating Dierdre's problem-centered story that "nothing" was going right, the exception-finding task invited her to reconsider things through the broader lens of what was right and working in her life. While not all students respond as Dierdre did, this simple task works well with most students and most concerns.

Stakeholder Example: Maria, Fourth-Grade Teacher. Solution-focused practice with teachers, parents, families, and other stakeholders involves the same process as SFC with students. As illustrated throughout the chapter, solution-focused counselors are very intentional about building and validating collaborative relationships from the outset of their work with students and caregivers. The school counselor's validation of people's struggles, perceptions, and feelings goes a long way toward building alliances and enhancing outcomes. Validation plays a large role in the following example of SFC with a fourth-grade teacher named Maria.

Maria consulted the counselor in the middle of the school year to discuss Alberto, a student she described as defiant and skilled at "pushing her buttons." Maria was an experienced, respected teacher with a strong reputation for handling difficult students. She apologized for bothering the counselor and was embarrassed about seeking help. Maria described Alberto's problem behaviors and said she became angry and recently "lost it" with Alberto and his parents. This prompted her to question her overall ability as a teacher and to wonder if she still had what it took to do the job. It started a few days earlier when she caught Alberto taking pens from another student's desk. She uncharacteristically raised her voice and scolded him in front of the other students. Later that same morning, she argued with his father by phone when he did not recognize the seriousness of Alberto's behavior.

After listening to Maria's concerns, the school counselor offered validating comments.

sc: I get that you did not respond to Alberto or his father the way you would have liked to and the way you usually respond to these situations. I also get how frustrating it is to work with someone every day and get very little in return.

MARIA: But I'm the teacher and adult in this relationship.

sc: Yes, and you're also a human being and not a machine programmed to respond the same way to every situation. No wonder you lost it. I'm surprised it hasn't happened earlier. This student has disrupted your class for several months now. You're not getting cooperation from his parents despite multiple phone calls requesting their help. On top of all that, you've got a handful of tough kids that would challenge anyone's patience.

The counselor's comments invited Maria to consider a broader, more flexible perspective of her responses and her overall competency as a teacher. The use of validation in SFC is based on the idea that solving difficult problems is challenging enough without having to justify or defend oneself to the counselor. In this example, the counselor's validation allowed Maria to relax and focus her attention and energy on developing a behavior plan for Alberto. When asked about previous strategies she had used in similar situations, Maria offered several ideas. Maria and the counselor cobbled her ideas into a practical behavior plan that enhanced Alberto's classroom behavior and overall school performance.

LIMITATIONS AND CHALLENGES

There are potential limitations and challenges in implementing SFC in schools. Some classic solution-focused techniques, such as the miracle question, have become so popular and formulaic that school counselors may be reluctant to adapt them or may abandon them when they are not working for students or teachers. Some authors suggest counselors may become overly enamored of solution-focused techniques and minimize the importance of the therapeutic relationship (Corey, 2017; Murphy, 2013). Like any school counseling approach, SFC is most effective when applied with ample flexibility and careful attention to the responses of students and caregivers.

Another potential limitation of SFC is that it sounds deceptively simple. SFC's core clinical premise—find what works and encourage more of it—can mislead counselors into thinking it is easy to do. As illustrated in this chapter, implementing a client-directed approach like SFC requires a major shift in traditional ways of conceptualizing problems, solutions, and clients, along with a corresponding skill set that includes precise use of language, collection and discussion of client feedback, alliance-building strategies, and a host of other therapeutic nuances and skills. SFC is a radically cooperative approach that gives students of all ages a significant voice in their care—easier said than done in the face of traditions, agencies, and co-workers with very different ideas about counseling children and adolescents.

School counselors who implement SFC also face the challenge of properly acknowledging people's concerns and not rushing them into solution talk before they are ready. This chapter advocates a both/and perspective for SFC in which counselors hear and validate both types of client stories—possibility and pain, strength and struggle, success and failure—rather than prematurely pressuring students and caregivers into discussing their strengths and successes. Shifting from problem-focused to solution-focused practice is challenging, which is why school counselors need to be persistent and patient with themselves and their colleagues. It helps to adopt a solution-focused approach to becoming a solution-focused counselor. For example, just as SFC invites students to build on resources, school counselors can identify and build on local resources that support the use of SFC in their settings—ideas, actions, policies, people, and anything else that enhances or expands the implementation of SFC.

Working with struggling students and serious problems is difficult and frustrating at times; it is also highly gratifying and enjoyable. Young people are very skilled at sizing up helping professionals, and they can tell whether we approach counseling as a burden or a joy. Effective school counselors approach students and counseling with a respectful sense of humility, appreciation, and adventure. I recommend the same as you apply the principles and practices of SFC in schools.

REFERENCES

American School Counselor Association. (2012). *The ASCA national model: A framework for school counseling programs* (3rd ed.). Alexandria, VA: American School Counselor Association.

Bohart, A. C., & Tallman, K. (2010). Clients: The neglected common factor in therapy. In B. L. Duncan, S. D. Miller, B. E. Wampold, & M. A. Hubble (Eds.), *The heart and soul of change: Delivering what works in therapy* (2nd ed., pp. 83–111). Washington, DC: American Psychological Association.

Bohart, A. C., & Wade, A. G. (2013). The client in psychotherapy. In M. J. Lambert (Ed.), *Bergin and Garfield's handbook of psychotherapy and behavior change* (6th ed., pp. 219–257). Hoboken, NJ: Wiley.

Cane, F. (2016). Whose problem? Everyone's solution: A case study of a systemic and solution-focused approach to therapeutic intervention in a secondary school. *Educational & Child Psychology, 33*(4), 66–79.

Corey, G. (2017). *Theory and practice of psychotherapy and counseling* (10th ed.). Boston, MA: Cengage Learning.

de Shazer, S., (1985). *Keys to solution in brief therapy*. New York: Norton.

de Shazer, S., Dolan, Y., Korman, H., Trepper, T., McCollum, E., & Berg, I. K. (2007). *More than miracles: The state of the art of solution-focused brief therapy.* New York, NY: Haworth Press.

Duncan, B. L. (2014). *On becoming a better therapist* (2nd ed.). Washington, DC: American Psychological Association.

Everall, R. D., & Paulson, B. L. (2006). The therapeutic alliance: Adolescent perspectives. *Counseling and Psychotherapy Research: Linking Research with Practice, 2,* 78–87.

Fiske, S. T., & Taylor, S. E. (2008). *Social cognition: From brains to culture.* New York, NY: McGraw-Hill.

Franklin, C., Streeter, C. L., Kim, J. S., & Tripodi, S. J. (2007). The effectiveness of a solution-focused, public alternative school for dropout prevention and retrieval. *Children & Schools, 29,* 15–26.

Freake, H., Barley, V., & Kent, G. (2007). Adolescents' views of helping professionals: A review of the literature. *Journal of Adolescence, 30,* 639–653.

Frederickson, B. L. (2001). The role of positive emotions in positive psychology: The broaden-and-bend theory of positive emotions. *American Psychologist, 56,* 218–226.

Garland, E. L., Fredrickson, B., Kring, A. M., Johnson, D. P., Meyer, P. S., & Penn, D. L. (2010). Upward spirals of positive emotions counter downward spirals of negativity: Insights from the broaden-and-build theory and affective neuroscience on the treatment of emotion dysfunctions and deficits in psychopathology. *Clinical Psychology Review, 30,* 849–864.

Gassman, D., & Grawe, K. (2006). General change mechanisms: The relation between problem activation and resource activation in successful and unsuccessful therapeutic interactions. *Clinical Psychology and Psychotherapy, 13*(1), 1–11.

Gergen, K. (2009). *An invitation to social construction.* London, England: Sage.

Gingerich, W. J., Kim, J. S., Stams, G. J. J., & MacDonald, A. J. (2012). Solution-focused brief therapy outcome research. In C. Franklin, T. S. Trepper, W. J. Gingerich, & E. E. McCollum (Eds.), *Solution-focused brief therapy: A handbook of evidence-based practice* (pp. 95–111). New York, NY: Oxford University Press.

Hook, J. N., Davis, D. E., Owen, J., Worthington Jr., E. L., & Utsey, S. O. (2013). Cultural humility: Measuring openness to culturally diverse clients. *Journal of Counseling Psychology, 60*(3), 353–366.

Kim, J. S. (2008). Examining the effectiveness of solution-focused brief therapy: A meta-analysis. *Research on Social Work Practice, 18,* 107–116.

Kim, J. S. (Ed.). (2014). *Solution-focused brief therapy: A multicultural approach.* Thousand Oaks, CA: Sage.

Kim, J. S., & Franklin, C. (2009). Solution-focused brief therapy in schools: A review of the outcome literature. *Children and Youth Services Review, 31,* 464–470.

Lambert, M. J. (Ed.) (2013). The efficacy and effectiveness of psychotherapy. In *Bergin and Garfield's handbook of psychotherapy and behavior change* (6th ed., pp. 169–218). Hoboken, NJ: Wiley.

Lipchik, E., Derks, J., Lacourt, M., & Nunnaly, E. (2012). Origins and treatment manual for solution-focused brief therapy. In C. Franklin, T. S. Trepper, W. J. Gingerich, & E. E. McCollum (Eds.), *Solution-focused brief therapy: A handbook of evidence-based practice* (pp. 3–19). New York, NY: Oxford University Press.

Miller, S. D., & Duncan, B. L. (2000). *Outcome Rating Scale.* Retrieved from https://heartandsoulofchange.com/content/measures/download.php

Miller, S. D., Duncan, B. L., & Johnson, L. D. (2002). *Session Rating Scale.* Retrieved from https://heartandsoulofchange.com/content/measures/download.php

Murphy, J. J. (2013). *Conducting student-driven interviews: Practical strategies for increasing student involvement and addressing behavior problems.* New York, NY: Routledge.

Murphy, J. J. (2015). *Solution-focused counseling in schools* (3rd ed.). Alexandria, VA: American Counseling Association.

Ridley, C. R. (2005). *Overcoming unintentional racism in counseling and therapy: A practitioner's guide to intentional intervention* (2nd ed.). Thousand Oaks, CA: Sage.

Shapiro, J. P., Friedberg, R. D., & Bardenstein, K. K. (2006). *Child and adolescent therapy: Science and art.* New York, NY: Wiley.

Sue, D. W., & Sue, D. (2016). *Counseling the culturally diverse: Theory and practice* (7th ed.). New York, NY: Wiley.

Tervalon, M., & Murray-García, J. (1998). Cultural humility versus cultural competence: A critical distinction in defining physician training outcomes in multicultural education. *Journal of Health Care for the Poor and Underserved, 9,* 117–125.

Wachtel, P. L. (2011). *Therapeutic communication: Knowing what to say when.* New York, NY: Guilford Press.

Wampold, B. E., & Imel, Z. E. (2015). *The great psychotherapy debate: The evidence for what makes psychotherapy work* (2nd ed.). New York, NY: Routledge Press.

SUGGESTED RESOURCES ON SOLUTION-FOCUSED COUNSELING IN SCHOOLS

Murphy, J. J. (2015). *Solution-focused counseling in schools* (3rd ed.). Alexandria, VA: American Counseling Association.

The newest edition of this widely adopted text provides practical, step-by-step guidelines for using SFC to help preschool through secondary students resolve a wide range of school problems. The book includes over 50 real-life examples, dialogue from counseling sessions, practice exercises, and hands-on appendixes to help counselors and counselors-to-be put SFC into immediate action.

http://www.drjohnmurphy.com (Change-Focused Practice in Schools)

This website offers books, videos, training information, and other materials on client-directed SFC and applications with children, adolescents, families, and schools.

http://www.heartandsoulofchange.com (Heart and Soul of Change Project)

Comprehensive information and resources on the Partners in Change Outcome Management System (PCOMS) and other materials on client feedback and outcome-informed services.

http://www.sfbta.org (Solution-Focused Brief Therapy Association)

This site includes a variety of links and information on solution-focused brief therapy (SFBT).

PART THREE

School Counseling Metatheories

10

Strengths-Based School Counseling 2.0

PATRICK AKOS, CLARE MERLIN-KNOBLICH,
AND KEVIN DUQUETTE

In 2004, Galassi and Akos suggested school counselors should be developmental advocates—that the core focus of school counselor advocacy should be on the optimal development of students (Galassi & Akos, 2004). The shifting mission and ever-expanding role and expectations of school counselors were frustrating. The focus on development appeared to have faded; instead, school counseling scholarship appeared to center on problem remediation. Externally and within the profession, school counselors were pushed to be psychological clinicians or mental health specialists (albeit many may not see this as negative). More damaging, school counselors were expected to do everything—from suicide/crisis intervention to 504/ IEP leadership to college admissions counseling to lunch monitoring to test coordination. The core functions around development had been crowded out by remediation, administration, and inappropriate roles. In 2001, Akos had utilized the American School Counselor Association (ASCA) National Standards (e.g., academic, personal/social, and career development) as a middle school counselor in practice—to facilitate normal development— yet felt pressure to pathologize the normal developmental struggles of early adolescents.

In 2007, Galassi and Akos wrote *Strengths-Based School Counseling (SBSC): Promoting Student Development and Achievement.* SBSC became a framework and philosophical approach to school counselor practice. It was built on the emerging body of research in positive psychology (Seligman & Csikszentmihalyi, 2000), social work (Saleeby, 1996), resilience (Benard, 1991), positive youth development (Larson, 2000), and more. Contemporary developmental research evolved and expanded. Galassi and Akos (2007) believed that traditional developmental stage theories were insufficient and instigated remedial perspectives. In addition to individual development, a theory for school counseling practice must include the social context to account for the bidirectional pressures that influence child and adolescent development (Walsh, Galassi, Murphy, & Park-Taylor, 2002). This broader perspective on development expanded the traditional view of what it meant for school counselors to promote optimal development for students.

This chapter includes a brief review, update, and examples of the SBSC framework. The fundamental premise of focusing efforts and advocacy on student development remains. The SBSC framework/philosophy is also integrated within the context of the ASCA National Model (2012). SBSC is not an isolated theory; it is a meta-theory or approach that influences or informs the application of the ASCA National Model or any comprehensive developmental guidance program. All of the authors have used SBSC in practice as school counselors in elementary, middle, and high schools in varied ways and we share the research-informed practice strategies we utilized.

EPISTEMOLOGY AND THEORY OF CHANGE

The basis for SBSC combines contemporary developmental knowledge with strengths and protective factors for youth. This framework is fundamentally humanistic (e.g., encompassing self-actualization, wellness, personal growth) and influences the work school counselors do at both a micro level (individual counseling) and a macro level (consultation, programming, changing the school environment). The six guiding principles are briefly described, with examples that illustrate them.

1. **Promote Context-Based Development for All Students**.
   Contemporary developmental theorists and researchers emphasize the influential and interactive role that context (e.g., culture) and environment play in human development. Thus, school counselors should acknowledge and seek to incorporate contextual factors in their efforts to facilitate positive development for all students. For example, the strengths-based school counselor recognizes the influence that culture and contextual factors exert on students of color and students from inner city, urban environments. One successful program is The Model Program for students K-12 (Tucker & Herman, 2002). This program endeavors to link academic and other success behaviors to students' cultural identities as African Americans. Meetings take place in an African American church in a low-income African American community.

2. **Promote Individual Student Strengths**. SBSC focuses on helping
   students to build on, or further enhance, their current culturally
   relevant strengths and competencies as well as to develop additional
   strengths and competencies that have been shown to be associated
   with positive development. For example, SBSC utilizes counseling
   theories like solution-focused brief counseling, a theory that
   encourages students of all ages to identify positive goals, to recognize
   strengths, and to continue to do in the future what has worked in
   the past. Furthermore, promoting strengths such as hope, optimism,
   and persistence, are the focus of interventions designed to help youth
   thrive.

3. **Promote Strengths-Enhancing Environments.** Strengths-enhancing
   environments are associated with positive youth development;
   therefore, an important function of the school counselor is to actively
   promote these environments through leadership, collaboration,
   advocacy, and other system-level interventions. For example, the
   strengths-based school counselor could establish a career academy
   in his or her school to promote students' engagement and career
   development. Career academies usually include a smaller learning
   community format (e.g., school-within-a-school), a college-prep
   curriculum with a career theme (e.g., health care, business), and
   partnerships with employers (Stern, Dayton, & Raby, 1992).

4. **Emphasize Strengths Promotion over Problem Reduction and
   Problem Prevention**. Rather than placing the school counselor in a
   reactive mode by focusing on problem prevention and remediation,
   SBSC focuses on promoting positive development, which allows the
   school counselor to assume a more proactive role and to serve a much
   larger number of students. For example, SBSC promotes teaching all
   students to be self-regulated learners and to increase academic self-
   efficacy. As self-regulated learners, students evaluate the results of their
   learning and adjust their efforts accordingly. They set higher goals,
   learn more effectively, and achieve at higher levels in the classroom
   (Omrod, 1999). By teaching students early how to self-regulate, school
   counselors take a proactive role in enabling students to succeed in the
   classroom.

5. **Emphasize Evidence-Based Interventions and Practice**. Adhering to
   the premise that research knowledge provides the most reliable source
   of guidance in determining appropriate and effective interventions, the
   strengths-oriented school counselor is committed to evidence-based
   and research-informed practice. SBSC encourages school counselors
   to utilize research in academic journals, publications by professional

organizations (e.g., the American School Counselor Association), reputable online resources, and other high-quality resources to inform their interventions and programs. For example, one program that has garnered very positive support in the research is Second Step, a social and emotional learning program for students in kindergarten through eighth grade.

6. **Emphasize Promotion-Oriented Developmental Advocacy at the School Level**. In SBSC, school counselor's advocacy efforts focus primarily on lobbying for system policies and environments that enhance development for all students and secondarily on identifying and removing barriers. The school counselor's advocacy is concerned with ensuring access, equity, and educational justice for all students, with a primary focus on the school or school system. For example, school counselors can advocate for the inclusion of students with special needs in regular education classes and for providing both the classroom teacher and the students with the necessary instructional resources to be academically successful in that environment. This is not the same as advocating against a policy of self-contained classes for these students. With an emphasis on the former, school counselors can push for and contribute to solutions, rather than merely expose problems.

For parsimony, we elaborate on three core components of the six guiding principles of SBSC. The core components serve as a practitioner-focused guide for both individual counseling and school counseling programming broadly.

Component 1: Promote Individual Student Strengths

Perhaps the most challenging SBSC component for school counselors to implement is a persistent and explicit focus on promoting strengths, rather than reducing or preventing problems (SBSC principle 4). Problem reduction and problem prevention have been consistently the norm for decades, but an emphasis on problems requires a deficit perspective that only focuses on a portion of the student body—those who are in trouble or are expected to be in trouble (or failing). Even in working to prevent problems, school counselors fail to enhance student development because they are solely focusing on what students might do wrong in the future. Neither working to remediate students' problems nor focusing on preventing problems allows students to thrive. However, focusing on strengths, instead of deficits, allows students to thrive based on their own assets. By focusing on strengths, school counselors can encourage students to grow along positive developmental pathways, no matter the pace. For example, if school counselors emphasize building a character trait like empathy in children, children can gradually understand, practice, and master the quality over time. Although it may be typical developmentally for students to develop a capacity for empathy by age 5 or 6, nurturing the quality in all students over time can emphasize mastery.

Although the focus in SBSC is promoting strengths over deficits, remediation of deficits remains an inevitable part of practice in school counseling, including in SBSC. However the primary emphasis is on promoting strengths in order to minimize the need for remediation. For example, a non-strengths-based school counselor might conduct small counseling groups and individual counseling sessions regularly with students who display misbehavior in their classrooms. Although well-intended, these efforts center on reducing negative behaviors. A strengths-based school counselor would meet individually with students referred for misbehaving in their classrooms, but the counselor would focus the bulk of his or her efforts on promoting positive classroom behaviors like self-discipline and responsibility. Although deficit remediation is inevitable in the life of a school counselor, strengths-based school counselors deliberately emphasize strengths promotion in their comprehensive school counseling program.

This strengths-based approach is not just a good idea—it is evidence-informed practice. For example, after years of child abuse prevention efforts, the organization Prevent Child Abuse America concluded that their work could be more effective if it focused on promoting strengths with individuals and families instead of emphasizing abuse prevention (Pollard & Rosenberg, 2003). In fact, in the process of promoting positive attitudes, skills, and knowledge among students, school counselors are likely to reduce and prevent problems anyway (Galassi & Akos, 2007).

REFLECTION MOMENT

Reflect on your own educational and work experiences to date. What instances can you recall when educators, mentors, or employers emphasized your strengths instead of your weaknesses? How did these experiences feel? How did you react to this emphasis?

There is abundant research demonstrating that strengths help students succeed. Galassi and Akos (2007) provided a comprehensive review of research on strengths in academic, personal/social, and career development. The ASCA *Mindsets & Behaviors* (2014) document uses similar research (e.g., belonging, self-efficacy, delayed gratification) recommended for the foundation of school counseling. School counselors promote strengths when they build students' assets, such as knowledge, attitudes, and skills, that are empirically shown to contribute to positive development. The development could be educationally focused, for academic achievement, or it may be socially/emotionally based or career and purpose-focused.

RESOURCES

The ASCA *Mindsets & Behaviors for Student Success: K-12 College- and Career-Readiness Standards for Every Student* (2014) are available from https://schoolcounselor.org/asca/media/asca/home/MindsetsBehaviors.pdf.

The *Mindsets & Behaviors* are based heavily on work from schools in Chicago and The University of Chicago report available from https://consortium.uchicago.edu/sites/default/files/publications/Noncognitive%20Report.pdf.

Component 2: Promote Strengths-Enhancing Environments

Aspects from children's environment play important roles in many counseling theories and approaches. SBSC is no different. The second component in SBSC practice is promoting a strengths-enhancing environment. Environment is a determining factor in human development, beginning with prenatal care, through childhood, adolescence, and young adulthood (Broderick & Blewitt, 2015). Given the important role that environment plays in human development, it is not sufficient to solely promote strengths individually with students (Galassi & Akos, 2007). On average, school counselor ratios exceed 400:1 (ASCA, 2014). Although individual counseling is an important tool, student development can be most impacted and sustained when the school environment is strengths-enhancing. School counselors can utilize the tools of comprehensive school counselor programs to create strengths-enhancing environments. They may use school counseling core curricula, small-group curricula, schoolwide initiatives, and faculty professional development to shape the school environment to promote strengths.

Research supports the value of strengths-enhancing environments in schools. Christensen and Anderson (2002) suggested that student academic achievement is improved when teachers and caregivers make performance expectations clear, provide high amounts of structure and support, allow multiple opportunities for learning, create positive climates, and model a commitment to learning. Although school counselors can build deep relationships individually with students who are struggling academically, contextual and cultural classroom aspects promote academic success for all students. Enrichment may still be needed for some, but a positive classroom/school climate must be present for academic thriving.

SBSC advocacy focuses on ensuring equity among students, rather than solely eliminating gaps. Instead of pathologizing the consequence of restricted academic enrichment for low-income students, strengths-based school counselors identify opportunities for students who are historically oppressed and restricted. Equity means creating asset-rich environments (e.g., access to Advanced Placement courses, African American male college-student mentors) and recognition of differential talents (e.g., bilingual skills of some Latino students). Strengths-based school counselors construct the necessary supports for students to thrive and to avoid stigmatizing and labeling students with life challenges. When taking a more environmentally focused approach, school counselors would be wise to utilize research on contextual factors that prompt optimal development. Some of this research includes schoolwide evidence-informed programs that benefit students by building their assets (Geltner & Leibforth, 2008) or protective factors, such as the Search Institute's (2017) 40 developmental assets that help youth thrive.

REFLECTION MOMENT

When you reflect on your own academic experience up to the present moment, can you identify the strengths-enhancing environments to which you were exposed? If so, what characterized these environments? If not, how could your context have been more focused on promoting strengths?

Component 3: Emphasize Evidence-Informed Interventions and Practice

As noted for the first two components, empirical evidence supports strengths-based practice. School counselors will always need to rely on clinical wisdom built upon experience, but it is essential that evidence influence practice—in particular for the promotion of development. By implementing interventions that have previously been substantiated by research, school counselors and other school stakeholders can trust that interventions are likely to lead to positive outcomes (Galassi & Akos, 2007). Hence, the third component of SBSC is to utilize evidence-informed interventions and practices. While evidence-based practice is ideal, randomized controlled trials in diverse school settings are too limited at this juncture for the full range of school counselor practice.

School counselors can access evidence-informed interventions in several ways. One way is to regularly explore information at the Ronald H. Fredrickson

Center for School Counseling Outcome Research and Evaluation (CSCORE) at the University of Massachusetts Amherst. Researchers at this center conduct and review education research on the effectiveness of counseling and education interventions (CSCORE, 2017). A comprehensive list of the research and useful evidence-informed practices for school counselors can be found on their website (www.umass.edu/schoolcounseling).

Also, school counselors can benefit from the resources available through their professional organizations, including the American School Counselor Association and the American Counseling Association. Each of these organizations has monthly magazines, which often contain articles about evidence-informed interventions (see their websites, www.schoolcounselor.org and www.counseling.org). Another way school counselors can locate evidence-informed interventions is by searching research databases, such as the Education Resource Information Center, Education Research Complete, Google Scholar, What Works Clearinghouse, and PsycINFO. These databases contain published peer-reviewed journal articles about education and psychology research, including those of interest to school counselors. School counselors seeking to implement interventions on specific topics may find such databases useful.

It is important to recognize that evidence-informed practice is not confined to school counseling research alone. Research about effective classrooms and school leadership is as relevant to creating nurturing contexts. Further, because school counselors interact with families and communities, research on broader topics (e.g., parent coaching/training, developmentally appropriate extracurricular activities) guides school counselors to make systemic and sustained impact. School counselors hoping to adopt a strengths-based approach need not feel like they are reinventing the wheel. There are a number of increasingly popular programs and interventions that would fall within the purview of a strengths-based school counselor and that could be used across all levels of P-12 education.

For example, schoolwide Positive Behavior Interventions and Supports (PBIS) programs follow a multitiered system of support (MTSS) framework to enhance positive behavior in schools. Rather than focusing on what students should not be doing, PBIS programs positively define desired behaviors and reward students for displaying them. Adopting this nondeficit approach to classroom behavior could be a way that school counselors change their school environment to be more strengths-based. Not only are PBIS programs popular, but also they are supported by evidence and have been found to improve school environments (Bradshaw, 2013; Bradshaw et al., 2008), as well as students' academic (Luiselli, Putnam, Handler, & Feinberg, 2005) and social/mental health functioning (Cook et al., 2015; Sprague et al., 2001). The benefits of a PBIS system go beyond traditional markers of school success and may lead to more equitable environments (Bradshaw), whereas traditional school discipline programs disproportionately target students of color (Rudd, 2014). Further, despite ASCA's insistence that dealing with discipline is inappropriate for school counselors, research shows that administrators may still see it as an important role for the counselor (Davis, 2006; Kolodinsky et al., 2009). PBIS systems, therefore, may be especially attractive to school counselors because they provide a strengths-based approach to an otherwise inappropriate duty.

As these three components demonstrate, SBSC applies comprehensively to schools. The framework can shape the work school counselors do with individual students, the schoolwide interventions counselors implement, and even the work that other educators do in schools. In fact, school counselors can be most effective in implementing SBSC if they work collaboratively with school administrators, teachers, staff members, and other support services members (Galassi & Akos, 2007). School counselors will need familiar counseling/relationship skills and familiar roles—such as leader, advocate, and collaborator—to implement SBSC in schools. The persistent focus on strengths and student development in SBSC provides a clear mission for school counselors in any function or role.

STRENGTHS-BASED APPROACHES FOR EARLY CHILDHOOD

The nature and focus of SBSC will change depending on the developmental needs of the population being served. Therefore, SBSC with students in early childhood will look different than SBSC with students in early or late adolescence. It can be argued that providing strengths-based programs to young children may be most important, considering that early childhood experiences can have long-lasting effects on children's learning, behavior, health, and life outlook (Armstrong, Missall, Shaffer, & Hojnoski, 2009; Masten & Tellegan, 2012). Schools also play a significant role in child development (Masten, Herbers, Cutuli, & LaFavor, 2008). Despite this importance, research on the effects of strengths- or asset-based programs in elementary school counseling is somewhat new.

Most strengths-based programs for young children have focused on the importance of community involvement and the establishment of community programs, as well as parent coaching/training. This is squarely in line with the promotion of context-based development and strength-enhancing environments, both of which are characteristics of the SBSC framework (SBSC principles 1 and 3; Akos & Galassi, 2008; Galassi & Akos 2007). Ecological focus in early childhood is due in part to young children's limited awareness of personal strengths (Park & Peterson, 2005). Even so, studies suggest that even very young children already possess assets to draw on, including curiosity, persistence (Park & Peterson, 2005), kindness, creativity, and humor (Park & Peterson, 2006).

APPLICATION

Given the weaknesses of self-report measures for young children, if you were an elementary school counselor, how might you go about identifying and building students' strengths? Consider how you could use individual counseling, small-group counseling, classroom curriculum, and schoolwide or extracurricular offerings.

Strengths-based programs at the pre-K and elementary school levels should elicit and build on children's existing strengths and develop their sense of value, empowerment, and efficacy (VanderVen, 2008). Strengths-based programs for young children should also be nurturing and warm, because this environment provides the context for children to practice expressing and regulating their emotions (Armstrong et al., 2009). Such interventions may involve working with children directly, but more often involve school counselors working alongside significant adults in children's lives.

Though much of the work in early childhood is done at the school level, school counselors can also utilize the SBSC framework for promotion of individual student strengths (SBSC principle 2; Galassi & Akos, 2007). Creating and fostering individual strengths in young children involve providing developmentally appropriate opportunities for children to contribute in their communities, homes, and schools. VanderVen (2008) suggested letting young children visit people who are isolated, thereby bringing pleasure with their presence. In their homes, children may perform chores to feel important and contributive. Chores can be based on the children's strengths (e.g., organization, cleaning) or they can be adapted to a school setting through the creation of classroom roles and jobs. Other school-based projects for early childhood include allowing children to work together on goal-oriented projects to foster and utilize problem-solving skills, curiosity, and resiliency (Helm & Beneke, 2003), and facilitating peer interaction to build social networks and social skills, both of which influence young children's school adjustment socially and academically (Armstrong et al., 2009).

Strengths can also be emphasized to children through character education, which can have lasting positive effects beyond elementary school (Watson, 2006). Values in Action Inventory of Strengths (VIA Strengths) is a strengths-based character education tool that school counselors can utilize in elementary schools. VIA Strengths are 24 character strengths across six categories (wisdom & knowledge, courage, humanity, justice, temperance, and transcendence; VIA

Survey, n.d.). In line with the research on strengths-based work in early childhood, Shoshani and Aviv (2012) conducted a study using VIA Strengths with first graders and their parents. Their results showed that parent strengths and child strengths were positively correlated with school adjustment, including children's curiosity, cognitive adjustment, motivation, and feelings about school.

Context and environment are important throughout life, but especially during early childhood when quality of child care greatly affects the child's thriving, development, and well-being (Comfort, Gordon, & Naples, 2011; Lombardi, 2003). Work at this stage of development often involves school counselors' collaboration with communities and parents to develop and implement strengths-based programs because children rarely have autonomy to make major decisions. The collaborations, commonly called school-family-community-partnerships, help school counselors create strengths-enhancing environments for young children (SBSC principle 3). School-family-community-partnerships focus on empowering families and communities (Sheridan & Kratochwill, 2007), and can be explicitly strengths-based through the use of "asset mapping," in which communities identify existing strengths and resources (Griffin & Farris, 2010). The use of existing community institutions (e.g., museums, zoos, libraries, playgrounds) to support positive development (Stipek & Seal, 2001) has long been suggested. Although differences in household and community income influence the extent to which this is possible (VanderVen, 2008), asset mapping combats this by putting aside the differences and focusing on what communities do have. Asset mapping also fosters connections between schools and communities to promote additional educational opportunities for students at the school level, which is one of the focuses of the SBSC framework. Unlike interventions that focus on asset building within the community, SBSC uses existing resources and programs to bring promotion-oriented opportunities to students (SBSC principle 6).

Throughout the past decade, researchers have argued that school counselors should play a large part in these partnerships (Bryan & Griffin, 2010; Bryan & Holcomb-McCoy, 2007), with some authors suggesting that 20% of counselors' time should be dedicated to creating and fostering school-family-community collaborations (Epstein & Van Voorhis, 2010). Bryan and Henry (2008) argued that strengths-based family work is especially important for low-income African American families, and Sheely-Moore and Sue found that a ten-session strengths-based parent–child training program led to fewer child behavioral problems and lower levels of relationship stress for this population.

School counselors who feel apprehensive about undertaking school-family-community-partnerships all at once may prefer smaller strengths-based interventions. Parent education programs that recognize and build family strengths are one way that school counselors can begin collaboration with communities. Such programs have been used with diverse family populations as well as families of children with chronic illness or an autism spectrum disorder and were found to be effective (Comfort et al., 2011; Steiner, 2010).

APPLICATION

Collaboration is an essential part of the school counseling role. With a partner, brainstorm ways that as a school counselor you would enhance parent engagement in promoting student/child strengths (in or out of school). Discuss:

- Potential obstacles you may encounter
- How you could overcome the obstacles
- Other stakeholders that you could include in your efforts

REFLECTION MOMENT

Think back to the elementary school you attended as a child. If you were a school counselor in that school, what community supports or institutions would you engage in promoting students' strengths? Discuss your reflections with a partner, then share what made this task easy or difficult for you.

STRENGTHS-BASED APPROACHES FOR ADOLESCENCE

The shift from childhood to adolescence brings a series of unique challenges that may make SBSC even more relevant and arguably preferable with this age group. For more than 50 years, adolescence has been conceptualized as a time for individuals to form a coherent and unique identity (Erikson, 1968). It is also a time of identity maturation (Klimstra, Hale, Raaijmakers, Branje, & Meeus, 2009; Meeus, Van De Schoot, Keijsers, Schwartz, & Branje, 2010) marked by the formation of skills and attitudes that persist through the rest of life (Allison & Shultz, 2001; Finkenauer, Engels, Meeus, & Oosterwegel, 2002; Masten & Tellegen, 2012). Often characterized as storm and stress, normal adolescent development has been pathologized. The SBSC approach is therefore most challenged in the application to adolescents. The strengths-based framework for school counseling (Akos & Galassi, 2008; Galassi & Akos, 2007) emphasizes the complex, reciprocal interplay between individuals and their environments. As in early childhood, the environment plays an important role in healthy development of adolescents (Benson, Scales, & Syvertsen, 2011; Lerner, von Eye,

Lerner, Lewin-Bizan, & Bowers, 2010; Mueller, Lewin-Bizan, & Urban, 2011). It is during adolescence, however, that individuals begin to assert more autonomy, to make independent decisions, and to impact the ecology itself (Theokas et al., 2005; Thomson, Schonert-Reichl, & Oberle, 2015). SBSC can capitalize on these strengths to help students self-advocate for changes at the school level (SBSC principles 2 and 6).

Further, in conjunction with changes in individual factors, adolescents' relationships are also often in flux (Lord, Eccles, & McCarthy, 1994). Peer relationships may become a priority (Carlisle, 2011), but parents still meet adolescents' need for attachment (Moretti & Peled, 2004). In-school and out-of-school activities play an important role in development, socialization, and subjective well-being (SWB; Kern, Waters, Adler, & White, 2014; Mueller et al., 2011), which encompasses the frequency of a person's positive emotions, infrequent negative emotions, and evaluations of overall life circumstances (Diener, Suh, Lucas, & Smith, 1999). SWB has been consistently correlated with positive academic, social, and family outcomes (Hotard, McFatter, McWhirter, & Stegall, 1989; Sari & Ozkan, 2016; Suldo & Shaffer, 2008). With budding autonomy and more choice, adolescence is a time for complex interplay between self, family, peers, school, and out-of-school factors.

REFLECTION MOMENT

Think back to the most important relationships that you had as an adolescent. What made these relationships meaningful? As a strengths-based school counselor, how can you capture these principles in creating meaningful relationships with students? How might you utilize the power of positive peer influence to promote development?

School counselors should keep in mind that strengths are not fixed traits, and developmental stage expectations built on norms provide little utility in helping students thrive. Instead, strengths are dynamic and may present themselves differently (e.g., computational skills in math class versus music class) and on different schedules based on context or developmental level (Biswas-Diener, Kashdan, & Minhas, 2011).

Evidence suggests that adolescents are open to, and appreciate, strengths-based frameworks (Harris et al., 2012) but are often unfamiliar with such approaches. When school counselors ask students about strengths in individual counseling, they may appear confused. Most adolescents have not been asked about strengths by adults, and are more familiar with interactions with adults focused on restricting and containing risk instead. Therefore, strengths-based school counselors should intentionally teach students about the framework and introduce it to significant adults in adolescents' lives. Persistent focus on eliciting strengths and capacity is needed for adolescents to enable awareness and utilization of strengths. In this way, SBSC creates strength-enhancing environments intentionally by promoting strengths with students and adults over simply reducing "problems" (SBSC principles 3 and 4).

SBSC programs at the secondary level may require creation or encouragement for student collaboration in organized out-of-school activities (Bird & Markle, 2012; Mueller et al., 2011). For example, school counselors may work with teachers to create groups of students to cooperate on homework, study skills, and executive skills (Bird & Markle, 2012). This collaboration would benefit students personally and academically and may increase peer connections and school satisfaction, which have been shown to influence subjective well-being (Long, Huebner, Wedell, & Hill, 2012).

School counselors should also work to ensure that all students are working on achievable, self-chosen goals. The presence of goal setting alone is not sufficient for positive development. Students must be personally invested so that they are willing to spend prolonged concentration on their goals (Bird & Markle, 2012). Depending on school level, school counselors could work with local high schools or universities to create mentoring programs to assist students in reaching their goals and to foster connections with role models (Bird & Markle, 2012) because some adolescents may have few role models to emulate (Larson, 2000).

DELIVERY: SELECTED SBSC EXAMPLES IN SCHOOLS

Elementary

Students in elementary school, who are generally 5 to 12 years old, are in a critical time in their lives for positive moral, cognitive, and social development (Broderick & Blewitt, 2015). School counselors can take advantage of this capacity and help build student strengths that will assist them for years to come. School counselors can utilize their roles as leaders, as well as their classroom curriculum skills (ASCA, 2012), to implement evidence-informed strengths-focused interventions (SBSC principle 5).

As a meta-theory, SBSC can include other counseling theories, so long as they align with the core SBSC principles. If a counseling theory and its techniques emphasize strengths promotion over problem reduction (SBSC principle 4) or promote strengths-enhancing environments (SBSC principle 3), it may be appropriate for use by a strengths-based school counselor. For example, solution-focused brief counseling (SFBC; also called focused brief therapy) is a strengths-focused approach good for use individually with elementary school students (Lines, 2006; Sklare, 2014). SFBC is often utilized by school counselors because of its brevity, and its tenets fit well within the context of SBSC, as SFBC looks to highlight and build upon the strengths that students already have (McLeod, 2005). School counselors can also use cognitive-behavioral therapy (CBT) in SBSC. CBT is an evidence-informed/based counseling approach that can be used to help students develop strengths like positive coping skills and social skills (Joyce-Baulie & Sulkowski, 2015). By selecting theoretically based techniques and tools from CBT and SFBC that align with the core ideas of SBSC, school counselors can widen their supply of relevant, effective tools.

Another way elementary school counselors can use SBSC in their practice is by incorporating evidence-informed curricula into their school counseling core curriculum, so long as the curricula align with the guiding principles of SBSC. Elementary school counselors are expected to spend 35% to 45% of their time delivering core curriculum lessons that span a range of academic, career, and social/emotional topics (ASCA, 2012). Using a strengths-based approach calls for ensuring that much of the curriculum used is evidence-informed and promotes strengths among students in the academic, career, and social/emotional domains.

Box 10.1 gives an example of a dialogue between an elementary school counselor and a third-grade teacher. In this conversation, the teacher describes her students' problem behaviors from a deficit perspective. The school counselor, informed by SBSC, is able to make suggestions for the teacher to use strengths promotion to improve the classroom environment.

Like PBIS, the growth mindset (Dweck, 2006) has become an increasingly popular strengths-based approach to working with students. School-based growth mindset interventions have been used with children as young as 4 years old (Pawlina & Stanford, 2011) and with elementary, secondary, and college students (Esparza, Shumow, & Schmidt, 2014; Grant & Dweck, 2003; McCutchen, Jones, Carbonneau, & Mueller, 2016). The growth mindset focuses on building students' resiliency and perseverance in the face of challenges by viewing intelligence and abilities as malleable traits that can be developed over time, and it is especially useful in helping students to combat negative racial and gender stereotypes (Dweck, 2008). Jensen (2013) argued that the growth mindset's focus on effort makes its use particularly important for students in poverty. The growth mindset has primarily been used as a means of boosting academic achievement (Blackwell, Trzesniewski, and Dweck, 2007; Grant & Dweck, 2003; McCutchen et al., 2016), although more recently, Duquette, Akos, and Harrison (2016) discussed the use of the growth mindset as a means of creating strengths-based school environments to combat bullying and to foster students' relationship-building skills.

Box 10.1.

Using SBSC in Consultation with Teachers

Teacher: [Stops by school counselor's office.] Hi. Could I talk to you for a minute about my class this year?

Counselor: Of course. Tell me about it.

Teacher: I have had a really hard year so far. This is my fifth year of teaching but easily my worst behaved class. I have at least six students who constantly are out of their seats. They are always running to the trash can or the pencil sharpener or just moving around the room. And when I try to correct them it takes forever to get them back in their seats. And three of my students stay put but never stop talking. I can't put them anywhere in the classroom without them talking constantly with the students next to them. I just don't know what to do. I try to take away recess and assign extra homework when they get really bad, but that doesn't seem to help. So then I try to just ignore it, but my patience only lasts so long before I get frustrated and send some of the troublemakers out of the room.

Counselor: Wow. That sounds like quite a frustrating experience. I can tell that even just describing it to me feels exhausting.

Teacher: It does. Yeah.

Counselor: How can I help you most given this challenging class?

Teacher: Well I know you're not a teacher, but you seem to do really well with my class when you do classroom guidance. Do you have any suggestions on how to help them calm down?

Counselor: You're right. I'm not a teacher, and you have a lot of expertise in content and pedagogy that I don't. But I do use an approach in my work called strengths-based school counseling. The approach can also apply to teachers to help improve classroom environments.

Teacher: Interesting. What's involved in the approach?

Counselor: It's a broad approach, but one aspect that may be most helpful to you is focusing on when students are on task in your class, as well as building up students' strengths instead of focusing on their deficits.

Teacher: Hm. I have to pay more attention when they are on task. Hard for me to see their strengths right now.

Counselor: It can be a hard switch when we're used to disciplining bad behaviors instead of good ones. But I wonder if it could help in your classroom. For example, I could set up a time to consult with you about some evidence-based strengths to promote, like self-management skills, which we can teach your over-talking and wandering students so that they have the skills to behave better.

Teacher: That would be wonderful.

Counselor: Great! When should we meet again?

Middle School

A strengths-based focus may be especially important to students in the transition to middle school, a transition that has been widely studied as a significant milestone in students' lives. The transition coincides with changes in school ecology, including fewer meaningful student–teacher interactions (Juvonen, 2007). The success of students' middle school transitions can also have long-term implications for students academically and socially (Goldstein, Boxer, & Rudolph, 2015). Though many researchers outline the challenges students face in transition (Gilmore & Boulton-Lewis, 2009), others describe the scaffolding and engagement to promote continuity and belonging (Akos, Rose, & Orthner, 2014).

The VIA strengths inventory and Search Insititue's 40 developmental assets again provide useful frameworks. To elaborate on them, we examine how a strengths-based school counselor may elicit students' personal strengths and begin conversations about their utility. The dialogue in Box 10.2 demonstrates how a school counselor may introduce the idea of personal strengths to a group of incoming sixth-grade students through a classroom curriculum lesson. By first normalizing the varying degrees of "feeling lost," the counselor allows students to honestly examine the quality of their transition. Rather than focusing on what has been difficult (a deficit-based focus), the counselor places attention on what students have done to be successful despite difficulties. When a student answers that something external (e.g., a sibling) has helped her transition, the counselor validates this response, and prompts students to think about individual strengths. When a student answers with a personal strength, the counselor asks the student to elaborate and to specify when the strength has been used before, highlighting its applicability, which leads into the larger focus of the lesson.

RESOURCES

The Student Success Skills program is one evidence-informed program that school counselors can use to build students' cognitive, self-management, and social skills. Learn more about this program at www.studentsuccessskills. com.

The VIA Inventory of Strengths is available at http://www.viacharacter.org/ www/.

Developmental Assets is another evidence-informed framework of characteristics that lead to student success. Learn more about this program at http:// www.search-institute.org/research/developmental-assets.

Use of VIA Inventory of Strengths in Classroom Curriculum Lesson as a Means of Promoting Individual Student Strengths

Counselor: The transition to middle school is an awesome opportunity. Also some students may feel lost at first, but most get excited about possibilities. Think about how the transition from elementary school to middle school has been for you, and give me a "fist to five" in terms of how hard it's been. A fist means you hold up zero fingers, and that you've had absolutely no difficulties with the transition. Holding up five fingers means that the transition has been the hardest thing you've ever done. Remember there's no wrong answer, I just want to get an idea of what it's been like for you. So, give me a fist to five on the transition for you, personally.

[Students hold up corresponding number of fingers, mostly ranging from one to four with a few zeroes and fives sprinkled throughout the classroom.]

Counselor: Wow, alright, so it looks like we have a pretty good range, and it looks like some of you are really cruising three core components. Someone tell me, even if it's been difficult for you, and especially if it's been difficult for you, what's helped you be able to make it this far?
Student 1: My older siblings gave me some tips about using lockers and changing clothes for gym class.
Counselor: Yeah, so having a sibling or friend who's done the transition might make it easier—how about something within yourself, personally, that's helped you get through some of the hard parts?
Student 2: I always tell myself never to give up.
Counselor: Excellent! Where else have you told yourself not to give up?
Student 2: Sometimes if I'm taking a hard test, and if I get to a question that I don't know, I tell myself that I can get through it if I keep trying.
Counselor: Good, so it sounds like you have a personal strength of "perseverance." Does anyone else here feel like they also have perseverance as a strength?

[Several other students raise their hands.]

Counselor: Great, and even if you don't know if you have perseverance as a strength, today will be a great way to find out if you do, as well as other strengths that you might have. Part of our lesson today will be taking a survey to figure out what your personal strengths are, and ways that you can use those personal strengths when you come across difficult situations.

Hope-based interventions are also supported by research. Although the word *hope* is commonly used in popular discourse, its use in research is based on Snyder and colleagues' (1991) conceptualization of hope as having three parts, including people's ability to conceptualize and set goals, as well as their beliefs about whether they have the pathways and agency to actually reach those goals.

Marques, Lopez, and Pais-Ribeiro (2011) intervened with sixth-grade students after the middle school transition through a 5-week hope-based program. The program consisted of five weekly, 60-minute sessions delivered in a small-group setting. The overall aim of the intervention was to help students set personally meaningful goals, examine multiple ways to attain their goals, harness the motivation and drive to achieve them, and reframe seemingly insurmountable obstacles as temporary setbacks. The group utilized modeling of techniques and continually reinforced the ideas that students were learning from session to session. In addition to taking part in the intervention group, Marques and colleagues also provided a manual for participants' parents and teachers in order to increase their awareness of the components of the program and to utilize them as sources of support for students. The researchers found that students who took part in the intervention reported significantly higher life satisfaction as well as higher levels of hope and self-worth than control-group students, who showed no changes in these dimensions. The positive effects of the intervention were also still in place at an 18-month follow-up. Further, the researchers found that students in the intervention group had higher levels of academic achievement than those in the control group.

Similarly, Akos and Kurz (2016) replicated this approach for counselor-led intervention utilizing hope-theory-based interventions during the middle school transition. Citing the unique developmental possibilities of early adolescence (e.g., abstract thought, metacognition, problem-solving capabilities), the authors outlined classroom curriculum and small-group interventions that helped students set sequential goals through hopeful thinking while building on their agency and budding autonomy. These particular interventions align well with the tenets of the SBSC framework in that they enhance developmental student strengths while also using the influence of teachers and parents to create environments that reinforce student gains with an emphasis on strengths over problem prevention (SBSC principle 4).

For students in the later years of middle school, Shoshani and Steinmetz (2014) examined how a positive psychology intervention would affect mental health and well-being. They studied more than 1,000 seventh to ninth grade students in Israel who participated in 15 classroom lessons on the core components of positive psychology. Lessons included interactive activities, discussions, and multimodal examples (e.g., poems, stories, movie clips). Students were also asked to keep reflective journals and to share their positive experiences with other students, both of which are recommended means of increasing students' SWB and of promoting strengths (Bird & Markle, 2012).

The results showed that students who took part in the positive psychology intervention had decreased symptoms of anxiety, depression, general distress, and interpersonal sensitivity, whereas students in the control group had increased general distress and depression. More importantly, students in the intervention group reported higher levels of self-esteem and self-efficacy, both of which decreased for control students. In addition to individual benefits, the intervention also had schoolwide implications. Students in the intervention group advocated for a new school bell that played a self-empowerment song, and they decorated the walls of the school with positive affirmations. Furthermore, the intervention led to student-initiated community service activities and a reframing of parent–teacher meetings to "strengths-based meetings."

APPLICATION

Based on what you now know of the SBSC framework, which of the six principles do you think Shoshani and Steinmetz (2013) utilized in their positive psychology intervention? Refer to the six principles and discuss with a partner which ones you see in action.

Shoshani and Steinmetz (2013) promoted context-based development for all students through strengths-enhancing environments, and they even helped students advocate for changes at the school level (SBSC principles 1, 3, and 6; Akos & Galassi, 2007). The results of the Shoshani and Steinmetz (2013) study also provide further evidence for Fredrickson's (2001) broaden-and-build theory, which highlights the role that positive emotions (e.g., contentment, pride, joy) play in fueling resiliency, well-being, and building of physical and intellectual strengths (in addition to reducing negative emotions). Positive emotions also broaden thought–action repertoires, meaning that boosting positive emotions for students also leads to more flexible and creative thinking (Fredrickson, 2001). Therefore, increasing positivity can increase the efficacy of individual counseling (e.g., increased capacity to solve problems) and promote a strengths-enhancing environment.

SBSC programs can also capitalize on the shifting ecological dynamics of middle school to harness the power of students' peer relationships to promote positive development (Akos, Hamm, Mack, & Dunaway, 2007). Systemically, school counselors may collaborate with teachers to create classroom ecologies that are organized, attuned to student needs, and emotionally supportive and to ensure that classroom seating and grouping patterns promote peer acceptance (Bierman, 2011). Counselors may also utilize classroom curriculum lessons to promote prosocial behaviors among students, which can lead to more positive school climates and an increase in helping behaviors (Caprara et al., 2014).

High School

High school counselors are well positioned to build strengths among adolescents ages 14 to 18, who are in a critical period of self-exploration and identity development. For students of color, late adolescence can be an especially salient time for racial identity development (Broderick & Blewitt, 2015). In this process, individuals progress through rejecting their own race and over-identifying with the majority race (Conformity Stage), entirely endorsing the values of their own race and excluding those of the majority race (Resistance and Immersion Stage), and selectively ascribing to values in both their own race and the majority race (Synergetic Articulation and Awareness Stage; Morten & Atkinson, 1983). The process usually begins when individuals become aware of racial stereotypes and discrimination, which are often magnified in high school, as students typically are exposed to a more diverse group of peers than when they were younger (Aldana & Byrd, 2015). Some research suggests that adolescents in other minority groups, such as those from low socioeconomic backgrounds, those with disabilities, and those who identify as LGBTQ, may experience similar identity development processes (Broderick & Blewitt, 2015).

   Given this critical time for identity development, high school is an important opportunity for school counselors to focus on enhancing strengths among students and their environments. Kern, Waters, Adler, and White (2015) found evidence of the important role that personal strengths play in adolescents' lives. For the purposes of their study, the researchers utilized the PERMA framework. (PERMA, an acronym, stands for Positive emotions, Engagement, Relationships, Meaning, and Achievement, all of which are important to well-being and happiness. More on the PERMA framework is available at http://www.gostrengths.com/whatisperma/.) Students with higher reported levels of positive emotions generally had higher levels of life satisfaction, hope, school engagement, gratitude, physical activity, and physical vitality. Although this sample was limited to males, Kern and colleagues suggested that schools utilize multidimensional measures of student well-being to gain a more thorough understanding of whole students, beyond what current measures (such as GPA) provide.

   In building student assets, school counselors using SBSC should rely on evidence-informed tools for individual work with students, as well as group work or schoolwide interventions (SBSC principle 5). For example, school counselors can use their advocacy and leadership skills (ASCA, 2012) to advocate for the adoption of Just Communities, an evidence-informed schoolwide program in which all students and staff in a school have an equal voice. Regular school community meetings also allow students in Just Communities schools to participate in school decisions and to provide input on school policies (Kuther & Higgins-D'Alessandro, 2000). This type of approach views adolescents as resources to be cultivated (as in Positive Youth Development), rather than problems to be managed. Although such a comprehensive schoolwide program may not easily be led by a single school counselor, collaborating with other school stakeholders and advocating for such a program could be effective in creating an evidence-informed strengths-enhancing school environment (SBSC principles 3 and 5).

High school is also an important time for adolescents to develop college or career plans. Career development is relevant at all levels, and it is becoming increasingly common for students to begin concrete planning for later life employment as early as ninth grade. Career concepts like meaning, purpose, and interests are inherently strengths-based. Doren and Kang (2016) found that strengths like autonomy, self-realization, and self-advocacy are positively associated with college and career-related adjustment. The Missouri Center for Career Education offers access to more than 400 classroom curriculum lessons on their website (www.missouricareereducation.org) that may assist school counselors in this work.

School counselors may also elect to conduct individual sessions to help students identify and solidify their understanding of strengths prior to leaving for college. The dialogue in Box 10.3 demonstrates how a school counselor can use a strengths-based approach to address a student's fears about transitioning to college. The counselor first recognizes and validates the student's understanding of the differences between high school and college, then asks her to think about the strengths that she utilized throughout high school and into the college application process. In this example, the counselor uses the Search Institute's (2017) 40 Developmental Assets as shared language with the student. The counselor also helps the student recognize different types of strengths (e.g., internal versus external assets) and prompts her to explore how existing strengths may be used in a new setting. This changes the focus of the conversation from deficit-based (i.e., what the student lacks in terms of knowledge about college) to strengths-based by having the student think about how she may be able to use her strengths in novel situations.

Box 10.3.

Use of Individual Counseling to Identify and Conceptualize Student Strengths in a New Setting

Student: I'm worried about what being in college is actually going to look like. I've heard that professors don't really care about their students, and no one really checks in on how you're doing.

Counselor: I can understand your worry. Transitioning to college can be intimidating, as there is more responsibility on you as a student than there was in high school. But thinking about that, you're going into college with some experiences under your belt, and a lot of strengths that allowed you to get into college. What are some of the strengths you see yourself using once you're there?

Student: What do mean, like, academically?

Counselor: Yeah, for sure, academic strengths are important, but aside from what you'll do academically, what are some strengths you've drawn upon to get through high school?

Student: I guess I'm pretty thoughtful. I researched a bunch of schools to find the right fit for me.

Counselor: Do you remember which one of the Developmental Assets that was?

Student: Probably planning and decision making. I think another strength would be that I'm close with my mom. Is that allowed?

Counselor: It's absolutely allowed—remember, strengths aren't just internal, but can also be how we use resources outside of ourselves to help us when we're stuck or come across a new challenge. How do you think your strengths may look different in a college setting versus how they looked in high school?

APPLICATION

In this chapter, SBSC has been applied to the elementary, middle, and high school levels. In which of these levels do you believe it would be easiest to apply SBSC? In which level would it be most challenging to apply SBSC? Form a group with your classmates based on preferred school level and discuss your anticipated challenges in applying SBSC to that level.

LIMITATIONS AND SUMMARY OF SBSC

The evidence base regarding strengths and strengths-promoting interventions for school counselors is not nearly as robust as research on remedially focused practice. Although humanistic traditions are present in our identity, the challenges youth face often take precedence and blind us to our developmental and wellness roots. Therefore, the main limitation of SBSC is inadequate longitudinal testing and the need for empirically driven programs that school counselors can implement with fidelity to empower youth with strengths to cope and thrive amid life's challenges.

In the updated conceptualization of SBSC, it remains a framework or metatheory. Indeed, CBT and SFBC can be important components in selected school counseling roles (e.g., consultation, individual counseling), but a framework is more pervasive. It requires school counselors to approach grief and loss with a focus on positive coping. It requires school counselors to acknowledge that success for students does not necessitate entry into Harvard—that excellence as a machinist, in the military, or in community service can also be optimal development.

SBSC is not idealism or false optimism. Promoting evidence-informed strengths or strengths-enhancing environments as a school counselor does not automatically resolve poverty, discrimination, or mental illness. But pervasive challenges require pervasive attention to what is possible or what is right in individuals. Without counselors' envisioning and promoting optimal development, students merely survive rather than thrive.

REFERENCES

Akos, P., & Galassi, J. P. (2008). Strengths-based school counseling: Introduction to the special issue. *Professional School Counseling, 12*(2), 66–67.

Akos, P., Hamm, J., Mack, S., & Dunaway, M. (2007). Utilizing the developmental influence of peers in middle school groups. *Journal for Specialists in Group Work, 32*(1), 51–60.

Akos, P., & Kurz, M. S. (2016). Applying Hope Theory to support middle school transitions. *Middle School Journal, 47*(1), 13–18.

Akos, P., Rose, R., & Orthner, D. (2014). Sociodemographic moderators of middle school transition effects on academic achievement. *Journal of Early Adolescence, 41*, 320–332. doi: 10.1177/0272431614529367

Aldana, A., & Byrd, C. M. (2015). School ethnic-racial socializations: Learning about race and ethnicity among African American students. *Urban Review, 47*, 563–576. doi: 10.1007/s11256-014-0319-0

Allison, B. N., & Schultz, J. B. (2001). Interpersonal identity formation during early adolescence. *Adolescence, 36*(143), 509–523.

American School Counselor Association. (2012). *The ASCA National Model: A framework for school counseling programs* (3rd ed.). Alexandria, VA: American School Counselor Association.

American School Counselor Association. (2014). *Mindsets & Behaviors for Student Success: K-12 college- and career-readiness standards for every student.* Alexandria, VA: American School Counselor Association.

Armstrong, K., Missall, K., Shaffer, E., & Hojnoski, R (2009). Promoting positive adaptation during the early childhood years. In R. Gilman, E. S. Huebner, & M. Furlong (Eds.), *Handbook of positive psychology in schools* (pp. 339–352). New York, NY: Routledge.

Benard, B. (1991). *Fostering resiliency in kids: Protective factors in the family, school, and community.* Portland, OR: Western Regional Center for Drug-Free Schools and Communities.

Benson, P. L., Scales, P. C., & Syvertsen, A. K. (2011). The contribution of the developmental framework to positive youth development theory and practice. In R. M. Lerner, J. V. Lerner, & J. B. Benson (Eds.), *Advances in child development and behavior: Positive youth development: Research and applications for promoting thriving in adolescence* (pp. 198–232). London, UK: Elsevier.

Bierman, K. L. (2011). The promise and potential of studying the "invisible hand" of teacher influence on peer relations and student outcomes: A commentary. *Journal of Applied Developmental Psychology, 32*(5), 297–303.

Bird, J. M., & Markle, R. S. (2012). Subjective well-being in school environments: Promoting positive youth development through evidence-informed assessment and intervention. *American Journal of Orthopsychiatry, 82*(1), 61–66.

Biswas-Diener, R., Kashdan, T. B., & Minhas, G. (2011). A dynamic approach to psychological strength development and intervention. *The Journal of Positive Psychology, 6*(2), 106–118.

Blackwell, L. S., Trzesniewski, K. H., & Dweck, C. S. (2007). Implicit theories of intelligence predict achievement across an adolescent transition: A longitudinal study and an intervention. *Child Development, 78*(1), 246–263.

Bradshaw, C. (2013). Preventing bullying through Positive Behavioral Interventions and Supports (PBIS): A multitiered approach to prevention and integration. *Theory into Practice, 52*(4), 288–295.

Bradshaw, C. P., Koth, C. W., Bevans, K. B., Ialongo, N., & Leaf, P. J. (2008). The impact of school wide Positive Behavioral Interventions and Supports (PBIS) on the organizational health of elementary schools. *School Psychology Quarterly, 23*(4), 462.

Broderick, P. C., & Blewitt, P. (2015). *The life span: Human development for helping professionals* (4th ed.). Upper Saddle River, NJ: Pearson.

Bryan, J., & Griffin, D. (2010). A multidimensional study of school-family-community partnership involvement: School, school counselor, and training factors. *Professional School Counseling, 14*(1), 75–86.

Bryan, J., & Henry, L. (2008). Strengths-based partnerships: A school-family-community partnership approach to empowering students. *Professional School Counseling, 12*(2), 149–156.

Bryan, J., & Holcomb-McCoy, C. (2007). An examination of school counselor involvement in school-family-community partnerships. *Professional School Counseling, 10*(5), 441–454.

Caprara, G. V., Kanacri, B. P. L., Gerbino, M., Zuffianò, A., Alessandri, G., Vecchio, G., . . . Bridglall, B. (2014). Positive effects of promoting prosocial behavior in early adolescence: Evidence from a school-based intervention. *International Journal of Behavioral Development, 38*(4), 386–396.

Carlisle, M. (2011). Healthy relationships and building developmental assets in middle school students. *Canadian Journal of Education, 34*(3), 18–32.

Christenson, S. L., & Anderson, A. R. (2002). Commentary: The centrality of the learning context for students' academic enabler skills. *School Psychology Review, 31*(3), 378–393.

Comfort, M., Gordon, P. R., & Naples, D. (2011). KIPS: An evidence-informed tool for assessing parenting strengths and needs in diverse families. *Infants & Young Children, 24*(1), 56–74.

Cook, C. R., Frye, M., Slemrod, T., Lyon, A. R., Renshaw, T. L., & Zhang, Y. (2015). An integrated approach to universal prevention: Independent and combined effects of PBIS and SEL on youths' mental health. *School Psychology Quarterly, 30*(2), 166–183.

Davis, T. (2006). Looking forward by going back: A school counselor educator's return to school counseling. *Professional School Counseling, 10*(2), 217–223.

Diener, E., Suh, E. M., Lucas, R. E., & Smith, H. L. (1999). Subjective well-being: Three decades of progress. *Psychological Bulletin, 125*(2), 276–302.

Doren, B., & Kang, H. J. (2016). Autonomy, self-realization, and self-advocacy and the school- and career-related adjustment of adolescent girls with disabilities. *Career Development and Transition for Exceptional Individuals, 39*, 132–143. doi: 10.1177/2165143415574875

Duquette, K., Akos, P., & Harrison, R. (2016). Eliminating social homelessness: Providing a house to GROW. *Middle Grades Review, 2*(6), 1–10.

Dweck, C. (2006). Mindset: The new psychology of success. New York, NY: Random House.

Dweck, C. (2008). Mindsets and math/science achievement. Carnegie Corporation of New York—Institute for Advanced Study Commission on Mathematics and Science Education. Lecture conducted from Institute for Advanced Study, New York.

Epstein, J. L., & Van Voorhis, F. L. (2010). School counselors' roles in developing partnerships with families and communities for student success. *Professional School Counseling, 14*(1), 1–14.

Erikson, E. H. (1968). *Identity: Youth and crisis.* New York, NY: Norton.

Esparza, J., Shumow, L., & Schmidt, J. A. (2014). Growth mindset of gifted seventh grade students in science. *NCSSSMST Journal, 19*(1), 6–13.

Finkenauer, C., Engels, R., Meeus, W., & Oosterwegel, A. (2002). Self and identity in early adolescence: The pains and gains of knowing who and what you are. In T. M. Brinthaupt & R. P. Lipka (Eds.), *Understanding early adolescent self and identity: Applications and interventions* (pp. 91–131). Albany, NY: State University of New York Press.

Fredrickson, B. (2001). The role of positive emotions in positive psychology the broaden-and-build theory of positive emotions. *American Psychologist, 56*(3), 218–226.

Galassi, J., & Akos, P. (2004). Developmental advocacy: 21st century school counseling. *Journal of Counseling and Development, 82*(2), 146–157.

Galassi, J. P., & Akos, P. (2007). *Strengths-based school counseling: Promoting student development and achievement.* New York, NY: Routledge.

Geltner, J., & Leibforth, T. (2008). Advocacy in the IEP process: Strengths-based school counseling in action. *Professional School Counseling, 12*(2), 162–165.

Gilmore, L. A., & Boulton-Lewis, G. M. (2009). "Just try harder and you will shine": A study of 20 lazy children. *Australian Journal of Guidance and Counselling, 19*(2), 95–103.

Goldstein, S. E., Boxer, P., & Rudolph, E. (2015). Middle school transition stress: Links with academic performance, motivation, and school experiences. *Contemporary School Psychology, 19*(1), 21–29.

Grant, H., & Dweck, C. S. (2003). Clarifying achievement goals and their impact. *Journal of Personality and Social Psychology, 85*(3), 541–553.

Griffin, D., & Farris, A. (2010). School counselors and collaboration: Finding resources through community asset mapping. *Professional School Counseling, 13*(5), 248–256.

Harris, N., Brazeau, J. N., Clarkson, A., Brownlee, K., & Rawana, E. P. (2012). Adolescents' experiences of a strengths-based treatment program for substance abuse. *Journal of Psychoactive Drugs, 44*(5), 390–397.

Helm, J., & Beneke, S. (Eds.). (2003). *The power of projects: Meeting contemporary challenges in early childhood classroom.* New York, NY: Teachers College Press.

Hotard, S. R., McFatter, R. M., McWhirter, R. M., & Stegall, M. E. (1989). Interactive effects of extraversion, neuroticism, and social relationships on subjective well-being. *Journal of Personality and Social Psychology, 57*, 321–331.

Jensen, E. (2013). How poverty affects classroom engagement. *Educational Leadership, 70*(8), 24–30.

Joyce-Baulie, D., & Sulkowski, M. L. (2015). *Cognitive behavioral therapy in K-12 settings: A practitioners' toolkit.* New York, NY: Springer.

Juvonen, J. (2007). Reforming middle schools: Focus on continuity, social connectedness, and engagement. *Educational Psychologist, 42*(4), 197–208.

Kern, M. L., Waters, L. E., Adler, A., & White, M. A. (2015). A multidimensional approach to measuring well-being in students: Application of the PERMA framework. *Journal of Positive Psychology, 10*(3), 262–271.

Klimstra, T. A., Hale, W. W. III, Raaijmakers, Q. A., Branje, S. J., & Meeus, W. H. (2009). Maturation of personality in adolescence. *Journal of Personality and Social Psychology, 96*(4), 898–912.

Kolodinsky, P., Draves, P., Schroder, V., Lindsey, C., & Zlatev, M. (2009). Reported levels of satisfaction and frustration by Arizona school counselors: A desire for greater connections with students in a data-driven era. *Professional School Counseling, 12*(3), 193–199.

Kuther, T. L., & Higgins-D'Alessandro, A. (2000). Bridging the gap between moral reasoning and adolescent engagement in risky behavior. *Journal of Adolescence, 23*, 409–422.

Larson, R. W. (2000). Toward a psychology of positive youth development. *American Psychologist, 55*(1), 170–183.

Lerner, R. M., von Eye, A., Lerner, J. V., Lewin-Bizan, S., & Bowers, E. P. (2010). Special issue introduction: The meaning and measurement of thriving: A view of the issues. *Journal of Youth and Adolescence, 39*(7), 707–719.

Lines, D. (2006). *Brief counselling in schools: Working with young people from 11 to 18* (2nd ed.). Thousand Oaks, CA: Sage Publications.

Lombardi, J. (2003). *Time to care: Redesigning child care to promote education, support families, and build communities.* Philadelphia, PA: Temple University Press.

Long, R. F., Huebner, E. S., Wedell, D. H., & Hills, K. J. (2012). Measuring school-related subjective well-being in adolescents. *American Journal of Orthopsychiatry, 82*(1), 50–60.

Lord, S. E., Eccles, J. S., & McCarthy, K. A. (1994). Surviving the junior high school transition family processes and self-perceptions as protective and risk factors. *The Journal of Early Adolescence, 14*(2), 162–199.

Luiselli, J. K., Putnam, R. F., Handler, M. W., & Feinberg, A. B. (2005). Whole-school positive behaviour support: effects on student discipline problems and academic performance. *Educational Psychology, 25*(2-3), 183–198.

Marques, S. C., Lopez, S. J., & Pais-Ribeiro, J. L. (2011). "Building hope for the future": A program to foster strengths in middle-school students. *Journal of Happiness Studies, 12*(1), 139–152.

Masten, A. S., & Tellegen, A. (2012). Resilience in developmental psychopathology: Contributions of the project competence longitudinal study. *Development and Psychopathology, 24*(2), 345–361.

Masten, A., Herbers, J., Cutuli, J., & Lafavor, T. (2008). Promoting competence and resilience in the school context. *Professional School Counseling, 12*(2), 76–84.

McCutchen, K., Jones, M., Carbonneau, K., & Mueller, C. (2016). Mindset and standardized testing over time. *Learning and Individual Differences, 45*, 208–213.

McLeod, J. (2005). *An introduction to counselling* (5th ed.). Philadelphia, PA: Open University Press.

Meeus, W., Van De Schoot, R., Keijsers, L., Schwartz, S. J., & Branje, S. (2010). On the progression and stability of adolescent identity formation: A five-wave longitudinal study in early-to-middle and middle-to-late adolescence. *Child Development, 81*(5), 1565–1581.

Moretti, M. M., & Peled, M. (2004). Adolescent-parent attachment: Bonds that support healthy development. *Paediatrics & Child Health, 9*(8), 551–555.

Morten, G., & Atkinson, D. R. (1983). Minority identity development and preference for counselor race. *Journal of Negro Education, 52*, 156–161.

Mueller, M. K., Lewin-Bizan, S., & Urban, J. B. (2011). Youth activity involvement and positive youth development. In R. M. Lerner, J. V. Lerner, & J. B. Benson (Eds.), *Advances in child development and behavior: Positive youth development: Research and applications for promoting thriving in adolescence* (Vol. 41, pp. 231–249). London, UK: Elsevier Publishing.

Omrod, J. (1999). *Human learning* (3rd ed). Upper Saddle River, NJ: Prentice Hall.

Park, N., & Peterson, C. (2005). The values in action inventory of character strengths for youth. In K. A. Moore & L. Lippman (Eds.), *What do children need to flourish?: Conceptualizing and measuring indicators of positive development* (pp. 13–23). New York, NY: Springer.

Park, N., & Peterson, C. (2006). Character strengths and happiness among young children: Content analysis of parental descriptions. *Journal of Happiness Studies, 7*(3), 323–341.

Pawlina, S., & Stanford, C. (2011). Preschoolers grow their brains: Shifting mindsets for greater resiliency and better problem solving. *YC Young Children, 66*(5), 30–35.

Pollard, E. L., & Rosenberg, M. L. (2003). The strengths-based approach to child well-being: Let's begin with the end in mind. In M. H. Bornstein, L. Davidson, C. L. M. Keyes, & K. A. Moore (Eds.), *Well-being: Positive development across the life course* (pp. 13–21). Mahwah, NJ: Lawrence Erlbaum Associates.

Ronald H. Fredrickson Center for School Counseling Outcome Research. (2017). About us. Available from http://www.umass.edu/schoolcounseling/about-us.php

Rudd, T. (2014). Racial disproportionality in school discipline: Implicit bias is heavily implicated. Kirwan Institute for the Study of Race and Ethnicity. Available from http://kirwaninstitute. osu. edu/wp-content/uploads/2014/02/racial-disproportionalityschools-02. pdf

Saleeby, D. (1996). The strengths perspective in social work practice: Extensions and cautions. *Social Work, 41*(3), 296–305.

Sari, T., & Ozkan, I. (2016). An investigation of the relationship between adolescents' subjective well-being and perceived parental attitudes. *Dusunen Adam, 29*(2), 155–162.

Search Institute (2017). Developmental assets. Available from http://www.search-institute.org/content/40-developmental-assets-adolescents-ages-12-18

Seligman, M., & Csikszentmihalyi, M. (2000). Positive psychology: An introduction. *American Psychologist, 55*, 5–14.

Sheridan, S. M., & Kratochwill, T. R. (2007). *Conjoint behavioral consultation: Promoting family-school connections and interventions.* New York: Springer.

Shoshani, A., & Aviv, I. (2012). The pillars of strength for first-grade adjustment– Parental and children's character strengths and the transition to elementary school. *The Journal of Positive Psychology, 7*(4), 315–326.

Shoshani, A., & Steinmetz, S. (2014). Positive psychology at school: A school-based intervention to promote adolescents' mental health and well-being. *Journal of Happiness Studies, 15*(6), 1289–1311.

Sklare, G. B. (2014). *Brief counseling that works: A solution-focused therapy approach for school counselors and other mental health professionals* (3rd ed.). Thousand Oaks, CA: Corwin.

Snyder, C. R., Harris, C., Anderson, J. R., Holleran, S. A., Irving, L. M., Sigmon, S. T., Yoshinobu, L., Gibb, J., Langelle, C., & Harney, P. (1991). The will and the ways: Development and validation of an individual-differences measure of hope. *Journal of Personality and Social Psychology, 60* (4), 570–585.

Sprague, J., Walker, H., Golly, A., White, K., Myers, D. R., & Shannon, T. (2001). Translating research into effective practice: The effects of a universal staff and student intervention on indicators of discipline and school safety. *Education and Treatment of Children, 24*(4), 495–511.

Steiner, A. M. (2010). A strength-based approach to parent education for children with autism. *Journal of Positive Behavior Interventions, 13*(3), 178–190.

Stern, D., Dayton, C., & Raby, M. (1992). *Career academies: Partnerships for reconstructing American high schools.* San Francisco, CA: Jossey-Bass.

Stipek, D., & Seal, D. (2001). *Motivated minds: Raising children to love learning.* New York, NY: Owl Books.

Suldo, S. M., & Shaffer, E. J. (2008). Looking beyond psychopathology: The dual-factor model of mental health in youth. *School Psychology Review, 37*(1), 52–68.

Theokas, C., Almerigi, J. B., Lerner, R. M., Dowling, E. M., Benson, P. L., Scales, P. C., & von Eye, A. (2005). Conceptualizing and modeling individual and ecological asset components of thriving in early adolescence. *The Journal of Early Adolescence, 25*(1), 113–143.

Thomson, K. C., Schonert-Reichl, K. A., & Oberle, E. (2015). Optimism in early adolescence: Relations to individual characteristics and ecological assets in families, schools, and neighborhoods. *Journal of Happiness Studies, 16*(4), 889–913.

Tucker, C., & Herman, K. (2002). Using culturally sensitive theories and research to meet the academic needs of low-income African American children. *American Psychologist, 57,* 762–773.

VanderVen, K. (2008). *Promoting positive development in early childhood: An ecological framework.* New York, NY: Springer.

VIA Survey. (n.d.). Retrieved May 17, 2018, from http://www.viacharacter.org/www/Character-Strengths-Survey

Walsh, M., Galassi, J., Murphy, J., & Park-Taylor, J. (2002). A conceptual framework for counseling psychologists in the schools. *The Counseling Psychologist, 30,* 682–704.

Watson, M. (2006). Long-term effects of moral/character education in elementary school: In pursuit of mechanisms. *Journal of Research in Character Education, 4*(1/2), 1–18.

11

Ecological School Counseling

H. GEORGE MCMAHON AND E. C. M. MASON

REFLECTION MOMENT

Picture yourself as a middle school counselor. During summer planning sessions, as all the teachers are busy putting the final touches on their classrooms, you are reviewing the school achievement data from the previous year. You notice that African American males are being cited for discipline infractions, including both in-school and out-of-school suspension, at much higher rates than other student groups. As you look further, you notice this trend has been consistent for at least that last 3 years. What do you think might be contributing to the discipline disproportionality? What can you do to address this issue?

Our K-12 system largely still adheres to the century-old, industrial-age factory model of education. A century ago, maybe it made sense to adopt seat-time requirements for graduation and pay teachers based on their educational credentials and seniority. . . . But the factory model of education is the wrong model for the 21st century.

—FORMER U.S. SECRETARY OF EDUCATION ARNE DUNCAN (2010)

The American educational system is in need of a paradigm shift from a rigid, mechanical model to a flexible, organic approach to better meet the needs of all students, and school counselors will need to be part of that process (McMahon, Mason, Daluga-Guenther, & Ruiz, 2014). Leadership, advocacy, collaboration, and systemic change are part of school counselors' training, and indeed the counselor's professional identity (Mason, Ockerman, & Chen-Hayes, 2013). School counselors have a unique skill set that enables them to articulate and to advocate for innovative visions of education, as well as specific strategies for helping all students be successful (McMahon et al., 2014). In fact, recent efforts to transform school counseling practice (e.g., Transforming School Counseling

Initiative, ASCA National Model) have led to a new vision of school counseling that asks school counselors to use leadership and advocacy skills to help all students succeed (Amatea & West-Olatunji, 2007; Mason & McMahon, 2009; Mason, Ockerman, & Chen-Hayes, 2013; Singh, Urbano, Haston, & McMahan, 2010) and to use data to assess and address systemic inequities leading to achievement gaps (Holcomb-McCoy, 2007). In order to meet these goals, school counselors are expected to work more systemically (Dahir & Stone, 2009) and to collaborate with other educators as well as with family and community members to promote student success (Bryan & Henry, 2012).

Working and thinking systemically are articulated by the definition of school counseling offered by The Education Trust in 2009: "School counseling is a profession that focuses on the relations and interactions between students and their school environment to reduce the effects of environmental and institutional barriers that impede student academic success" (para. 3). This definition represents a movement toward a more ecological approach. Although an ecological perspective has been used as a foundation for practice in a variety of other helping professions (Conyne & Cook, 2004; Sallis, Owen, & Fisher, 2008; Sheridan & Gutkin, 2000; Unger, 2002), it has not been used as an intentional or systemic theoretical approach for school counselors until very recently (McMahon et al., 2014).

WHAT IS ECOLOGICAL SCHOOL COUNSELING?

Ecological school counseling (ESC) is a paradigm that conceptualizes schools as ecosystems, operating under systemic principles such as interactional causality, interconnectedness, and dynamic balance. The role of the school counselor is to understand and to work with students within and across their multiple ecosystems (e.g., families, peer groups, classrooms, neighborhoods) as well as to create healthier systems in which students can learn and grow. School counselors working from this perspective (ecological school counselors) are focused on helping students develop the awareness and skills to be successful in a variety of their ecosystems, including school, and advocating for systemic change on behalf of, and with, students. In order to meet this goal, ecological school counselors must work directly with students as well as collaborate with stakeholders across ecosystems. In articulating the model of ecological school counseling, McMahon et al. (2014) identified four primary functions of ecological school counselors:

1. Ecological school counselors understand their students within their multiple and unique contexts. Ecological school counselors must work to develop what Cook and Conyne (2004) described as "ecological empathy"; that is, a complex and contextualized understanding of

students, their experiences, their situation, their cultural backgrounds, and their values—including intragroup differences. In addition, ecological school counselors must understand that sometimes the values and messages within groups contradict one another and how such mixed messages can affect a student. For instance, what is the experience of a student who has to interpret and manage potentially contradictory messages from teachers, counselors, parents, and friends about the importance of college?

2. Ecological school counselors work directly with their students from an ecological perspective. Working with students from an ecological perspective means working with students directly, educating them about the multiple systems in which they live, and providing them with the necessary tools to work within systems, as well as advocating for their needs.

3. Ecological school counselors employ repeated cycles of multilevel assessment and multilevel interventions. Seeking to understand a variety of factors contributing to a problem and attempting to address those factors across several tiers of influence are crucial to promoting student success. Therefore, working with students to develop needed skills, helping teachers create better climates for learning, working with parents to develop self-advocacy skills, and advocating for more inclusive educational policies could all be part of a multilevel intervention targeting a systemic issue.

4. Ecological school counselors create and maintain healthy schools as systems. According to ESC theory, the fit between students and their school environment is crucial to the students' ultimate success. Therefore, ecological school counselors must help ensure that the school, as a system, is healthy, balanced, and sustainable so that it can be successful in its goal of graduating students who are fully prepared to contribute in a variety of ways to the larger community (McMahon et al., 2014). Ecological school counselors can employ many of the skills identified in the ASCA National Model (American School Counselor Association, 2012), including leadership, collaboration, and advocacy, to help build a safe and welcoming, strengths-based culture that values a variety of contributions.

Foundations of ESC

The term *ecology* is used in a variety of academic fields, including biology, psychology, anthropology, sociology, and economics. The key to ecological thought across scientific and academic perspectives is a focus on the reciprocal and interactive exchanges between entity and physical environment, and how those exchanges influence each constituent over time (Germain & Gitterman, 1996; Saleebey, 2001). Although the term *ecological* gained popularity through the general systems theory movement (Odum, 1994) and in the environmental conservation movement (Shrader-Frechette & McCoy, 1993), the term was originally coined by the English botanist Sir Arthur Tansley in the early 20th century to describe the interdependence that plants and animals have on each other and on their physical surroundings in any natural habitat (Saleebey, 2001). What stands out about an ecological perspective, regardless of the specific content area, is the core belief that in order to fully understand an ecosystem, not only must one look at the structure of the components within a system, but also one must understand the interactive patterns between constituents that serve to promote the health of the whole (Capra, 1996).

The name most commonly associated with ecological models in psychology is Urie Bronfenbrenner. Drawing from a range of fields, such as child psychology, sociology, anthropology, and economics, Bronfenbrenner built on Kurt Lewin's (1951) ideas to formulate his theory of human development, suggesting that people do not develop in isolation, but in relationship to the many settings in which they are embedded (Bronfenbrenner, 1979). His social ecology of human development centered on understanding the multiple systems that influence human development and how those systems affect one another through transactional relationships. Bronfenbrenner defined four major types of systems arranged in concentric circles around the individual: microsystems, mesosystems, exosystems, and macrosystems. In Bronfenbrenner's conceptualization, microsystems are the closest interpersonal relations experienced by an individual in a given setting, such as a child's family (Bronfenbrenner, 1979). As a person develops and matures, their microsystems expand to include settings like school and peer groups. Mesosystems are the interactive relationships among the microsystems in which an individual participates, such as the relationship between a student's family and the school. Exosystems are settings that do not directly involve the individual, but that affect and are affected by the individual's microsystems. Examples include parents' work environments and peer networks, peers' relationships with their parents, siblings' peer groups, and local school board activities. Finally, macrosystems are the broader social forces that have a pervasive impact on the three lower-order systems, including laws, political systems, social and economic conditions, and cultural values.

An application of Bronfenbrenner's model that is particularly interesting comes from the field of public health. In 1980, Rudolph Moos used Bronfenbrenner's ideas as a foundation of his social-ecological model health-related behavior. Grounded in the idea that health behavior is shaped across multiple levels of influence (e.g., intrapersonal, interpersonal, institutional, community, and public policy; McLeroy et al., 1988), this perspective led to a new approach to large-scale behavior change that included multilevel assessment and multilevel intervention as the new gold standard of practice (Sallis, Owen, & Fisher, 2008). Although outside of the fields of psychology and education, this public health model is relevant to school counseling because it is increasingly common that school counselors are asked not just to help individuals change their behavior, but to instigate large-scale behavior change throughout a system.

ECOLOGICAL COUNSELING

To date, the most thorough example of applying a comprehensive ecological perspective to counseling is found in Conyne and Cook's model of ecological counseling (2004). Counseling is seen as "contextualized help-giving that is dependent on the meaning clients derive from their environmental interaction" (Conyne & Cook, 2004, p. 6). The goal of ecological counseling is to promote the client's full interdependence and cooperation with the ecological climate. This approach builds on previous work by Conyne and Clack (1981), which asserted the importance of understanding the role of the ecological climate in behavior. The ecological climate is seen as the medium through which individuals both create and experience their world (Cook, 2012). Thus, behavior cannot be understood as separate from the client's environment, nor can the client's environment be perceived as a static or impotent background within which actions are taking place (Conyne & Clack, 1981; Cook, 2012). Conyne and Cook's ecological counseling model is built on concepts from Lewin and Bronfenbrenner, but it also integrates a social constructivist perspective into its theoretical approach. Specifically, Conyne and Cook's ecological counseling model states that whatever happens during clients' interactions with their environments is subject to the clients' interpretations of the ongoing process of interaction.

Epistemological Foundations of ESC

ESC draws from a variety of scientific and applied practice fields. Although each of the models has different origins, one of the tenets they share is a focus on holism. That is, the models all hold that, to fully understand an entity (e.g., organism, client, student), one must understand it within its larger context. This is in opposition to a reductionist approach, which contends that one can know an entity by breaking it down and evaluating its parts.

Similar to holism, systems thinking has heavily influenced ESC, particularly in the fundamental belief in interactive causality and interdependence of components within and across systems. Finally, ESC also draws from postmodern thought, particularly in the understanding that individual meaning is constructed through social interactions and can also be either maintained or changed through them. Synthesizing these epistemological foundations is important for the school counselor who adopts an ecological perspective. The counselor can then understand the student within the multiple contexts in which the student lives and grows (holism), remember that small change in any system can lead to significant change in another system, and understand that there is no "objective reality" about the larger system; instead, the ways in which smaller groups and individuals experience, interpret, and socially construct meaning about the system lead to multiple realities.

THE ECOLOGICAL SCHOOL COUNSELOR

Becoming an ecological school counselor often requires a paradigm shift. However, putting ESC into practice does not necessarily mean that school counselors must change the roles they play in a school or change the strategies they use. In fact, many of the trends within school counseling (e.g., collaboration, advocacy, and leadership) are necessary to ESC. Ecological school counselors can easily adopt the ASCA National Model or similar scaffolds for comprehensive counseling programs. What is different is the way in which ecological school counselors understand their students and the attention they give to change at the systemic level as well as the individual level. Below are some core assumptions that an ecological school counselor would adopt. After each assumption is described, we discuss how the assumptions might inform the important tasks that an ecological school counselor would focus on within a school.

REFLECTION MOMENT

Think back to your experiences in elementary school. What systems were you a part of that influenced your learning and growth? Family? Friends? Classroom? Faith-based groups? Sports teams? Other activities? How did those groups change as you entered middle school? Did some become more or less influential? How did things change as you entered high school? Were there times when the messages you were receiving from one group about what you should do and what you should prioritize contradicted the messages you received from another group? How did you manage those conflicting messages across those spheres of influence?

Assumptions of ESC

ESC is grounded in several academic and scientific disciplines, including ecology, systems theories, psychology, counseling, and public health. Core principles are borrowed from each of these fields to create the under-lying assumptions of ESC, first articulated by McMahon, Mason, Daluga-Guenther, and Ruiz (2014). A primary assumption is that schools are, in fact, ecosystems. If this is true, then the following seven assumptions must also be true.

Schools are part of an interconnected web of subsystems and suprasystems. Schools are systems in and of themselves, with boundaries that help identify what and who is within and outside of the school. However, schools are also nested within larger systems, such as neighborhoods, school feeder patterns, districts, counties, and states. Schools are their own entities, but they are clearly affected by what happens in those larger systems. Similarly, schools are made up of smaller subsystems, each of which operates by its own norms to some degree. Grade levels, classrooms, teaching teams, sports teams, and administrators all represent some of the more official subsystems that make up a school. Some subsystems are more organic, however, such as student cliques. Although not a formal part of the school structure, these subsystems also affect, and are affected by, changes in the larger systems.

Healthy, well-functioning schools are dynamic, balanced, and flexible. Like most systems, schools strive to maintain balance and relative order in the midst of constant change. Students graduate, new students matriculate, faculties turn over, and districts are redrawn. Healthy schools manage these changes by having semipermeable boundaries that accept and work with the "new," whether it is information, trends, or students, while maintaining a strong enough boundary to remain fairly constant in terms of values, goals, and affiliation. Schools that struggle with change, like families that struggle with change, often do so because their boundaries are either too permeable or too rigid. Schools with permeable boundaries may lose identity too quickly with any change in the larger system, and students may not feel as affiliated with, or connected to, the school and just "come and go" as visitors, rather than belonging as students. On the other side, rigid schools may resist all new infor-mation in a struggle to defy any change, leaving the school more and more iso-lated from the world outside, often leaving students with a feeling that school is irrelevant to their lives.

Diversity within school systems is necessary and adaptive. Change is the one constant across ecosystems. In order for a system to remain balanced in the midst of change, it must have diversity of people, ideas, and experiences inclusive of multiple characteristics, including sociocultural traits like eth-nicity and language as well as more fundamental aspects like talents and interests. This is true at the student level as well as the faculty, administra-tion, and parent levels. This diversity, at its core, is about resilience. In order to meet emerging challenges, schools must have a diverse pool of workers and students who can take on emerging roles or quickly adapt to new tasks and expectations. A more homogeneous system may be well suited to produce a certain type of graduate who is successful at one thing, but as the larger context shifts, the more rigid schools will not be able to quickly adapt to emerging needs.

Everyone contributes. In any healthy, balanced system, the constituents are active and all have a role. The overall health of the system, in fact, is reliant upon a wide range of meaningful contributions from all participants. Just as the diversity of the members is adaptive, it is important that there is diversity among the contributions students and others make to the school. This may contrast with the norms of many current schools in the United States, where a few contributions (e.g., academic achievement, athletic ability) are given far more value than many other contributions (e.g., peer leadership, artistic accomplishments). From an ecological perspective, it is important both that the system provide opportunities for a wide range of contributions and that those contributions be truly valued by the system. This notion of meaningful contribution is strikingly similar to other concepts common in counseling, such as Adler's sense of belonging and social interest (see Dreikurs, 1971). Meaningful contribution promotes both the health of individuals, by providing a purpose and a role to play within the school, and the health of the system, by ensuring a wide range of diverse skills and expertise that can help the system address emerging disruptions.

Schools use feedback to identify and address emerging issues. Information about how well a school is functioning is readily available if the school is able to interpret it productively. Much of the data collected by, or made available to, schools, although often seen as achievement or achievement-related data, can be viewed as feedback about the health of the school. Schools often look at low attendance, low graduation rates, high retention rates, and high discipline referrals as problems that need to be fixed. From an ecological perspective, however, these data are feedback or "signals" that the system is struggling in some way. Often, in fact, this feedback is actually an attempted solution to a problem. A student's staying home from school can be understood as an attempt at a solution to a problem that is present but not identified (e.g., the student is being bullied, or the student is quickly losing self-confidence, or the student feels that he can be more helpful to his family at home than at school).

Meaning is both constructed and experienced within schools and their subsystems. Grounded in the idea of social constructivism, this assumption posits that people are meaning-making creatures, built to make sense of the world and their place in it (Cook, 2012). The meaning-making function is vital to human experience (Hayes & Oppenheim, 1997) and is a crucial part of our well-being (Cook, 2012). Conyne and Cook (2004) promoted the idea that in Lewin's (1938) formula $B = f(p \times e)$ [*Behavior is a function of the interaction between a person (p) and the person's environment (e)*], the × refers not only to the interaction of the person with their environment, but also to the meaning the individual makes out of that interaction. The meaning-making function plays out in schools in two important ways. First, students, as well other stakeholders, interpret the meaning of school as an institution in their lives. Is it a valuable endeavor on its own merit? Is it an investment in one's future? Is it a requirement that is mostly meaningless but needs to be done to move on in life? Is it irrelevant, or even a distraction from what matters most? According to Hayes and Oppenheim (1997), the process of interpreting what it means to be part of a school and the central purpose of the school at any given point in time is occurring within various subsystems simultaneously, and the more congruent the individual interpretations are with the actions of the system, the more balanced a system will be. Although diversity of ideas, experiences, perspectives, and skills is important in creating a healthy system that utilizes and values a variety of assets, the more consensus there is on what the fundamental purpose of the school is (e.g., to create a community where students can learn and prepare for postsecondary life) across members of the system, the more effective the system can be in fulfilling that purpose.

Second, the school and its constituent subsystems are constantly interpreting feedback and updating their interpretation of the school. This feedback is both formal (e.g., achievement data, test scores, and graduation rates) and informal (e.g., narratives that graduates maintain about the school and the reputation of the school in the community). Educators spend a great deal of energy worrying about what outcome data say about their school, yet from an ecological perspective, it's the interpretation of, and the school's response to, the data that says far more than the data. The data are used to validate previously held beliefs about the school, and in some cases, to challenge these beliefs and the role that school is thought to play in students' lives. For example, a decline in college-attendance rates of seniors might have a negative interpretation. However, stronger efforts by military branches to recruit more women, for example, might account for this change. If the community at large supports students going into the military, this might create less upset in the system.

Healthy schools are sustainable. One of the core features of ecosystems in nature is that they seek sustainability. Sustainable systems are very efficient, with all components contributing and the system as a whole producing very little waste. In schools, this would mean that a healthy school would have a reciprocal, symbiotic relationship with the larger community, so that the school graduates students who will contribute to the larger community and produce and nurture the next generation of healthy students, sustaining both systems. Going a little deeper, this changes the goal of school from producing graduates to preparing students to actively contribute to the larger community in meaningful ways. Communities, as ecosystems, are diverse, thus graduates must be prepared to contribute in myriad ways, from working in local industry to innovation and entrepreneurship, from building and maintaining infrastructure to creating beauty and powerful art, and from performing civic duties to raising the next generation of families. Rather than graduating a single type of student, schools are charged to help all students develop their unique abilities and to encourage them to pursue their goals so that they will be ready to perform a wide array of functions upon graduation, helping to sustain a healthy community.

PROMOTING ECOLOGICAL CHANGE IN SCHOOLS

Change is a complex phenomenon, and the ecological perspective is a complex approach. There is no standard formula to determine a change strategy, no "if x, then y" in ESC. Rather, an ecological school counselor is constantly assessing—formally and informally—how students are doing in relation to other students and within the larger ecosystems in a school (classroom, social networks, etc.), and how the school as a system is doing in relation to the larger community context. Once an accurate assessment is initiated, an ecological school counselor may use several strategies to promote change, many of which are very familiar to school counselors (e.g., individual counseling, group counseling, classroom lessons, teacher consultation, collaboration, advocacy, etc.). Specific intervention strategies are available, but first it is important to discuss in more detail the accurate assessment of factors contributing to the identified issue.

Assessment of Contributing Factors Across Systems and Levels

For school counselors adopting an ecological perspective, understanding students within their multiple and unique environments, and how their experiences in each arena may manifest in school behavior is a crucial part of the counseling process. Building on both Bronfenbrenner's systems model (1979) and McLeroy et al.'s (1988) reconceptualization of his model, school counselors must understand and empathize with their students from multiple contextual perspectives, taking into account intrapersonal variables (e.g., learning style, personality variables), interpersonal/primary group variables (e.g., cultural upbringing, family dynamics, peer interactions), school variables (e.g., class structure, teaching style), community variables (e.g., neighborhood composition, access to resources, cultural norms of larger community), and public policy variables (e.g., school board policy, changes in funding/support related to political shifts).

Understand student eco-webs. Ecological school counselors are constantly monitoring how students are doing across the multiple systems. Ecological school counselors understand that there are multiple factors across levels that may contribute to—or impede—student learning. To further compound the process, these factors not only affect student learning but also affect each other. To illustrate this concept, an eco-web depicts many factors across systems that may affect student success (or any similar variable), as well as the relationship that the factors have to each other. A fairly simple eco-web created by practicing school counselors in an ESC training is portrayed in Figure 11.1. (For more information on creating eco-webs, see Williams, McMahon, & Goodman, 2015.)

When using eco-webs, it is often useful to sort the factors across systems or levels. For instance, influences can be identified and sorted across intrapersonal factors (e.g., specific learning needs, cognitive abilities, confidence), interpersonal/primary group factors (e.g., parent expectations, cultural values and perspectives, peer group influences), institutional factors (e.g., school resources, teacher quality, school policy), community factors (e.g., access to resources, safety, extracurricular opportunities), and public policy (e.g., political climate,

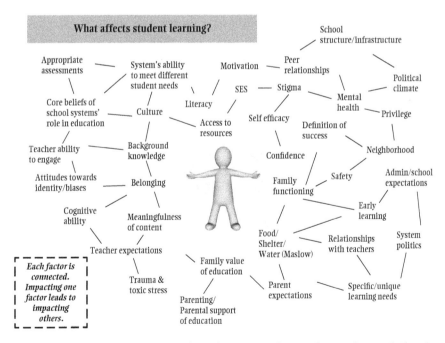

Figure 11.1. Eco-web created by Ariel Gordon, Sam Hicks, Heathery Jarboe, and Cheryl Sewell during a workshop led by George McMahon. Used with permission.

laws affecting personal freedoms, policy regarding treatment of marginalized populations).

Identifying and understanding these systemic factors requires knowledge, awareness, and assessment across multiple levels. For example, intrapersonal factors, such as learning styles, abilities and disabilities, motivation, self-efficacy, and goals, are part of the interaction. So, too, are interpersonal factors, such as the influence of peer groups, family expectations, teacher relationships, and larger family factors, including SES, family structure and dynamics, and educational level/experience. Having both a broad understanding of cultural and power dynamics as well as a deep understanding of cultural perspectives of the particular student population is paramount. Factors existing in the student's larger context, including exposure to violence, abuse, and trauma, or environmental hazards, larger sociopolitical and macro-environmental forces, such as political attitudes, the economy, and even natural disasters, can all affect student learning.

A common reaction school counselors have to the eco-map is to feel overwhelmed, as there appear to be so many potential barriers to student success that no one can address them all. It is useful to remember, however, that because all of the factors interact with each other, the goal is not to find "the cause," it is to look for practical, realistic places to intervene. Furthermore, starting in multiple places simultaneously may be useful. For example, a school counselor might begin by gathering data from students with a shared experience, such as those receiving disciplinary measures in the scenario described at the beginning of the chapter, while also examining the school's discipline policy to determine if there is a practice that accounts for the disproportionality.

Assessing student/environment "fit." Another important concept in assessment is the idea of student/environment "fit." Remember that, from an ecological perspective, it is not just the multisystemic factors themselves, but the relationship among those larger systemic factors and the individual that is fundamental (Conyne & Cook, 2004). Thus, when working with a student who is struggling to be successful in school, an ecological school counselor may ask, "How do the expectations of the school fit with the student's abilities, culture, circumstances or worldview?" As an example, consider the diverse neighborhoods in which many public schools are embedded. Public schools have become a hub of intersecting cultures within communities—often the place within a given neighborhood where people from different cultural backgrounds and perspectives interact more than any other. Although schools can be very culturally diverse in terms of their students and families, public schools themselves usually have a very Eurocentric perspective, and the core values that underlie the process and goals of education are still overwhelmingly Western. Preschool-12 schools in the United States tend to value achievement over process, individual responsibility over group work, hierarchical over collective learning, receiving information over generating knowledge, and standardization over creativity—all values consistent with a historically white, North American culture. While there is nothing inherently wrong with any of those values in and of themselves, they are not universal values, and thus may not be a good fit with the values or behavioral norms for any given student or family. A student who comes from a collectivist culture that values cooperative learning over individual work, for instance, might struggle with the idea that at school individual achievement is prized over group productivity, or the student may feel uncomfortable being recognized for individual success.

REFLECTION MOMENT

Consider your own experiences in K-12 education. Can you recall a time in which you or someone you knew had an experience of not fitting in? How might this experience have been true for others like you or someone you knew? What elements in the school system were indications of this lack of fit? What data could have been collected to demonstrate this lack of fit as a means of helping to address it?

Reframing "problem" to "feedback." Although the concept of feedback comes from general systems theory (Hanson, 2014), it has been widely used as a key variable in family therapy (Dallos & Draper, 2010). The general idea of feedback is that it is a signal that the system is out of balance or otherwise not functioning properly. In fact, what many schools see as "problems" to be addressed (e.g., test scores, graduation rates, attendance, or discipline referrals, to name a few) can be conceptualized as feedback. That is, test scores are feedback about how much/what students are learning, and if used properly, can inform changes in teaching strategies and/or curricula. From a linear perspective, however, too often this feedback is used only as the final evaluation. This becomes a lost opportunity, and the focus often becomes how to get the final evaluation schools want rather than to use the feedback to better understand and address deeper systemic issues. As an example, consider that for many schools experiencing low attendance, the typical reaction (and one consistent with an industrial perspective) is to implement interventions like incentive programs (e.g., class with the highest attendance rate gets an ice cream party), punishment (students who miss more than X days cannot participate in special events), or psychoeducation (a group for students who miss more than 10 days during a grading period that teaches the value of school and the importance of attending school on their future). However, by taking time to understand the experiences of those who are not attending, educators may discover the larger issues contributing the low attendance. Concerns about bullying, transportation challenges, medical issues, student beliefs about the relevance of school, family needs, fear of a government agency (e.g., family and children services, immigration, etc.), a low sense of belongingness, lack of hope, or any combination of these could be present, and not attending school could be an attempted solution, rather than the problem itself.

Initiating Change from an Ecological Perspective

Once a multilevel assessment is complete, and the ecological school counselor believes he or she has a sense of what the feedback is revealing, it is time to intervene. To illustrate what change might look like across various scenarios, we discuss strategies for initiating change in different systems, including the individual student, a classroom, a school, and a community. It is important to remember that change can be initiated in any system and at any level because in an interconnected web of multiple factors, there is no singular "cause," and thus no singular "right" place to initiate change. An ecological school counselor can start wherever it makes the most practical sense. Taking into account factors like access to resources, social capital, political leverage, and return on investment becomes important.

Outlined below are potential strategies for initiating change across levels. To help make these ideas more tangible, the scenario presented at the beginning of the chapter is repeated here for easy access.

> REFLECTION MOMENT REVISITED
>
> *Picture yourself as a middle school counselor. During summer planning sessions, as all the teachers are busy putting the final touches on their classrooms, you are reviewing the school achievement data from the previous year. You notice that African American males are being cited for discipline infractions, including both in-school and out of school suspension, at much higher rates than other student groups. As you look further, you notice this trend has been consistent for at least last 3 years.*

When a school counselor is working with a student in individual counseling, crisis counseling, or student advisement, it is imperative that ecological school counselors invest time to understand the student within the multiple contexts in which students live and learn in order to accurately identify factors that may be contributing to the presenting challenge. Remember that, from an ecological perspective, the student does not "have" the problem, but neither does the problem solely exist in the environment. Most often, both the struggle and the eventual solution exist in the dynamics between the student and the environment(s). Therefore, any intervention, whether remedial, preventative, or goal-directed, is about promoting student fit. Rather than "fixing" the student, ecological school counselors focus on helping students meet their goals within multiple contexts and on supporting them in addressing the challenges that may exist across those contexts.

Intrapersonal change. Intrapersonal change comes from developing the students' insight into the system through deconstructing system norms, expectations, and values, and then from helping students to develop the agency to work more effectively within the system to meet their goals. As a first step in working with students individually, ecological school counselors can help build their students' awareness of the contextual challenges to meeting their goals and can demystify the "rules of the game" (e.g., build critical consciousness and deconstruct systemic power dynamics). Although highlighting systemic challenges to students may seem counterintuitive to some, research has shown that self-efficacy can be enhanced when students develop the critical awareness of societal inequities and understand these challenges as systemic rather than intrapersonal (Diemer & Blustein, 2005). For example, ecological school counselors can help students understand potential systemic forces at play by encouraging them to examine data. While school and district staff and board personnel may analyze data to understand trends in student achievement and behavior, students themselves are likely to be aware of only their own individual data (e.g., grades, GPA, attendance, etc.). An ecological school counselor sharing aggregate data (e.g., schoolwide attendance records, discipline trends, etc.) with students and asking them how they might make sense of it, empowers a process for understanding outcomes from a systemic rather than individual perspective.

As students become more aware of the expectations and cultural norms, ecological school counselors can help students to develop new skills and build the social capital needed in order to more effectively navigate the system. Counselors and students should simultaneously be working together to change the system in order to make it more appropriate and welcoming for all students. This can be done through advocacy as well as through building self-advocacy competencies within the student. As an example, when the second author of this chapter was a new school counselor, she was approached by a group of female students in her middle school about starting a step (dance) team. These particular students did not fit in with the two primary athletic activities in the school, basketball and cheerleading, but they wanted to contribute to school spirit in their own way. They asked if the counselor would sponsor the team; although the counselor agreed to be the sponsor, she gave the students the task of finding out what school policies and people needed to be consulted in order to begin their endeavor. Based on their investigation, the students pitched a proposal to the principal and some active members of the parent association to gain approval and start-up funds. Ultimately, approval was granted and they founded the school's first step team, which ran successfully for many years.

Change in children. Developmentally, the theory of change for children in ESC means the school counselor recognizes that there is a need to help children to understand the systems in which they live. Thus, for children, change comes through experiences that broaden their understanding of the systems in their own world and how they interact with one another. The school counselor may serve as a guide through this process and help students at this age to gain exposure and work through the cognitive and emotional processes (e.g., self-awareness, insight, cognitive restructuring, etc.) that accompany understanding new experiences. In essence, the school counselor's work is to help children to learn the nature of ecology and the interaction of systems as it applies to their own lives.

To apply a more common individual theory, the ecological school counselor may draw on the tenets of Adlerian theory. Young students' sense of belonging and contributing (or not-belonging and not-contributing) is important feedback for ecological school counselors as they assess the health of the school. Ecological school counselors will look for opportunities to enhance students' opportunities to contribute and their sense of belonging—not just for individual students, but for groups of students as well. Promoting agency and belonging might take the form of classroom lessons on social-emotional concepts like fairness, responsibility, goal setting, respect for diversity, self-advocacy, and caring, or might include establishing and training a group of students who serve as school ambassadors for new students or school visitors. It may also include working at the systemic level to develop more opportunities for students to utilize their talents and interests to contribute to the well-being of the school. Creating a culture where a variety of achievements (e.g., arts, technology, community service) are appreciated could go a long way to improve school climate and increase school engagement.

Sample Dialogue

COUNSELOR: Laquita, you seem to be upset about something. What happened in the classroom just now? Maybe we can problem-solve together.

LAQUITA: The teacher asked Maven to be the line leader to lunch again today. She already did it last week, too, and she wasn't even here every day!

COUNSELOR: I see. You're upset that Maven was asked and you were not, and that she's had more than one opportunity to be line leader. Is there anything else going on that would help me understand?

LAQUITA: My mom doesn't let me do anything at home. She says I'm not old enough and my sister gets to help with everything because she's oldest. I only get to feed the dog and take him out. I'm tired of being the baby!

COUNSELOR: It seems like you want to have some responsibility in the classroom. You seem to notice when your classmates are absent. What would you think about volunteering to help take attendance next week? Perhaps your teacher might like some help with that, since she's filling in and still learning your names.

Change in adolescents. When the ESC theory of change is extended to adolescents, and Adlerian principles are again used to conceptualize individual change, it becomes clear that developing a personal identity and building social interest are core goals for healthy student development. Adolescents will have more abstract thinking patterns and will be more interested in, and attuned to, concepts that are essential to healthy systems functioning, such as diversity, feedback, equilibrium, and boundaries. Ecological school counselors working with adolescents can help students go beyond their understanding of the contexts of their own immediate systems, help them think about more distal systems, and encourage them to begin to take action to create change. This work fits well with adolescents' developing sense of justice and promotes individual agency through building their sense of social interest. Adolescents care deeply about fairness and equity, and thus they have the cognitive structures to observe incongruities between how systems claim to operate and how they actually operate. Similarly, adolescents may be more receptive to feedback within systems and may be compelled to challenge it or act on it. The ecological school counselor working with adolescents needs to be conscious of opportunities to nurture this more sophisticated sense of agency and to help students develop into advocates who are wise to the dynamics of the systems within a global world. Teaching self-advocacy and social justice might take the form of establishing a buddy program in which general education students assist students with severe disabilities during parts of the school day, sponsoring an after-school club that organizes recycling or beautification efforts in the community, or presenting classroom lessons in which a classroom from another part of the world is video-conferenced in for discussion on a global topic.

Sample Dialogue

COUNSELOR: Hey Michael, just checking in with you. Your history teacher says you've been "acting up" in class recently. Just wondering what's going on and if I can help.

STUDENT: Yeah, some of my friends in class are buggin' me. They've been making jokes about Juan, and I've been trying to get them to stop. He has

CP just like my cousin. My friends don't seem to get that Juan is really smart even though he is in a wheelchair. I'm so tired of putting up with them. They just don't get it.

COUNSELOR: Seems like this is really bothering you and you are trying to stand up for Juan. If you came up with an idea for how to increase your friends' understanding of CP, and to get to know Juan, I might be able to help you pull it off. What ideas do you have?

STUDENT: Maybe if they just spent time with him outside of class it would help, like playing cards or something. I play cards with my cousin and just hang out. I could show them how. Juan isn't the only one, though. I think we need some sort of club or group in the school so kids like Juan can socialize more. Would you help me with that?

APPLICATION

Referring back to the scenario about discipline disproportionality, how might you work directly with students who have received multiple discipline notices? What knowledge might they benefit from? What systemic dynamics (e.g., school/district policies, historical practices, cultural values, etc.) could you deconstruct that may be helpful? What skills could they benefit from developing? How might you empower them through the process of examining aggregate data about disciplinary referrals?

Interpersonal change. An ecological school counselor working to promote interpersonal change is concerned with the relationships that exist in the school, both within systems (e.g., peer relationships) and between systems (e.g., between teachers and students). A key piece of affecting interpersonal change is developing "ecological empathy" (Conyne & Cook, 2004), or a contextualized understanding of an individual within their multiple contexts, and appreciation for how those roles and identities may play out in other relationships.

For example, consider a student who repeatedly comes to school late, missing part of the first-period class. If her teacher interprets her repeated tardiness as a lack of commitment to her education or a lack of respect, the teacher would likely be disappointed and even angry. Without further inquiry, this could lead to an adversarial relationship between the teacher and student. However, if the teacher were to ask the student about what led to her tardiness, the teacher might find out that the student is the eldest sibling in a single-parent home and is often in charge of getting younger siblings to school, which starts later than the high school. Even if the teacher could not excuse the tardiness for this reason, it is far more likely the interpersonal relationship between the student and the teacher would become more collaborative, thus leading to the student's getting the help she needs to be successful.

School counselors can help to build these more empathic and collaborative relationships within a school by advocating for the students or teaching students self-advocacy skills. Through individual sessions, role plays, or small groups, school counselors can coach students on how to talk to teachers when personal issues arise, attending to such skills as the best time to approach teachers, how to read their nonverbal language for ideal opportunities, and practicing how and what to say. Staff and parent consultations with the school counselor are another way to broker these relationships. On behalf of students, or even with them present if they agree, school counselors can consult with teachers to increase awareness and empathy regarding individual student situations. In addition, providing professional development, developing mentoring programs, teaching nonviolent communication skills, and developing empathy skills in students through the school counseling curriculum could all help to create positive interpersonal change.

APPLICATION

Thinking back to the disproportionate discipline scenario, what role might interpersonal relationships play in addressing the disproportionality? What are some strategies ecological school counselors could use to help strengthen the "ecological empathy" that teachers (and counselors) can have for their students? How could ecological school counselors help strengthen interpersonal relationships between teachers and students? How could a school counselor address interpersonal relationships in multiple ways for the benefit of students?

Change in schools. Recent trends within the profession have led to school counselors' being asked to work more systemically (Dahir & Stone, 2009), to use data to identify and address schoolwide inequities (Holcomb-McCoy, 2007), and to utilize leadership and advocacy skills to serve all students (Amatea & West-Olatunji, 2007; Mason & McMahon, 2009). This shift fits well with the ecological model, as it focuses on creating change within the school culture in order to better serve all students. In particular, using schoolwide data to highlight achievement and opportunity gaps is a crucial step in identifying needs. However, it is important to remember that the data must be seen as feedback or a signal, rather than as the problem itself. For an ecological school counselor to design and lead schoolwide intervention strategies, an in-depth understanding of the systemic factors is crucial.

Consider the common example of administrators who want to reduce bullying in a school. Administrators may look at discipline data, including suspensions, but they may also consider data from school climate assessment or even data on student or parent perceptions of school safety. Many schools would likely utilize the data by trying to identify and work with those identified as bullies and to address the problem through the discipline system. Viewing the data as evidence of an imbalance within the system, however, would lead an ecological school counselor to become curious about the multiple factors that contribute to the situation. Therefore, interventions at the systemic level could include presenting data to administrators, policymakers, and other stakeholders to raise awareness of contributing factors (areas of the school where bullying tends to take place; victims who identify as LGBTQ, have disabilities, or belong to other targeted groups; school or district policy that may be exacerbating the issue) or providing professional development opportunities for teachers and/or administrators. Whatever the intervention, it is clear that this is where the advocacy, leadership, and systemic change skills highlighted in the ASCA National Model (ASCA, 2012) become essential.

APPLICATION

Thinking back to the example of discipline disproportionality, what are some of the school-level factors that might be explored to get a clearer picture of the issue? What policy factors might be playing a role in the situation? What historical norms may be contributing? How might you exercise your leadership skills and identity to promote change at a school level?

Change in communities. School counselors working from an ecological perspective understand the school as a system, but they also understand that the school itself is embedded within a larger community, and that the school and the community are interconnected. A healthy community can provide valuable resources to help promote a healthy school. Likewise, a healthy school system prepares individuals to contribute to the health of the community in myriad ways. Therefore, an ecological school counselor cannot limit his or her focus to what goes on in the building. Helping to strengthen the community, and in particular the relationship between the school and the community, becomes a vital part of the school counselors' job. For example, the second author received several displaced students at her school in the aftermath of Hurricane Katrina in 2005. After assessing the particular needs of this population, the counselor worked with the school social worker and several community agencies and churches to provide clothing, school supplies, and household items to the students and their families. During the holidays, she obtained a grant through the local rotary club and was able to provide each family with a gift card. Other examples of actions that school counselors can take to promote healthy communities include advocating for extracurricular activities for youth in the community, collaborating with community workforce development agencies, partnering with law enforcement agencies, and working with community groups to support viable business infrastructure initiatives.

Fortunately, the ASCA model includes components like advisory councils to help ensure that the school counseling program, as well as the school itself, remains aware of, and responsive to, the immediate and long-term needs of families and the community. Ecological school counselors, especially when they begin at a new school, can start by mapping the potential partnerships and resources in the area and touring neighborhoods to better understand the landscape of the community. In addition, there are excellent models for building collaborative relationships with communities, including Bryan and Henry's model for building school-family-community partnerships (2012). What is important in these models is a consensus that true collaboration is built on mutual understanding, focuses on mutual goals, and strives for mutual benefit. For instance, schools that take leadership roles in creating food or clothing drives to meet the needs of community members or that take on responsibility for the cleaning of a road or park in the community would demonstrate the schools' investment in the community. This type of collaboration also means that school counselors must let go of the idea that they are solely responsible for all interventions. Building relationships with partners who have diverse skills and abilities, influence within diverse communities, and access to necessary resources is a vital responsibility of ecological school counselors, and ideally these relationships will be built before the need for them emerges.

APPLICATION

Referring to the example of discipline disproportionality one last time, what are some ways in which the school counselor might collaborate with community members to raise awareness of this issue and to brainstorm strategies? What could the community provide the students, faculty, or administration that would help redefine the issue and lead to new collaborative strategies to make school discipline equitable and beneficial for all students?

CONCLUSION

Reading through the theoretical model of ESC, it probably seems like a lot to remember, and a lot of work to do. Truthfully, it is. When school counselors

Table 11.1. Ecological School Counselor Tasks

Ecological Level	Assessment	Intervention	ASCA Model Alignment
Individual	Testing (nondiagnostic), career assessment, suicide assessment, psychosocial counseling, clinical interview	Individual counseling, student planning, goal setting, crisis intervention, behavioral management, teaching self-advocacy	Delivery System, Accountability
Interpersonal/Group	Collecting and examining perception data (focus groups, student/ faculty surveys) and outcome data (school achievement, achievement gap)	Small-group services, core counseling curriculum, closing-the-gap projects, advocacy	Delivery System, Accountability
Institutional	Reviewing school improvement plans, program assessment, examining process, school counselor competencies assessment, examining school process data (opportunity gaps)	Committee, building, district, or organizational leadership; advocating for policy change on behalf of students, families, or staff; providing professional development	Foundation, Management System, Accountability
Community	Advisory boards, collecting and analyzing community perception data (focus groups, surveys), needs assessments, examining census data	Collaboration with school staff, families, and community; community social justice activism; political activism	Foundation, Management System, Accountability

Source: McMahon, Mason, Daluga-Guenther, and Ruiz (2014).

first become aware of all of the relevant contributing factors across ecosystems, and the idea that they should intervene across levels, many feel overwhelmed. The good news is that school counselors are already doing much of this work, even if it is not being conceptualized this way. Therefore, the approach is less about doing new things and learning new skills and more about streamlining and strategizing much of what school counselors already do, and focusing it on desired outcomes. Table 11.1 provides overview of what school counselors already to do assess and intervene across levels.

Interpersonally, the school counselor adapts and changes as he or she works to create change within systems. The ecological school counselor understands well that, as only one individual, he or she is not (and cannot be) the sole cause of change in a system, either for good or for bad. Rather, the counselor understands that there are multiple factors at play, and school counseling is simply one of them. The ecological school counselor's role—putting things in motion and ideally driving toward a healthier system—is a vital one.

Change itself is interdependent and recursive—as individuals within a system change, the system itself is changed. Likewise, as systems change, so do the individuals in them. The vital role of the ecological school counselor with the individual student as well as within the system is to identify the feed-back that is signaling some distress, to identify ecological factors that are likely contributing to the issue, and to initiate the change process across multiple levels to facilitate the systems' changing themselves.

SUGGESTED READINGS

Bronfenbrenner, U. (1979). *The ecology of human development: Experiments by nature and design*. Cambridge, MA: Harvard University Press.

Capra, F. (1996). *The web of life: A new scientific understanding of living systems*. New York, NY: Doubleday.

Conyne, R. K., & Clack, R. J. (1981). *Environmental assessment and design: A new tool for the applied behavioral scientist*. New York, NY: Praeger.

Conyne, R. K., & Cook, E. P. (2004). *Ecological counseling: An innovative approach to conceptualizing person-environment interaction*. Alexandria, VA: American Counseling Association.

Cook, E. P. (2012). *Understanding people in context: The ecological perspective in counseling*. Alexandria, VA: American Counseling Association.

McMahon, H. G., Mason, E. C. M., Daluga-Guenther, N., & Ruiz, A. (2014). An ecological model of professional school counseling. *Journal of Counseling and Development*, *92*, 459–471.

REFERENCES

Amatea, E., & West-Olatunji, C. A. (2007). Joining the conversation about educating our poorest children: Emerging leadership roles for school counselors in high-poverty schools. *Professional School Counseling, 11,* 81–89.

American School Counselor Association. (2012). *ASCA National Model: A framework for school counseling programs* (3rd ed.). Alexandria, VA: American School Counselor Association.

Bronfenbrenner, U. (1979). *The ecology of human development: Experiments by nature and design.* Cambridge, MA: Harvard University Press.

Bryan, J., & Henry, L. (2012). A model for building school–family–community partnerships: Principles and process. *Journal of Counseling & Development, 90*(4), 408–420.

Capra, F. (1996). *The web of life: A new scientific understanding of living systems.* New York, NY: Doubleday.

Conyne, R. K., & Clack, R. J. (1981). *Environmental assessment and design: A new tool for the applied behavioral scientist.* New York, NY: Praeger.

Conyne, R. K., & Cook, E. P. (2004). Understanding persons within environments: An introduction to ecological counseling. In R. K. Conyne & E. P. Cook (Eds.), *Ecological counseling: An innovative approach to conceptualizing person-environment interaction.* Alexandria, VA: American Counseling Association.

Cook, E. P. (2012). *Understanding people in context: The ecological perspective in counseling.* Alexandria, VA: American Counseling Association.

Dahir, C. A., & Stone, C. B. (2009). School counselor accountability: The path to social justice and systemic change. *Journal of Counseling and Development, 87,* 12–20.

Dallos, R., & Draper, R. (2010). *An introduction to family therapy: Systemic theory and practice.* Buckingham, UK: McGraw-Hill Education (UK).

Diemer, M. A., & Blustein, D. L. (2005). Critical consciousness and career development among urban youth. *Journal of Vocational Behavior, 68*(2), 220–232.

Dreikurs, R. (1971). *Social equality: The challenge of today.* Chicago, IL: Regnery.

The Education Trust. (2009). *The new vision for school counseling.* Available from http://www.edtrust.org/dc/tsc/vision

Germain, C. B., & Gitterman, A. (1996). *The life model of social work practice: Advances in theory and practice.* New York, NY: Columbia University Press.

Hanson, B. G. (2014). *General systems theory—Beginning with wholes.* Philadelphia, PA: Taylor & Francis.

Hayes, R. L., & Oppenheim, R. (1997). Constructivism: Reality is what you make it. In T. Sexton & B. Griffin (Eds.), *Constructivist thinking in counseling practice, research, and training* (pp. 19–41). New York, NY: Teachers College Press.

Holcomb-McCoy, C. C. (2007). *School counseling to close the achievement gap: A social justice framework for success.* Thousand Oaks, CA: Corwin.

Lewin, K. (1938). *Contributions to psychological theory. The conceptual representation and the measurement of psychological forces.* Durham, NC, US: Duke University Press.

Lewin, K. (1951). *Field theory in social science.* New York, NY: Harper.

Mason, E. C. M., & McMahon, H. G. (2009). Leadership practices in school counselors. *Professional School Counseling, 13,* 107–115.

Mason, E., Ockerman, M. S., & Chen-Hayes, S. F. (2013). Change-Agent-for-Equity (CAFE) model: A framework for school counselor identity. *Journal of School Counseling, 11*(4), n4.

McLeroy, K. R., Bibeau, D., Steckler, A., & Glanz, K. (1988). An ecological perspective on health promotion programs. *Health Education & Behavior, 15,* 351–377.

McMahon, H. G., Mason, E. C. M., Daluga-Guenther, N., & Ruiz, A. (2014). An ecological model of professional school counseling. *Journal of Counseling and Development, 92,* 459–471.

Moos, R. H. (1980). Social-ecological perspectives on health. In G. C. Stone, F. Cohen, & N. E. Adler (Eds.), *Health psychology: A handbook* (pp. 523–547). San Francisco, CA: Jossey-Bass.

Odum, H. T. (1994). *Ecological and general systems: An introduction to systems ecology.* Niwot, CO: University Press of Colorado.

Saleebey, D. (2001). *Human behavior and social environments: A biopsychosocial approach.* New York, NY: Columbia University Press.

Sallis, J. F, Owen, N., & Fisher, E. B. (2008). Ecological models of health behavior. In K. Glanz, B. K. Rimer, & K. Viswanath (Eds.), *Health behavior and health education: Theory, research, and practice* (4th ed., pp. 465–486). San Francisco, CA: Jossey-Bass.

Sheridan, S. M., & Gutkin, T. B. (2000). The ecology of school psychology: Examining and changing our paradigm for the 21st century. *School Psychology Review, 29,* 485–502.

Shrader-Frechette, K. S., & McCoy, E. D. (1993). *Method in ecology: Strategies for conservation.* New York, NY: Cambridge University Press

Singh, A. A., Urbano, A., Haston, M., & McMahan, E. (2010). School counselors' strategies for social justice change: A grounded theory of what works in the real world. *Professional School Counseling, 13,* 135–145.

Unger, M. (2002). A deeper, more social ecological social work practice. *Social Service Review, 76,* 480–497.

Williams, J. M., McMahon, H. G., & Goodman, R. D. (2015). Eco-webbing: A teaching strategy to facilitate critical consciousness and agency. *Counselor Education & Supervision, 54,* 82–97.

12

An Advocating Student-within-Environment Approach to School Counseling

MATTHEW E. LEMBERGER-TRUELOVE AND HANNAH BOWERS

School environments are incredibly unique and complex. Each school environment includes scores of children and adolescents who make up complex social arrangements in classrooms, playgrounds, and myriad other educational settings. Furthermore, each school includes multiple adult educators and stakeholders. The latticework that is a school environment is even more challenging given that each child and adult is bound to a variety of expectations related to learning and social interaction. Considering the uniqueness and complexity of schools, it is curious that professional school counselors have largely imported theories of practice that were developed and matured outside of the school context in particular.

While there is nothing inherently inappropriate in school counselors' adoption of classical counseling theories, it might be inferred that such theories and related practices lack the specific nuances that account for the behaviors required of a school counselor. A school counselor is obliged to provide direct services that include "activities that promote academic, career and personal/social development" (ASCA, 2012, p. 85), as delivered in individual, small-group, classroom, or large-group educational settings. Furthermore, many school counselors are encumbered with multitudinous noncounseling activities, not limited to administrative and supportive roles (Dollarhide & Lemberger, 2006). In this way, it is reasonable that a theory for school counseling must include axioms related to student learning, social support, and career construction while also proving adaptable enough to operate within formal counseling and noncounseling contexts. Additionally, such a theory must be relevant to the cultural complexities within a given school system as well as in the larger surrounding milieu.

REFLECTION MOMENT

Consider your experiences in schools. What were some unique features you witnessed? What idiosyncrasies pertaining to school environments, students, or educators might a school counselor need to consider when identifying and utilizing a counseling theory?

Advocating Student-within-Environment (ASE; Lemberger, 2010; Lemberger & Hutchison, 2014) is a theoretical perspective that was devised to assist school counselors in their support of children and adolescents in schools, particularly students who are situated in disenfranchised communities. The ASE perspective was crafted to include humanistic and social justice ideologies to guide the delivery of direct and indirect school counseling services, including individual and group counseling, guidance lessons, and consultation activities. The philosophic basis of the ASE approach proceeds from the belief that school counselors can best support the student by working with that student to maximize her or his internal capacities as they coalesce with education and social opportunities in and beyond the school environment. The best articulation of the aim of ASE can be found in the following quote:

To best prepare young children in poverty for later life challenges, professional counselors must make every attempt to improve social conditions; however, it is equally important that young children's internal capacities be strengthened either to accommodate improved social conditions or to maximize resilience in the face of persistent adversity. (Lemberger, Carbonneau, Atencio, Zieher, & Palacios, 2018)

A school counselor who employs the ASE approach as a theory for practice will help students to elicit and sharpen aptitudes that were either not fully nurtured or were generally impeded. In turn, an ASE school counselor believes that the cultivation of student resources is generative enough to thrive across a variety of learning and social challenges. The ASE approach necessitates that, as students are nurtured, any individual change must be accompanied by parallel efforts at various system levels (e.g., school, family, community). As an orientation for practice, ASE was originally established to support students who hailed from challenging economic environments. Although this orientation persists, the developers of ASE believe that the approach is germane to the challenges that confront all students, across all types of schools. In fact, the ASE approach assumes that all opportunities of living are challenging. Moreover, the ubiquity of challenges provides each individual the opportunity for deepening experiences and prosperity.

FOUNDATION AND EPISTEMOLOGY OF ASE

Given the educational mission of elementary, middle, and secondary schools, school counseling theories must include axioms that are equal parts educational, therapeutic, and socially responsive. As such, the developers of the ASE perspective suggest that school counselors employ operations from contemporary learning and developmental sciences that are germane to the needs of students in difficult social and school environments. Such operations embolden the student to be self-reflective and self-directive in learning and social behaviors, thereby increasing the likelihood that the schooling experience will be personally meaningful and transformative to the student even beyond the classroom.

A basic philosophical supposition of the ASE approach is that each student is her or his own best resource, even in turbulent learning and social environments. Correspondingly, ASE theory deviates from counseling approaches that prioritize the perspective of the counselor or any other educational stakeholder; in this way, ASE theory reflects the suggestions offered by the critical education theorist Paulo Freire (1970), who posited that "This, then, is the great humanistic and historical task of the oppressed: to liberate themselves and their oppressors as well" (p. 44). As such, counseling from an ASE perspective requires a counselor to join with the inner perceptual reality of the student, to relate to that student's particular social circumstance, and to provide counseling praxis that encourages the student to exert inner resources in meaningful ways in various environments. In parallel, the ASE counselor must prime and challenge aspects of the school environment that are not prepared or willing to support the student's development. The promise of this form of school counseling is that everyone will benefit from the unfettered enfranchisement of the student, particularly the student.

The ASE-influenced school counselor is not tied to any particular learning or social outcomes for students or school systems, especially the pursuit of academic achievement as an end in itself. Fixed school goals can be incredibly dehumanizing, as they generally reflect the values of educators or the external society. Instead, ASE requires profound trust in the student. It is assumed that a student who is genuinely supported will in turn identify and pursue personally and socially valuable ends. In this way, the ASE approach further reflects the ideas of Freire (1970), particularly his concept of *conscientização*, or critical consciousness, which is the manifestation of the student's earnest understanding of, and response to, oppressive or constrictive educational and social scenes.

The theoretical bases for the ASE approach are predicated on the reflexivity between an active and sentient agent (e.g., student) and the surrounding environment (e.g., teachers, peers, family members, epoch). Certain other counseling theories prize the individual's autonomy and capacity to alter internal and external experiences. These theories espouse that individual development is sufficient for counseling change, thereby leading to more useful affect, cognition, or behaviors for living in solidarity with the world. Alternatively, other theories proceed from the belief that the individual's experience results from interaction with the environment, which largely affects and dictates how she or he experiences and acts.

The ASE approach reconciles the tension between the individual self and the adjacent environment by trapping each in an inescapable relationship with the other. An adherent to the ASE approach believes that placing greater significance on individual experience or agency threatens to create hegemonic dynamics where individuals are always at odds and competing for personal and social significance. Contrariwise, a counselor influenced by ASE theory is equally critical of largely social epistemologies where the individual is relegated as a consequential being, perpetually victimized by circumstance. In this manner, any personal wellness or social prosperity must be nurtured in reflexivity.

The ASE perspective evades the solipsism problem by affirming that consciousness is shared between individuals and, in varying ways, the aspects of the surrounding environment. Therefore, conscious executive control, such as a learning and social development, is neither fully autonomous nor wholly responsive (Oakley & Halligan, 2017) but is more akin to a kaleidoscope, where individual capacities are affected by environmental conditions (and environments are similarly affected by a multiplicity of individuals). Consider one student's consciousness and agency as if it were represented by a yellow crystal in the kaleidoscope. That same yellow crystal appears orange if its environment is a red crystal (e.g., threatening school environment), or it appears green if its presenting environment is blue (e.g., comforting school environment). The yellowness that is the individual student's consciousness and agency are stable and can influence what is manifest, yet it is concurrently altered by the influence of the environment.

Conceptualizing students-within-environments has dramatic implications for school counseling practice. Foremost, the approach abandons traditional approaches that initiate or focus counseling on either the individual or system levels. There are risks in counseling the individual student as fully autonomous being, just as there are risks in demanding that the student conform to the school or surrounding environment (Lemberger, 2010). ASE provides an alternative, where the school counselor focuses practice on cultivating indwelling capacities and equanimity between the individual and the environment, and there is less risk of desolation for either the student or school environment. Instead, in collaboration with the student and elements from her or his surroundings, the counselor advocates an adaptive and impartial relatedness between student and aspects of the school environment.

To fashion harmony between the student and environment, a school counselor influenced by ASE focuses on enriching inherent attributes and awareness within each student and within various players in relevant environments. The school counselor trusts that these pursuits will result in an inclination for personal accomplishment and social activism for the student. Additionally, these school counseling foci are not held as specific ends; rather, each is a mechanism designed to amplify capacities without predetermined attachments to how the capacities manifest.

A school counselor who employs ASE theory operates from the epistemic belief that amplified attributes and awareness shared between individuals and environments are more personally able and socially just. This approach to school counseling is an attempt to vivify the spirit of *conscientização* (critical consciousness; Freire, 1970) using specific and school-relevant ideas and practices. Some of these ideas are presented here, but the list is not exhaustive, because a school counselor can adopt any relevant ideas and practices that are consistent with the credo to amplify student-within-environment.

Dialogical Humanism

The ASE school counseling perspective draws from an incipient version of humanistic psychology, namely dialogical humanism (Hansen, Speciale, & Lemberger, 2014; Lemberger & Lemberger-Truelove, 2016). Traditional humanistic psychology proceeds from the following maxims: the individual is intentional and meaning-driven, humans have choice and related responsibilities, individuals are conscious of themselves and others, and humans are holistic and cannot be reduced to parts (Greening, 2006). Dialogical humanism largely embraces these ideas but extends each by explicitly binding individual human interests with larger societal considerations.

Humanistic psychology has been erroneously criticized as being a self-centric approach; nonetheless, dialogical humanism fortifies against this critique by unequivocally anchoring the individual self within the larger cultural context. At the individual level, the student is encouraged to examine personal goals and values, but to challenge these initial impulses as they operate in relationship to the broader school and social contexts. For example, in my (first author) first year as a high school counselor, a freshman student entered my office with the goal of receiving a schedule change because she believed that her math teacher was "evil." Engaging the student in a dialogue led to a new proposition: that the student feared and avoided any adult who challenged her. As a consequence, our initial meeting related to a schedule change led to a yearlong counseling relationship that improved not only her experiences in the math class, but also her peer and family relationships.

Executive Functioning

Although neurobiological constructs like self-regulated behavior and heightened levels of executive functioning are associated with school success (Jacobson, Willford, & Pianta, 2011; Sesma et al., 2009), these constructs are generally not represented in the social justice or counseling literature. From an ASE perspective, they are two of many examples of human operations that are potentially useful for social justice education and counseling because they are a means for student agency that might result in learning and social liberation. Furthermore, neurobiological processes are often associated with school-centric outcomes (e.g., academic achievement, behaviors complicit with authority), which may reflect the oppressive ideologies opposed by ASE and other social justice approaches. Alternatively, these intrinsic human factors can be refocused as assets in the student to affect her or his beingness in the world in personal and transformative ways.

Educational scholars have consistently found that a student's capacity to reflect and to act on reflections is associated with school and life successes (Bransford, Brown, & Cocking, 1999; Masten, & Coatsworth, 1998). These skills are understood as the student's capacity to self-regulate learning or behavior, a skill deemed appropriate for counselor intervention by school counseling scholars (e.g., Lapan, Kardash, & Turner, 2002; Lemberger, Selig, Bowers, & Rogers, 2015). From a neurological perspective, self-regulatory expressions are associated with cognitive processes, such as the use of executive functions (Hofmann, Schmeichel, & Baddeley, 2012)—that is, the cognitive activities necessary for goal-directed behavior and appropriate social conduct, including the use of one's working memory, shifting focus, planning, organizing, and behavioral control (Best & Miller, 2010; Hofmann, Schmeichel, & Baddeley, 2012). For a school counselor who practices using ASE theory, executive functions and self-regulating behaviors are vital ingredients in the support of a student who is self-reflective and intentional in action. Self-regulating behaviors are not mechanisms of repression: instead, they are antecedent features of a person who can deconstruct learning and social situations while preparing to reconstruct opportunities and experiences in more apposite ways.

The ripening of the student's executive functions can be understood as a mechanism of critical consciousness. Each of the executive functions pertains to attention and activity, or, as Freire (1970) suggested, "reflection and action directed at the structures to be transformed" (p. 126). Although Freire never mentioned executive functions specifically, it appears that they are the ingredients for the types of praxis in student learning and social change that he urged.

School Connectedness

From an epistemological perspective, it is unlikely that a student will be able to activate executive functions and other self-regulatory behaviors if she or he feels disconnected, threatened, or extraneous to the school environment. Therefore, a school counselor inspired by ASE theory believes that student and social consciousness require shared experiences of acceptance, safety, encouragement, and respect from both peers and adults in the school environment (Resnick et al., 1997). Propitiously, feelings of connectedness to others in the school or the overall school environment are associated with learning and social successes even in high poverty environments (Niehaus, Moritz Rudasill, & Rakes, 2012; Witherspoon, Schotland, Way, & Hughes, 2009) and are considered within the professional purview of school counselors (Hernández & Seem, 2004).

From an ASE perspective, a school counselor is charged with eliciting and supporting the student's perceived experiences of the school community, but also with ameliorating the conditions so that every student can exercise her or his agency to experience belonging, safety, predictability, and the conditions for self-defined successes. Furthermore, an ASE counselor is compelled to collaborate with the student so that each student contributes to the total connectedness across the school community, generally by confronting and transforming restrictive systems, and expressing genuine personal and social compassion.

Just as a school counselor must appreciate a student's unique disposition and culture when focusing on that student's executive functions, the counselor must also attend to these student factors when focusing on feelings of connectedness to the school community (Furlong, O'Brennan, & You, 2011). An ASE school counselor invites the student and aspects of the environment to find common ground without imposing the values or authority of one at the expense of the other. Instead, authentic connection occurs when each participant within an environment is valued and prized in such a manner that dialogue and development can be distributed and shared.

REFLECTION MOMENT

Recollect your experiences as a student. What personal attributes assisted you in your school successes? What additional abilities or resources do you believe would have changed your experiences? In what ways did people or conditions present within your school environments affect your abilities or experiences in learning or socializing as a student?

THEORY OF CHANGE

A school counselor who utilizes ASE theory believes that a quality counseling relationship that targets essential student capacities as they relate to aspects of the school environment can lead to improved personal and social outcomes. Consistent with the Plato's theory of anamnesis, students and members of the school environment do not necessarily learn or ascertain new ways of functioning; instead, new end-states manifest as a consequence of bringing attention and vitality to inbuilt abilities. In short, it is spurious to assume that a student can learn something if there were not an inbuilt potential. As such, the goal of ASE theory is to encourage each student and other members of the school environment to pursue the most apposite version of her- or himself, as mediated by their experiences within diverse social settings.

The ASE theory of change proceeds from the belief that a counselor must first engage in an authentic and mutual relationship with the student. Using that relationship as a base, the counselor will assist the student in amplifying essential capacities, such as self-regulatory and social-emotional functioning. Development also requires that the school counselor work with relevant parties in the school system so that the student is more willing and safe, and able to express, to refine, and to assert her or his amplified capacities.

To stimulate the student's capacities and related critical consciousness in a school, the ASE-influenced school counselor will elicit the student's internal perspective and resources, juxtapose them with the external realities specific to that student (in a strength-focused manner), and abet a new position that is useful as student-within-environment. It is essential that the counselor promote the means for amplifying the student's internal and social abilities so that she or he can best affect her or his relevant environment; this is categorically different than the experiences of oppressed or dehumanized students, who are often governed by forces that limit a student's sense of agency as a learner and social being. For example, relative to academic content, the counselor might ask a middle school student to discuss her or his understanding of a concept and contrast this understanding to the expectations of the teacher or test material. In this way, the counselor can work with the student to elucidate misconceptions within the learning experience (Bransford, Brown, & Cocking, 1999) and use new learning strategies that are unencumbered by any impediments that might have manifested in the classroom setting. This dialogical process can then be generalized for the student so that she or he can use the new strategy in other circumstances, but more importantly she or he can refer to the experience of looking within oneself and the designs of the school environment to create a new reality that is personally and socially meaningful.

In addition to working within the perceptual reality of the student, whenever possible and appropriate, an ASE-influenced school counselor must perform corresponding work at the school level to reinforce and celebrate the student's capacities and successes. Returning to the aforementioned example, using con-sultation processes with the classroom teacher, the school counselor would then describe only the relevant events of the student counseling with the teacher (e.g., the learning strategy). In so doing, this would amplify the likelihood that the teacher prompts the student in such a way that the opportunity to use the strategy is clear to the student, but it will further increase the likelihood that the teacher will notice and reinforce the successful use of the skill by the student.

The ASE approach to school counseling shifts the nature of school coun-seling praxis as ancillary to the school curriculum to that of a primary com-ponent of the education community. From the ASE perspective, the school counselor is charged with helping students and educators enrich learning skills and social relationships. The ASE approach does not necessarily endorse a set of prescribed counseling techniques or student outcomes; rather, the school counselor uses traditional humanistic and social justice strategies, coupled with contemporary advances in the learning and developmental sciences, to redirect all counseling activities toward the transformational learning and lib-erated relational experiences for each student and related adult. Simply put, the role of the school counselor is to assist in the deepening of experiences, understanding, and expression for students and related adults in their lives. To vivify these broad schooling outcomes, operations like heightened levels of stu-dent executive functioning, feelings of connectedness and engagement in the school, radical personal acceptance, and so on are used by an ASE-influenced school counselor. Together, these and other theoretically consistent counseling practices can point the student toward a critical consciousness.

ASE theorists endorse the advocacy recommendations offered by critical educators (e.g., Freire, 1970; Giroux, 1983; Ladson-Billings & Tate, 1995) and social justice advocates in the counseling field (see Bemak & Chung, 2005; Goodman et al., 2004), but we suggest a further step offering intermediate counseling praxis. That is, an ASE-informed school counselor is readied with more than simply *what* to do as a humanistic social justice advocate in the school: she or he also maintains *how* to enact these ends as they pertain to the inner cognitive and affective capacities implicit to each student's humanness. Furthermore, the counselor places the authority of learning and expression in the student, rather than on the counselor, who, even if equipped with the desire to impart equity and empowerment, would simply be replacing one educator's agenda with another. The ASE-influenced counselor believes that top-down schooling is potentially dehumanizing, which in turn threatens the sustainability and relevance of any educational practice or outcome.

Theory of Change Applied to Young Children

Young children rapidly pass through a number of developmental periods, each of which requires support from the surrounding environment. Personal aptitudes are either fortified or jeopardized. What results is a kaleidoscopic combination of personal capacity intermingled with external circumstances. In the most ideal circumstances, the types of early opportunities posed to young children will validate their inherent abilities. Unfortunately for many children, interactions with the social environment require the child to adjust or to compromise. From an ASE perspective, a school counselor is primarily charged with providing age-appropriate preventative and responsive services that draw out indwelling abilities and priorities.

In practice, school counselors who work with young children primarily focus their attention on enriching emergent abilities in young children. For example, I (first author) was once employed in a school where an administrator wanted to expel a sixth grader from the district as a result of persistent fighting. I was told that this student was unreachable. Using the concept of magic as a device to illustrate empathy, the young student began to use his "magic" in the classroom to create more useful relationships with peers and his teacher. Shortly thereafter, his teacher was convinced that he was "transformed." While his individual development illustrated that his innate social abilities were as ample as they were hampered by his experiences, I reminded the teacher that it would be impossible to expect him to sustain his transformation always, and in all ways. In fact, I suggested that we maintain the same type of empathy for him as he was then sharing with us. If, after his next slip-up, we respond to him as we did in the past, there would be no incentive for him to return to his newfound behaviors. Our aspiration as educators is to accept the humanity of the student, regardless of her or his behaviors or circumstances that are temporarily inconvenient. This brief example demonstrates the ASE theory of change for young children: that is, the counselor helps to draw out individual student capacities while concurrently priming the environment to receive and reinforce those capacities.

Theory of Change Applied to Adolescents

Many of the challenges that confront young children persist into adolescence. For many students, the emerging capacities that first manifest in early childhood begin to take hold and deepen during the teenage years. Many adolescents endure personal, social, or learning trauma, causing them to believe that they are stuck or inconsequential. In addition, adolescence is a time when students are affected by conflicting drives (e.g., the desire for autonomy while anticipating connectedness to others) and external pressures ripen.

The ASE theory of change for adolescents still pertains to the manner in which the student operates within the environment. Whereas the focus with younger children is to expose inner capacities as they pertain to external realities, a school counselor employing ASE theory with an adolescent is generally more concerned with helping the student ripen her or his agency to respond to these realities. For example, I (first author) once worked with a high school senior who wanted me to convince her parents to allow her to forgo a year of college to volunteer abroad. From an ASE perspective, my role was not to guide the student or her parents; rather, it was to support each as they considered the individual and social factors implicit to any decision.

DELIVERY OF ASE

The American School Counselor Association National Model (ASCA, 2012) includes a number of delivery approaches, each intended to focus the types of services offered by school counselors. The delivery of programs requires that the counselor integrate a theory of practice into group activities, individual student planning (i.e., appraisal and advisement), and responsive services (i.e., short-term counseling and crisis response). The ASCA National Model appears to align with the dialogical approach implicit to ASE theory, in that both suggest that a school counselor deliver practices intended to empower each student while making efforts to affect systems that influence student development.

Direct Services

The ASCA National Model (2012) advises that a school counselor adopt a core curriculum, that is, a formal scheme to deliver content pertaining to the support of students' academic and learning achievement, career development, and personal and social growth. A school counselor using ASE theory can work directly with students in each of these areas using individual or group counseling approaches, as consistent with the National Model. Furthermore, the National Model prioritizes preventative services, which are also congruous with ASE in supporting students' internal capacities as the most apposite approach to improve students' experiences and schooling conditions.

Indirect Services

Direct services are the bedrock of school counseling. While working directly with students is central to the ASCA National Model and ASE theory, each acknowledges the importance of including adult participants in the school counselor's delivery of a program. Providing consultation and collaboration services to adult stakeholders increases the likelihood of success and shared investment. Finally, both ASCA and the ASE approach acknowledge that there are circumstances when the needs of the students exceed the resources available in the school, therefore requiring the inclusion of responsive services in the delivery of a comprehensive school counseling program.

Hidden Curriculum

There are aspects implicit to each school milieu that are not necessarily covered specifically in the ASCA National Model yet are nonetheless essential for the delivery of ASE. Concurrent with the formal curricula rendered by educators, there is a ubiquitous hidden curriculum that includes all the factors that contribute to the context, processes, and social dynamics within a given school (Vallance, 1974). It is as if the school is its own culture that operates within a multitude of other outside cultures. Each of these cultures affects the school and the students within the school, culminating in a curriculum that each student must navigate. Utilizing ASE theory, a school counselor can assist a student as she or he confronts these clandestine and perplexing aspects of the school. Consistent with the critical consciousness goal of ASE theory, a school counselor collaborates with the student to draw attention to elements within the hidden curriculum. With a clearer conception of the informal operations within the school, the student is more likely to enact personal capacities in a socially relevant and personally meaningful way.

THEORY OPERATIONALIZED

Most theories of counseling were designed with suppositions pertaining to normal functioning or wellness (personal or societal), pathology or psychological disturbance, and therapeutic practices intended to confront pathology and contribute to more "normal" functioning. However, an adherent to ASE theory is generally cautious to arrogate guileless suppositions relative to how a human endures living and, instead, conceptualizes so-called normality, pathology, and even counseling practice in a more dialogical and incalculable manner. There are certainly moral assumptions within ASE theory, yet an ASE counselor maintains that life is riddled with challenges that disrupt living. In this way, rather than striving to support students in the most perfunctory way, a school counselor who utilizes ASE is willing to tolerate the profound ambiguity of people, schools, and counseling practice, while remaining steadfast to beliefs that students and educators possess profound untapped potentials and, also, that social interactions are often governed by personal and social limiters.

A school counselor adopting ASE theory is a skeptic, not a cynic. A skeptic is one who maintains doubt with optimism, whereas a cynic doubts with persistent pessimism. In practice, an ASE school counselor is skeptical that students (and their related stakeholders) have actualized their potential. Furthermore, the school counselor is skeptical that the various social systems, not limited to members of the school community and the surrounding culture, have best enriched students' capacities. Nonetheless, the school counselor is optimistic that capacities can be nurtured, ruptures can be mended, and students-within-environments can thrive.

A primary mechanism for enlivening the spirit of ASE theory is found in the potency of radical curiosity. As a school counselor, if one is radically curious about the history, ability, and pursuits of a student, generally that student will feel validated and empowered. If the school counselor is radically curious about the workings of the social system, she or he is better equipped and able to unearth impediments and resources to schooling. If this radical curiosity is distributed between the student and the members of the school environment, each is more likely to accept the other and to commit to personal and social prosperity.

It must be noted that the type of social solidarity pursued by an ASE-informed school counselor should not be confused with the pursuit of consensus among the student and members of the environment. Too often, consensus reflects the goals and authority of the more powerful agent in the environment, for example the educational outcomes expected by a teacher or parent, the assertiveness of a bullying classmate, and so on. Instead, ASE theory involves amplifying personal abilities and social access so that diverse students and stakeholders can better pursue ends that they deem meaningful.

Some outcomes of ASE might not necessarily reflect the prevailing schooling ethos. A student who has sharpened her or his capacities might choose scholarship, art, athletics, or something altogether different. In fact, a student might choose to disengage with typical school behaviors and outcomes. As long as the student's choice is not a consequence of obstructed abilities or social delimiters, the ASE counselor can support the student's abilities to pursue multiple goals that are flexible and personally meaningful.

This said, with increased access to personal agency and social equity, most students pursue laudable goals with a greater likelihood of success and social value.

Generally speaking, ASE is a broad and inclusive therapeutic focus, rather than a system with built-in specific and structured practices. With this in mind, there are certain counseling behaviors that are most illustrative of the ASE focus. A school counselor's use of curriculum or technique can be considered consistent with ASE theory insofar as his or her efforts attempt to invigorate the abilities and actions of students while concurrently ameliorating school and other social systems.

ASE Operationalized in Elementary, Middle, and High Schools

The practice of ASE theory requires that the school counselor support the development of the individual student's abilities as they interface with various aspects of the school environment. Although a school counselor maintains this general focus for all students, the school counselor adapts practice in a nuanced manner to meet the developmental needs of students and school climate differences at the elementary, middle, and high school levels.

In an elementary school, students generally enter school with the expectation that they will quickly adapt to new social and learning expectations. Increasingly, within the first few years of formal schooling, behavioral and learning expectations evolve, and it is a school counselor's job to help foster students' social and cognitive skills. In a similar way, a school counselor is required to collaborate with professional educators and other stakeholders in creating the most worthwhile school environments possible.

A school counselor utilizing ASE theory in early education settings can provide support using each of the suggested delivery approaches. For example, many elementary school counselors provide large- and small-group psychoeducational activities at the student level and parallel offerings to teachers, administrators, staff, and parents/guardians. These counseling activities are designed to include activities that sharpen students' learning and social abilities while providing adults with the resources to reinforce and enrich students' opportunities to practice and refine the abilities.

In middle schools, students often experience multiple personal and social transitions, such as sustaining attention across different classrooms, peer dynamics, and physical changes. An ASE school counselor helps students and the adults in their lives to identify these changes and the various factors that influence how they manifest. Small-group counseling, as one example, could be a great way to assist students in asserting their individual identities within new and increasingly complex social arrangements.

The transition to high school can be marked by dramatic changes for youth. For many students, personal and social challenges feel more daunting and abiding. Using individual counseling, for example, a school counselor can help a student consider career or educational possibilities and identify strategies to confront difficult personal or social circumstances. At the school environment level, a school counselor can work with teachers to improve learning conditions or with parents to help them learn new strategies to support adolescents. Across all educational levels, the school counselor using ASE theory attempts to amplify the dialogical connection shared between the student and various aspects of the environment.

Establishment of a Dialogical Connection

A quality counseling relationship is a necessary ingredient in the support of students and others in the school environment. Researchers have consistently reported that a strong counseling relationship and feelings of connection contribute to desirable therapeutic outcomes (Horvath, Del Re, Flückiger, & Symonds, 2011; Lapan, Wells, Petersen, & McCann, 2014). Gelso (2011) suggested that counseling is a "personal relationship existing between two or more persons as reflected in the degree to which each is genuine with the other and perceives the other in ways that befit the other" (p. 12–13). Others have suggested that there are common factors to counseling relationships that contribute to client outcomes, not limited to the emotive bond shared between counselor and client as delivered in a healing setting with culturally useful beliefs about distress and healing (Laska, Gurman, & Wampold, 2014). From an ASE perspective, a connected relationship is required in establishing trust and safety with the student, especially since counseling will ultimately entail engagement with the school environment.

To enact the connected counseling relationship, the school counselor engages the student or stakeholder with radical curiosity. The counselor is open to the experiences of the conversant, regardless of what content is shared in the counseling dialogue.

From an ASE perspective, all counseling activity is dialogical. Dialogical philosophy assumes the truthfulness of incidence, while further accepting that each incidence entails diverse perspectives, sociohistorical influencers, and modification over time and circumstance. When a school counselor is listening to a student's story, it is linguistically dialogical. When a school counselor is delivering a small- or large-group psychoeducational activity, it is experientially dialogical. The quality counseling relationship is dialogical when the counselor concurrently apprehends the genuine lived experience of the student (or stakeholder) from her or his vantage point and further believes that this perspective is prone to expansion, revision, and continual growth. This belief is consistent with the research related to the growth mindset (Yeager & Dweck, 2012); individuals who commit to activities with persistence generally accomplish their intent or adjust in such a manner that new intentions are created and pursued.

Quality counseling relationships are threatened when the student or stakeholder does not believe that she or he is connected. Human beings are generally tribal in nature; we seek out perceived allies and try to avoid or repel perceived threats. Furthermore, from a neurocognitive perspective, when we perceive someone or a belief as threatening, we typically create beliefs about that other person or their ideology to keep them at bay.

A school counselor using ASE theory attempts to reverse this human proclivity toward separation in effort to build a quality counseling relationship. Drawing from wisdom offered by the philosopher Blaise Pascal (1995), an ASE dialogue begins with validating the unique manner in which the student (or stakeholder) constructs her or his belief. Validation does not necessarily mean always agreeing with the student, but it does mean making it apparent that you understand the rationale behind the student's belief. Consider the following example:

STUDENT: My teacher is so mean!!! He really doesn't care about me at all and hates me.

COUNSELOR: You believe that when your teacher is disappointed in your classroom behaviors it means that your teacher hates you.

STUDENT: Yeah, he just gets mad for no reason and then doesn't ever believe that I can do anything good.

COUNSELOR: I can see how that is frustrating. After your teacher gets upset, you suppose that he doesn't provide you the same support and chances later to show that you can be successful.

STUDENT: Exactly. He just hates me.

COUNSELOR: I can see how not being attended to can lead you to feel hated. You experience his anger after a certain incident, but you say that you believe that this carries over into other things in the class.

In this brief example, the school counselor reflects the student's feelings. Only after the student believes that there is connection and understanding can the counselor begin to introduce dialogical alternatives. With that in mind, again consistent with Pascal, the alternative explored must be meaningful and initiated from within the student's perspective.

The goal in this example is not to minimize or to justify the teacher's behaviors. Rather, it is important that the school counselor does not inadvertently diminish the student's experiences or appear to take sides. The aim is to illustrate empathy and to introduce possible means for the student to influence her or his situation.

Socially Useful Executive Functions

With the establishment of a quality relationship, a school counselor inspired by ASE theory utilizes techniques designed to foster the student's innate executive capacities. Executive functions are mental processes that promote goal-directed behaviors, such as inhibiting, shifting from task to task, emotional control, initiating activities, working memory, planning and organizing materials, and monitoring, which in turn are related to learning and social outcomes in students (Barker & Munakata, 2015). The school counselor believes that nurturing the student's cognitive abilities will enable the student to better navigate learning and social situations in the school.

The school counselor who commits to ASE theory can adopt a number of related practices to nurture a student's executive functioning. For example, there are connections between executive functioning and social-emotional learning (Liew, 2012), physical activity (Best, 2010), and learning and social performance (Clark, Prior, & Kinsella, 2002). More than simply looking for techniques or curricular activities that potentially promote executive functions, a school counselor utilizes these approaches in all ways to promote the student's agency within the school environment.

Social-Emotional Learning. Social-emotional learning (SEL) is a comprehensive intervention approach that can inform how school counselors help children in schools manage their emotions, experience empathy, pursue goals, and effectively navigate interpersonal relationships (Collaborative for Academic, Social, and Emotional Learning [CASEL], 2012). Durlak and colleagues (2011) performed a meta-analysis of 213 school-based SEL interventions and found that students who received high-quality SEL interventions experienced increases in social-emotional functioning and learning outcomes. To pursue these experiences and outcomes, a school counselor utilizing ASE can import the five key areas of social-emotional competence as suggested by the CASEL (2003) using the following:

- *Self-awareness* is when a student identifies his or her emotions, recognizes strengths in him- or herself and in others, and maintains a sense of self-efficacy and self-confidence. A school counselor can reflect the student's feelings to stoke this type of self-awareness. For example, the counselor might say, "Janelle, you are feeling frustrated because someone else is taking a turn on the swing and you really wanted to swing." Or "I can see how elated you are when you invest so much effort and figure out a solution that works for you."

- *Self-management* is when a student addresses impulse control, stress management, persistence, goal setting, and motivation. To assist the student, a school counselor can ask an open-ended question pertaining to a student's initial goals or behavior:

> COUNSELOR: It appears that you're upset because you have to wait your turn for the milk to be poured by the teacher; tell me, if you want milk in your cup how must you hold it for teacher to pour it?
>
> STUDENT: [Indicating an open-side-up position.] I guess I have to hold it this way.
>
> COUNSELOR: Okay, when you're banging the cup upside down against the table, what might that be telling the teacher?
>
> STUDENT: That I want my milk now.
>
> COUNSELOR: Yes, it could certainly be letting her know that you are eager to get your drink. But if your cup is upside down, your teacher might not be able to pour the milk in. I wonder, if the cup is moving and up-side down, what might be another belief that your teacher has about you banging the cup?
>
> STUDENT: That I am not waiting my turn.
>
> COUNSELOR: I can see that as a possibility, too. You want your milk as fast as possible, and you are describing how not waiting your turn might slow you down from getting what you really want.

- *Social awareness* is when a student establishes empathy, respect for others, and perspective taking. A counselor can help with social awareness by connecting goals or choices with others in the school environment, by saying, for example, "You're sorry about what happened with James. What do you think he wanted when he went over there to play?" Or "Are you feeling better? Can you find someone else in class who you believe could use your strategy for feeling better? Is this a person who you believe would appreciate your strategy? What things could you do to make it successful?"
- *Relationship skills* include cooperation, willingness to seek and provide assistance to others, and enacting useful communication behaviors.
- Similarly, *responsible decision-making* includes opportunities for the student to evaluate and reflect on personal responsibilities. A counselor can reflect appropriate choices and relationship habits with the following examples: "I can tell that you're very excited about going to gym, but before you can start a new activity what must you do

in the area you just left?" Or "Being a sophomore can be really hard, lots of new things to consider. You seem to have identified some traits in others that you admire. While you admire these traits, you seem to be a bit cautious in seeking help from these people who you admire, especially when it pertains to some pretty important choices that confront you."

Movement and Mindfulness. Encouraging physical activity and instilling contemplative mindfulness practices in schools are two examples of effective approaches to heightening executive functioning in school-age children (Diamond & Lee, 2011; Lemberger, Carbonneau, Atencio, Zieher, & Palacios, 2018). In contemporary classrooms, there is a predominant focus on learning skills and behavior management. Paradoxically, each of these classroom focus areas might hinder the natural proclivities of young learners. For example, humans have adapted to learning while moving, but schools require students to sit passively for many consecutive hours.

Similarly, students are generally situated in large classrooms, with myriad devices of judgment and pernicious evaluation. As an alternative, mindfulness-based practices are concerned with how one maintains awareness of current experiences in a curious and nonjudgmental manner (Bishop et al., 2004). Just as the body and mind do not function optimally while dormant, the student's mind is neurologically and experientially compromised when confronted with persistent judgment and reactivity.

A school counselor who utilizes ASE theory must operate within the typical practices and customs of a school environment. In this way, it is unlikely that a school counselor can expand the number of hours and types of activities that go on during recess or even in the typical classroom settings. This said, a counselor can infuse appropriate movement (e.g., stretching, dance) and mindfulness practices (e.g., contemplative breathing) in standard counseling activities, such as large- and small-group counseling.

In addition to supplying formal curricular activities that include movement and mindfulness, ASE-informed school counseling can integrate these practices in the general counseling dialogue with students. For example, a school counselor can subtly introduce the value of nonjudgmental mindfulness by encouraging the student to accept his or her abilities while pursuing new goals or choices:

COUNSELOR: That strategy didn't work the way you hoped, but that outcome certainly doesn't reflect your ability to come up with other strategies that will get you closer to your desired goal.

STUDENT: I don't know. Things don't seem to work out for me, especially when I try real hard.

COUNSELOR: You believe it is difficult to try new strategies because you haven't had much success in the past. But maybe you have accomplished something. Have you considered that the outcomes might not reflect your ability to get what you want, but these past strategies did help you figure out what didn't work?

STUDENT: I am sure that that's possible. I just don't know.

COUNSELOR: Fair, you mentioned that you haven't had many good experiences when you try hard. Let's try and make things easier instead. Can we stop, take a few deep and intentional breaths together, and try and separate what we judge as ability and what is simply just a strategy we use that might not reflect your real ability to get your goals met?

ASE theory is germane to contemporary mindfulness in that each endorses the concept of radical acceptance (akin to radical curiosity discussed earlier). That is, the school counselor does not necessarily accept all student behaviors or accept the unjust things that happen to students in and beyond schools; instead, the counselor accepts that the experience of the event was real and personal, and yet transient. In a similar way, emotional movement reflects physical movement; the ultimate aspiration of ASE is to draw attention while apprehending new, more intentional, and liberated possibilities physically, psychologically, or socially.

Integration of Theoretically Related Techniques. More than a set of techniques or practices, ASE is a focus of school counseling that can integrate myriad approaches from classical counseling theories and education practices. This focus is not eclecticism, as it does not randomly meld divergent ideas and doings. Instead, insofar as a practice can be applied in a manner that is consistent with dialogical philosophy, a school counselor can fuse it into ASE theory.

For example, from a dialogical perspective, the CBT technique of the downward arrow can be refocused to be consistent with ASE theory. In classical CBT, the downward arrow is a way of challenging the student's core beliefs with progressive questions in effort to ascertain a more specific and fixed core belief. A school counselor who uses the downward arrow technique within an ASE framework does not necessarily assume linearity of the student's experience or even that core beliefs are fully personal or sustainable. Rather, a school counselor would use the multiple progressive questions of the downward arrow to explore and validate multiple possibilities within context (see Box 12.1).

Box 12.1.

Application of the Downward Arrow

CBT Application of the Downward Arrow

Counselor: You are saying that you feel that you are stupid if you fail another test. I am curious, what makes a person stupid?

Student: Being stupid means that other people, my parents, others in class, see me as incapable of doing well in my classes.

Counselor: Then, if that's true, that being stupid means others will see you as incapable, then what does that say about you?

Student: I don't know. I guess [pause], others believing I am stupid and incapable just dominates what I think about and do.

Counselor: Right, okay, then that says you are more concerned about what others think than what you believe about yourself. Then that tells you what about yourself?

Student: I guess it means that I have focused on what I believe others believe about me. If I believe that they think I am stupid, I guess—to me—it must mean I am stupid.

Counselor: That means that you are only of value if others see you doing things right.

ASE Application of the Downward Arrow

Counselor: I hear that you are concerned that the last test didn't turn out the way you hoped. After that result you are now calling yourself stupid?

Student: Yeah, I tried really hard and I still failed. Everyone, my parents, other kids in class, they all think I am stupid. It's not one test, it's all of them. They must be right, I must be stupid.

Counselor: That's a lot of disappointment. Can you tell me what your beliefs were going into the test?

Student: I know school is hard for me. Sometimes I don't feel as smart as others. But I studied hard because I felt a little more optimistic. But see, that didn't work out.

Counselor: It must be frustrating when new optimism doesn't translate into new outcomes. But I wonder about the optimistic belief itself rather than the outcome of this most recent test. Might it be that optimism is a new outcome?

Student: What do you mean?

Counselor: You told me that everyone thinks you're unable to do well in school. You also told me that you believe them; you even go so far as to adopt the belief that you are stupid. Yet, on the other hand, there is this other possible belief, that is some tentative optimism that you can perform differently. I wonder if there is a way that we can use the truth of either belief to help create new, more helpful beliefs and strategies in the future.

In the ASE application of the downward arrow, there is no pursuit of a single or stable defining core belief. Instead, the ASE approach is more concerned with diverse influencers and possibilities. In a similar manner, a school counselor can integrate techniques drawn from other counseling theories and educational practices. For example, teachers often adopt learning mnemonics and graphic organizers. A school counselor can integrate these devices into the counseling dialogue to append individual student capacities as they are relevant to the learning expectations of the classroom.

Social Advocacy. Students who have sharpened their executive cognitive, social, or emotional functions are readied to pursue schooling outcomes that are most apposite to their inherent proclivities. While these personal pursuits are worthwhile, an ASE school counselor encourages students to share and distribute their aptitudes with others in need.

Returning to the philosopher Plato, in the famous Allegory of the Cave, a newly freed and enlightened slave leaves a cave of ignorance only to return and free others. Plato called these enlightened individuals Philosopher Kings. Correspondingly, a means of deepening the maturation of students' capacities is for the students to share in their expression with others. The reciprocal benefit to such pursuits is shared in solidarity among the initiating student, the receiving peers, and other members of the environment.

In practice, a school counselor will help facilitate social advocacy activities in support of students. Social advocacy might include the school counselor directly challenging unscrupulous aspects of the school environment or it might include the school counselor supporting students to actuate their internal resources to challenge social limiters either autonomously or in tandem with other advocates. For example, a school counselor can collaborate with students in volunteer activities in and beyond the school walls. Or, more simply, a school counselor can serve as a ready ear when a student identifies and engages in social advocacy opportunities.

ASE Operationalized with Adult Stakeholders

In many ways, ASE theory is a type of liberation psychology (see Martín-Baró, 1994). The goal is to amplify an individual student's capacities so that the student might define and pursue her or his own life course, neither encumbered by restrictive social agents nor beholden to prescribed expectations. While this type of self-determination is laudable, to accomplish such ends, the student is still bound to the social environment. The hope is that the individual can persist without compromise and yet remain responsive to the environment. For this to occur, the various aspects of the environment must entail corresponding conditions for the student to blossom.

As much as is possible, and consistent with ethical counseling practices, a school counselor informed by ASE will work directly with members of the school environment to create useful learning and social conditions for students. A school counselor will serve as a conduit between student, educators, family, and even appropriate members of the broader community (Bryan & Henry, 2012). The primary focus remains the connection experienced by the student, but the members of the community are accountable for the type of equity, access, and reinforcement so that the student's capacities rise within more connected environments.

In practice, a school counselor will provide individual consultation and other relevant direct services to educators, family, and community members. For example, in my first year as a school counselor, I (first author) was working with a young child on a mnemonic designed to help him in class. After our time together, he returned to class and waited for his teacher to call on him and provide him the opportunity to use the mnemonic in the exact way that his counselor introduced it. The teacher did not know that the student was waiting to use the new technique, nor what the technique was. The student sat in class waiting. He was then disappointed that he didn't get to use it, moreover that he put in more effort than others, to no avail. The teacher was likely disappointed because the student left class and nothing seemed to change. In that instance, I learned that there must be reciprocal intervention.

It is important to note that reciprocal intervention must be handled with care. There are ethical requirements, such as that a student's privacy and autonomy be protected. This said, considering the aforementioned example, I could have consulted with the teacher about general strategies to prompt and reinforce the student without compromising the student's confidence. In a similar way, while it is incumbent on a counselor to provide systemic support parallel to student counseling, all activities with the adult stakeholders must elevate the student.

APPLICATION

Consider your current relationship with schools. Given your current role as a graduate student, practicing school counselor, counselor educator, or stakeholder, what are some specific actions that you can identify to improve the qualities of schools and/or students' experiences in schools? For example, can you influence education policy? List three feasible, immediate, and accomplishable goals to improve one or more schools. Pick the single goal that is most meaningful and attainable in the immediate future and create a specific plan to pursue.

LIMITATIONS

In an era when school counselors are required to provide evidence for how their behaviors pertain to student and school outcomes (see ASCA, 2012; Bemak, Williams, & Chung, 2014), it is important that school counseling theories and related practices are shown to mediate desired outcomes. The ASE approach to school counseling does provide very specific and relevant constructs that can be measured and analyzed to illustrate accountable school counseling practice not limited to students' changes in executive functioning, feelings of connectedness, and academic or behavioral growth (see Bowers & Lemberger, 2016). One example of how such an investigation might be performed reflects select studies performed with the Student Success Skills (SSS) curriculum, which is consistent with the bases of the ASE approach (e.g., Lemberger, Carbonneau, Selig, & Bowers, 2018; Lemberger & Clemens, 2012). Unfortunately, while the SSS curriculum is consistent with ASE, it is inappropriate to describe SSS as a thoroughgoing example of ASE theory. As such, one major limitation of the ASE approach is that it is still nascent in the literature, especially relative to empirical support.

In addition to the dearth of empirical studies that explicitly describe results from a fully implemented ASE school counseling program, the prospect of carrying out such a study might appear dubious for some practicing school counselors. The type of action research that is customary to school counselors is generally linear (see Rowell, 2006); that is, a school counselor delivers an intervention, collects practical data, and then reports to stakeholders how that intervention affected a desired outcome. A practicing school counselor can certainly be influenced by the ASE approach as she or he captures and reports data in a very linear manner, yet the multifaceted axioms of ASE will certainly be sacrificed. In this way, a major limitation of the ASE focus is that it doesn't lend itself to the types of action research practices familiar to most practitioners.

The multifaceted nature of the ASE approach might limit more than measurement, in that its philosophical nature might curb its attractiveness to certain school counselors. For example, the focus on dialogical reasoning and dynamic systems might overwhelm practitioners. Additionally, concepts like executive functioning or growth mindset might appear too academic or even too durable for a school counselor to take on. Given the rapid pace of school counselors' schedules, some might believe that it is impossible to account for the amalgamation of diverse student needs and capacities and how each interfaces with innumerable social factors. Similarly, the ASE approach requires school counselors to promote individual student change while concurrently working for larger social change. Social change is daunting and often controversial. The ASE approach requires that the school counselor adopt a leadership position in the total school culture, while at the same time encouraging the students to be empowered.

There are other practical limitations related to ASE. The ASE approach incorporates practices influenced by the SEL literature, among others. While the SEL literature support is strong (e.g., Durlak, Weissberg, Dymnicki, Taylor, & Schellinger, 2011), some critiques have proposed that focusing on individual change might neglect systemic inequalities that confront marginalized students. Also, it has been claimed that targeting individual student abilities, such as students' SEL functioning, might erroneously imply that they are somehow deficient or responsible for school or societal inadequacies (Ecclestone & Lewis, 2014).

Critiques of self-centric approaches to counseling are consistent with ASE theory, yet it is reasonable to be cautious that misuses of ASE practices might occur. If school counselors focus on cultivating individual student functioning without making efforts to improve the multiple systems that affect that student, the counselors have inadvertently created a hegemonic approach to change.

Concluding Thoughts on the ASE Approach

The ASE perspective for school counseling challenges the school counselor to adopt a leadership role in the curricular content and climate of the school community. This means that, on some occasions, the counselor will be the chief deliverer of direct counseling services to students and, at other times, she or he will act in support of teachers, administrators, or parents. Also, a school counselor is explicitly charged with influencing school policy and other forms of social advocacy. With this in mind, the counselor's chief responsibility from an ASE perspective is to invest in all individuals so that each individual can define and embody her or his optimal functioning within more hospitable social environments.

There are a number of direct counseling practices germane to ASE theory, yet the school counselor assumes that the ends can extend beyond their intent. For example, a school counselor can translate SEL into counseling activities and language. In synchrony with counseling practices aimed at individual students, a school counselor will work with teacher, administrators, or other stakeholders so that they might witness the value of these skills. While these specific counseling applications can have a boosterish influence on students and entire systems, the counselor's efforts are metamorphic, in that more emboldened students and systems can thrive in myriad ways.

The ASE approach requires a steadfast belief in the student and the wherewithal to challenge often-unrelenting social and educational systems. In an almost paradoxical manner, the school counselor who adopts the ASE approach maintains an almost imperturbable stance—accepting each student genuinely, but readied with the mindset that potential is always emerging; grasping the complexities of social and school systems, yet unrelentingly demanding greater equity, access, and support; and the trust that individuals and environments can operate in harmony, while maintaining healthy curiosity so that this end can be met.

ADDITIONAL RESOURCES

READINGS

Bowers, H., Lemberger-Truelove, M. E., & Brigman, G. (2018). A social emotional learning leadership framework for school counselors. *Professional School Counselor.*

Buber, M. (1958). *I & thou* (2nd ed., R. G. Smith, Trans.). New York, NY: Charles Scribner.

Freire, P. (1970). *Pedagogy of the oppressed.* New York, NY: Continuum.

Lemberger, M. E., & Lemberger-Truelove, T. L. (2016). Bases for a more socially just humanistic praxis. *Journal of Humanistic Psychology, 56*(6), 571–580.

Bransford, J., Brown, A., & Cocking, R. (1999). *How people learn: Brain, mind, experience and school.* Washington, DC: National Research Council.

Siegel, D. J., & Bryson, T. P. (2011). *The whole-brain child: 12 revolutionary strategies to nurture your child's developing mind.* New York: Delacorte Press.

WEBSITES

Center on the Developing Child: https://developingchild.harvard.edu

Center for Healthy Minds: https://centerhealthyminds.org

Collaborative for Academic, Social, and Emotional Learning—https://casel.org

Mind and Life Institute: https://www.mindandlife.org

Ronald H. Fredrickson Center for School Counseling Outcome Research & Evaluation—http://www.umass.edu/schoolcounseling/

Student Success Skills—http://studentsuccessskills.com

REFERENCES

American School Counselor Association. (2012). *The ASCA National Model: A framework for school counseling programs* (3rd ed.). Alexandria, VA: American School Counselor Association.

Barker, J. E., & Munakata, Y. (2015). Developing self-directed executive functioning: Recent findings and future directions. *Mind, Brain, and Education, 9*(2), 92–99.

Bemak, F., & Chung, R. C. Y. (2005). Advocacy as a critical role for urban school counselors: Working toward equity and social justice. *Professional School Counseling, 8*(3), 196–202.

Bemak, F., Williams, J. M., & Chung, R. C. Y. (2014). Four critical domains of accountability for school counselors. *Professional School Counseling, 18*(1), 100–110.

Best, J. R. (2010). Effects of physical activity on children's executive function: Contributions of experimental research on aerobic exercise. *Developmental Review, 30*(4), 331–351.

Best, J. R., & Miller, P. H. (2010). A developmental perspective on executive function. *Child Development, 81*(6), 1641–1660.

Bishop, S. R., Lau, M., Shapiro, S., Carlson, L., Anderson, N. D., Carmody, J., . . . Devins, G. (2004). Mindfulness: A proposed operational definition. *Clinical Psychology: Science and Practice, 11*, 230–241.

Bowers, H., & Lemberger, M. E. (2016). A person-centered humanistic approach to performing evidence-based school counseling research. *Person-Centered & Experiential Psychotherapies, 15*(1), 55–66.

Bransford, J., Brown, A., & Cocking, R. (1999). *How people learn: Brain, mind, experience and school.* Washington, DC: National Research Council.

Bryan, J., & Henry, L. (2012). A model for building school–family–community partnerships: Principles and process. *Journal of Counseling & Development, 90*(4), 408–420.

Clark, C., Prior, M., & Kinsella, G. (2002). The relationship between executive function abilities, adaptive behaviour, and academic achievement in children with externalising behaviour problems. *Journal of Child Psychology and Psychiatry, 43*(6), 785–796.

Collaborative for Academic, Social, and Emotional Learning (CASEL). (2012). *2013 CASEL guide to effective social and emotional learning programs: Preschool and elementary school edition.* Chicago, IL: Collaborative for Academic, Social, and Emotional Learning.

Diamond, A., & Lee, K. (2011). Interventions shown to aid executive function development in children 4 to 12 years old. *Science, 333*(6045), 959–964.

Dollarhide, C. T., & Lemberger, M. E. (2006). "No Child Left Behind": Implications for school counselors. *Professional School Counselor, 9*(4), 295–304.

Durlak, J. A., Weissberg, R. P., Dymnicki, A. B., Taylor, R. D., & Schellinger, K. B. (2011). The impact of enhancing students' social and emotional learning: A meta-analysis of school-based universal interventions. *Child Development, 82*, 405–432.

Ecclestone, K., & Lewis, L. (2014). Interventions for resilience in educational settings: Challenging policy discourses of risk and vulnerability. *Journal of Education Policy, 29*(2), 195–216. doi:10.1080/02680939.2013.806678

Freire, P. (1970). *Pedagogy of the oppressed.* New York, NY: Continuum.

Furlong, M. J., O'Brennan, L. M., & You, S. (2011). Psychometric properties of the ADD Health School Connectedness Scale for 18 sociocultural groups. *Psychology in the Schools, 48*(10), 986–997.

Gelso, C. J. (2011). *The real relationship in psychotherapy: The hidden foundation of change.* Washington, DC: American Psychological Association.

Giroux, H. (1983). *Theory and resistance: A pedagogy for the opposition.* Hadley, MA: Bergin & Garvey.

Goodman, L. A., Liang, B., Helms, J. E., Latta, R. E., Sparks, E., & Weintrab, S. R. (2004). Training counseling psychologists as social justice agents: Feminist and multicultural principles in action. *The Counseling Psychologist, 32*(6), 793–837.

Greening, T. (2006). Five basic postulates of humanistic psychology. *Journal of Humanistic Psychology, 46*(3), 239.

Hansen, J. T., Speciale, M., & Lemberger, M. E. (2014). Humanism: The foundation and future of professional counseling. *Journal of Humanistic Counseling, 53*(3), 170–190.

Hofmann, W., Schmeichel, B. J., & Baddeley, A. D. (2012). Executive functions and self-regulation. *Trends in Cognitive Sciences, 16*(3), 174–180.

Horvath, A. O., Del Re, A. D., Flückiger, C., & Symonds, D. (2011). Alliance in individual psychotherapy. In J. C. Norcross & J. C. Norcross (Eds.), *Psychotherapy relationships that work: Evidence-based responsiveness* (2nd ed., pp. 25–69). New York, NY: Oxford University Press.

Jacobson, L. A., Willford, A. P., & Pianta, R. C. (2011). The role of executive funtion in children's competent adjustment to middle school. *Child Neuropsychology, 17*(3), 255–280. doi:10.1080/09297049.2010.535654

Ladson-Billings, G. & Tate, W. F. (1995) Toward a critical race theory of education. *Teachers College Record, 97*(1), 47–68.

Lapan, R. T., Kardash, C. A. M., & Turner, S. (2002). Empowering students to become self-regulated learners. *Professional School Counseling, 5*, 257–266.

Lapan, R. T., Wells, R., Petersen, J., & McCann, L. A. (2014). Stand tall to protect students: School counselors strengthening school connectedness. *Journal of Counseling & Development, 92*(3), 304–315.

Laska, K. M., Gurman, A. S., & Wampold, B. E. (2014). Expanding the lens of evidence-based practice in psychotherapy: A common factors perspective. *Psychotherapy, 51*(4), 467–481.

Lemberger, M. E. (2010). Advocating Student-within-Environment: A humanistic theory for school counseling. *The Journal of Humanistic Counseling, Education and Development, 49*(2), 131–146.

Lemberger, M. E., Carbonneau, K. J., Atencio, D. J., Zieher, A. K., & Palacios, A. (2018). Self-regulatory growth effects for young children participating in a combined social-emotional learning and mindfulness-based intervention. *Journal of Counseling and Development, 96*(3).

Lemberger, M. E., Carbonneau, K., Selig, J. P., & Bowers, H. (2018). The role of social-emotional mediators on middle school students' academic growth as fostered by an evidence-based intervention. *Journal of Counseling and Development, 96*(1), 27–40.

Lemberger, M. E., & Clemens, E. V. (2012). Connectedness and self-regulation as constructs of the Student Success Skills program in inner-city African-American elementary students. *Journal of Counseling and Development, 90*(4), 450–458.

Lemberger, M. E., & Hutchison, B. (2014). Advocating Student-within-Environment: A humanistic approach for therapists to animate social justice in the schools. *Journal of Humanistic Psychology, 54*(1), 28–44.

Lemberger, M. E., & Lemberger-Truelove, T. L. (2016). Bases for a more socially just humanistic praxis. *Journal of Humanistic Psychology, 56*(6), 571–580.

Lemberger, M. E., Selig, J. P., Bowers, H., & Rogers, J. E. (2015). The influence of the Student Success Skills program on the executive functioning skills, feelings of connectedness, and academic achievement in a predominately Hispanic, low-income middle school district. *Journal of Counseling and Development, 93*(1), 25–37.

Liew, J. (2012). Effortful control, executive functions, and education: Bringing self-regulatory and social-emotional competencies to the table. *Child Development Perspectives, 6*(2), 105–111.

Masten, A. S., & Coatsworth, J. D. (1998). The development of competence in favorable and unfavorable environments: Lessons from research on successful children. *American Psychologist, 53*(2), 205–220.

Martín-Baró, I. (1994). *Writings for a liberation psychology.* Cambridge, MA: Harvard University Press.

Niehaus, K., Moritz Rudasill, K., & Rakes, C. (2012). A longitudinal study of school connectedness and academic outcomes across sixth grade. *Journal of School Psychology, 50*(4), 443–460.

Oakley, D. A., & Halligan, P. W. (2017). Chasing the rainbow: the non-conscious nature of being. *Frontiers in Psychology, 8,* 1924.

Pascal, B. (1995), *Pensées.* (A.J. Krailsheimer, Trans.). London: Penguin Books.

Resnick, M. D., Bearman, P. S., Blum, R. W., Bauman, K. E., Harris, K. M., Jones, J., . . . Udry, J. R. (1997). Protecting adolescents from harm: Findings from the National Longitudinal Study on Adolescent Health. *Journal of the American Medical Association, 278*(10), 823–832.

Rowell, L. (2006). Action research and school counseling: Closing the gap between research and practice. *Professional School Counseling, 9*(4), 376–384.

Hernández, T. J., & Seem, S. R. (2004). A safe school climate: A systemic approach and the school counselor. *Professional School Counseling, 7,* 256–262.

Sesma, H. W., Mahone, E. M., Levine, T., Eason, S. H., & Cutting, L. E. (2009). The contribution of executive skills to reading comprehension. *Child Neuropsychology, 15*(3), 232–246.

Vallance, E. (1974). Hiding the hidden curriculum: An interpretation of the language of justification in nineteenth-century educational reform. *Curriculum Theory Network, 4*(1), 5–22.

Witherspoon, D., Schotland, M., Way, N., & Hughes, D. (2009). Connecting the dots: How connectedness to multiple contexts influences the psychological and academic adjustment of urban youth. *Applied Developmental Science, 13*(4), 199–216.

Yeager, D. S., & Dweck, C. S. (2012). Mindsets that promote resilience: When students believe that personal characteristics can be developed. *Educational Psychologist, 47*(4), 302–314.

PART FOUR

Supervising School Counselors

13

The Discrimination Model for School Counseling Supervision

MELISSA LUKE AND KRISTOPHER M. GOODRICH

A substantive supervision literature has emerged in the last 25 years (Bernard & Goodyear, 2014; Bernard & Luke, 2015), with a wide range of theoretical and empirical content to support and promote clinical supervision (Lazovsky & Shimoni, 2007). While supervision is an essential component of the training of professional counselors (Luke, Ellis, & Bernard, 2011), there are differing opinions about the standardized characterization, purpose, models, and processes of clinical supervision (Miller & Dollarhide, 2006). The impressive body of literature related to supervision has distinguished administrative and clinical supervision (Bernard & Goodyear, 2014; Dollarhide & Miller, 2006), but the varied definitions of supervision have been implicated as obstructive to the development of supervision theory, related research, and the translation of models into practice (Goodyear, Nelson, Bunch, & Clairborn, 2006; Whitman, Ryan, & Rubenstein, 2001), particularly with respect to school counseling (Luke et al., 2011).

A frequently cited definition of supervision as offered by Bernard and Goodyear (2014, p. 9) is:

> Supervision is an intervention provided by a more senior member of a profession to a more junior colleague or colleagues who typically (but not always) are members of that same profession. This relationship is evaluative and hierarchical, extends over time, and has the simultaneous purposes of enhancing the professional functioning of the more junior person(s); monitoring the quality of professional services offered to the clients that she,

he, or they see; and serving as a gatekeeper for the particular profession the
supervisee seeks to enter.

In addition to the functions included in this definition, supervision is also
recognized as a social process through which professional mores, attitudes,
values, thinking patterns, and problem-solving strategies are acquired (Auxier,
Hughes, & Kline, 2003; Luke & Gordon, 2012). Moreover, the Discrimination
Model is recognized as the most widely researched and implemented model of
supervision (Bernard & Goodyear, 2014). That said, to date, supervision has yet
to establish itself as a requisite practice in school counseling contexts outside of
training (Luke et al., 2011).

This chapter begins with a review of the theory of supervision, followed
by an application of the theory to school counseling supervision. Then the
Discrimination Model is presented for use in school counselor supervision; although it was conceived as a transtheoretical model, its use can be anchored
in the epistemology of social role models of supervision. Next, the theory of
change within the Discrimination Model is delineated as it applies to school
counselors, and how the Discrimination Model can be implemented in both
the training and practice of school counselors is illustrated. Following this
operationalization, the empirical support is reviewed and concomitant limitations are identified. Throughout the chapter, reflection moments are provided
wherein readers are encouraged to draw connections between the material and
their personal experiences. The chapter concludes with opportunities for the
reader to apply the Discrimination Model and the chapter content to school
counseling case vignettes. Last, the chapter provides a list of related resources.

THEORETICAL OVERVIEW OF SUPERVISION

Early approaches to supervision emerged out of various schools of counseling
and therapy (Holloway, 1992; Leddick & Bernard, 1980). Prior to the conceptualization of supervision as a distinct and separate practice from counseling and psychotherapy, supervisors transferred their knowledge about the
processes and procedures of a particular theoretical orientation into the domain of supervision. Eckstein and Wallerstein (1958) were among the earliest
to formalize a model of supervision. They presented definitive stages through
which the psychodynamic supervisor assisted the supervisee in increasing
self-awareness, which, in turn, was theorized to lead to a more effective therapeutic use of self. Kell and Mueller (1966) and Boyd (1978) offered the first
discussions of supervision that were not attached to a specific theoretical orientation. Embedded within even these initial supervisory theories were several
developmental assumptions: clinical skills can be refined through experiential

and didactic learning, theory and practice can be integrated through reflective practice, and the development of professional identity occurs through professional socialization (Bernard & Goodyear, 2014; Dollarhide & Miller, 2006; Holloway & Neufeldt, 1995; Watkins, 1995). Contemporary supervisory theory recognizes clinical supervision as a unique intervention that differs from teaching, counseling, or consultation (Bernard & Goodyear, 2014; Luke & Bernard, 2006). Although opinions vary about how long supervision should last, how much supervision is needed, and what the content should be, there is concurrence about its necessity (Holloway & Neufeldt, 1995; Robiner & Schofield, 1990). Consequently, multiple complex theories of supervision have emerged. However, most lack a solid empirical foundation (Green & Dye, 2002; Watkins, 1998).

Supervision of School Counselors

The literature is replete with discussions of the importance of clinical supervision for school counselors (Dollarhide & Miller, 2006; Luke & Bernard, 2006; Luke et al., 2011; Wood & Rayle, 2006). The recommended practicum and internship training experiences for school counselors include both individual and group supervision (American School Counselor Association, 2012, 2016; CACREP, 2016). Yet, in practice, school counselors receive little or no clinical supervision after graduation (American Association for Counseling and Development: School Counseling Task Force, 1989; Luke et al., 2011); instead, they tend to receive more administrative supervision. Administrative supervision can be seen as work-task-focused supervision, typically including personnel or program management and traditional day-to-day administrative tasks (Henderson, 1994); this differs from clinical supervision, which tends to be student- or client-focused supervision, which has a greater focus on the supervisee's clinical skills (or skills deficits), student/client conceptualization, and personalization issues of the counselor that might affect the therapeutic relationship (Bernard, 1979, 1997; Luke & Bernard, 2006). Numerous studies have documented the discrepancy between the numbers of practicing school counselors desiring supervision and those actually receiving it (Borders & Usher, 1992; Dollarhide & Miller, 2006; McMahon & Patton, 2000; Miller & Dollarhide, 2006; Page et al., 2001; Roberts & Borders, 1994; Sutton & Page, 1994). It has been speculated that the lack of access to supervision may contribute to the fact that roughly one third of the surveyed school counselors reported no need for clinical supervision (Dollarhide & Miller, 2006; Wilkerson, 2006).

A plethora of reasons have been suggested for the gaps between real and ideal supervisory practice, as well as for the disparity in perceptions of the need for supervision within a school counseling context (Dollarhide & Miller, 2006;

Luke & Bernard, 2006; Luke et al., 2011; Wilkerson, 2006; Wood & Rayle, 2006). Lazovsky and Shimoni (2007) described the "ongoing dialogue regarding theoretical models and concepts on the one hand, and perceived ideal and real roles, on the other" (p. 313) as vital for the professionalism of supervision in a school counseling context. However, the lack of available education or training in school counselor supervision has continually been cited in the school counseling literature as problematic (Herlihy, Gray, & McCollum, 2002; Luke et al., 2011). The same master's level school counselor practitioners who lack education or training in supervision are serving as site supervisors for school counseling students' internship experiences (DeKryf & Pehrsson, 2011; Luke et al., 2011), furthering the field's education and supervision gap.

REFLECTION MOMENT

What were your experiences of supervision? How much supervision did you receive? How much did you want? As a professional, have you had supervision? How might you utilize supervision now, differently than you have in the past?

Conceptualizations of Supervision

In the first edition of their text, *Fundamentals of Clinical Supervision*, Bernard and Goodyear (1992) differentiated among psychotherapy-based, developmental, and conceptual models of supervision. They later deleted their reference to conceptual models and, instead, referred to social role models (Bernard; 1997; Bernard & Goodyear, 2014). The term *social role model* has been further revised, and social role models are currently referred to as process models (Bernard & Goodyear, 2014). These three categories are now commonly used to distinguish supervision models (Bernard & Goodyear, 2014; Borders & Brown, 2005; Bradley & Ladany, 2001; Falender & Shafranske, 2004). The earliest conceptualizations of supervision largely depended on models of the counseling relationship (Eckstein & Wallerstein, 1958) and were described as psychoanalytic supervision, client-centered supervision, and so on. Developmental and process-based models emerged later (Bernard, 1979; Hawkins & Shohet, 1989; Holloway, 1995; Littrell, Lee-Borden, & Lorenz, 1979; Loganbill, Hardy, & Delworth, 1982).

Thirty years ago, Holloway (1987) described developmental models of supervision as having become "the zeitgeist of supervision thinking and research" (p. 209), with underlying assumptions of predictable, but dynamic and ongoing, growth. Though developmental models of supervision are intuitively appealing and remain widely used to conceptualize contemporary supervision,

several reviews of the related literature concluded that there is empirical un-
certainty regarding their validity (Goodyear & Robyak, 1982; Holloway, 1992;
Steven et al., 1998; Worthington, 1987).

While developmental models of supervision hinge upon the evolving needs of
the supervisee throughout training, process models of supervision emphasize the
roles and functions of counseling supervisors. Glidden and Tracey (1992) distinguished the value of social role (now process) models as providing structure to supervision, including direction for the supervisor in the use of supervisory foci and
roles. Other scholarly writing in supervision has categorized these same models
as eclectic, integrated, and process-based (Borders & Leddick, 1987; Bradley &
Ladany, 2001; Falender & Shafranske, 2004; Norcross & Halgin, 1997). Though the
referent terminology varies, there is general agreement that the included models
serve as "conceptual tools for understanding the interrelated forces that contribute
to the process of supervision" (Falender & Shafranske, 2004, p. 19).

According to Holloway (1995), the goal of supervision is to establish an ongoing relationship wherein the supervisor uses specific tasks and functions to
promote supervisee development. Process models of supervision, including
the Discrimination Model (Bernard, 1979, 1997), the Hawkins and Shohet
model (Hawkins & Shohet, 1989) and the Systems Approach to Supervision
model (Holloway, 1995), summarize supervisory behaviors, particularly the
component tasks and processes related to the role of the supervisor (Bernard &
Goodyear, 2014). As early as 1958, Apfelbaum introduced the roles of the critic,
model, and nurturer to distinguish varied therapeutic approaches. Much the
same way, Bernard (1979) used the supervisory foci and roles, and Hawkins and
Shohet (1989) and Holloway (1995) used supervisory goals, function, and style
to describe the supervisory activity embedded within the individualized work
between the supervisor and supervisee. While supervisors may have a predi-
lection for a particular role or style of supervision (Bernard, 1981; Holloway,
1995; Lazvosky & Shimoni, 2007; Putney, Worthington, & McCullough, 1992;
Shoffner & Briggs, 2001), the decision about which combination to use is best
informed by supervisee need and the context of the supervisory experience
(Bernard, 1997; Holloway, 1995; Stoltenberg, McNeill, & Delworth, 1998).

REFLECTION MOMENT

*Think about how you learn best. What enables you to learn? Now relate
that to supervision. What kind of supervisor behaviors did, or would best,
contribute to your learning? What are your preferred mechanisms and
modalities for receiving feedback? How might prior experiences with supervision influence your expectations for learning in supervision in the future?*

Although the formerly used term *social role model* accentuates the roles used by the supervisor, the role is only one variable in the equation of supervision. The empirical literature differs about the constructs on which the selection of supervisory role or style is based and includes the working alliance (Martin, Garske, & Davis, 2000), social influence attributes, such as expertness, trustworthiness, and attractiveness (Neufeldt, Beutler, & Ranchero, 1997), supervisee development (Ellis & Dell, 1986; Ellis et al., 1988; Gysbers & Johnston, 1965; Heppner & Roehlke, 1984), supervision setting and context (Lazvosky & Shimoni, 2007), and the theoretical orientation of both the supervisor and supervisee (Goodyear et al., 1984; Goodyear & Bradley, 1983; Goodyear & Robyak, 1982; Putney et al., 1992; Whitman et al., 2001). Regardless of how it is selected, each supervisory role or style implies a distinctive distribution of power between the supervisor and supervisee (Holloway, 1995).

There is considerable contemporary discussion and application of process models of supervision (e.g., Pearson, 2001, 2004, 2006), as these models outline the behaviors and expectancies associated with the styles and roles supervisors enact in relation to their supervisees (Bernard & Goodyear, 2014; Holloway, 1992). However, research has not supported a clear supervisee preference for any one supervisory role or style (Fernando & Hulse-Killacky, 2005; Lazvosky & Shimoni, 2007; Shechtman & Wirtzberger, 1999), nor have there been consistent supervisor-reported benefits in productivity, efficiency, or learning attributed to a particular role (Holloway & Wampold, 1983). As process models tend to be atheoretical, like the Discrimination Model (Bernard, 1979, 1997), they can be used in conjunction with developmental approaches and within various other theoretically aligned models (Bernard & Goodyear, 2014). The Discrimination Model remains one of the most widely used conceptual frames for supervision (Bernard & Goodyear, 2014; Borders & Brown, 2005). Indicators of its influence in the conceptualization and practice of supervision are the facts that the Discrimination Model is one of the most extensively researched supervision models in general (Lazvosky & Shimoni, 2007) and that it is the only model in its category that has been extensively empirically examined. Although other process models have been developed specifically for school counselor supervision (Luke & Bernard, 2006; Nelson & Johnson, 1999; Struder, 2005; Wood & Rayle, 2006), many school counselor supervisors rely upon the Discrimination Model to support their school counseling supervisory practice (Luke et al., 2011).

THE DISCRIMINATION MODEL

The Discrimination Model (Bernard, 1979, 1997) is generally accepted as "one of the best-known models of supervision" (Borders & Brown, 2005, p. 7). In reference to the effects of various supervision models, Lazovsky and Shimoni (2007) described the Discrimination Model as having "been most influential in designing and understanding the supervisor role" (p. 305). Rooted in technical eclecticism, the Discrimination Model was so named because it relies upon the supervisor to discriminate among possible areas of focus in supervision according to supervisee need and, subsequently, to adjust the selected supervisor role to most effectively approach this material with the supervisee. The transtheoretical origin of the Discrimination Model enables it to stand alone as a three-focus (i.e., intervention skills, conceptualization skills, and personalization skills) and three-role (i.e., teacher, counselor, and consultant) conceptual map for supervisors to organize and track their supervisory efforts or to be combined with other, perhaps more theoretically oriented, supervisory frameworks.

The Discrimination Model (Bernard, 1979, 1997) was developed as "the simplest of maps" (Bernard, 1997, p. 310) for supervisors-in-training to conceptualize the categories of counselor behavior that would benefit from supervisory interventions and the forms the interventions would take. It proposed three foci of supervision and three role postures of the supervisor (Bernard, 1979). The three areas of focus include intervention skills (originally labeled process skills), conceptualization skills, and personalization skills. Within the clinical supervision of counseling, intervention skills are said to "include all observable counselor behaviors that distinguish counseling as an intentional interpersonal activity" (Luke & Bernard, 2006, p. 284). These counseling techniques and strategies are implemented for the client's therapeutic gain.

Conceptualization skills are less obvious and may require indirect assessment on the part of the supervisor through discussion with the supervisee. These cognitive skills involve the supervisee's ability to detect, organize, and respond to the client-generated data and case material. Personalization skills may also require initial supervisor interpretation and include the supervisee's personal responses and attributes used within counseling and supervision, as well as the ability of the supervisee to use the self of the therapist within these relationships. Lanning (1986) proposed the addition of a fourth focus category for professional behavior, but Bernard (1997) subsumed these activities within the original model. Although each focus is discussed as a separate area for supervisory attention, in counseling practice, these skills may appear in combination.

Reflecting its classification as a social role model of supervision (Bernard & Goodyear, 2014), the Discrimination Model identifies the three potential supervisor approaches as the roles (or metaphor) of teacher, counselor, and consultant. Although all three foci can be addressed through any of the three roles, Bernard (1979) suggested that each role has differential effects on the supervision provided. In the teacher role, the supervisor uses a didactic and structured approach and is concerned with instruction, modeling, and evaluation. In the role of the counselor, the supervisor facilitates, as opposed to directs, the supervisory interaction. In this role, the supervisor assists with reflection on, and exploration of, the supervisee's internal reality as related to the counseling case. Operating from a consultant role, the supervisor shares the responsibility and control of the supervisee's learning and development within supervision and encourages the supervisee to develop, access, and utilize an internal frame of reference.

Bernard's (1979, 1997) Discrimination Model is widely utilized in the supervision of counselors in both training and practice settings (Borders & Benshoff, 1999; Borders & Brown, 2005). Advantages of the Discrimination Model include its simple and straightforward identification of supervisor roles in relation to supervisee needs (Ellis & Ladany, 1997). The purpose of the Discrimination Model is to give supervisors a cognitive map that tracks the focus of supervision and determines the best supervisory approach for accomplishing supervision goals. While supervisors often have a preference for focus or role (Bernard, 1981; Holloway, 1995; Putney et al., 1992), and there are some focus-role pairs that for practical reasons may be used more than others (Stenack & Dye, 1982, 1983), all of the nine-cell combinations within the Discrimination Model are both independent and feasible (Ellis & Dell, 1986; Luke et al., 2011). Further, Ellis and Ladany (1997) asserted that the model's straightforward conceptual approach to supervisory foci and roles make it a useful tool in the examination of supervisory processes.

School Counseling Supervision Model

Although the Discrimination Model by itself may have great utility for practicing school counselors and their supervisors, new models of supervision have taken the Discrimination Model and applied it to the field of school counseling more specifically. This type of clinical supervision extension models have been called "target issue" models by Bernard and Goodyear (2014) because they are focused on a specific task or target; in this case, it is the application of school counseling. The School Counseling Supervision Model (SCSM; Luke & Bernard, 2006) further applied the Discrimination Model by targeting and describing how supervision can take place utilizing the roles and responsibilities of professional school counselors as discussed by the American School Counselor Association (ASCA; 2012).

The SCSM is built off an application of the ASCA National Model, namely one of the four components making up the model, the Delivery System. The Delivery System consists of the services the school counselor provides to school stakeholders (students, families, school staff, and community) and includes both direct and indirect services. Utilizing the Delivery System from the ASCA National Model (2012), the SCSM is a 3 × 3 × 4 model that supervisors use as a "point of entry" to initate the supervisory relationship. Points of entry are described by the authors of this model as the specific roles or tasks in which the school counseling supervisee is engaged when applying school counseling services. They include counseling and consultation, large-group intervention, individual and group advisement, and planning, co-ordinating, and evaluation. From the identified point of entry, supervisors then work with their supervisees using the roles (teacher, consultant, and counselor) and foci (intervention, conceptualization, and personalization) of the Discrimination Model to explore, understand, and challenge their supervisees across the various functions of school counselors in a comprehensive, developmental school counseling model to ensure appropriate and intentional services for the students whom they serve. As such, the SCSM is different from the Discrimination Model in that, as opposed to the Discrimination Model, which is flexible in adaption by design, the SCSM has a specific focus on the delivery of school counseling services across the ASCA National Model (2012). The SCSM adapts the roles and foci of the Discrimination Model but adds the points of entry to steer the supervisor to explore across the dimensions of direct and indirect services, to ensure that school counselors provide a comprehensive, developmental program to the students they serve.

Theory of Change

The theory behind providing supervision of counseling services is that supervision will have a positive influence on supervisee behavior and, through this intervention, client outcomes will improve. In the contexts of school counseling, one would surmise that the theory of change is that, through use of the SCSM, supervisors of school counselors will see increased professional functioning across the four points of entry (areas of professional functioning) across the ASCA National Model's (2012) Delivery System by school counselors, and those school counselors will see improved outcomes of their P-12 students. For example, the supervisory dyad must first make a determination about the identified point of entry from the four possible across the ASCA National Model Delivery System, and then the area of focus is selected (intervention, conceptualization, personalization). Dependent on the supervisor's ascribed theoretical positioning, the context of supervision, and the level of development of the supervisee and his or her needs, these decisions may be more or less collaboratively determined. That said, the supervisor then utilizes clinical and educational judgment to select the most appropriate supervisory role through which to operate in order to maximize the opportunities for supervisee growth and development. While Bernard (1979) cautioned about the importance of supervisory transparency and clarity with respect to the identified focus, scholars have subsequently highlighted advantages in supervisory flexibility across roles (Luke & Bernard, 2012, Luke et al., 2011), as this provides a broader range of opportunities for change. Although the SCSM has up to this point not been widely empirically researched, Luke, Ellis, and Bernard (2011) did find preliminary support for the model. Additionally, it should be noted that the Discrimination Model (Bernard, 1979, 1997), on which the SCSM is based, is one of the most empirically explored models of clinical supervision currently available (Bernard & Goodyear, 2014).

Exploring clinical supervision in general, empirical research has found direct effects of supervision on supervisee competence (Bernard & Goodyear, 2014). Utilizing the Discrimination Model as a framework, Bernard and Goodyear claim that supervisors indirectly influence supervisees' professional competence by focusing on issues related to the supervisee's self, case conceptualization, and skills and strategies. Although this association has not been directly examined, Bernard and Goodyear (2014) noted that because so much supervision research has focused on the direct outcomes with supervisees, this indirect association has been well established.

REFLECTION MOMENT

How would you capture the outcomes of supervisees in a school? How would you study the effect of supervision on student learning? What evidence do you use to measure your own or others' growth and development in supervision?

Less well established is the effect of supervision on client outcomes. As noted by numerous scholars (Callahan, Almstrom, Swift, Borja, & Heath, 2009; Freitas, 2002; Hill & Knox, 2013; Watkins, 2011), this has been the most difficult to establish. Supervision research up to this point in time has focused on process variables, including supervisory alliance, but less attention has been paid to outcome variables. This may be due to the complexities and challenges of supervision research, as many supervisory pairs involve one supervisor, one or more supervisees, and then a host of supervisees' students or clients. Therefore, supervisory outcome-based research shares similar challenges as found when researching nested variables involved in classroom or group processes. However, scholars have found an influence of supervision on supervisee–client interactions. For example, Patton and Kivlighan (1997) found that the quality of the working alliance between supervisor and supervisee affected the quality of the working alliance between supervisee and client. In a related finding, a positive supervisory relationship has been found to increase supervisory modeling and accommodation of observed supervisor behavior; lower supervisory anxiety and role ambiguity, while increasing supervisee confidence; contribute to the development of basic counseling skills; and assist in managing challenging therapeutic impasses or disruption in the counselor–client working alliance (Bambling, King, Raue, Schweitzer, & Lambert, 2015). Thus, although we do not currently know the exact mechanisms for change that may come from the clinical supervision process, it is clear that change does occur through the process of receiving clinical supervision.

Application

Lucy is a 20-year veteran school counselor working in an urban middle school setting. Felicia is a school counselor-in-training, completing her first internship under Lucy's supervision. Felicia has previously informed her classmates and professors in the counseling program that she decided to pursue a career in school counseling because she "likes kids," "adults scare her," and she likes individual interaction so she can have an influence on children's development.

REFLECTION MOMENT

What are some areas of focus that immediately come to mind when Felicia discusses her interest in the field of school counseling? Might there be other ideas or paths you may wish to follow? If so, what roles or foci might you employ to understand this supervisee more?

In exploring Felicia's work as an intern, Lucy began to notice that Felicia has either shied away from, or avoided, large-group guidance interventions when offered the opportunity. Additionally, when Felicia's assigned students were found to struggle in certain classrooms, Lucy noticed that Felicia would not seek outside support or consultation from the students' teachers or attempt to engage the student's parents. Lucy noted that she has had least two different points of entry that she could attend to.

REFLECTION MOMENT

What points of entry might you attend to in this moment? How would each potential point of entry shift the subsequent focus? How might you utilize the varied roles the SCSM to address some of these concerns raised?

Using the Large-Group Intervention as a point of intervention (see Figure 13.1 for more details), Lucy could explore with Felicia what was informing her lack of engagement with guidance curriculum. If Felicia noted that she struggled to understand how to frame and prepare for the interventions, Lucy could utilize either the consultant role (to brainstorm with her) or teacher role (to instruct Felicia how to frame and prepare for the intervention) to focus Felicia on how to conceptualize (the focus) the intervention. If Felicia noted

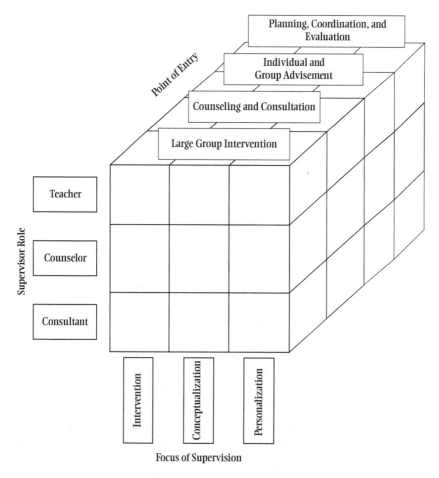

Figure 13.1. School Counseling Supervision Model (SCSM).

that she had deficits in speaking to large groups, Lucy could use her teacher role to instruct Felicia in the different skills (focus) she would need to have to successfully facilitate the program. Finally, if fear was motivating Felicia's lack of engagement with large-group intervention, Lucy could take on the counselor role with a personalization focus to understand what motivated Felicia's fear of speaking in front of large groups and work to explore ways that Felicia may find symptom relief so that she could move past her fear to fulfill that function of a school counselor.

REFLECTION MOMENT

Has there ever been a time in your life when you might have identified with Felicia and her concerns? If so, how might you use that in your supervisory relationship to support Felicia in her growth as a school counselor? How might you infuse your understanding of counselor development or specific counseling theories into your approach?

Another potential point of entry for Lucy is Counseling and Consultation, as Felicia appeared to struggle to engage with teachers or parents to support the needs of her students. As described above, Lucy could select a role (teacher, consultant, or counselor) based upon how active or supportive the supervisee needed the supervisor to be. The teaching role could be employed if Felicia did not know what consultation was, or how it could be useful in the school counseling setting. The consultant role might be employed if Felicia knew conceptually about consultation, but needed help brainstorming ways in which it could occur. Finally, the counselor role could be utilized if Lucy needed to probe Felicia to understand what was motivating her functioning (or lack of functioning) in this domain. After selecting a role, the supervisor would then decide what focus to take. This could either be around conceptualization (knowledge or knowledge deficits around consultation), skills (behavioral interventions that could be employed either in consulting with others, or skills working with adults), or personalization (fears, anxieties, countertransference, or other personalization issues that guide supervisee behavior).

REFLECTION MOMENT

If you were the supervisor, what roles or foci might you employ with Felicia and why? How might you anticipate the role and focus selected would support Felicia in her growth? What focus might be harder for you to address? In what ways might you struggle to enact certain roles and why?

It should be noted that across both examples, Lucy would not select one role or focus and stick with it throughout the supervisory session; instead, Lucy would fluidly move across the different roles and foci to better understand the full picture of Felicia and her work. This way, Lucy would have a more comprehensive picture of Felicia's functioning as a school counselor and ensure that all the learning needs of the supervisee could be attended to. This also ensures that the theories and beliefs of the supervisor do not inadvertently lead the session, so that incorrect assumptions are challenged and revised to best understand intervention needed by the supervisee (for example, a supervisor might believe a supervisee was anxious when a large-group intervention does not go well, and instead find it was an issue around organization and preparation). It is worthwhile to point out that the model provides a highly useful way to map out or document supervisory interventions to track supervisee reactions and responses to supervision. For example, some scholars report that they take notes and map the notes onto the model to better see what themes emerge in the supervisee's work. This can help to indicate areas that supervisors need to attend to (e.g., areas of supervisee need), as well as to ensure that no area has gone unexplored throughout the supervisory process.

Research

The Discrimination Model has received at least partial support in a variety of studies (Clingerman & Bernard, 2004; Ellis & Dell, 1986; Ellis, Dell, & Good, 1988; Fall & Sutton, 2004; Glidden & Tracey, 1992; Goodyear, Abadie, & Efros, 1984; Goodyear & Robyak, 1982; Lazovsky & Shimoni, 2007; Luke et al., 2011; Stenack & Dye, 1982, 1983; Yager, Wilson, Brewer, & Kinnetz, 1989). Specifically, research has supported that the three foci of the Discrimination Model are distinguishable from one another (Goodyear & Robyak, 1982; Stenack & Dye, 1982, 1983). However, the emphasized focus of supervision was inconsistent across the reviewed studies, with three studies reporting personalization (Clingerman & Bernard, 2004; Freeman & McHenry, 1996; Henry, Hart, & Nance, 2004) and three others reporting conceptualization (Goodyear & Robyak, 1982; Fall & Sutton, 2004; Putney et al., 1992) as the most frequently used focus. Although clear distinctions were repeatedly found between the supervisory roles of teacher and counselor, the role of consultant has appeared less discernable (Goodyear et al., 1984; Lazovsky & Shimoni, 2007; Stenack & Dye, 1982). Yet, the egalitarian role of consultant stood out as the role of choice for both supervision of entry-level counselors in practice settings (Fall & Sutton, 2004; Hart & Nance, 2003) and supervisees in the school context (Shechtman & Wirtzberger, 1999), as well as for supervisors with a cognitive-behavioral theoretical orientation (Putney et al., 1992). Another noteworthy finding is that use of the supervisory roles, such as teacher, counselor, and consultant, differentially affected the supervision (Stenack & Dye, 1983). Similarly, the adjunctive theoretical orientation of the supervisor was shown to influence supervision processes, including the selection of supervisory foci and roles (Freeman & McHenry, 1996; Goodyear et al., 1984; Goodyear & Robyak, 1982; Putney et al., 1992). Because a general preference or advantage for a particular focus or role remains unclear, it is assumed that effective supervision entails a flexible use of all foci and roles (Goodyear & Robyak, 1982; Struder, 2005).

In their study of school counseling supervisors' conceptualization of the Discrimination Model, Luke et al. (2011) found that school counselor supervisors share some of the same conceptualizations as their university counterparts, but they also differ as well. Furthermore, Goodrich and Luke (2011) extended the Discrimination Model to facilitate supervision of group work. Luke and Goodrich (2013) utilized discourse analysis to test the supervision of group work with school counselors-in-training and found empirical support for the model. As such, there appears to be empirical support in extending the Discrimination Model to target issue models, specifically with school counseling. Future scholars could utilize quantitative techniques, such as multilevel modeling, to explore supervisory outcomes of the use of SCSM on supervisee while concurrently attending to statistical fixes for the violation of independence assumption inherent in grouped data and which is not often addressed by researchers in designing their work (Boyle et al., 2017; McCarthy, Whittaker, Boyle, & Eyal, 2017; Selig et al., 2017). Qualitatively, scholars might interview practicing supervisors of school counselors, as well as those who have been supervised, using the SCSM to explore how this model has been implemented in the supervisory relationship and ways in which supervisors might more intentionally attend to supervisee and student needs while engaged in its practice.

SUGGESTED READINGS

American Association for Counseling and Development, School Counseling Task Force. (1989). *School counseling: A profession at risk* [Final report]. Alexandria, VA: American Association for Counseling and Development.

American School Counselor Association (ASCA). (2016). *Why school counseling directors/coordinators?* Available from https://www.schoolcounselor.org/school-counselors-members/careers-roles/why-school-counseling-directors-coordinators

Dollarhide, C. T., & Miller, G. M. (2006). Supervision for preparation and practice of school counselors: Pathways to excellence. *Counselor Education and Supervision, 45*(4), 242–252. doi:10.1002/j.1556-6978.2006.tb00001.x

Glaes, J. M. (2010). *Implementing an ASCA-informed school counselor supervision model: A qualitative field-based study* (Doctoral dissertation). Retrieved from ProQuest Dissertations Publishing. (Accession No. 3410401)

Sunde-Peterson, J., & Deuschle, C. (2006). A model for supervising school counseling students without teaching experience. *Counselor Education and Supervision, 45*(4), 267–281. doi:10.1002/j.1556-6978.2006.tb00003.x

Wood, C., & Dixon-Rayle, A. (2006). A model of school counseling supervision: The goals, functions, roles, and systems model. *Counselor Education and Supervision, 45*(4), 253–266. doi:10.1002/j.1556-6978.2006.tb00002.x

REFERENCES

American School Counselor Association. (2012). *ASCA National Model: A framework for school counseling programs* (3rd ed.). Alexandria, VA: Author.

American School Counselor Association. (2016). *ASCA ethical standards for school counselors.* Available from https://www.schoolcounselor.org/asca/media/asca/Ethics/EthicalStandards2016.pdf

Auxier, C. R., Hughes, F. R., & Kline, W. B. (2003). Identity development in counselors-in-training. *Counselor Education and Supervision, 43*(1), 25–38. doi:10.1002/j.1556-6978.2003.tb01827.x

Bambling, M., King, R., Raue, P., Schweitzer, R., & Lambert, W. (2015). Clinical supervision: Its influence on client-related working alliance and client symptom reduction in the brief treatment of major depression. *Psychotherapy Research, 16*(3), 317–331. DOI: 10.1080/10503300500268524

Bernard, J. M. (1979). Supervisor training: A Discrimination Model. *Counselor Education and Supervision, 19*, 60–68.

Bernard, J. M. (1981). Inservice training for clinical supervisors. *Professional Psychology, 12*(6), 740–748. doi:10.1037//0735-7028.12.6.740

Bernard, J. M. (1997). The Discrimination Model. In C. E. Watkins, Jr. (Ed.), *Handbook of psychotherapy supervision* (pp. 310–327). New York, NY: Wiley.

Bernard, J. M., & Goodyear, R. K. (2014). *Fundamentals of clinical supervision.* Boston, MA: Pearson.

Bernard, J. M., & Luke, M. (2015). A content analysis of 10 years of clinical supervision articles in counseling. *Counselor Education and Supervision, 54*(5), 242–257. doi:10.1002/ceas.12024

Borders, L. D., & Benshoff, J. M. (1999). *Clinical supervision: Learning to think like a supervisor* [Video recording and guide booklet]. Produced by the Department of Counseling and Educational Development, University of North Carolina, Greensboro.

Borders, L. D., & Brown, L. L. (2005). *The new hand of counseling supervision.* Mahwah, NJ: Lahaska Press.

Borders, L. D., & Leddick, G. R. (1987). *Handbook of counseling supervision.* Washington DC: Author.

Borders, L. D., & Usher, C. H. (1992). Post-degree supervision: Existing and preferred practices. *Journal of Counseling & Development, 70*(5), 594–599. doi:10.1002/j.1556-6676.1992.tb01667.x

Boyd, J. (1978). *Counselor supervision: Approaches, preparation, practices.* Muncie, IN: Accelerated Development.

Boyle, L. H., Whittaker, T. A., Eyal, M., & McCarthy, C. J. (2017). What really happens in quantitative group research? Results of a content analysis of recent quantitative research in JSGW. *The Journal for Specialists in Group Work, 42*(3), 243–252. http://dx.doi.org/10.1080/01933922.2017.1338812

Bradley, L. J., & Ladany, N. (2001). *Counselor supervision: Principles, process, and practice* (3rd ed.). Philadelphia, PA: Brunner-Routledge.

Callahan, J. L., Almstrom, C. M., Swift, J. K., Borja, S. E., & Heath, C. J. (2009). Exploring the contribution of supervisors to intervention outcomes. *Training and Education in Professional Psychology, 3*(2), 72–77. doi:10.1037/a0014294

Clingerman, T. L., & Bernard, J. M. (2004). An investigation of the use of e-mail as a supplemental modality for clinical supervision. *Counselor Education and Supervision, 44*(2), 92–95. doi:10.1002/j.1556-6978.2004.tb01862.x

Council for the Accreditation of Counseling and Related Educational Standards (CACREP). (2016). CACREP 2016 Standards. Available from http://www.cacrep.org/wp-content/uploads/2016/06/2016-Standards-with-Glossary-rev-2.2016.pdf

DeKruyf, L., & Pehrsson, D. (2011). School counseling site supervisor training: An exploratory study. *Counselor Education and Supervision, 50*(5), 314–327.

Dollarhide, C. T., & Miller, G. M. (2006). Supervision for preparation and practice of school counselors: Pathways to excellence. *Counselor Education and Supervision, 45*(4), 242.

Eckstein R., & Wallerstein, R. S. (1958). *The teaching and learning of psychotherapy.* New York, NY: International Universities Press.

Ellis, M. V., & Dell, D. M. (1986). Dimensionality of supervisor roles: Supervisors' perceptions of supervision. *Journal of Counseling Psychology, 33*(3), 282–291. doi:10.1037//0022-0167.33.3.282

Ellis, M. V., Dell, D. M., & Good, G. E. (1988). Counselor trainees' perceptions of supervisor roles: Two studies testing the dimensionality of supervision. *Journal of Counseling Psychology, 35*, 315–324.

Ellis, M. V., & Ladany, N. (1997). Inferences concerning supervisees and clients in clinical supervision: An integrative review. In C. E. Watkins (Ed.), *Handbook of psychotherapy supervision* (pp. 447–507). Hoboken, NJ: John Wiley & Sons.

Falender, C. A., & Shafranske, E. P. (2004). *Clinical supervision: A competency-based approach.* Washington, DC: American Psychological Association. doi:10.1037/10806-000

Fall, M., & Sutton, J. M. (2004). FallSupervision of entry level licensed counselors: A descriptive study. *The Clinical Supervisor, 22*(2), 139–151. doi:10.1300/J001v22n02_09

Fernando, D. M., & Hulse-Killacky, D. (2005). The relationship of supervisory styles to satisfaction with supervision and the perceived self-efficacy of a master's-level counseling students. *Counselor Education and Supervision, 44*(4), 293–304. doi:10.1002/j.1556-6978.2005.tb01757.x

Freeman, B., & McHenry, S. (1996). Clinical supervision of counselors-in-training: A nationwide survey of ideal delivery, goals, and theoretical influences. *Counselor Education and Supervision, 36*(2), 144–158. doi:10.1002/j.1556-6978.1996.tb00382.x

Freitas, G. J. (2002). The impact of psychotherapy supervision on client outcome: A critical examination of 2 decades of research. *Psychotherapy: Theory, Research, Practice, Training, 39*(4), 354–367. doi:10.1037//0033-3204.39.4.354

Glidden, C. E., & Tracey, T. J. (1992). A multidimensional scaling analysis of supervisory dimensions and their perceived relevance across trainee experience levels. *Professional Psychology: Research and Practice, 23*(2), 151–157. doi:10.1037/0735-7028.23.2.151

Goodrich, K. M., & Luke, M. (2011). The LGBTQ responsive model for supervision of group work. *The Journal for Specialists in Group Work, 36*(1), 22–40. doi:10.1080/01933922.2010.537739

Goodyear, R. K., Abadie, P. D., & Efros, F. (1984). Supervisory theory into practice: Differential perception of supervision by Ekstein, Ellis, Polster, and Rogers. *Journal of Counseling Psychology, 31*(2), 228–237. doi:10.1037/0022-0167.31.2.228

Goodyear, R. K., & Bradley, F. O. (1983). Theories of counselor supervision: Points of convergence and divergence. *The Counseling Psychologist, 11*(1), 59–67. doi:10.1177/0011000083111010

Goodyear, R. K., Nelson, M. L., Bunch, K., & Clairborn, C. D. (2006). Current supervision scholarship in psychology: A five year review. *The Clinical Supervisor, 24*(1-2), 137. doi:10.1300/J001v24n01_07

Goodyear, R. K., & Robyak, J. E. (1982). Supervisors' theory and experience in supervisory focus. *Psychological Reports, 51*(3), 978–978. doi:10.2466/pr0.1982.51.3.978

Green, D., & Dye, L. (2002). How should we best train clinical psychology supervisors? A Delphi survey. *Psychology Learning and Teaching, 2*, 108–115.

Gysbers, N. C., & Johnston, J. A. (1965). Expectations of a practicum supervisor's role. *Counselor Education and Supervision, 4*(2), 68–74. doi:10.1002/j.1556-6978.1965.tb02182.x

Hart, G. M., & Nance, D. (2003). Styles of counselor supervision as perceived by supervisors and supervisees. *Counselor Education and Supervision, 43*(2), 146–158. doi:10.1002/j.1556-6978.2003.tb01838.x

Hawkins, P., & Shohet, R. (1989). *Supervision in the helping professions: An individual, group, and organizational approach.* Philadelphia, PA: Open University Press.

Henderson, P. (1994). Administrative skills in counseling supervision. Available from https://www.counseling.org/Resources/Library/ERIC%20Digests/94-24.pdf

Henry, P. J., Hart, G. M., & Nance, D. W. (2004). Supervision topics as perceived by supervisors and supervisees. *The Clinical Supervisor, 23*(2), 139–152.

Heppner, P. P., & Roehlke, H. J. (1984). Differences among supervisees at different levels of training: Implications for a developmental model of supervision. *Journal of Counseling Psychology, 31*(1), 76–90. doi:10.1037/0022-0167.31.1.76

Herlihy, B., Gray, N., & McCollum, V. (2002). Legal and ethical issues in school counselor supervision. *Professional School Counseling, 6*(1), 55–60.

Hill, C. E., & Knox, S. (2013). Training and supervision in psychotherapy. In M. J. Lambert (Ed.), *Bergin and Garfield's handbook of psychotherapy and behavior change* (6th ed., pp. 775–811). Hoboken, NJ: John Wiley & Sons.

Holloway, E. L. (1987). Developmental models of supervision: Is it development? *Professional Psychology: Research and Practice, 18*(3), 209–216. doi:10.1037/0735-7028.18.3.209

Holloway, E. (1992). Supervision: A way of teaching and learning In S. Brown & R. Lent (Eds.), *The handbook of counseling psychology* (2nd ed.). New York, NY: Wiley.

Holloway, E. L. (1995). *Clinical supervision: A systems approach.* Thousand Oaks, CA: Sage.

Holloway, E. L., & Neufeldt, S. A. (1995). Supervision: Its contributions to treatment efficacy. *Journal of Consulting and Clinical Psychology, 63*(2), 207–213. doi:10.1037/0022-006X.63.2.207

Holloway, E. L., & Wampold, B. E. (1983). Patterns of verbal behavior and judgments of satisfaction in the supervision interview. *Journal of Counseling Psychology, 30*(2), 227–234. doi:10.1037/0022-0167.30.2.227

Kell, B. L., & Mueller, W. J. (1966). *Impact and change: A study of counseling relationships.* New York, NY: Appleton-Century-Crofts.

Lanning, W. (1986). Development of the supervisor emphasis rating form. *Counselor Education and Supervision, 25*, 191–196.

Lazovsky, R., & Shimoni, A. (2007). The on-site mentor of counseling interns: Perceptions of ideal role and actual role performance. *Journal of Counseling & Development, 85*(3), 303–316. doi:10.1002/j.1556-6678.2007.tb00479.x

Leddick, G. R., & Bernard, J. M. (1980). The history of supervision: A critical review. *Counselor Education and Supervision, 20*, 186–196.

Littrell, J. M., Lee-Borden, N., & Lorenz, J. (1979). A developmental framework for counseling supervision. *Counselor Education and Supervision, 19*, 129–136.

Loganbill, C., Hardy, E., & Delworth, U. (1982). Supervision: A conceptual model. *The Counseling Psychologist, 10*(1), 3–42. doi:10.1177/0011000082101002

Luke, M., & Bernard, J. M. (2006). The school counseling supervision model: An extension of the Discrimination Model. *Counselor Education and Supervision, 45*(4), 282–295. doi:10.1002/j.1556-6678.2006.tb00004.x

Luke, M., Ellis, M. V., & Bernard, J. M. (2011). School counselor supervisors' perceptions of the Discrimination Model of Supervision. *Counselor Education and Supervision, 50*(5), 328–343. doi:10.1002j.1556-6978.2011.tb01919.x

Luke, M., & Goodrich, K. M. (2013). Investigating the LGBTQ responsive model for supervision of group work. *The Journal for Specialists in Group Work, 38*(2), 121–145. doi:10.1080/01933922.2013.775207

Luke, M., & Gordon, C. (2012). Supervisors' use of reinforcement, reframing, and advice to re-author the supervisory narrative through e-mail supervision. *The Clinical Supervisor, 31*(2), 159–177. doi:10.1080/07325223.2013.730020

Martin, D. J., Garske, J. P., & Davis, M. K. (2000). Relation of the therapeutic alliance with outcome and other variables: A meta-analytic review. *Journal of Consulting and Clinical Psychology, 68*(3), 438–450. doi:10.1037/0022-006X.68.3.438

McCarthy, C. J., Whittaker, T. A., Boyle, L. H., & Eyal, M. (2017). Quantitative approaches to group research: Suggestions for best practices. *The Journal for Specialists in Group Work, 42*(1), 3–16.

McMahon, M., & Patton, W. (2000). Beyond 2000: Incorporating the constructivist influence into career guidance and counselling. *Australian Journal of Career Development, 9*(1), 25–29. doi:10.1177/103841620000900106

Miller, G. M., & Dollarhide, C. T. (2006). Supervision in schools: Building pathways to excellence. *Counselor Education and Supervision, 45*(4), 296–303. doi:10.1002/j.1556-6978.2006.tb00005.x

Nelson, M. D., & Johnson, P. (1999). School counselors as supervisors: An integrated approach for supervising school counseling interns. *Counselor Education and Supervision, 39*(2), 89–100.

Neufeldt, S. A., Beutler, L. E., & Ranchero, R. (1997). Research on supervisor variables in psychotherapy supervision. In C. E. Watkins, Jr. (Ed.), *Handbook of psychotherapy supervision* (pp. 508–525). New York, NY: John Wiley & Sons.

Norcross, J. C., & Halgin, R. P. (1997). Integrative approaches to psychotherapy supervision. In C. E. Watkins (Ed.), *Handbook of psychotherapy supervision* (pp. 203–222). New York, NY: Wiley.

Page, B. J., Pietrzak, D. R., & Sutton, J. M. (2001). National survey of school counselor supervision. *Counselor Education & Supervision, 41*, 142–150. doi:10.1002/j.1556-6978.2001.tb01278.x

Patton, M. J., & Kivlighan, D. M. (1997). Relevance of the supervisory alliance to the counseling alliance and to treatment adherence in counselor training. *Journal of Counseling Psychology, 44*(1), 108–115. doi:10.1037/0022-0167.44.1.108

Pearson, Q. M. (2001). A case in clinical supervision: A framework for putting theory into practice. *Journal of Mental Health Counseling, 23*, 147–183.

Pearson, Q. M. (2004). Getting the most out of clinical supervision: Strategies for mental health counseling students. *Journal of Mental Health Counseling, 26*, 361–373.

Pearson, Q. M. (2006). Psychotherapy-driven supervision: Integrating counseling theories into role-based supervision. *Journal of Mental Health Counseling, 28*, 241–253.

Putney, M. W., Worthington, E. L., & McCullough, M. E. (1992). Effects of supervisor and supervisee theoretical orientation and supervisor-supervisee matching on interns' perceptions of supervision. *Journal of Counseling Psychology, 39*(2), 258–265. doi:10.1037/0022-0167.39.2.258

Roberts, E. B., & Borders, L. D. (1994). Supervision of school counselors: Administrative, program, and counseling. *The School Counselor, 41*(3), 149–157.

Robiner, W. N., & Schofield, W. (1990). References on supervision in clinical and counseling psychology. *Professional Psychology: Research and Practice, 21*(4), 297–312. doi:10.1037/0735-7028.21.4.297

Selig, J. P., Trott, A., & Lemberger, M. E. (2017). Multilevel modeling for research in group work. *The Journal for Specialists in Group Work, 42*(2), 1–17.

Shechtman, Z., & Wirtzberger, A. (1999). Needs and preferred style of supervision among Israeli school counselors at different stages of professional development. *Journal of Counseling & Development, 77*, 454–464.

Shoffner, M. F., & Briggs, M. K. (2001). An interactive approach for developing interprofessional collaboration: Preparing school counselors. *Counselor Education and Supervision, 40*(3), 193–202. doi:10.1002/j.1556-6978.2001.tb01252.x

Stenack, R. J., & Dye, H. A. (1982). Behavioral descriptions of counseling supervision roles. *Counselor Education and Supervision, 21*, 295–304.

Stenack, R. J., & Dye, H. A. (1983). Practicum supervision roles: Effects on supervisee statements. *Counselor Education and Supervision, 23*, 157–168.

Steven, D., Goodyear, R., & Robertson, P. (1998). Supervisor development: An exploratory study in changes in stance and emphasis. *Clinical Supervisor, 16*, 73–88.

Stoltenberg, M. C. D., Neill, B. W., & Delworth, U. (1998). *IDM supervision: An integrated developmental model for supervising counselors and therapists.* San Francisco, CA: Jossey-Bass.

Struder, J. R. (2005). Supervising school counselors-in-training: A guide for field supervisors. *Professional School Counseling, 8*, 353–359.

Sutton, J. M., & Page, B. J. (1994). Post-degree clinical supervision of school counselors. *The School Counselor, 42*(1), 32–39.

Watkins, C. E. (1995). Psychotherapy supervisor and supervisee: Developmental models and research nine years later. *Clinical Psychology Review, 15*, 647–680.

Watkins, C. E. (2011). Does psychotherapy supervision contribute to patient outcomes? Considering thirty years of research. *The Clinical Supervisor, 30*(2), 235–256. doi:10.1080/07325223.2011.619417

Watkins, Y. (1998). Quality supervision theory and practice for clinical supervisors. *Physiotherapy, 84*(3), 151–151. doi:10.1016/S0031-9406(05)66534-0

Whitman, S. M., Ryan, B., & Rubenstein, D. F. (2001). Psychotherapy supervisor training: Differences between psychiatry and other mental health disciplines. *Academic Psychiatry, 25*(3), 156–161. doi:10.1176/appi.ap.25.3.156-6978.2006.tb00002.x

Wilkerson, K. (2006). Peer supervision for the professional development of school counselors: Toward an understanding of terms and findings. *Counselor Education and Supervision, 46*(1), 59–67. doi:10.1002/j.1556-6978.2006.tb00012.x

Wood, C., & Rayle, A. D. (2006). A model of school counseling supervision: The goals, functions, roles, and systems model. *Counselor Education and Supervision, 45*(4), 253–266. doi:10.1002/j.155

Worthington, E. L. (1987). Changes in supervision as counselors and supervisors gain experience: A review. *Professional Psychology: Research and Practice, 18*(3), 189–208. doi:10.1037//0735-7028.18.3.189

Yager, G. G., Wilson, F. R., Brewer, D., & Kinnetz, P. (1989). The development and validation of an instrument to measure counseling supervisor focus and style. Paper presented at the annual meeting of the American Education Research Association, San Francisco, CA: Unpublished instrument.

Index

students of diversity
  deficit narrative, 4
  nonacademic barriers to learning, 4
  school counseling and, 3–5
Student Success Skills (SSS), 112, 115,
    227, 289
students-within-environments. *See*
    Advocating Student-within-
    Environment approach
Stulmaker, Hayley L., xxv
style of life, Adlerian school
    counseling, 78–79
subjective well-being (SWB), 223
subsystems, in school ecosystem, 247
superiority, striving for, 82–83
supervision of school counseling
  conceptualizations of, 300–2
  defined, 297–98
  Discrimination Model, 298, 302–11
  overview, 297–98
  in practice, 299
  theoretical overview, 298–302
suprasystems, in school ecosystem, 247
sustainability, of school ecosystem, 249–50
systems, schools as. *See* school ecosystem,
    in ESC
systems area, CCPTP, 21
systems model, 250–51
systems theory, 185–86, 245–46
system support, in CDGP, 16–17

Tansley, Arthur, 243–44
target issue models, 304
task setting technique, 93
teachers
  ASE approach, 274, 288
  ecological school counseling, 258–59
  person-centered school counseling,
    60–61, 63, 67–68
  Reality Therapy class meetings, 148, 149
  SBSC in consultation with, 226
  supervisors as, 303–4, 308–9
theories of school counseling delivery. *See*
    also specific theories
  ASCA National Model and, xi, 6
  book setup, xi

intentions of authors, x
  need for, x, 7, 9–11
  overview, xi
  strengths-based school counseling
    and, 224–25
  use in school counseling work, xi
theory of change
  Adlerian school counseling, 87–90
  ASE approach, 273–76
  cognitive-behavioral therapy, 108–10
  Discrimination Model of
    supervision, 305–6
  existentialism, 162–65, 167–70
  person-centered school
    counseling, 50–56
  solution-focused counseling, 186–95
  strengths-based school
    counseling, 212–19
thinking, in Reality Therapy, 135. *See also*
    cognitive-behavioral therapy
Thompson, C. L., 110
Tier One (classroom guidance)
    interventions, CBT, 115
Tier Three (individual counseling)
    interventions, CBT, 115, 116
Tier Two (small-group counseling)
    interventions, CBT, 115–16
tonic behaviors, Reality Therapy, 130–31
total behavior, Choice Theory, 129
total knowledge filter, Choice Theory, 129
total school climate (Lebenswelt)
  elementary school applications, 170, 172
  high school applications, 173–75, 176
  middle school applications, 171–73, 174
  overview, 167
toxic behaviors, Reality Therapy, 130–31
toys, for child-centered play therapy, 57
Tracey, T. J., 301
training, school counselor, 20–22
transition stage of group development, 146

Überwelt (spiritual existential dimension),
    163, 167, 170
Umwelt. *See* physical existential dimension
U.S. Department of Education
    (DOE), 33–34